# FIREFIGHTER EXAM

# Firefighter
# Exam

## 4th Edition

LEARNINGEXPRESS®

NEW YORK

Copyright © 2009 LearningExpress, LLC.

All rights reserved under International and Pan-American Copyright Conventions.
Published in the United States by LearningExpress, LLC, New York.

Library of Congress Cataloging-in-Publication Data:
Firefighter exam. —4th ed.
    p. cm.
  ISBN-13: 978-1-57685-671-0 (pbk. : alk. paper)
  ISBN-10: 1-57685-671-2 (pbk. : alk. paper)
    1. Fire extinction—Examinations—Study guides. 2. Fire extinction—United States—Examinations, questions, etc. 3. Fire extinction—Vocational guidance. I. LearningExpress (Organization)
TH9157.F525 2009
628.9'25076--dc22

                                        2008041286

Printed in the United States of America

9 8 7 6 5 4 3 2 1

Fourth Edition

  ISBN-10 1-57685-671-2
  ISBN-13 978-1-57685-671-0

**Regarding the Information in This Book**

We attempt to verify the information presented in our books prior to publication. It is always a good idea, however, to double-check such important information as minimum requirements, application and testing procedures, and deadlines with your local fire department, as such information can change from time to time.

For more information or to place an order, contact LearningExpress at:
    2 Rector Street
    26th Floor
    New York, NY 10006

Or visit us at:
    www.learnatest.com

# Contents ▶

List of Contributors      vii

How to Use This Book      ix

**CHAPTER 1**      What Firefighters Really Do      1

**CHAPTER 2**      How Firefighters Are Selected      13

**CHAPTER 3**      The LearningExpress Test Preparation System      29

**CHAPTER 4**      Firefighter Practice Exam 1      51

**CHAPTER 5**      Firefighter Practice Exam 2      95

**CHAPTER 6**      Reading Text, Tables, Charts, and Graphs      125

**CHAPTER 7**      Memory and Observation      141

**CHAPTER 8**      Math      149

**CHAPTER 9**      Judgment and Reasoning      181

**CHAPTER 10**      Mechanical Aptitude      193

**CHAPTER 11**      Spatial Relations and Map Reading      209

**CHAPTER 12**      Verbal Expression      219

**CHAPTER 13**      Firefighter Practice Exam 3      235

**CHAPTER 14**      Firefighter Practice Exam 4      287

**CHAPTER 15**      The Candidate Physical Ability Test      319

**CHAPTER 16**      The Oral Interview      329

# List of ▶ Contributors

**Thomas Anthony, PE,** is the captain of the Adamsburg Volunteer Fire Department and is a Structures Specialist with Pennsylvania Task Force 1. He is a Project Manager for HDR Engineering, has a Master of Science Degree in Civil Engineering from the University of Pittsburgh, and is a licensed Professional Engineer in PA, OH, and WV. He has served for 26 years in fire and emergency medical services and is a licensed Emergency Medical Technician–Paramedic in Pennsylvania.

**Michael Dortenzo, BA/MEd,** is the fire chief at the Guyasuta Fire Department of O'Hara Township, a Pennsylvania Suppression Fire Service Instructor, Pennsylvania Department of Health Rescue/EMS instructor, and certified police officer. He has 21 years in fire service, and is currently a high school teacher for a vocationally based public safety program in New Stanton, PA.

**Tim Hautamaki, MS/HRM,** is the assistant fire chief at the City of Lauderhill Fire Rescue, a Fire Service Instructor, and a member of the American Heart Association Regional Faculty. He has 22 years in fire service, and his current responsibilities focus on human resources issues, recruitment, testing, screening, hiring, and promotions.

**Darryl Jones, MS/Public Management,** is the Chief of the Pittsburgh Bureau of Fire and former chief of the Aliquippa Fire Department. He is a graduate of the Executive Fire Officer Program at the National Fire Academy and an Adjunct Instructor for the Pennsylvania State Fire Academy. He has 22 years in the fire service.

**George Munkenbeck** is a fourth-generation member of New York's volunteer fire service. He presently teaches at American Public University in the Fire Science program. As a member of the Coast Guard and Coast Guard Reserve, George has served in the operations and port security branches of the Coast Guard and held three commands. He now trains and educates emergency responders in the areas of emergency planning and response.

# ▶ How to Use This Book

**F**irefighting is more than a job or career; it is a calling. Perhaps you remember the first time that you saw a fire truck pass by, rushing to some emergency, or watched as firefighters worked to save a life in peril. That day, you began to dream of a career as a firefighter.

The fire service of today is a far cry from the organization it was only a few years ago. Firefighters, while still relied upon by the community for routine emergency response, are now also on the front lines of homeland defense. The fire service of today is more likely to render medical aid or carry out difficult rescues than fight fires. New tasks such as conducting building inspections, giving safety education classes, responding to hazardous materials incidents, and performing difficult technical rescues mean that the firefighter of today must be better educated and trained than ever before.

For you to earn the rank of firefighter, you must first prepare for the highly competitive examinations that mark the beginning of an increasingly difficult selection process. Today, this selection process also includes physical ability tests, medical qualification, and personal interviews before you can be placed on the list. The length of the process can vary from a few months to a few years before you can take the oath. For that reason, you must make sure that you are committed to the career—and never lose sight of the dream that inspired you as you move through the process.

This book will guide you through each stage of the selection process and will help you strengthen your test-taking skills to improve your chances of success. The following chapters are filled with useful information, advice, and practice exercises that will help you understand both how the hiring process works and how you can best meet the requirements.

You will want to begin your preparation by reading Chapter 1, "What Firefighters Really Do." This chapter gives a summary of the duties and responsibilities of a firefighter. You will have the opportunity to evaluate your own interests and abilities as you learn about getting hired, trained, paid, and promoted. It's important to read this chapter carefully so that you understand how to prepare yourself to become a part of this vital and challenging career.

Next, in Chapter 2, "How Firefighters Are Selected," you will read a summary of the selection process, from the initial application to the training academy. By learning the exact steps you will need to take in order to become a firefighter, you will have an edge over those applicants coming in cold.

Chapter 3, "The LearningExpress Test Preparation System," will give you invaluable advice on how to organize your time before and during the written exam. If you have had trouble with written exams in the past (anxiety, bad study habits, running out of time), you definitely don't want to skip this chapter—it even gives you great tips on how to choose the right multiple-choice answer when you are unsure. Even if written exams aren't that hard for you, be sure to take advantage of the sample study plans in this chapter. The best way to succeed on your exam is to be well prepared, and these study schedules will help you organize your time.

After devising a study plan for yourself, you will want to jump right in and take a practice exam. Note that not all of the exams test the same skills. Because fire departments around the country use different types of exams, four different exams are included in this book.

To use your study time most efficiently, you should find out what skills the department you want to apply to will be testing. (Chapter 3 shows you how.) Then you can concentrate on the practice exams in this book that correspond to those skills. At the beginning of each exam, you will find a description of the skills tested.

Once you have taken one or two exams and know which areas need the most work, you can begin studying the different subjects covered in Chapters 6–12. After substantial review of your problem subjects, move on to another practice exam to see if your score improves. From there, you can determine how much more preparation you need and whether you want to seek help from a friend, a book on the subject, or a tutor.

Finally, don't forget to read Chapters 15 and 16, which cover the ins and outs of the Physical Ability Test and the oral interview.

This book is here to help. It covers all the basics of what fire departments across the country are looking for in a candidate, and it gives you examples of what typical firefighter exams are like. You've given yourself a big advantage by choosing to use this book. One essential ingredient that this book doesn't provide, however, is specific requirements for the fire department in your city of interest. It's important for you to get all the information your fire department provides and make a few phone calls to clarify exactly what steps you need to take. Your success in becoming a firefighter depends largely on your desire to become one, and the amount of work you are willing to do to achieve this goal.

Good luck!

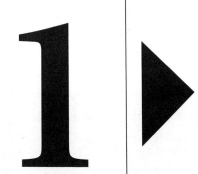

# What Firefighters Really Do

## CHAPTER SUMMARY

If you are looking for a vital and challenging career, you are on the right track. Firefighters are true champions of the public good—with hefty doses of bravery and skill mixed in. This chapter describes the duties and demands of the job. You will learn about getting hired, trained, paid, and promoted. You will also find information on how this profession is changing—and how you can prepare yourself to become a part of it.

You see flames. You smell smoke. An alarm goes off. Someone yells "fire." For most people, this would be the time to evacuate the premises. But if you happen to be a firefighter, it's time to go to work. Describing firefighters without using the word "hero" would be tough. After all, their ultimate goal is to prevent or relieve human suffering and loss. They regularly put their own lives on the line to save other lives and protect property. Much of their work is physically exhausting, mentally demanding, and highly dangerous. When a fire or other emergency strikes, they are on the scene battling flames, smoke, collapsing walls, chemical explosions, and numerous other threats. Unlike civilians, they can't evacuate the premises. They are working hard until the crisis has passed.

Behind every heroic moment, of course, are countless hours of preparation. Career firefighters are highly trained professionals. Their services are essential to every community and every stretch of land across this country. If you make this your career choice, rest assured that the need for firefighters is constant and the job prospects are promising. But this is a competitive field. Wherever you apply, you will need to show that you have what it takes to meet the demands of the job—and succeed in every stage of the hiring process.

## Where the Jobs Are

There were approximately 361,000 individuals employed in the fire service in the United States in 2006. About 293,000 were line firefighters, whereas the rest were supervisors or other support staff. The majority of these individuals, about nine out of ten according to the Bureau of Labor Statistics (BLS), are employed by municipal or county fire departments serving communities of 25,000 people or more. Large cities are the largest employers, but many intermediate-sized municipalities also employ career firefighters.

---

### Just the Facts

There are four building blocks—fuel, heat, air, and chemical reaction—that must be present for a fire to occur. This can be pictured as a four-sided figure (referred to as a *tetrahedron*) —if one side is removed, the figure collapses. This is used to illustrate the point that if any one of these building blocks is removed, the fire is extinguished, which is the basis of fire attack.

---

Full-time firefighters are also hired by federal and state government agencies to protect government-owned property and special facilities. For example, the U.S. Forest Service, Bureau of Land Management, and Park Service offer both year-round and seasonal fire service jobs to protect the country's national parks, forests, and other lands.

In the private sector, many large industrial companies have their own firefighting forces, especially companies in the oil, chemical, aircraft, and aerospace industries. Other employers include airports, shipyards, and military bases. A growing number of companies are in the business of providing fire protection services—including on-call or on-site firefighting teams—to other businesses and institutions.

In addition to career firefighters, there are thousands of volunteer firefighters nationwide. In fact, of the almost 1.1 million firefighters in the United States,

about 71% of them are volunteers. Volunteers protect the majority of the nation's territory, but career firefighters protect the majority of the nation's population. Volunteer service is a good way to get training and experience for a career in the fire service. Many suburban communities have a cadre of career firefighters who are supplemented by volunteers at an alarm. These departments, called *combination departments*, are becoming more common and frequently give preference in hiring to those who have served in their volunteer ranks.

## On the Job

The foremost duty of a firefighter is exactly what the job title says—to fight fires. Whether a fire breaks out at a two-story home, a 700-room hotel, or a 10,000-acre farm, the next sound you will hear is the familiar wail of those massive red trucks barreling their way to the scene, loaded with firefighters in protective equipment, helmets, and self-contained breathing apparatus.

But firefighters today do a lot more than put out fires. Natural disasters, bombing incidents, gas pipe explosions, and hazardous waste spills are just a few of the situations in which firefighters are called on to provide emergency services. Sometimes, these circumstances pose the threat of fire. Other times, a rescue operation may be the main order of business. Whatever the crisis at hand, firefighters are also trained to administer and coordinate basic medical care to any injured persons.

Increasingly, fire departments are finding themselves called on as the lead responders to and planners for natural and manmade disasters. In the post-9/11 world, the fire service frequently finds itself on the front line in homeland defense. What this means is that each firefighter has to be trained and cross-trained to work with agencies in adjacent communities and with federal and state agencies to fulfill these new tasks.

Fire departments are also playing an increased role in providing emergency medical services in many areas. Budget constraints have led to many municipalities combining or supplementing their emergency medical services with their fire departments. Fire departments provide a wide range of medical response, from immediate first response that provides basic first aid or cardiopulmonary resuscitation (CPR), to full advanced life support response with paramedics who will accompany the ambulance crew to the hospital. Fire departments are often able to arrive at medical calls more quickly than the ambulance, and can make the difference between life and death in many emergencies.

Fire departments also provide many nonemergency services. One highly important task is to inspect buildings and facilities for compliance with fire codes and safety regulations. Another is to educate the public about fire prevention and safety procedures. This could include giving presentations to local schools and community groups or sponsoring campaigns aimed at making people more aware of fire hazards—sort of a local version of Smokey the Bear's "Only you can prevent forest fires" campaign! Firefighters often participate in public education efforts, but building inspection more often is handled by higher-ranked fire service personnel who have had special training.

What the average person may not be aware of is simply how much knowledge and training goes into firefighting. We see them driving the red truck, attaching a hose to a hydrant, dousing flames, breaking through windows with a pickax, and climbing tall ladders. These activities alone require a high level of technical skill and a great deal of physical stamina and strength. Firefighters also face serious physical risks from being exposed to flames, smoke, fumes, and explosive or toxic materials, as well as from walls and buildings caving in or collapsing.

To reduce those risks, it is critical that firefighters stay in top physical condition and master the use of various equipment and tools. But it is equally critical that they have a knowledge bank filled with scientific and technical information about combustible materials, building construction, ventilation systems, sprinkler systems, electrical circuitry, chemical reactions, and a host of other subjects. Firefighters are educated, trained, and drilled again and again in each of these critical areas.

Computers and other forms of advanced technology are becoming more common in firefighting. Computers are typically used for documenting call reports, staff activities, and other administrative functions. Most fire training is conducted using presentation software such as PowerPoint. There is a wide variety of training available over the Internet, including courses on incident command and many other subjects. There are database programs available for hazardous materials responses that provide information on how to deal with fires or leaks of harmful substances. Many chief's vehicles, and an increasing number of other fire trucks, now carry laptop computers. Other forms of advanced technology such as thermal imaging devices are common in the modern fire service. To be successful as a firefighter, you will need a good, basic understanding of computers and technology.

Much of this preparation and learning goes on back at the station house. In departments with full-time personnel, on-duty firefighters usually eat, sleep, and make a home away from home at the station. Although most rotate between day and night shifts, the length of their tour of duty and their shifts varies from department to department. For example, they may work four days on, then four days off, putting in anywhere from 10- to 16-hour shifts. Or they may work a 24-hour shift, followed by 48 hours off, then the cycle repeats. Whatever the work schedule, it's not the corporate nine-to-five routine.

Clearly it's not every day that a firefighter rescues a child from a burning building, and nobody hopes for disaster to strike. But since there is no predicting when it might, a firefighting force must be on alert 24 hours a day, 365 days a year. Between sirens, their on-duty time is devoted to practice drills, training and education programs, equipment maintenance, and other routine activities.

Because of the many demands on a firefighter's abilities, many departments now emphasize some secondary education beyond the simple basics requried for the job. For example, many departments require training in such areas as driver/engineer courses, Fire Officer 1 and Fire Officer 2, and even Fire Science degrees for promotion through the ranks. Most advanced positions in the fire service require a college education, up to and including advanced degrees such as a Master's of Art or Science degree. Degrees in public policy, business management, or other areas are often required. There are also Bachelor of Science degrees available in Fire Science and Fire Protection Engineering, which deals with the design of fire safety systems in buildings.

### Just the Facts

In the days of steamers and horses, dogs were a welcome occupant of the fire house. They not only kept the horses company, but also rid the fire house of rats and mice that were attracted by the horse feed. Dalmatians were long associated with horse-drawn coaches. They were trained to run alongside or ahead of the team and drive off animals that would otherwise scare the horses. They came to be used by the fire service for the same purpose and thus entered firefighting lore.

## The Payback: Salary and Benefits

As with nearly every job, firefighters earn different salaries depending on where they work and who they work for. The size and location of the department or agency makes a difference, and so does a firefighter's level of experience and time on the job. Salary data for several municipal departments in your state are provided in later chapters. The statistics that follow will give you a sense of the "big picture" nationwide.

The U.S. Department of Labor's Bureau of Labor Statistic (BLS), in its 2006 edition of *Occupational Employment and Wages*, cites the median annual wage for firefighters as $41,190, with the middle 50% earning between $29,550 and $54,120. These are average figures based on national and regional reports and are calculated on a 40-hour week. These figures do not consider that most firefighters work a longer week, nor do they account for significant benefits such as health insurance, sick days, vacations, and retirement benefits.

The current trend is to offer certain incentives, thus increasing the pay range for firefighters who choose to expand their professional horizons. This includes incentives for paramedic pay, advanced education, and increases for technical certifications such as CPR Instructor or Fire Service Instructor.

If you work in a small city, you can expect a smaller annual salary than is paid in large cities. Geographically speaking, salaries tend to be lowest in the southern region of the United States and highest out west.

Typical working hours for full-time firefighters range from 40 to 56 hours a week. They are entitled by law to overtime pay, which kicks in at an average of 53 or more hours a week during a work period. Many departments also offer longevity pay to career firefighters, usually around $1,000 a year. This extra pay is generally separate from any salary increase that comes with a promotion.

Scheduling varies from one department to another. Many departments operate on variations of 24-hour schedules, either 24 hours on and 48 off or 24 on and 72 off. Some departments operate on more traditional 40-hour work weeks with shifts from 7:00 A.M. until 3:00 P.M., and so on. These scheduling differences can also affect how overtime is paid.

Employee benefit packages for firefighters also vary from department to department, but they tend to be substantial. Common benefits include medical, disability, and life insurance; sick leave, vacation, and holiday pay; educational incentives; and a generous pension plan. Departments also supply the uniforms and personal equipment that firefighters use on the job.

Unions play a large role in negotiating and protecting the salaries and benefits that firefighters earn. The BLS notes that most firefighters in medium to large departments are members of the International Association of Fire Fighters (IAFF), which maintains a national office and local chapters. The IAFF and other professional organizations also work to resolve labor disputes and sponsor governmental legislation on behalf of their members.

## Hiring Trends

Employment of firefighters is expected to increase about 12% between 2006 and 2016. Some new jobs will be created in suburban communities where populations are on the rise. New positions will open up with suburban departments as they add career positions to their volunteer departments to form combination departments. These new positions will provide more rapid response to emergencies and supplement the volunteer response. Employment in large urban departments will be stable—not producing many new jobs, but holding steady on the large numbers they already employ. Overall, the majority of job openings will come about simply to replace firefighters who retire or leave the job for other reasons.

For the most part, firefighting certainly can be called "a steady job." Although budget cuts have reduced some departments, community pressure has been supportive of better fire and rescue services. Even when local governments call for budget cuts, communities generally rally to keep or increase the number of firefighters their tax dollars support. For the most part, too, the job market is not subject to seasonal fluctuations. One exception is forestry firefighting, which offers mostly seasonal employment and is available almost exclusively through state and federal agencies.

Along with job security, you have the other advantages described earlier: relatively high wages, good benefits, a generous pension, and the chance to do challenging, exciting, and important work. All these benefits add up to steep competition for these jobs. Most fire departments—especially large urban departments—have many more applicants than they do job openings.

### Just the Facts

Firefighters used to slide down a brass pole to respond to alarms. The first of these fire poles was installed on April 21, 1878, by Captain David B. Kenyon in New York's Engine 21. Fire poles are one of the dying traditions in the fire service, because while they allowed a rapid response, they caused injuries. Some are kept in place or even installed in new construction for tradition's sake, but for the most part, they are no longer used.

## Applying for the Job

Because municipal and county fire departments operate independently, no one set of qualifications and hiring procedures is used by each and every department nationwide. However, though the particulars may vary, certain standards are likely wherever you plan to apply. For example, most departments:

- have a minimum age requirement between 18 and 21
- require a high school education or a General Equivalency Diploma (GED); some departments have a higher education requirement
- run a background check on your employment and education and a criminal record check
- require that you pass a series of tests, including a written examination, a physical ability test, a medical exam (often with drug screening), an oral interview, and possibly psychological testing.

Departments often have residency requirements stating that you must live in the city or county in which you apply. Experience as a volunteer firefighter or an Emergency Medical Technician (EMT) or paramedic is always a plus and is sometimes a requirement for employment, either at the time you apply and test for the job or to be satisfied before you begin active duty. Affirmative Action or other hiring requirements may also factor into the selection process.

Many types of previous work experience look good on the application form. Jobs in construction, mechanics, landscaping, masonry, and plumbing are some that demonstrate the physical strength and dexterity needed to be a firefighter. But the basic idea is to show that you have held a responsible job, have followed a boss's orders, and are a team player. Also, whether it is required or not, departments tend to look favorably on applicants who have attended college. Even better is having taken courses in fire science. Keep in mind how much competition you are apt to have for a firefighting job. Any advantage you have or can give yourself—which includes preparing yourself for the written exam—can really make the difference in getting hired.

Military service is also beneficial to an applicant. The fire service is basically a paramilitary organization, with ranks and a structure similar to the military.

Although service in any area of the military would be a benefit to the applicant, training as a military firefighter may be even better. All of the major services have firefighting opportunities. The U.S. Navy typically provides some amount of firefighting training to all of its personnel because firefighting is a critical function for damage control aboard ship. Military service is an excellent way to serve your country in addition to preparing you for a career in the fire service.

The National Fire Protection Association (NFPA) has established standards that have been adopted by many jurisdictions, and the two certifying agencies, the National Board on Fire Service Professional Qualifications and the International Fire Service Accreditation Congress, use these as a basis for their national certifications. Many jurisdictions have based their hiring, physical, and training requirements on the standards developed by the NFPA. Also, some states require applicants to pass state certification tests, in addition to meeting requirements and passing tests at the local (city or county) level. Normally this certification testing is also available to volunteer firefighters, so if you are a volunteer or are considering becoming a volunteer to gain experience for your career, you should investigate becoming certified. A word of caution, however: Some states have training requirements that do not necessarily follow NFPA or other national guidelines. Certification from one state may not transfer to another. You should carefully investigate this if you plan to relocate to another state.

As for federal and state firefighter jobs, you can expect similar requirements and testing procedures. Application procedures for these jobs are handled by the individual hiring agencies, state civil service commissions, local branches of the Office of Personnel Management (OPM), or other government organizations. In the private sector, you will find more variation in the employment procedures. Basically, it's like looking for a job in any private business: Companies make their choices based on an applicant's education, experience, and ability to handle the responsibilities and physical demands of the job.

Benjamin Franklin founded this country's first volunteer fire department in 1736 in Philadelphia, Pennsylvania. He also became its first volunteer fire chief.

## Starting Out and Moving Up

Once you are hired as a firefighter, your department will make sure you get all the training you need to do the job. Many large urban departments run their own on-site formal training programs or fire academy. Smaller departments may send new recruits to a fire academy in their region. Some stick mostly to on-the-job training supervised by experienced fire service personnel.

Academy training generally lasts several weeks, with part of the time spent on classroom instruction and part on practical training. You will cover areas such as firefighting and prevention techniques, hazardous and combustible materials, local building codes, and emergency medical procedures. You will also learn how to use various kinds of firefighting and rescue equipment.

As you continue on the job, you will regularly receive training to learn new skills and keep you up to date on the latest equipment and firefighting techniques. This ongoing training is aimed at improving your overall performance as a firefighter. If, down the road, you want to move up the ranks, you will have to meet a different set of training, education, and testing requirements.

For any rank promotion, factors such as your on-the-job performance, a recommendation from your supervisor, and how long you've been on the job are taken into account. You will also need to pass a writ-ten exam for most promotions—to become a driver operator, lieutenant, captain, battalion chief, assistant chief, deputy chief, or chief. You will probably have to pass a physical performance test in which you demonstrate techniques or use equipment relative to the position you want. You might have to become certified in specialized areas, usually through a combination of skills training and knowledge-based education programs, followed by a written certification exam.

Higher education is another requirement you may face for promotion. If you haven't done so already, you may need to take certain college classes or earn a college degree. For example, many departments require an associate's degree to become a lieutenant or captain. The BLS reports that generally a master's degree in public administration, business administration, or a related field is required for any rank at or above battalion chief. Advanced education and training programs are available through a variety of sources, including community colleges and universities, professional organizations, and state-sponsored fire academies.

**Just the Facts**
One of the legends told of the Great Chicago Fire of 1871 is that it was started by Mrs. Catherine O'Leary's cow when it kicked over a kerosene lantern in her barn. Most historians now discount that story as urban legend. The facts show that the hot, dry weather combined with an overworked and understaffed fire department made conditions perfect for a conflagration. This fire and the larger deadly fire in Peshtigo, Wisconsin, on the same day in October, provided a date for what would become Fire Prevention Week. The first Fire Prevention Week was proclaimed by President Calvin Coolidge in 1925.

## The Future

The days of fighting fires by bucket brigade are long gone. Professional firefighters are here to stay, a permanent fixture in every community. Meanwhile, their job is becoming more sophisticated all the time.

You can see this happening even with the tools of the job. It's true that there may be no substitutes for basic firefighting equipment like hoses, pumps, and ladders. Yet even the most basic equipment continues to be improved—made more lightweight or built to operate electronically instead of manually. The same thing applies to developing better materials for uniforms, ones that are more lightweight, heat-resistant, and flame-retardant.

When it comes to the job itself, experts in the field are constantly at work developing new methods to prevent and control fires. They are coming up with chemical solutions to quench fires and computerized models that simulate and solve fire-related problems. They are also perfecting devices such as smoke detectors and indoor sprinkler systems, which are widely used and can help to avoid full-scale destruction by fire.

Not all changes in society work to the firefighter's advantage, however. For example, the size, design, construction, and high-tech elements of buildings today can make the firefighter's job a whole lot tougher. We also have chemical spills, bombings, and large aircraft crashes—firefighters play a big role in handling these and many other kinds of crises. After the Oklahoma City bombing in 1995, for instance, firefighters were a significant force in the search-and-rescue operation. Firefighters also played a major role in saving thousands of lives after the terrorist attacks of September 11, 2001.

As a firefighter, it is important to stay aware of changes and advancements in society that affect your profession. Any number of hot items in the news— from antigovernment groups and toxic waste dumping to the latest pesticide or home security system—may pose new job-related challenges for you. To keep up with these challenges, you can expect to see fire departments boosting their standards for hiring, training, and educating firefighters. That is why it is so important

for you to show, right from the start, your willingness and ability to constantly develop new skills and knowledge.

---

**Just the Facts**

St. Florian, born in 256 A.D., is considered to be the patron saint of the fire service in countries around the world. Legend has it that a person can be saved from fire by invoking his name.

---

## Making the Commitment

What would we do without firefighters? Somebody has to snuff out major fires. Somebody has to make a dedicated effort to prevent them in the first place. Somebody has to be there to lend an expert hand during all types of emergencies. These "somebodies" are the fire service professionals who have the knowledge, training, and courage to do the job.

If that is the kind of somebody you want to be, there's no time like the present to begin preparing for the application and selection process. Along with all the tips and practical guidance you will find in this book, here are five steps to help you get headed in that direction.

1. **Get fit.** Make a physical fitness program part of your daily routine. You will need to be in top shape to pass the physical performance test in the hiring process and to do the job once you are part of the force. High-energy activities, like recreational sports, weightlifting, and jogging will help you build endurance. You might also want to try the martial arts. Karate, judo, and the like are great for improving your endurance and strength, but also for developing a mind/body connection that can help you stay in control and focused under stressful circumstances. (For some specific training tips, see Chapter 15 on the Physical Ability Test.)

2. **Do some networking.** The best resources for learning about a career as a firefighter are people now working in the field. Start with your family and friends and then move on from there —you are bound to find someone who knows or who can lead you to fire service professionals. Ask them questions. Get some pointers. Find out what it's really like to be a firefighter from people who have first-hand knowledge.

3. **Do some research.** Spend some time at local and college libraries or on the Web reading about the fire service profession. Contact professional organizations for any newsletters, articles, and papers they publish. Subscribe to magazines in the field. Don't forget to scan the daily newspaper for articles about firefighting and on topics that affect the profession.

4. **Prepare for the written exam.** Your test score on the written exam really counts. It's not just a matter of passing the exam. Your goal is to wind up with a score that gives you an advantage over the competition. So give yourself plenty of time to get ready—in other words, start studying and taking the practice exams in this book as far in advance of the exam as you can.

5. **Prepare for the oral interview.** Naturally you want to feel confident and comfortable when you are interviewed for this job. To help your cause, put in some practice time. Think about why you want to become a firefighter. Think about the abilities, knowledge, and experience you can bring to the force. Think about your long-term goals. Then have a friend or family member run you through a practice interview. The point isn't to memorize what you plan to say. It's to get a good sense of your talents and goals and to help you feel comfortable talking about yourself. (You will find out more about what's involved in the oral interview, and how to prepare for it in Chapter 16, The Oral Interview, which covers this part of the selection process.)

If you really want to be a firefighter, it's up to you to make the commitment. So take these next steps. Get yourself ready. Take charge of your future. A career in firefighting promises many challenges and rewards. All of them could be yours.

**The Firefighter's Prayer**

*When I'm called to duty, God,*
*wherever flames may rage,*
*give me strength to save a life,*
*whatever be its age.*

*Help me to embrace a little child*
*before it is too late*
*or save an older person from*
*the horror of that fate.*

*Enable me to be alert*
*to hear the weakest shout*
*and quickly and efficiently*
*to put the fire out.*

*I want to fill my calling and*
*to give the best in me;*
*to guard my neighbors and*
*protect their property.*

*And if, according to your will,*
*While on duty I must answer*
*death's call,*
*Bless with your protecting hand*
*My family, one and all.*

—Anonymous

## ▶ Helpful Resources

Listed below are several major professional organizations, publications, and websites in the fire service field. You may want to take advantage of the information and assistance that these organizations have to offer regarding fire service opportunities, training and education, union activities, and other career-related matters. You can also learn more and keep up on the latest fire-service news by reading dedicated magazines, journals, and websites.

### Organizations

International Association of Fire Chiefs
4025 Fair Ridge Drive
Fairfax, VA 22033
703-273-0911
www.iafc.org

International Association of Fire Fighters
1750 New York Avenue, NW
Washington, D.C. 20006
202-737-8418
www.iaff.org

International Fire Service Training Association
930 N. Willis
Stillwater, OK 74078
405-744-5723
www.ifsta.org

National Fire Protection Association
1 Batterymarch Park
Quincy, MA 02169
617-770-3000
www.nfpa.org

### Publications

*Fire Chief Magazine*
330 North Wabash Avenue, Ste. 2300
Chicago, IL 60611
312-595-1080
www.firechief.com

*Fire Technology and NFPA Journal*, published by the National Fire Protection Association. See the previous information listed for the National Fire Protection Association.

*Fire Engineering Magazine*
PennWell Corporation
21-00 Route 208 South
Fairlawn, NJ 07410
973-251-5055
www.fireengineering.com

*FireHouse Magazine*
3 Huntington Quad
Suite 301 N
Melville, NY 11747
800-308-6397
www.firehouse.com

**Web sites**

National Fire Sprinkler Association
www.nfsa.org

National Institute of Occupational Safety and Health
(NIOSH)
Main Page: www.cdc.gov/niosh/homepage
Fire Specific: www.cdc.gov/niosh/firehome.html

National Institute of Standards and Technology
Main Site: www.nist.gov
Building and Fire Research Library: www.brfl.nist.gov

U.S. Fire Administration
Main Site: www.usfa.gov
Publications: www.usfa/publications
Technical Reports:
www.usfa.gov/publications/techreps.cfm

U.S. Forest Service
www.fs.fed.us

# How Firefighters Are Selected

## CHAPTER SUMMARY

Throughout the country, fire departments use a number of different ways to assess firefighter candidates. This chapter provides a summary of the process of selecting recruits, from the initial application to the training academy.

There are few careers that are as demanding and require expertise in as many disciplines as firefighting. Although improved safety equipment and modern apparatus have made emergency response safer in many ways, there is still the potential of uncertainty and danger in even the most routine response.

Today, the fire service is an all-hazards response agency. Firefighters might find themselves at a trash fire and, before returning to quarters, have to render medical aid to a child who fell from her bike. If a problem or emergency is not clearly assigned to other agencies, the fire service is sent. In the twenty-first century, firefighters are on the front line of community protection. Hazardous materials require knowledge of chemistry. Terrorism, both homegrown and domestic, requires cross-training with law enforcement. Natural threats, such as floods, storms, and earthquakes, require knowledge of emergency management.

A career in the fire service is no longer a part-time career that provides benefits and the ability to run a side business, but rather requires a full-time commitment to lifelong learning. As a group, firefighters are seen by the community as heroes who are able to treat injuries like a combat medic; mitigate spilled chemicals as a professional chemist would; defeat terrorism alongside homeland defense responders; plan for emergencies at the level of a military planner; fight every fire, and rescue all who are in danger. For all of these reasons, communities are very careful whom they hire for fire department openings. All applicants must go through a rigorous testing and selection process that may last a few months to a year or more, so as to select only those who are qualified and prepared for the commitment. Although physical strength is still required, firefighters today must also have the academic skills to apply mathematics and sciences. Municipalities seek candidates with all the necessary skills, but they also seek potential firefighters who are trustworthy. When all is said and done, a firefighter occupies a position in which people must trust him or her with their lives and property.

In most cases, there are far more applicants for each position than can be appointed. The selection process may be made up of an initial application, background checks, a written examination, an oral interview or board, a physical ability test, a drug screening, and psychological tests. Being informed and prepared will help you to remain confident through every stage of the process.

That's one reason you are reading this book: It will tell you what to expect, so you will know exactly what the steps are in becoming a firefighter. Knowing those steps, you will have an edge over applicants coming in cold, and you can make a realistic assessment of your skills and abilities.

During this assessment, you might discover challenges that make becoming a firefighter unrealistic for you. However, you might instead find weaknesses that you can correct—and you can address them now, before you get involved in the selection process.

## ▶ The Eligibility List

Most fire departments, or the city personnel departments that handle the selection process for them, establish a list of eligible candidates; many such lists rank candidates from highest to lowest. How ranks are determined varies from place to place; sometimes the rank is based solely on the written exam score, sometimes on the physical ability test, and sometimes on a combination of factors. Many municipalities are now combining scores on all the steps to develop an overall rating based on all aspects of the selection process. The point is, even if you make it through the entire selection process, the likelihood that you will be hired as a firefighter often depends on the quality of your performance in one or more parts of the selection process.

Make a commitment now: You need to work hard, in advance, to do well on the written exam, the physical ability test, and the oral interview (if there is one), so that your name will stand out at the top of your agency's eligibility list.

First, though, you need information. You need to know about the selection process for firefighters. This chapter outlines the basic process in its many steps. Not every fire department includes all of the steps discussed. The particulars of the process in the city where you are applying are usually available from the city human resources department or the fire department itself.

## ▶ Basic Qualifications

The basic qualifications you need to even think about becoming a firefighter vary from city to city. It's worthwhile to find out what those qualifications are in the agency you want to serve. Some qualifications are pretty standard:

- A minimum age—sometimes this can be as low as 18, but 21 is the age that seems to be most common today. In some departments, there is a maximum age, but for the most part, these have been replaced by the requirements of physical ability tests and health.

- A high school diploma, or its equivalent, but now many departments require some college, and a few are looking for an associate's degree or perhaps a professional certification.
- A clean criminal record
- Excellent physical and mental health
- A valid driver's license and a satisfactory driving record

Many jurisdictions, but not all, require that you live nearby or in the jurisdiction. Some fire departments give preference to otherwise qualified veterans over civilians. This may take the form of a policy, sometimes called a "Veteran's Preference" policy, whereby points are automatically added to the written exam. Is this unfair? No. Fire companies are a lot like military units. They follow a strict chain of command, and firefighters on the line work as a team, knowing that their lives are in each other's hands. Military personnel have learned the discipline and teamwork that are vital to firefighting and emergency services, making them very well qualified.

Increasingly, fire departments are also giving preference to applicants with fire and emergency medical certifications, such as National Board on Fire Professional Qualifications or ProBoard Accreditation Firefighter I, National Registry Emergency Medical Technician, or Paramedic or other fire service certifications, such as vehicle and technical rescue. Some fire departments have successfully used these to screen candidates or as entry requirements. As fire departments continue to shift to all-hazards response agencies, these certifications and higher levels of education will be important for service.

## ▶ The Exam or Position Announcement

Applying to be a firefighter differs from applying for most other jobs. The differences begin with the exam or position announcement. You rarely see fire department openings advertised in the Help Wanted ads. Instead, the city usually starts looking for potential firefighters by means of a special announcement. This announcement will outline the basic qualifications for the position as well as the steps you will have to go through in the selection process. It often tells you some of the duties you will be expected to perform. It may give the date and place of the written exam, which for most positions is the first step in the selection process. Search the Web, looking for the area where you desire to be a firefighter, and determine if the fire department or department of public safety has a Web site. Very often these sites will post calendars stating when the hiring process will begin and if and when they are hiring.

Get a copy of this announcement. Often your public library will have a copy, or you can get one directly from the fire department, city human resources department, or from the Internet. If exams are held irregularly, the fire or personnel department may maintain a mailing list so that you can receive an exam announcement the next time an exam is scheduled. If exams are held frequently, you will sometimes be told to simply show up at the exam site on a given day of the week or month. In those cases you usually get more information about the job and the selection process if you pass the written exam. Study the exam announcement, as well as any other material, such as brochures, that the department sends you. You need to be prepared for the whole selection process to be successful.

One very useful exercise is to create a table with two columns—one column should contain each individual requirement of the announcement in its own box; in the second column, you should fill in your qualifications at the time of application. This will give you a graphic view of how well you fulfill the job requirements contained in the announcement.

# City of Newburg Fire Department Firefighter Job Description

## General Definition of the Classification:

The firefighter performs responsible work in service to our city protecting citizens and their property against fire and other life safety risks. This title is engaged in life safety response that includes, but is not limited to, fire suppression, emergency medical responses, rescue, hazardous materials, and artificial and natural hazard mitigation or other related work as assigned. The work required by this classification is performed under the supervision of officers and managers appointed by the common council.

## Examples of the Tasks and Work Performed by This Class:

- Responds to alarms for the purpose of fire suppression, rescue, advancing hose lines, performing entry into hazardous conditions, ventilation, laddering a structure, salvage of property, extrication of trapped individuals, providing emergency medical care and emergency hazard mitigation.
- Performs clean-up and overhaul work on emergency scenes.
- Conducts required water supply tests, including, but not limited to, hydrants and installed systems in structures and on apparatus.
- Responds to all emergency and nonemergency calls as dispatched, including service calls.
- Assists in the maintenance and repair of fire apparatus and equipment.
- Assists in the maintenance and cleaning of fire stations and grounds.
- Under the supervision of the company officers and other supervisors, conducts code inspections of residences and businesses to enforce fire codes and to develop prefire plans.
- Participates in continuing technical education and training programs both as an individual and through attendance at scheduled drills and classes.
- Conducts fire and life safety training classes, demonstrations, and station tours for public, school and community individuals, and groups.
- Backs up dispatchers and communications personnel when needed.
- Performs related tasks as assigned by supervisors.

## Knowledge, Skills, and Abilities:

### All candidates for this position must:

- Be at least 18 years of age.
- Be a resident of this city or Kings County.
- Have the ability to understand and follow written and oral instructions.
- Be able to establish and maintain cooperative relationships with fellow employees and the public.
- Be able to write reports and prepare records.
- Possess a strong mechanical aptitude.
- Be able to perform heavy manual labor and have skill in operating heavy equipment.

## Required Medical Qualifications, Education, and Licenses for Appointment:

### Upon appointment, the candidate must:

- Possess a valid driver's license.
- Be a high school graduate or hold an equivalent certificate.

## Medical Qualifications:

Candidates must be in excellent health and have no conditions that would restrict their ability to safely do fire suppression and rescue work. Weight (body fat content) must be proportionate to height for men and women. Uncorrected distance visual acuity of at least 20/100 in the poorer eye and 20/40 in the better eye, correctable to at least 20/40 in one eye and 20/20 in the other eye, is required. Regarding refractive surgery, most persons who have had these procedures will be passed. However, some may be deferred for several months or disqualified based on an individualized assessment of the surgical outcome. Color vision: Candidates must be able to accurately and quickly name colors and must be free of other visual impairments that would restrict the ability to perform firefighter duties.

Firefighters are required to be nonsmokers throughout their employment with the Newburg Fire Department.

**Job Announcement for Newburg FD**

**Required to Take the Written Examination**        **Me**

Be at least 18 years of age     _____

Be a resident of this city or Kings County     _____

Have the ability to understand and follow written
and oral instructions     _____

Be able to establish and maintain cooperative
relationships with fellow employees and the public     _____

Be able to write reports and prepare records     _____

Possess a strong mechanical aptitude     _____

Be able to perform heavy manual labor and have
skill in operating heavy equipment     _____

**Required for Appointment**

Possess a valid driver's license     _____

Be a high school graduate or hold an equivalent
certificate     _____

Candidates must be in excellent health and have no
conditions that would restrict their ability to safely
do fire suppression and rescue work     _____

Weight (body fat content) must be proportionate to
height for men and women     _____

Uncorrected distance visual acuity of at least 20/100
in the poorer eye and 20/40 in the better eye, correctable to at least 20/40 in one eye and 20/20 in the
other eye is required     _____

Regarding refractive surgery, most persons who
have had these procedures will be passed. However,
some may be deferred for several months or
disqualified based on an individualized assessment
of the surgical outcome     _____

Color vision: Candidates must be able to accurately
and quickly name colors and must be free of other
visual impairments that would restrict the ability to
perform firefighter duties     _____

Firefighters are required to be nonsmokers
throughout their employment with the
Newburg Fire Department     _____

- Neatness and accuracy count. Filling in your apartment number in the blank labeled "city" reflects poorly on your ability to follow directions.
- Most agencies don't want your resume. Save your time and energy for filling out the application form the agency gives you.
- Verify all information you put on the form. Don't guess or estimate; if you are not sure of, for instance, the exact address of the company you used to work for, look it up.
- If you are mailing your application, take care to submit it to the proper address. It might go to the personnel department rather than to the fire department. Follow the directions on the exam announcement.

## ▶ The Application

Often the first step in the process of becoming a firefighter is filling out an application. Sometimes this is a complete application, asking about your education, employment experience, personal data, and so on. Sometimes there is just an application to take the written or physical test, with a fuller application coming later. In any case, at some point, you will probably be asked some questions you wouldn't expect to see on a regular job application. You might be asked things such as whether you have ever received any speeding tickets or been in trouble with the law, whether you've used illegal drugs, or even whether any relatives work for the city or for the fire department. Your answers to these questions, as well as the more conventional ones, will serve as the starting point if the department conducts an investigation of your background, so it is important to answer all questions accurately and honestly. If you don't remember what year you worked for XYZ Company or your exact address your sophomore year of high school, don't guess; look it up.

## ▶ The Written Exam

In most jurisdictions, taking a written exam is the next step in the application process, though in some cases the physical ability test comes first.

The written exam is your first opportunity to show that you have what it takes to be a firefighter. As such, it is extremely important. Candidates who don't pass the written exam don't go any farther in the selection process. Furthermore, the written exam score often figures into applicants' rank on the eligibility list; in some cases, this score by itself determines your rank, whereas in others it is combined with other scores, such as physical ability or oral board scores. In those places, a person who merely passes the written exam with a score of, say, 70, is unlikely to be hired when there are plenty of applicants with scores in the 90s. The exam bulletin may specify what your rank will be based on.

### What the Written Exam Is Like

Most written exams simply test basic skills and aptitudes: how well you understand what you read, your ability to follow directions, your judgment and reasoning skills, your ability to read and understand maps and floor plans, and sometimes your memory or your math skills. In this preliminary written exam, you may

- Ask for and use any material the fire department or personnel department puts out about the written test. Some agencies have study guides; some even conduct study sessions. Why let others get a vital advantage while you don't?
- Practice, practice, practice. And then practice some more.
- Try to find some people who have taken the exam recently, and ask them what was on the exam. Their hindsight—"I wish I had studied . . ."—can be your foresight.

not be tested on your knowledge of fire behavior, fire-fighting procedures, or any other specific body of knowledge. This test is often designed only to see how well you can read, reason, and do basic math.

In some places, taking the exam involves studying written materials in advance and then answering questions about them on the exam. These written materials generally have to do with fire and firefighting—but all you have to do is study the guide you are given. You are still being tested on just your reading skills and memory, and there are good reasons for this.

Firefighters have to be able to read, understand, and act on complex written materials—not only fire law and fire procedures, but also scientific materials about fire, combustible materials, and chemicals. They have to be able to think clearly and independently because lives depend on decisions they make in a split second. They have to be able to do enough math to read and understand pressure gauges, or estimate the height of a building and the amount of hose needed to reach the third floor. They have to be able to read maps and floor plans so they can get to the emergency site quickly or find their way to an exit even in a smoke-filled building.

Most exams are multiple-choice tests of the sort you have often encountered in school. You get an exam book and an answer sheet where you have to fill in little circles (bubbles) or squares with a number 2 pencil.

## How to Prepare for the Written Exam

Pay close attention to any material the fire department or city human resources department puts out about the exam. If there is a study guide, study it. Pay close attention to what you are going to be tested on, and then practice with similar materials.

That's where this book comes in. There are four practice exams here that include the skills most commonly tested. There are also chapters on each kind of question you are most likely to encounter. Each chapter includes not only sample questions but also tips and hints on how to prepare for that kind of question and how to do well on the exam itself. You should also check out Chapter 3, "The LearningExpress Test Preparation System," which tells you all you need to know about preparing for and taking standardized tests.

## Finding Out How You Did

Some municipalities will send you information that shows you the questions you answered incorrectly or the areas where you were weaker than the other candidates. In other jurisdictions, the examination results list may be posted in order of the rank of the candidates with no grades shown. Most municipalities will send a letter with the test results and instructions on what to do next or how to appeal.

- Take advantage of any training sessions or test-course walk-throughs the fire department offers. The whole purpose of such sessions is to help you pass the physical test.
- Start exercising now. Yes, today. Work up to a 45-minute workout at least five times a week.
- Exercises that increase your upper-body strength are particularly useful. Consider lifting weights several times a week.
- If you smoke, stop.
- If you are overweight, eat a healthier diet along with your exercise.
- Exercise with a friend. Listen to tunes while you work out. Give yourself rewards for reaching milestones like shaving a minute off your mile-run time or bench pressing ten more pounds. Find out what will motivate you to work hard and do it.

## ▶ The Candidate Physical Ability Test (CPAT)

The Candidate Physical Ability Test is the next step in the process for many fire departments; some put this step first. You should expect to have a medical clearance, or at the very least sign a medical waiver stating that you are in good enough shape to undertake this stressful test, before you will be allowed to participate. The fire department wants to make sure that no one has a heart attack in the middle of the test. So, you can expect the test to be tough.

Firefighting is, after all, physically demanding work. Once again, lives depend on whether your strength, stamina, and overall fitness allow you to carry out the necessary tasks during an emergency. If you make it to the academy and later into a fire company, you can expect to continue physical training and exercises throughout your career. In fact, in some cities all firefighters are required to retake the Candidate Physical Ability Test every year.

Chapter 15 will give you a very detailed explanation of the Candidate Physical Ability Test.

## What the Candidate Physical Ability Test Is Like

The exact events that make up the Candidate Physical Ability Test vary from place to place, but the tasks you have to perform are almost always job-related—they are a lot like the physical tasks you will actually have to perform as a firefighter. Some tests are set up as obstacle courses; others consist of a group of stations. In some, you are timed from start to finish with no breaks; others allow a break period between stations. The tests are timed. Your performance on the test is scored depending on that time. Often you have to wear full (heavy) protective gear, including an air pack, throughout these events. Here is an example of the events in a test that you would typically have ten minutes, 20 seconds to complete:

- Stair climb with weighted vest
- Hose drag
- Equipment carry
- Ladder raise and extension
- Forcible entry
- Search
- Rescue dummy drag
- Ceiling breach and pull

In an obstacle-course setup like this one, you might be given the opportunity to walk the course before you actually have to take the test. During the test itself, you would be timed as you went through the events, and you would have to complete the events within a set time limit to pass. In departments where the Candidate Physical Ability Test figures into your rank on the eligibility list, merely meeting the maximum time to pass isn't good enough; people who have lower times will be hired before you are.

Different departments have different policies on retesting if you fail. Some allow you to retest on the same day after a rest period. Some allow you to come back another time and try again—usually up to a set maximum number of tries. And in some departments, your first try is the only chance you get; if you fail, you are out, at least until the next testing period. Few departments will allow you to retest, if you have already passed, simply to improve your time.

You can usually find out just what tasks are included in the Candidate Physical Ability Test from the exam announcement or related materials.

### How to Prepare for the Candidate Physical Ability Test

Many urban fire departments report that the Candidate Physical Ability Test is the one step of the process that most applicants fail. People come in unprepared, and they are simply not strong enough or fast enough to do all the events, while wearing heavy gear, in the time allotted. Female applicants, in particular, have high failure rates on physical ability tests because some of the events require a lot of upper-body strength. Improved techniques, not just improved strength, can help applicants pass this part of the exam.

The Candidate Physical Ability Test is one area where advance preparation is almost guaranteed to pay off. No matter how good the shape you are in, start an exercise program *now*. You can design your program around the requirements listed in the exam announcement if you want, but any exercise that will increase your strength and stamina will help. Because sheer brute force is required to drag a 150-pound dummy or to lift a 50-foot ladder, exercises that increase your strength are particularly important. But you will also want to include some aerobic exercise such as running or swimming to improve your stamina and overall fitness as well.

If you are not prepared, the stress of the test can lead to heat stress, which is a serious medical condition. If you are not in great shape, consult a doctor before you begin. Start slow and easy and increase your activity as you go. As you gain strength, start wearing weights on your ankles and wrists, and later add a heavy backpack. And remember that you don't have to do all this work alone. Working out with a friend is not only more fun, it also helps guard against the temptation to cheat by skipping a day or doing fewer repetitions.

Many fire departments conduct training sessions for would-be applicants to help them get up to the required level of fitness. Some allow you to walk through the course ahead of time. If any of these opportunities are available to you, be sure to use them.

For more information on the physical ability test and how to prepare for it, see Chapter 15, "The Candidate Physical Ability Test."

## ▶ The Background Investigation

Most fire departments conduct background investigations of applicants who pass the written and physical tests. Some departments prescreen applicants and may reject an applicant who has a criminal record. Firefighters have to be honest, upright citizens who can get along with both their company and the people they serve. You may not even know such an investigation is going on—until someone at the oral interview asks you why you wrote on your application that you never used drugs when your high school friends all say you regularly smoked marijuana on weekends. (That's why it is important to answer honestly on your application.)

## What the Background Investigation Is Like

The rigorousness with which your background will be checked depends on the policies of your department. Some conduct a fairly superficial check, calling your former employers and schools simply to verify that you were there when you say you were there and didn't have any problems during that time.

Other departments will investigate you in a great deal more depth, asking their contacts how long and how well they knew you and what kind of person they found you to be. Did you meet your obligations? How did you deal with problems? Did they find you to be an honest person? Do they know of anything that might affect your fitness to be a firefighter? The references you provided will lead the investigator to other people who knew you, and when the investigator is finished, he or she will have a pretty complete picture of what kind of person you are.

A few fire departments include a polygraph, or lie detector test, as part of the background investigation. As long as you have been honest in what you have said when your stress reactions weren't being monitored by a polygraph machine, a lie detector test is nothing to worry about.

## How to Prepare for the Background Investigation

The best way you can improve your chances of getting through a background investigation with flying colors is by working on any problems in your background. You can't change the past, but you can use the present to improve your chances in the future. You can address problems that might give a background investigator pause: Pay your old traffic tickets, document your full recovery from a serious illness, or establish your drug-free status since high school.

You can also take steps to make yourself a more attractive candidate by getting related experience. Join a local volunteer fire department to get training in the basics of firefighting skills and emergency medical services. Many local fire departments pay for emergency services training and some training is free to fire department members who reside in the county for which they volunteer. Most, if not all, career fire departments now require at a minimum certification as a Nationally Registered Emergency Medical Technician. Candidates who possess this certification will place higher on the eligibility list than those who do not.

## ▶ Oral Interviews and Boards

The selection process in your fire department is likely to include one or more oral interviews. There may be an individual interview with the chief or deputy chief, or there may be an oral board, in which you would meet with several people—or you may face both. Whether it is an individual interview or an oral board, the interviewers are interested in your interpersonal skills—how well you communicate with them—as well as in your qualifications to be a firefighter.

## What the Oral Interview Is Like

In some cities, applicants who get this far in the process meet with the chief or deputy chief, who may conduct something like a typical job interview. The chief or deputy chief might describe in detail what the job is like, ask you how well you think you can do a job like that, and ask you why you want to be a firefighter in the first place. In the process, the chief will also be

- Dress neatly and conservatively, as you would for a business interview.
- Be polite; say "please" and "thank you," "sir" and "ma'am."
- Remember, one-half of communication is listening. Look at board members or interviewers as they speak to you, and listen carefully to what they say.
- Think before you speak. Nod or say "OK" to indicate that you understand the question, and then pause a moment to collect your thoughts before speaking.
- If you start to feel nervous, take a deep breath, relax, and just do your best.
- Prepare by having a friend or family member ask you questions.

assessing your interpersonal skills, whether you seem honest and relatively comfortable in talking to him or her. You may also be asked questions about your background and experience.

This interview can be a make-or-break part of the process, with the chief approving or rejecting your candidacy, or the chief may rank you against other applicants, in which case the chief's assessment of you is likely to figure into your place on the eligibility list.

The chief's interview may also include situational questions like those typically asked by an oral board, or you may be facing an oral board in addition to your interview with the chief.

## What the Oral Board Is Like

The oral board typically assesses such qualities as interpersonal skills, communication skills, judgment and decision-making abilities, respect for diversity, and adaptability. The board itself consists of two to five people, who may be firefighters or civilian personnel or interview specialists. There is usually some variety in the makeup of the board: It usually consists of officers of various ranks and/or civilians from the personnel department or from the community.

The way the interview is conducted depends on the practices of the individual department. You may be asked a few questions similar to those you would be asked at a normal employment interview: Why do

you want to be a firefighter? What qualities do you have that would make you good at this job? You may be asked questions about your background, especially if your application or background investigation raised any questions in the board members' minds. Have answers prepared for such questions in advance.

In addition to such questions, you may be presented with hypothetical situations that you will be asked to respond to. A board member may say something like this: "A coworker on your shift is posting derogatory, racially based jokes in his gear rack and his locker. Another coworker on your shift finds the jokes tasteless and offensive. What would you do?" You would then have to come up with an appropriate response to this situation.

Increasingly, cities have standardized the oral board questions. The same questions are asked of every candidate, and when the interview is over, the board rates each candidate on a standard scale. This procedure helps the interviewers reach a somewhat more objective conclusion about the candidates they have interviewed and may result in a score that is included in the factors used to rank candidates in the eligibility list.

## How to Prepare for the Oral Board or Interview

If the agency you are applying to puts out any material about the oral board, study it carefully. It may tell you what the board is looking for. It may even give you some sample questions you can use for practice.

Whether you are facing an oral board or an individual interview, think about your answers to questions you might be asked. You might even try to write your own oral board questions and situations. Write down your answers if you want. Practice saying them in front of a mirror until you feel comfortable, but don't memorize them. You don't want to sound like you are reciting from a book. Your answers should sound conversational even though you've prepared in advance.

After practicing on your own, enlist friends or family to serve as a mock oral board or interviewer. If you know a speech teacher, get him or her to help. Give them your questions, tell them about what you have learned, and then have a practice oral board or interview. Start from the moment you walk into the room. Go through the entire session as if it were the real thing, and then ask your mock board or interviewer for feedback on your performance. It may even help to videotape your mock board session. The camera can reveal things about your body language or habits that you don't even know about.

For more information about the oral board or interview and how to prepare for it, see Chapter 16, "The Oral Interview."

## ▶ The Psychological Evaluation

Some cities, though not all, include a psychological evaluation as part of the firefighter selection process. The fire department wants to make sure that you are emotionally and mentally stable before putting you in a high-stress job in which you have to interact with peers, superiors, and the public. Don't worry, though; the psychological evaluation is not designed to uncover your deep dark secrets. Its only purpose is to make sure you have the mental and emotional health to do the job.

## What the Psychological Evaluation Is Like

If your fire department has a psychological evaluation, most likely that means you will be taking one or two written tests. A few cities have candidates interviewed by a psychologist or psychiatrist.

If you have to take a written psychological test, it is likely to be a standardized multiple-choice or true–false test licensed from a psychological testing company. The Minnesota Multiphasic Personality Inventory (MMPI) is one commonly used test. Such tests typically ask you about your interests, attitudes, and background. They may take one hour or several to complete; the hiring agency will let you know approximately how much time to allot.

If your process includes an oral psychological assessment, you will meet with a psychologist or psychiatrist, who may be either on the hiring agency's staff or an independent contractor. The psychologist may ask you questions about your schooling and jobs, your relationships with family and friends, your habits, and your hobbies. The psychologist may be as interested in the *way* you answer—whether you come across as open, forthright, and honest—as in the answers themselves.

## How to Prepare for the Psychological Evaluation

There is only one piece of advice we can offer you for dealing with a psychological evaluation, whether written or oral: Don't try to psych out the assessment. The psychologists who designed the written test set it up so that one answer checks against another to find out whether test takers are lying. Just answer honestly, and don't worry about whether your answers to some of the questions seem to you to indicate that you might be nuts after all. They probably don't.

Similarly, if you are having an oral interview, there is no point in playing psychological games with someone who is better trained at it than you are. Just answer openly and honestly, and try to relax. The psychologist isn't really interested in your feelings about your mother, unless they are so extreme that they are likely to make you unfit to be a firefighter.

## ▶ The Medical Examination

Before passage of the Americans With Disabilities Act (ADA), many fire departments conducted a medical examination early in the process, before the physical ability test. Now, the ADA says it is illegal to do any examinations or ask any questions that could reveal an applicant's disability until after a conditional offer of employment has been made. That means that in most jurisdictions you will get such a conditional offer before you are asked to submit to a medical exam.

You should know, however, that almost any disability can prevent you from becoming a firefighter, even under the protections provided by ADA. Firefighting requires a high level of physical and mental fitness, and a host of disabilities that would not prevent a candidate from doing some other job would prevent a firefighter from fulfilling essential job functions. For example, a skin condition that requires a man to wear facial hair would disqualify that man from being a firefighter because facial hair interferes with proper operation of the breathing apparatus.

## Drug Testing

Note, however, that a test for use of illegal drugs *can* be administered before a conditional offer of employment. Because firefighters have to be in tiptop physical shape, and because they are in a position of public trust, the fire department expects them to be drug-free. You may have to undergo drug testing periodically throughout your career as a firefighter.

## What the Medical Exam Is Like

The medical exam itself is nothing to be afraid of. It will be just like any other thorough physical exam. The doctor may be on the staff of the hiring agency or someone outside the department with his or her own practice, just like your own doctor. Your blood pressure, temperature, weight, and so on will be measured; your heart and lungs will be listened to and your limbs examined. The doctor will probably peer into your eyes, ears, nose, and mouth. You will also have to donate some blood and urine. Because of those tests, you won't know the results of the physical exam right away. You will probably be notified in writing in a few weeks, after the test results come in.

## ▶ If at First You Don't Succeed, Part One

The selection process for firefighters is a rigorous one. If you fail one of the steps, take the time for some serious self-evaluation.

The most common problem is that many candidates try to take too many examinations too close together. Not only is that stressful, it means that you will not be fully prepared for any. Try to avoid taking several examinations in a short period—pick those you really want and prepare specifically for them. You will have a better chance of passing.

**If you fail the written test,** look at the reasons you didn't do well. Was it just that the format was unfamiliar? Well, now you know what to expect.

Do you need to brush up on some of the skills tested? There are lots of books to help people with basic skills. You might start with the LearningExpress Skill Builders, a set of four books that help improve your practical math, writing, vocabulary and spelling, and reading comprehension. Enlist a teacher or a friend to help you, or check out the inexpensive courses offered by local high schools and community colleges.

Some fire departments allow you to retest after a waiting period—a period you should use to improve your skills. If the exam isn't being offered again for years, consider trying some other jurisdiction.

**If you fail the Candidate Physical Ability Test,** your course of action is clear. Increase your daily physical exercise until you know you can do what is required, and then retest or try another jurisdiction.

**If you fail the oral board or interview,** try to figure out what the problem was. Do you think your answers were good but perhaps you didn't express them well? Then you need some practice in oral communication. You can take courses or enlist your friends to help you practice.

Did the questions and situations throw you for a loop, so you gave what now seem like inappropriate answers? Then try to bone up for the next time. Talk to candidates who were successful and ask them what they said. Talk with firefighters you know about what might have been good answers for the questions you were asked. Even if your department doesn't allow you to redo the oral board, you can use what you learn in applying to another department.

**If the medical exam eliminates you,** you will usually be notified as to what condition caused the problem. Is the condition one that can be corrected? See your doctor for advice.

**If you don't make the list and aren't told why,** the problem might have been the oral board or, more likely, the psychological evaluation or the background investigation. Now, you really have to do some hard thinking.

Make sure your credit score is above 600 according to the FICO scale, one of the major credit bureaus that measure credit ratings. Nowadays, more often than not, career departments are requesting credit scores of applicants to ensure the candidate they are hiring is not overly in debt, which may equate to a higher potential risk of employee problems.

Can you think of *anything* in your past that might lead to questions about your fitness to be a firefighter? Could any of your personal traits or attitudes raise such questions? And then the hard question: Is there anything you can do to change these aspects of your past or your personality? If so, you might have a chance when you reapply or apply to another department. If not, it's time to think about another field.

If you feel you were wrongly excluded on the basis of a psychological evaluation or background check, most departments have appeals procedures. However, that word *wrongly* is very important. The psychologist or background investigator almost certainly had to supply a rationale in recommending against you. Do you have solid factual evidence that you can use in an administrative hearing to counter such a rationale? If not, you would be wasting your time and money, as well as the hiring agency's, by making an appeal. Move carefully and get legal advice before you take such a step.

## The Waiting Game

You went through the whole long process, passed all the tests, did the best you could, made the eligibility list—and now you wait. You could just sit on your hands. Or you could decide to do something with this time to prepare for what you hope is your new career. Do some networking. Talk to firefighters about what the job is really like. Find out if your fire department offers volunteer opportunities or a cadet program. Take a course in first aid or enroll in an Emergency Medical Technician program. Even if you don't get called, even if your rank on the score doesn't get you a job this time, you will be better qualified for the next try.

Here's one thing you don't want to do while you are waiting: Don't call to find out what your chances are or how far down on the list they have gotten or when they might call you. You probably won't get to talk to the people making those decisions, so you will just annoy some poor receptionist. If you did get through to the decision-makers, you'd be in even worse shape: You'd be annoying *them*.

## ▶ If at First You Don't Succeed, Part Two

If you make the list, go through the waiting game, and finally aren't selected, don't despair. Think through all the steps of the selection process, and use them to do a critical self-evaluation.

Maybe your written, physical, or oral board score was high enough to pass but not high enough to put you near the top of the list. At the next testing, make sure you are better prepared.

Maybe you had an excellent score that should have put you at the top of the list, and you suspect that you were passed over for someone lower down. That means someone less well qualified was selected while you were not, right? Maybe, maybe not.

There were probably a lot of people on the list, and a lot of them may have scored high. One more point on the test might have made the difference, or maybe the department had the freedom to pick and choose on the basis of other qualifications. Maybe, in comparison with you, a lot of people on your list had more education or experience. Maybe there were plenty of certified Emergency Medical Technicians on the list, and they got first crack at the available jobs.

What can you do? You may have heard or read about suits being brought against cities by people who thought their selection process was unfair. That's a last resort, a step you would take only after getting excellent legal advice and thinking through the costs of time, money, and energy. You would also have to think about whether you would want to occupy a position you got as the result of a lawsuit and whether you would be hurting your chances of being hired somewhere else.

Most people are better off simply trying again. And don't limit your options. There are lots of fire departments all over the country; there are volunteer and part-time positions available, particularly in smaller towns; and there are a growing number of private fire protection service agencies. Do your research. This book is a good start. Find out what's available. Find out who is hiring. Being turned down by one department need not be the end of your firefighting career.

There are many related careers that will open up in years to come, especially in the growing field of emergency management. Many of these require the same knowledge and qualifications, but require higher education. Do not give up, and keep researching employment opportunities in the emergency response field. You never know what will open up!

## ▶ And When You Do Succeed . . .

Congratulations! The end of the waiting game for you is notification to attend the fire service academy. You are on the road to your career as a firefighter.

The road is hardly over, though. First, you have to make it through the academy, where you can expect physical training as well as training in fire and emergency services. You will also have a lot of learning to do in your first year or so on the job. Throughout your career, you will need to keep up with new techniques, new equipment, and new procedures. And if you decide to go for a promotion, there will be more steps, more tests, and more evaluations. But you can do it, if you are determined and committed. You have already made a good start.

Never forget that fire service is no longer a part-time career. The new hazards and risks facing our communities will challenge firefighters to gain new skills and new knowledge. Lifelong learning is a commitment you will have to make to remain useful. New challenges mean new opportunities. The future is bright for those who are prepared today.

CHAPTER

# 3

# The LearningExpress Test Preparation System

## CHAPTER SUMMARY

Taking the firefighter written exam can be tough. It demands a lot of preparation if you want to achieve a top score. Your rank on the eligibility list is often determined largely by this score. The LearningExpress Test Preparation System, developed exclusively for LearningExpress by leading test experts, gives you the discipline and attitude you need to succeed, and to move forward in the selection process.

Taking the firefighter written exam is no picnic, and neither is getting ready for it. Your future career in fire fighting depends on your getting a high score on the various parts of the test, but there are all sorts of pitfalls that can keep you from doing your best on this all-important exam. Here are some of the obstacles that can stand in the way of your success:

- being unfamiliar with the format of the exam
- being paralyzed by test anxiety
- leaving your preparation to the last minute
- not preparing at all!
- not knowing vital test-taking skills: how to pace yourself through the exam, how to use the process of elimination, and when to guess
- not being in tip-top mental and physical shape
- being distracted on test day because you're hungry or the room is cold

What is the common denominator in all these test-taking pitfalls? One word: *control*. Who is in control, you or the exam?

Now, the good news: The LearningExpress Test Preparation System puts you in control. In just nine easy-to-follow steps, you will learn everything you need to know to make sure that you are in charge of your preparation and your performance on the exam. Other test takers may let the test get the better of them; other test takers may be unprepared or out of shape, but not you. You will have taken all the steps you need to take to get a high score on the firefighter exam.

Here's how the LearningExpress Test Preparation System works: Nine easy steps lead you through everything you need to know and do to get ready to master your exam. Each of the steps listed below includes both reading about the step and one or more activities. It is important that you do the activities along with the reading, or you won't be getting the full benefit of the system. Each step tells you approximately how much time that step will take you to complete.

We estimate that working through the entire system will take you approximately three hours, although it is perfectly OK if you work faster or slower than the time estimates assume. If you can take a whole afternoon or evening, you can work through the whole LearningExpress Test Preparation System in one sitting. Otherwise, you can break it up, and do just one or two steps a day for the next several days. It's up to you—remember, you are in control.

| | |
|---|---|
| Step 1. Get Information | 30 minutes |
| Step 2. Conquer Test Anxiety | 20 minutes |
| Step 3. Make a Plan | 50 minutes |
| Step 4. Learn to Manage Your Time | 10 minutes |
| Step 5. Learn to Use the Process of Elimination | 20 minutes |
| Step 6. Know When to Guess | 20 minutes |
| Step 7. Reach Your Peak Performance Zone | 10 minutes |
| Step 8. Get Your Act Together | 10 minutes |
| Step 9. Do It! | 10 minutes |
| **Total** | **3 hours** |

## ▶ Step 1: Get Information

**Time to complete: 30 minutes**
**Activities: Read Chapter 2, "How Firefighters Are Selected"**

Knowledge is power. The first step in the LearningExpress Test Preparation System is finding out everything you can about your firefighter exam. Contact the fire department you want to apply to and ask who you should speak to about applying to be a firefighter. In larger cities, you will be referred to a recruiting unit or to the human resources department. In smaller towns, you may speak to someone right there in the department. Request a position announcement or exam bulletin and ask when the next exam is scheduled. The exam bulletin usually gives a brief outline of what skills will be tested on the written exam.

### What You Should Find Out

The more details you can find out about the exam, either from the bulletin or from speaking with a recruiter, the more efficiently you will be able to study. Here's a list of some things you might want to find out about your exam:

- what skills are tested
- how many sections are on the exam
- how many questions each section has
- whether the questions are ordered from easy to hard, or if the sequence is random
- how much time is allotted for each section
- if there are breaks between sections
- what the passing score is, and how many questions you have to answer right to get that score
- whether a higher score gives you any advantages, like a better rank on the eligibility list
- how the test is scored; is there a penalty for wrong answers?
- whether you are permitted to go back to a prior section or move on to the next section if you finish early

- whether you can write in the test booklet or will be given scratch paper
- what you should bring with you on exam day

### What's on Most Firefighter Exams

The skills that the firefighter written exam tests vary from city to city. That's why it is important to contact the recruiting office or fire department to find out what skills are covered. Below are the most commonly tested subjects:

- Reading Text, Tables, Charts, and Graphs
- Verbal Expression
- Spatial Relations
- Judgment and Reasoning
- Map Reading
- Memory and Observation
- Mechanical Aptitude
- Math

If you haven't already done so, stop here and read Chapter 2 of this book, which gives you an overview of the entire selection process. Then move on to the next step and get rid of that test anxiety!

## ▶ Step 2: Conquer Test Anxiety

**Time to complete: 20 minutes**
**Activity: Take the Test Anxiety Quiz**

Having complete information about the exam is the first step in getting control of the exam. Next, you have to overcome one of the biggest obstacles to test success: test anxiety. Test anxiety can not only impair your performance on the exam itself, it can even keep you from preparing! In Step 2, you will learn stress management techniques that will help you succeed on your exam. Learn these strategies now, and practice them as you work through the exams in this book, so they will be second nature to you by exam day.

You only need to worry about test anxiety if it is extreme enough to impair your performance. The following questionnaire will provide a diagnosis of your level of test anxiety. In the blank before each statement, write the number that most accurately describes your experience.

0 = Never  1 = Once or twice  2 = Sometimes  3 = Often

____ I have gotten so nervous before an exam that I simply put down the books and didn't study for it.

____ I have experienced disabling physical symptoms such as vomiting and severe headaches because I was nervous about an exam.

____ I have simply not showed up for an exam because I was scared to take it.

____ I have experienced dizziness and disorientation while taking an exam.

____ I have had trouble filling in the little circles because my hands were shaking too hard.

____ I have failed an exam because I was too nervous to complete it.

____ **Total: Add up the numbers in the blanks above.**

### Your Test Anxiety Score

Here are the steps you should take, depending on your score. If you scored

- **below 3,** your level of test anxiety is nothing to worry about; it is probably just enough to give you that little extra edge.
- **between 3 and 6,** your test anxiety may be enough to impair your performance, and you should practice the stress management techniques listed in this section to try to bring your test anxiety down to manageable levels.
- **above 6,** your level of test anxiety is a serious concern. In addition to practicing the stress management techniques listed in this section, you may want to seek additional personal help. Call your local high school or community college and ask for the academic counselor. Tell the counselor that you have a level of test anxiety that sometimes keeps you from being able to take an exam. The counselor may be willing to help you or may suggest someone else you should talk to.

### Combating Test Anxiety

The first thing you need to know is that a little test anxiety is a good thing. Everyone gets nervous before a big exam—and if that nervousness motivates you to prepare thoroughly, so much the better. It is said that Sir Laurence Olivier, one of the foremost British actors of the 20th century, was ill before every performance. His stage fright didn't impair his performance; in fact, it probably gave him a little extra edge—just the kind of edge you need to do well, whether on a stage or in an examination room.

Stop here and answer the questions on the Test Anxiety Quiz to find out whether your level of test anxiety is something you should worry about.

## Stress Management before the Test

If you feel your level of anxiety getting the best of you in the weeks before the test, here is what you need to do to bring the level down again:

- **Get prepared.** There's nothing like knowing what to expect and being prepared for it to put you in control of test anxiety. That's why you are reading this book. Use it faithfully, and remind yourself that you are better prepared than most of the people taking the test.

- **Practice self-confidence.** A positive attitude is a great way to combat test anxiety. This is no time to be humble or shy. Stand in front of the mirror and say to your reflection, "I'm prepared. I'm full of self-confidence. I'm going to ace this test. I know I can do it." Say it into a tape recorder and play it back once a day. If you hear it often enough, you will believe it.

- **Fight negative messages.** Every time someone starts telling you how hard the exam is or how it is almost impossible to get a high score, start telling them your self-confidence messages. If it's you telling yourself *you don't do well on exams, you just can't do this*, don't listen. Turn on your tape recorder and listen to your self-confidence messages.

- **Visualize.** Imagine yourself reporting for duty on your first day of firefighter training. Think of yourself wearing your uniform with pride and learning skills you will use for the rest of your life. Visualizing success can help make it happen—and it reminds you of why you are doing all this work in preparing for the exam.

- **Exercise.** Physical activity helps calm your body down and focus your mind, and as you know, being in top shape physically will be important on the Candidate Physical Ability Test. Go for a run, lift weights, go swimming—and do it regularly.

## Stress Management on Test Day

There are several ways you can bring down your level of test anxiety on test day. They will work best if you practice them in the weeks before the test, so you know which ones work best for you.

- **Deep breathing.** Take a deep breath while you count to five. Hold it for a count of one, then let it out on a count of five. Repeat several times.

- **Move your body.** Try rolling your head in a circle. Rotate your shoulders. Shake your hands from the wrist. Many people find these movements very relaxing.

- **Visualize again.** Think of the place where you are most relaxed: lying on the beach in the sun, walking through the park, or whatever. Now, close your eyes and imagine that you are actually there. If you practice in advance, you will find that you only need a few seconds of this exercise to experience a significant increase in your sense of well-being.

When anxiety threatens to overwhelm you right there during the exam, there are still things you can do to manage the stress level:

- **Repeat your self-confidence messages.** You should have them memorized by now. Say them quietly to yourself, and believe them!

- **Visualize one more time.** This time, visualize yourself moving smoothly and quickly through the test, answering every question right and finishing just before time is up. Like most visualization techniques, this one works best if you have practiced it ahead of time.

- **Find an easy question.** Skim over the test until you find an easy question, and answer it. Getting even one circle filled in gets you into the test-taking groove.

- **Take a mental break.** Everyone loses concentration once in a while during a long test. It's normal, so you shouldn't worry about it. Instead, accept what has happened. Say to yourself, "Hey, I lost it there for a minute. My brain is taking a break." Put down your pencil, close your eyes, and do some deep breathing for a few seconds. Then you are ready to go back to work.

Try these techniques ahead of time, and find out which ones work best for you.

## ▶ Step 3: Make a Plan

**Time to complete: 50 minutes**
**Activity: Construct a study plan**

Maybe the most important thing you can do to get control of yourself and your exam is to make a study plan. Too many people are unprepared simply because they fail to plan. Spending hours on the day before the exam poring over sample test questions not only raises your level of test anxiety, it also is simply no substitute for careful preparation and practice over time.

Don't fall into the cram trap. Take control of your preparation time by mapping out a study schedule. There are four sample schedules on the following pages, based on the amount of time you have before the exam. If you are the kind of person who needs deadlines and assign-

ments to motivate you for a project, here they are. If you are the kind of person who doesn't like to follow other people's plans, you can use the suggested schedules here to construct your own.

In constructing your plan, you should take into account how much work you need to do. If your score on the sample test wasn't what you had hoped, consider taking some of the steps from Schedule A and getting them into Schedule D somehow, even if you do have only three weeks before the exam.

You can also customize your plan according to the information you gathered in Step 1. If the exam you have to take doesn't include verbal expression questions, for instance, you can skip Chapter 12 and concentrate instead on some other area that *is* covered. Below is a table that lists all the chapters you need to study for each exam.

Even more important than making a plan is making a commitment. You can't improve your skills in reading, writing, and judgment overnight. You have to set aside some time every day for study and practice. Try for at least 20 minutes a day. Twenty minutes daily will do you much more good than two hours once a week.

If you have months before the exam, you are lucky. Don't put off your study until the week before the exam! Start now. Even ten minutes a day, with half an hour or more on weekends, can make a big difference in your score—and in your chances of making the department!

| Exams | Study Chapters |
|---|---|
| Exam 1, Chapter 4<br>Exam 3, Chapter 13 | 6, "Reading Text, Tables, Charts, and Graphs"<br>7, "Memory and Observation"<br>9, "Judgment and Reasoning"<br>11, "Spatial Relations and Map Reading"<br>12, "Verbal Expression" |
| Exam 2, Chapter 5<br>Exam 4, Chapter 14 | 6, "Reading Text, Tables, Charts, and Graphs"<br>8, "Math"<br>9, "Judgment and Reasoning"<br>10, "Mechanical Aptitude"<br>12, "Verbal Expression" |

# Schedule A: The Leisure Plan

If no test has been announced yet in your city, you may have a year or more in which to get ready. This schedule gives you six months to sharpen your skills. If an exam is announced in the middle of your preparation, you can use one of the later schedules to help you compress your study program. Study only the chapters that are relevant to the type of exam you will be taking.

| Time | Preparation |
|------|-------------|
| Exam minus 6 months | Take one of the exams from Chapters 4 or 5. Then study the explanations for the answers until you know you could answer all the questions correctly. |
| Exam minus 5 months | Read Chapter 6 and work through the exercises. Start going to the library once every two weeks to read books or magazines about firefighting. Find other people who are preparing for the test and form a study group. |
| Exam minus 4 months | Read Chapters 7 and 8 and work through the exercises. Use at least one of the additional resources for each chapter. Start practicing your math by making up problems out of everyday events. Exercise your memory by making note of the buildings and rooms you see each day. |
| Exam minus 3 months | Read Chapters 9 and 10 and work through the exercises. Visit your local auto mechanic's shop and familiarize yourself with the tools you see there. Keep up your reading. |
| Exam minus 2 months | Read Chapters 11 and 12 and work through the exercises. Practice your map-reading skills by drawing a map of your neighborhood and finding the most direct routes to the places you frequent. |
| Exam minus 1 month | Take one of the practice exams in either Chapter 13 or 14. Use your score to help you decide where to concentrate your efforts this month. Go back to the relevant chapters and use the additional resources listed there, or get the help of a friend or teacher. |
| Exam minus 1 week | Review the practice exams. See how much you have learned in the past months. Concentrate on what you have done well and resolve to do your best in any areas where you still feel uncertain. |
| Exam minus 1 day | Relax. Do something unrelated to the exam and firefighting. Eat a good meal and go to bed at your usual time. |

# Schedule B: The Just-Enough-Time Plan

If you have three to six months before the exam, that should be enough time to prepare for the written test, especially if you score above 70 on the first sample test you take. This schedule assumes four months; stretch it out or compress it if you have more or less time, and study only the chapters that are relevant to the type of exam you will be taking.

| Time | Preparation |
|---|---|
| Exam minus 4 months | Take one practice exam from Chapter 4 or 5 to determine where you need most work. Read Chapters 6, 7, and 8 and work through the exercises. Use at least one of the additional resources listed in each chapter. Start going to the library once every two weeks to read books about firefighting. Exercise your memory by making note of the buildings and rooms you see each day. Practice your math by making up problems out of everyday events. |
| Exam minus 3 months | Read Chapters 9 and 10 and work through the exercises. Use at least one of the additional resources for each chapter. Visit your local auto mechanic's shop and familiarize yourself with the tools you see there. |
| Exam minus 2 months | Read Chapters 11 and 12 and work through the exercises. Practice your map-reading skills by drawing a map of your neighborhood and finding the most direct routes to the places you frequent. Keep up your reading. |
| Exam minus 1 month | Take one of the practice exams in Chapter 13 or 14. Use your score to help you decide where to concentrate your efforts this month. Go back to the relevant chapters and use the extra resources listed there, or get the help of a friend or teacher. |
| Exam minus 1 week | Review the practice exams. See how much you have learned in the past months. Concentrate on what you have done well, and resolve to do your best in areas where you still feel uncertain. |
| Exam minus 1 day | Relax. Do something unrelated to the exam and firefighting. Eat a good meal and go to bed at your usual time. |

# Schedule C: More Study in Less Time

If you have one to three months before the exam, you still have enough time for some concentrated study that will help you improve your score. This schedule is built around a two-month time frame. If you have only one month, spend an extra couple of hours a week to get in all these steps. If you have three months, take some of the steps from Schedule B and fit them in. Only study the chapters that are relevant to the type of exam you will be taking.

| Time | Preparation |
|---|---|
| Exam minus 8 weeks | Take one practice exam from Chapters 4 or 5 to find one or two areas you are weakest in. Choose the appropriate chapter(s) from among Chapters 6–12 to read in these two weeks. Use some of the additional resources listed there. When you get to those chapters in this plan, review them. |
| Exam minus 6 weeks | Read Chapters 6–9 and work through the exercises. |
| Exam minus 4 weeks | Read Chapters 10–12 and work through the exercises. |
| Exam minus 2 weeks | Take one of the second practice exams in either Chapter 13 or 14. Then score it and read the answer explanations until you are sure you understand them. Review the areas in which your score is lowest. |
| Exam minus 1 week | Review the practice exams, concentrating on the areas where a little work can help the most. |
| Exam minus 1 day | Relax. Do something unrelated to the exam and firefighting. Eat a good meal and go to bed at your usual time. |

# Schedule D: The Short-Term Plan

If you have three weeks or less before the exam, you have your work cut out for you. Carve half an hour out of every day for study. This schedule assumes that you have the whole three weeks to prepare in; if you have less time, you will have to compress the schedule accordingly. Study only the chapters that are relevant to the type of exam you will be taking.

| Time | Preparation |
|---|---|
| Exam minus 3 weeks | Take one practice exam from Chapter 4 or 5. Then read the material in Chapters 6–9 and work through the exercises. |
| Exam minus 2 weeks | Read the material in Chapters 10–12 and work through the exercises. Take one of the practice exams in either Chapter 13 or 14. |
| Exam minus 1 week | Evaluate your performance on the second practice exam. Review the parts of Chapters 6–12 that you had the most trouble with. Get a friend or teacher to help you with the section where you had the most difficulty. |
| Exam minus 2 days | Review the practice exams. Make sure you understand the answer explanations. |
| Exam minus 1 day | Relax. Do something unrelated to the exam and firefighting. Eat a good meal and go to bed at your usual time. |

## ▶ Step 4: Learn to Manage Your Time

**Time to complete: 10 minutes to read, many hours of practice!**

**Activities: Practice these strategies as you take the sample tests in this book**

Steps 4, 5, and 6 of the LearningExpress Test Preparation System put you in charge of your exam by showing you test-taking strategies that work. Practice these strategies as you take the practice exams in this book, and then you will be ready to use them on test day.

First, you will take control of your time on the exam. The first step in achieving this control is to find out the format of the exam you are going to take. Some firefighter exams have different sections that are each timed separately. If this is true of the exam you will be taking, you will want to practice using your time wisely on the practice exams and try to avoid mistakes while working quickly. Other types of exams don't have separately timed sections. If this is the case, just practice pacing yourself on the practice exams so you don't spend too much time on difficult questions.

- **Listen carefully to directions.** By the time you get to the exam, you should know how the test works, but listen just in case something has changed.
- **Pace yourself.** Glance at your watch every few minutes, and compare the time to how far you have gotten in the section. When one-quarter of the time has elapsed, you should be a quarter of the way through the section, and so on. If you are falling behind, pick up the pace a bit.
- **Keep moving.** Don't dither around on one question. If you don't know the answer, skip the question and move on. Circle the number of the question in your test booklet in case you have time to come back to it later.

- **Keep track of your place on the answer sheet.** If you skip a question, make sure you skip on the answer sheet too. Check yourself every 5–10 questions to make sure the question number and the answer sheet number are still the same.
- **Don't rush.** Though you should keep moving, rushing won't help. Try to keep calm and work methodically and quickly.

## ▶ Step 5: Learn to Use the Process of Elimination

**Time to complete: 20 minutes**

**Activity: Complete worksheet on Using the Process of Elimination**

After time management, your next most important tool for taking control of your exam is using the process of elimination wisely. It is standard test-taking wisdom that you should always read all the answer choices before choosing your answer. This helps you find the right answer by eliminating wrong answer choices. And, sure enough, that standard wisdom applies to your exam, too.

Let's say you are facing a vocabulary question that goes like this:

**13.** "Biology uses a *binomial* system of classification." In this sentence, the word *binomial* most nearly means
   **a.** understanding the law.
   **b.** having two names.
   **c.** scientifically sound.
   **d.** having a double meaning.

If you happen to know what *binomial* means, you don't need to use the process of elimination, but let's assume that, like most people, you don't. So you look at the answer choices. "Understanding the law" sure doesn't sound very likely for something having to do with biology. So you eliminate choice **a**—and now you only have three answer choices to deal with. Mark an **X** next to choice **a** so you never have to read it again.

On to the other answer choices. If you know that the prefix *bi-* means *two*, as in *bicycle*, you will flag choice **b** as a possible answer. Make a check mark beside it, meaning "good answer, I might use this one."

Choice **c**, "scientifically sound," is a possibility. At least it's about science, not law. It could work here, though, when you think about it, having a "scientifically sound" classification system in a scientific field is kind of redundant. You remember the *bi-* in *binomial*, and probably continue to like answer **b** better. But you are not sure, so you put a question mark next to **c**, meaning "well, maybe."

Now, choice **d**, "having a double meaning." You are still keeping in mind that *bi-* means *two*, so this one looks possible at first. But then you look again at the sentence the word belongs in, and you think, "Why would biology want a system of classification that has two meanings? That wouldn't work very well!" If you are really taken with the idea that *bi* means *two*, you might put a question mark here. But if you are feeling a little more confident, you will put an **X**. You already have a better answer picked out.

Now your question looks like this:

**13.** "Biology uses a *binomial* system of classification." In this sentence, the word *binomial* most nearly means
  X **a.** understanding the law.
  ✔ **b.** having two names.
  ? **c.** scientifically sound.
  ? **d.** having a double meaning.

You have just one check mark for a good answer. If you are pressed for time, you should simply mark choice **b** on your answer sheet. If you have the time to be extra careful, you could compare your check-mark answer to your question-mark answers to make sure that it is better. (It is: The *binomial* system in biology is the one that gives a two-part genus and species name like *homo sapiens*.)

It is good to have a system for marking good, bad, and maybe answers. We're recommending this one:

**X** = bad
**✔** = good
**?** = maybe

If you don't like these marks, devise your own system. Just make sure you do it long before test day—while you are working through the practice exams in this book—so you won't have to worry about it during the test.

Even when you think you are absolutely clueless about a question, you can often use the process of elimination to get rid of one answer choice. If so, you are better prepared to make an educated guess, as you will see in Step 6. More often, the process of elimination allows you to get down to only two possibly right answers. Then you are in a strong position to guess. And sometimes, even though you don't know the right answer, you find it simply by getting rid of the wrong ones, as you did in the example above.

Try using your powers of elimination on the questions in the Using the Process of Elimination worksheet. The answer explanations there show ways you might use the process to arrive at the right answer.

The process of elimination is your tool for the next step, which is knowing when to guess.

Use the process of elimination to answer the following questions.

**1.** Ilsa is as old as Meghan will be in five years. The difference between Ed's age and Meghan's age is twice the difference between Ilsa's age and Meghan's age. Ed is 29. How old is Ilsa?

   **a.** 4

   **b.** 10

   **c.** 19

   **d.** 24

**2.** "All drivers of commercial vehicles must carry a valid commercial driver's license whenever operating a commercial vehicle." According to this sentence, which of the following people need NOT carry a commercial driver's license?

   **a.** a truck driver idling his engine while waiting to be directed to a loading dock

   **b.** a bus operator backing her bus out of the way of another bus in the bus lot

   **c.** a taxi driver driving his personal car to the grocery store

   **d.** a limousine driver taking the limousine to her home after dropping off her last passenger of the evening

**3.** Smoking tobacco has been linked to

   **a.** increased risk of stroke and heart attack.

   **b.** all forms of respiratory disease.

   **c.** increasing mortality rates over the past ten years.

   **d.** juvenile delinquency.

**4.** Which of the following words is spelled correctly?

   **a.** incorrigible

   **b.** outragous

   **c.** domestickated

   **d.** understandible

## Answers

Here are the answers, as well as some suggestions as to how you might have used the process of elimination to find them.

**1. d.** You should have eliminated choice **a** off the bat. Ilsa can't be four years old if Meghan is going to be Ilsa's age in five years. The best way to eliminate the other answer choices is to try plugging them into the information given in the problem. For instance, for choice **b**, if Ilsa is 10, then Meghan must be 5. The difference in their ages is 5. The difference between Ed's age, 29, and Meghan's age, 5, is 24. Is 24 two times 5? No. Then choice **b** is wrong. You could eliminate choice **c** in the same way and be left with choice **d**.

**2. c.** Note the word *not* in the question, and go through the answers one by one. Is the truck driver in choice **a** "operating a commercial vehicle"? Yes, idling counts as "operating," so he needs to have a commercial driver's license. Likewise, the bus operator in choice **b** is operating a commercial vehicle; the question doesn't say the operator has to be on the street. The limo driver in **d** is operating a commercial vehicle, even if it doesn't have a passenger in it. However, the cabbie in choice **c** is not operating a commercial vehicle, but his own private car.

**3. a.** You could eliminate choice **b** simply because of the presence of the word *all*. Such absolutes hardly ever appear in correct answer choices. Choice **c** looks attractive until you think a little about what you know—aren't *fewer* people smoking these days, rather than more? So how could smoking be responsible for a higher mortality rate? (If you didn't know that *mortality rate* means the rate at which people die, you might keep this choice as a possibility, but you'd still be able to eliminate two answers and have only two to choose from.) And choice **d** seems like a stretch, so you could eliminate that one, too. And you're left with the correct choice, **a**.

**4. a.** How you used the process of elimination here depends on which words you recognized as being spelled incorrectly. If you knew that the correct spellings were *outrageous*, *domesticated*, and *understandable*, then you were home free. The odds are that you knew that at least one of those words was wrong!

## ▶ Step 6: Know When to Guess

**Time to complete: 20 minutes**
**Activity: Complete worksheet on Your Guessing Ability**

Armed with the process of elimination, you are ready to take control of one of the big questions in test taking: Should I guess? The answer is usually yes. Unless the exam has a so-called "guessing penalty," you have nothing to lose and everything to gain from guessing. The more complicated answer depends both on the exam and on you—your personality and your guessing intuition.

Most firefighter exams don't use a guessing penalty. The number of questions you answer correctly yields your score, and there is no penalty for wrong answers. So most of the time, you don't have to worry—simply go ahead and guess. But if you find that your exam does have a guessing penalty, you should read the section below to find out what that means to you.

### How the Guessing Penalty Works

A guessing penalty really works against only *random* guessing—filling in the little circles to make a nice pattern on your answer sheet. If you can eliminate one or more answer choices, as outlined in the previous section, you are better off taking a guess than leaving the answer blank, even on the sections that have a penalty.

Here's how a guessing penalty works: Depending on the number of answer choices in a given exam, some proportion of the number of questions you get wrong is subtracted from the total number of questions you got right. For instance, if there are four answer choices, typically the guessing penalty is one-third of a point for each wrong answer. Suppose you took a test composed of 100 questions. You answered 88 of them right and 12 wrong.

If there is no guessing penalty, your score is simply 88. But if there is a one-third point guessing penalty, the scorers take your 12 wrong answers and divide by 3 to come up with 4. Then they subtract that 4 from your correct-answer score of 88 to leave you with a score of 84. Thus, you would have been better off if you had simply not answered those 12 questions that you weren't sure of, leaving you with a total score of 88.

The following are ten really hard questions. You're not supposed to know the answers. Rather, this is an assessment of your ability to guess when you don't have a clue. Read each question carefully, just as if you did expect to know the answer. If you have any knowledge at all of the subject of the question, use that knowledge to help you eliminate wrong answer choices. Use this answer grid to fill in your answers to the questions.

1. (a) (b) (c) (d)
2. (a) (b) (c) (d)
3. (a) (b) (c) (d)
4. (a) (b) (c) (d)

5. (a) (b) (c) (d)
6. (a) (b) (c) (d)
7. (a) (b) (c) (d)
8. (a) (b) (c) (d)

9. (a) (b) (c) (d)
10. (a) (b) (c) (d)

**1.** September 7 is Independence Day in
   a. India.
   b. Costa Rica.
   c. Brazil.
   d. Australia.

**2.** Which of the following is the formula for determining the momentum of an object?
   a. $p = mv$
   b. $F = ma$
   c. $P = IV$
   d. $E = mc^2$

**3.** Because of the expansion of the universe, the stars and other celestial bodies are all moving away from each other. This phenomenon is known as
   a. Newton's first law.
   b. the big bang.
   c. gravitational collapse.
   d. Hubble flow.

**4.** American author Gertrude Stein was born in
   a. 1713.
   b. 1830.
   c. 1874.
   d. 1901.

**5.** Which of the following is NOT one of the Five Classics attributed to Confucius?
   a. the *I Ching*
   b. the *Book of Holiness*
   c. the *Spring and Autumn Annals*
   d. the *Book of History*

**6.** The religious and philosophical doctrine that holds that the universe is constantly in a struggle between good and evil is known as
   a. Pelagianism.
   b. Manichaeanism.
   c. neo-Hegelianism.
   d. Epicureanism.

**7.** The third Chief Justice of the Supreme Court was
   a. John Blair.
   b. William Cushing.
   c. James Wilson.
   d. John Jay.

**8.** Which of the following is the poisonous portion of a daffodil?
   a. the bulb
   b. the leaves
   c. the stem
   d. the flowers

**9.** The winner of the Masters golf tournament in 1953 was
   **a.** Sam Snead.
   **b.** Cary Middlecoff.
   **c.** Arnold Palmer.
   **d.** Ben Hogan.

**10.** The state with the highest per capita personal income in 1980 was
   **a.** Alaska.
   **b.** Connecticut.
   **c.** New York.
   **d.** Texas.

## Answers

Check your answers against the correct answers below.

**1.** c.
**2.** a.
**3.** d.
**4.** c.
**5.** b.
**6.** b.
**7.** b.
**8.** a.
**9.** d.
**10.** a.

## How Did You Do?

You may have simply gotten lucky and actually known the answers to one or two questions. In addition, your guessing was more successful if you were able to use the process of elimination on any of the questions. Maybe you didn't know who the third Chief Justice was (question 7), but you knew that John Jay was the first. In that case, you would have eliminated choice **d** and therefore improved your odds of guessing correctly from one in four to one in three.

According to probability, you should get $2\frac{1}{2}$ answers correct by guessing, so getting either two or three right would be average. If you got four or more right, you may be a really terrific guesser. If you got one or none right, you may not be a very good guesser.

Keep in mind, though, that this is only a small sample. You should continue to keep track of your guessing ability as you work through the practice questions in this book. Circle the numbers of questions you guess on as you make your guess, or, if you don't have time while you take the practice exams, go back afterward and try to remember which questions you guessed at. Remember, on a test with four answer choices for each question, your chances of getting a right answer is one in four. So keep a separate "guessing" score for each exam. How many questions did you guess on? How many did you get right? If the number you got right is at least one-fourth of the number of questions you guessed on, you are at least an average guesser, maybe better—and you should go ahead and guess on the real exam. If the number you got right is significantly lower than one-fourth of the number you guessed on, you should not guess on exams where there is a guessing penalty unless you can eliminate a wrong answer. If there's no guessing penalty, however, you would be safe in guessing anyway.

## What You Should Do about the Guessing Penalty

Now that you know how a guessing penalty works, you know that marking your answer sheet at random doesn't pay. If you are running out of time on an exam that has a guessing penalty, you should not use your remaining seconds to mark a pretty pattern on your answer sheet. Take those few seconds to try to answer one more question right.

But as soon as you get out of the realm of random guessing, the guessing penalty no longer works against you. If you can use the process of elimination to get rid of even one wrong answer choice, the odds stop being against you and start working in your favor.

Sticking with the example of an exam that has four answer choices, eliminating just one wrong answer makes your odds of choosing the correct answer one in three. That's the same as the one-out-of-three guessing penalty—even odds. If you eliminate two answer choices, your odds are one in two—better than the guessing penalty. In either case, you should go ahead and choose one of the remaining answer choices.

## When There Is No Guessing Penalty

As noted earlier, most firefighter exams don't have a guessing penalty. That means that, all other things being equal, you should always go ahead and guess, even if you have no idea what the question means. Your score won't be affected if you are wrong.

But all other things aren't necessarily equal. The other factor in deciding whether or not to guess, besides the exam and whether or not it has a guessing penalty, is you. There are two things you need to know about yourself before you go into the exam:

- Are you a risk-taker?
- Are you a good guesser?

Your risk-taking temperament matters most on exams with a guessing penalty.

Without a guessing penalty, even if you are a play-it-safe person, guessing is perfectly safe. Overcome your anxieties, and go ahead and mark an answer.

## ▶ Step 7: Reach Your Peak Performance Zone

**NOTE:** Consult a doctor for a full medical examination prior to beginning any serious exercise program.

**Time to complete: 10 minutes to read; weeks to complete!**

**Activity: Complete the Physical Preparation Checklist**

To get ready for a challenge like a big exam, you have to take control of your physical, as well as your mental, state. Exercise, proper diet, and rest will ensure that your body works with, rather than against, your mind on test day, as well as during your preparation.

### Exercise

If you don't already have a regular exercise program, the time during which you are preparing for an exam is an excellent time to start one. You will have to be pretty fit to pass your physical ability test anyway. And if you are already keeping fit—or trying to get that way—don't let the pressure of preparing for an exam fool you into quitting now. Exercise helps reduce stress by pumping wonderful, good-feeling hormones called endorphins into your system. It also increases the oxygen supply throughout your body, including your brain, so you will be at peak performance on test day.

A half hour of vigorous activity—enough to raise a sweat—every day should be your aim. If you are really pressed for time, every other day is OK. Choose an activity you like and get out there and do it. Jogging with a friend always makes the time go faster, or take a radio.

# Physical Preparation Checklist

During the week before the test, write down (1) what physical exercise you engaged in and for how long and (2) what you ate for each meal. Remember, you're trying for at least a half an hour of exercise every other day (preferably every day) and a balanced diet that's light on junk food.

**Exam minus 7 days**

Exercise: _____ for _____ minutes

Breakfast: _____

Lunch: _____

Dinner: _____

Snacks: _____

**Exam minus 6 days**

Exercise: _____ for _____ minutes

Breakfast: _____

Lunch: _____

Dinner: _____

Snacks: _____

**Exam minus 5 days**

Exercise: _____ for _____ minutes

Breakfast: _____

Lunch: _____

Dinner: _____

Snacks: _____

**Exam minus 4 days**

Exercise: _____ for _____ minutes

Breakfast: _____

Lunch: _____

Dinner: _____

Snacks: _____

**Exam minus 3 days**

Exercise: _____ for _____ minutes

Breakfast: _____

Lunch: _____

Dinner: _____

Snacks: _____

**Exam minus 2 days**

Exercise: _____ for _____ minutes

Breakfast: _____

Lunch: _____

Dinner: _____

Snacks: _____

**Exam minus 1 day**

Exercise: _____ for _____ minutes

Breakfast: _____

Lunch: _____

Dinner: _____

Snacks: _____

But don't overdo it. You don't want to exhaust yourself. Moderation is the key.

## Diet

First of all, cut out the junk. Go easy on caffeine and nicotine, and eliminate alcohol from your system at least two weeks before the exam.

What your body needs for peak performance is simply a balanced diet. Eat plenty of fruits and vegetables, along with lean protein and complex carbohydrates. Foods that are high in lecithin (an amino acid), such as fish and beans, are especially good "brain foods."

The night before the exam, you might "carbo-load" the way athletes do before a contest. Eat a big plate of spaghetti, rice and beans, or your favorite carbohydrate.

## Rest

You probably know how much sleep you need every night to be at your best, even if you don't always get it. Make sure you do get that much sleep, though, for at least a week before the exam. Moderation is important here, too. Extra sleep will just make you groggy.

If you are not a morning person and your exam will be given in the morning, you should reset your internal clock so that your body doesn't think you are taking an exam at 3 A.M. You have to start this process well before the exam. The way it works is to get up half an hour earlier each morning, and then go to bed half an hour earlier that night. Don't try it the other way around; you will just toss and turn if you go to bed early without having gotten up early. The next morning, get up another half an hour earlier, and so on. How long you will have to do this depends on how late you are used to getting up.

## ▶ Step 8: Get Your Act Together

**Time to complete: 10 minutes to read; time to complete will vary**

**Activity: Complete Final Preparations worksheet**

You are in control of your mind and body; you are in charge of test anxiety, your preparation, and your test-taking strategies. Now it's time to take charge of external factors, like the testing site and the materials you need to take the exam.

### Find Out Where the Test Is and Make a Trial Run

The exam bulletin will tell you when and where your exam is being held. Do you know how to get to the testing site? Do you know how long it will take you to get there? If not, make a trial run, preferably on the same day of the week and at the same time of day. Make note, on the Final Preparations worksheet, of the amount of time it will take you to get to the exam site. Plan on arriving 10–15 minutes early so you can get the lay of the land, use the bathroom, and calm down. Then figure out how early you will have to get up that morning, and make sure you get up that early every day for a week before the exam.

### Gather Your Materials

The night before the exam, lay out the clothes you will wear and the materials you have to bring with you to the exam. Plan on dressing in layers; you won't have any control over the temperature of the examination room. Have a sweater or jacket you can take off if it's warm. Use the checklist on the Final Preparations worksheet to help you pull together what you will need.

### Don't Skip Breakfast

Even if you don't usually eat breakfast, do so on exam morning. A cup of coffee doesn't count. Don't eat doughnuts or other sweet foods, either. A sugar high

### Getting to the Exam Site

Location of exam: _____

Date: _____

Time of exam: _____

Do I know how to get to the exam site?   Yes ___   No ___

(If no, make a trial run.)

Time it will take to get to exam site: _____

### Things to Lay out the Night Before

Clothes I will wear        ___

Sweater/jacket             ___

Watch                      ___

Photo ID                   ___

Admission card             ___

4 No. 2 pencils            ___

_____        _____

_____        _____

will leave you with a sugar low in the middle of the exam. A mix of protein and carbohydrates is best: Cereal with milk, or eggs with toast, will do your body a world of good.

## ▶ Step 9: Do It!

**Time to complete: 10 minutes, plus test-taking time**
**Activity: Ace the Firefighter Exam!**
Fast forward to exam day. You are ready. You made a study plan and followed through. You practiced your test-taking strategies while working through this book. You are in control of your physical, mental, and emotional state. You know when and where to show up and what to bring with you. In other words, you are better prepared than most of the other people taking the exam with you.

When you are done with the firefighter exam, you will have earned a reward. Plan a celebration. Call up your friends and plan a party, or have a nice dinner for two—whatever your heart desires. Give yourself something to look forward to.

And then do it. Go into the exam, full of confidence, armed with test-taking strategies that you have practiced until they are second nature. You are in control of yourself, your environment, and your performance on the exam. You are ready to succeed. Go in there and ace the exam. And look forward to your future career as a firefighter!

CHAPTER

4 ▶

# Firefighter
# Practice Exam 1

## CHAPTER SUMMARY

This is the first practice exam in this book, based on the most commonly tested areas on the firefighter written exams. Use this test to see how you would do if you had to take the exam today.

The skills tested on the exam that follows are the ones that have been tested in the past on firefighter exams that focus on job-related skills. The exam you take may look somewhat different from this exam, but you will find that this exam provides vital practice in the skills you need to pass a firefighter exam. For a somewhat different type of test, see Firefighter Practice Exam 2 in the next chapter.

This practice exam consists of 100 multiple-choice questions in the following areas: memory and observation, reading comprehension, verbal expression, spatial relations, judgment, and following procedures.

Normally, you would have about three hours for this test; however, for now, don't worry about timing. Just take the test in as relaxed a manner as you can. The answer sheet you should use for answering the questions is on the following page. Then comes the exam itself, and after that is the answer key, with each correct answer explained. The answer key is followed by a section on how to score your exam.

## Practice Exam 1

| 1. | ⓐ ⓑ ⓒ ⓓ | 36. | ⓐ ⓑ ⓒ ⓓ | 71. | ⓐ ⓑ ⓒ ⓓ |
|---|---|---|---|---|---|
| 2. | ⓐ ⓑ ⓒ ⓓ | 37. | ⓐ ⓑ ⓒ ⓓ | 72. | ⓐ ⓑ ⓒ ⓓ |
| 3. | ⓐ ⓑ ⓒ ⓓ | 38. | ⓐ ⓑ ⓒ ⓓ | 73. | ⓐ ⓑ ⓒ ⓓ |
| 4. | ⓐ ⓑ ⓒ ⓓ | 39. | ⓐ ⓑ ⓒ ⓓ | 74. | ⓐ ⓑ ⓒ ⓓ |
| 5. | ⓐ ⓑ ⓒ ⓓ | 40. | ⓐ ⓑ ⓒ ⓓ | 75. | ⓐ ⓑ ⓒ ⓓ |
| 6. | ⓐ ⓑ ⓒ ⓓ | 41. | ⓐ ⓑ ⓒ ⓓ | 76. | ⓐ ⓑ ⓒ ⓓ |
| 7. | ⓐ ⓑ ⓒ ⓓ | 42. | ⓐ ⓑ ⓒ ⓓ | 77. | ⓐ ⓑ ⓒ ⓓ |
| 8. | ⓐ ⓑ ⓒ ⓓ | 43. | ⓐ ⓑ ⓒ ⓓ | 78. | ⓐ ⓑ ⓒ ⓓ |
| 9. | ⓐ ⓑ ⓒ ⓓ | 44. | ⓐ ⓑ ⓒ ⓓ | 79. | ⓐ ⓑ ⓒ ⓓ |
| 10. | ⓐ ⓑ ⓒ ⓓ | 45. | ⓐ ⓑ ⓒ ⓓ | 80. | ⓐ ⓑ ⓒ ⓓ |
| 11. | ⓐ ⓑ ⓒ ⓓ | 46. | ⓐ ⓑ ⓒ ⓓ | 81. | ⓐ ⓑ ⓒ ⓓ |
| 12. | ⓐ ⓑ ⓒ ⓓ | 47. | ⓐ ⓑ ⓒ ⓓ | 82. | ⓐ ⓑ ⓒ ⓓ |
| 13. | ⓐ ⓑ ⓒ ⓓ | 48. | ⓐ ⓑ ⓒ ⓓ | 83. | ⓐ ⓑ ⓒ ⓓ |
| 14. | ⓐ ⓑ ⓒ ⓓ | 49. | ⓐ ⓑ ⓒ ⓓ | 84. | ⓐ ⓑ ⓒ ⓓ |
| 15. | ⓐ ⓑ ⓒ ⓓ | 50. | ⓐ ⓑ ⓒ ⓓ | 85. | ⓐ ⓑ ⓒ ⓓ |
| 16. | ⓐ ⓑ ⓒ ⓓ | 51. | ⓐ ⓑ ⓒ ⓓ | 86. | ⓐ ⓑ ⓒ ⓓ |
| 17. | ⓐ ⓑ ⓒ ⓓ | 52. | ⓐ ⓑ ⓒ ⓓ | 87. | ⓐ ⓑ ⓒ ⓓ |
| 18. | ⓐ ⓑ ⓒ ⓓ | 53. | ⓐ ⓑ ⓒ ⓓ | 88. | ⓐ ⓑ ⓒ ⓓ |
| 19. | ⓐ ⓑ ⓒ ⓓ | 54. | ⓐ ⓑ ⓒ ⓓ | 89. | ⓐ ⓑ ⓒ ⓓ |
| 20. | ⓐ ⓑ ⓒ ⓓ | 55. | ⓐ ⓑ ⓒ ⓓ | 90. | ⓐ ⓑ ⓒ ⓓ |
| 21. | ⓐ ⓑ ⓒ ⓓ | 56. | ⓐ ⓑ ⓒ ⓓ | 91. | ⓐ ⓑ ⓒ ⓓ |
| 22. | ⓐ ⓑ ⓒ ⓓ | 57. | ⓐ ⓑ ⓒ ⓓ | 92. | ⓐ ⓑ ⓒ ⓓ |
| 23. | ⓐ ⓑ ⓒ ⓓ | 58. | ⓐ ⓑ ⓒ ⓓ | 93. | ⓐ ⓑ ⓒ ⓓ |
| 24. | ⓐ ⓑ ⓒ ⓓ | 59. | ⓐ ⓑ ⓒ ⓓ | 94. | ⓐ ⓑ ⓒ ⓓ |
| 25. | ⓐ ⓑ ⓒ ⓓ | 60. | ⓐ ⓑ ⓒ ⓓ | 95. | ⓐ ⓑ ⓒ ⓓ |
| 26. | ⓐ ⓑ ⓒ ⓓ | 61. | ⓐ ⓑ ⓒ ⓓ | 96. | ⓐ ⓑ ⓒ ⓓ |
| 27. | ⓐ ⓑ ⓒ ⓓ | 62. | ⓐ ⓑ ⓒ ⓓ | 97. | ⓐ ⓑ ⓒ ⓓ |
| 28. | ⓐ ⓑ ⓒ ⓓ | 63. | ⓐ ⓑ ⓒ ⓓ | 98. | ⓐ ⓑ ⓒ ⓓ |
| 29. | ⓐ ⓑ ⓒ ⓓ | 64. | ⓐ ⓑ ⓒ ⓓ | 99. | ⓐ ⓑ ⓒ ⓓ |
| 30. | ⓐ ⓑ ⓒ ⓓ | 65. | ⓐ ⓑ ⓒ ⓓ | 100. | ⓐ ⓑ ⓒ ⓓ |
| 31. | ⓐ ⓑ ⓒ ⓓ | 66. | ⓐ ⓑ ⓒ ⓓ | | |
| 32. | ⓐ ⓑ ⓒ ⓓ | 67. | ⓐ ⓑ ⓒ ⓓ | | |
| 33. | ⓐ ⓑ ⓒ ⓓ | 68. | ⓐ ⓑ ⓒ ⓓ | | |
| 34. | ⓐ ⓑ ⓒ ⓓ | 69. | ⓐ ⓑ ⓒ ⓓ | | |
| 35. | ⓐ ⓑ ⓒ ⓓ | 70. | ⓐ ⓑ ⓒ ⓓ | | |

You will have five minutes to study the diagram on the following page, after which you must turn the page and answer questions 1–7 from memory. You will NOT be permitted to look back at the diagram to answer the questions.

PAINT STORE

28

24

After you have spent five minutes studying the diagram on the previous page, turn the page and answer questions 1–7 based on the diagram. DO NOT turn back to the diagram to answer these questions. When you have finished questions 1–7, you may go on to the next memory diagram.

**1.** Upon arriving at the scene, you can see flames inside the windows on which floor(s)?
  **a.** second floor only
  **b.** third floor only
  **c.** first and third floors
  **d.** second and third floors

**2.** How many victims can you see inside the building that is on fire?
  **a.** none
  **b.** one
  **c.** two
  **d.** three

**3.** What is the address of the business next door to the fire scene?
  **a.** 22
  **b.** 20
  **c.** 24
  **d.** 28

**4.** You must evacuate the victims in the fire building from the roof. What obstructions are in your way?
  **a.** a clothesline and two smoke stacks
  **b.** a TV antenna and two smoke stacks
  **c.** a clothesline and a TV antenna
  **d.** a clothesline and a smoke stack

**5.** How many people are standing in the windows of the dwelling adjacent to the fire?
  **a.** two adults
  **b.** three adults
  **c.** three adults and two babies
  **d.** two adults and two babies

**6.** When you arrive at the scene, you evacuate the business next door to the fire for all of the following reasons EXCEPT
  **a.** paints can be extremely flammable.
  **b.** the fire has spread to the roof of the store.
  **c.** smoke may endanger the employees and patrons of the store.
  **d.** the store shares the fire wall with the building on fire.

**7.** Firefighters do not have access to one of the windows in the fire building. Which floor is it on?
  **a.** first
  **b.** third
  **c.** basement
  **d.** second

You will have five minutes to study the diagram on the next page, after which you must turn the page and answer questions 8–15 from memory. You will NOT be permitted to look back at the diagram to answer the questions.

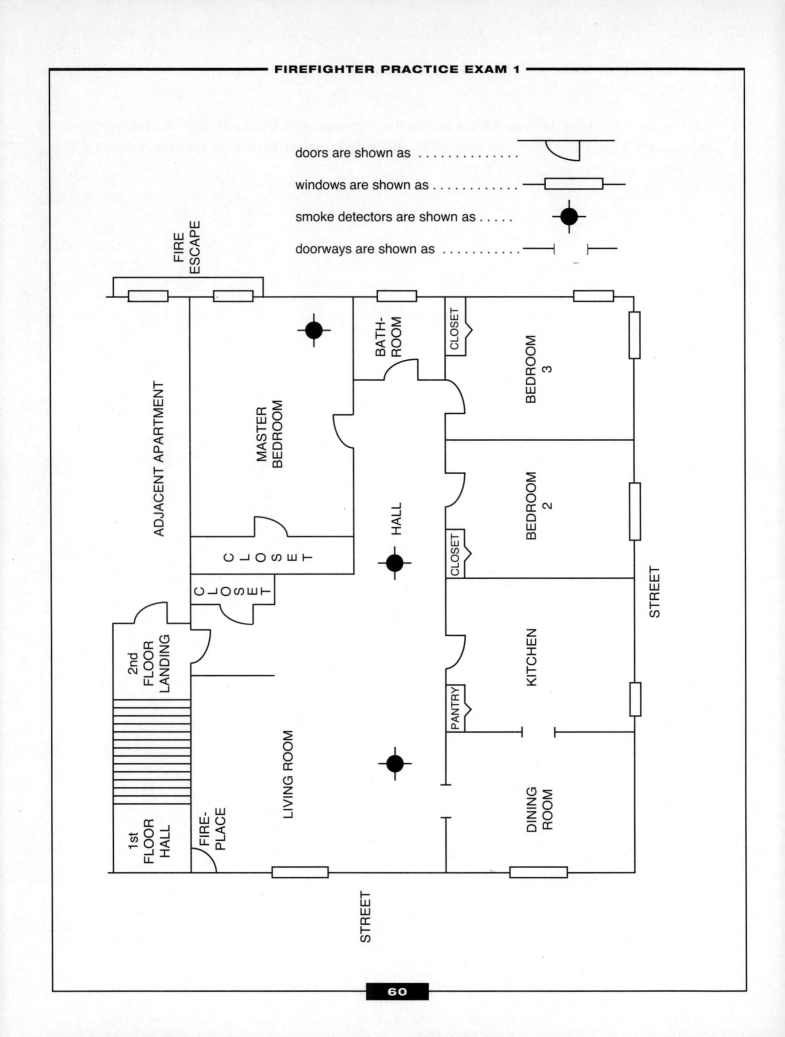

doors are shown as . . . . . . . . . . . . . .

windows are shown as . . . . . . . . . . .

smoke detectors are shown as . . . . .

doorways are shown as . . . . . . . . . .

FIRE ESCAPE

ADJACENT APARTMENT

MASTER BEDROOM

CLOSET

CLOSET

2nd FLOOR LANDING

1st FLOOR HALL

FIRE-PLACE

LIVING ROOM

HALL

BATH-ROOM

CLOSET

BEDROOM 3

BEDROOM 2

CLOSET

KITCHEN

PANTRY

DINING ROOM

STREET

STREET

After you have spent five minutes studying the diagram, turn the page and answer questions 8–15 based on the diagram. DO NOT turn back to the diagram to answer these questions. When you have finished questions 8–15, you may go on with the rest of the test.

**8.** The number of rooms in the apartment is
   **a.** eight.
   **b.** seven.
   **c.** six.
   **d.** five.

**9.** The firefighters enter the first floor hall and proceed up the stairs and into the apartment. What is the first room they encounter?
   **a.** the living room
   **b.** the master bedroom
   **c.** the bathroom
   **d.** the kitchen

**10.** How many smoke detectors are in the bedrooms?
   **a.** none
   **b.** one
   **c.** two
   **d.** three

**11.** While searching a room, firefighters notice that there are two windows. Which room are they in?
   **a.** bedroom 3
   **b.** the dining room
   **c.** bedroom 2
   **d.** the master bedroom

**12.** During the night, a spark from the fireplace starts the carpet smoldering, which causes the drapes to catch fire. The fire begins to spread. The areas most affected by the fire are the
   **a.** kitchen and bedroom 2.
   **b.** living room and bathroom.
   **c.** master bedroom and bedroom 2.
   **d.** living room and dining room.

**13.** The residents of the apartment like to smoke in bed. One of them falls asleep in the master bedroom and drops a lit cigarette on the floor. The smoke detector that will activate first is located in the
   **a.** hall.
   **b.** living room.
   **c.** master bedroom.
   **d.** bedroom 3.

**14.** The number of windows in the apartment is
   **a.** seven.
   **b.** eight.
   **c.** nine.
   **d.** ten.

**15.** The firefighters who need to get into the apartment can do so by the
   **a.** fire escape only.
   **b.** windows, hall stairway, and fire escape.
   **c.** hall stairway and fire escape only.
   **d.** windows and hall stairway only.

Answer questions 16–19 based on the following information.

The preferred order for removal of civilians from a fire building is as follows:
   1. Interior stairs
   2. Fire escape
   3. Adjacent building
   4. Aerial ladder or tower ladder
   5. Ground ladder
   6. Rescue rope

**16.** Which of the following is the preferred means of removing fire victims from a burning building?

a. leading them down a fire escape

b. using the aerial ladder or tower ladder

c. using the stairway inside the building

d. using a rescue rope

**17.** What means of saving civilians trapped by fire would be used only as a last resort?

a. using a roof rescue rope and removing the victims through a window

b. taking them out via an adjoining building

c. using a rescue rope

d. raising a grand ladder to a window

**18.** Several firefighters suddenly find that they are trapped by the fire they are fighting. They find that the interior stairway is blocked and they cannot reach the fire escape. What should they try next?

a. taking the fire escape

b. sliding down a rescue rope

c. trying to reach an adjoining building

d. using a ground ladder

**19.** Before resorting to using the ground ladder, a firefighter should try all the following escape methods EXCEPT

a. going through the adjoining building.

b. sliding down the roof rescue rope.

c. using the interior stairs.

d. using the fire escape.

Answer question 20 based on your best judgment and common sense.

**20.** Firefighters are required to check the air supply on their self-contained breathing apparatus (SCBA) each day. If there is any reduction in pressure, the firefighter should change the air tank and replace it with a full tank. The main reason firefighters should have full air tanks is that

a. a full air tank permits the firefighters to operate for a maximum length of time in a fire area.

b. firefighters won't have to check their air tank for the rest of the week if the tanks are not used.

c. a full air tank allows the firefighters to have a feeling of confidence and protection against heat, flame, and toxic gases.

d. checking and replacing tanks provides work for the firefighters assigned to the Mask Maintenance Unit.

Answer questions 21–23 based on the following information.

One of the most dangerous rescue situations faced by firefighters is searching burning structures. While searching burning structures, the best way to reduce the risk of danger is through training, practicing, and planning. The factors that the firefighter must evaluate include type of occupancy, time of day, fire and smoke conditions, and activity clues. Firefighters must always work in teams of two or more when entering an involved structure. A minimum of two fully equipped firefighters and a charged hose line should be ready to go in and assist the team if needed. This is known as the two-in/two-out rule. When conducting a search, firefighters should carry a forcible-entry tool, a flashlight, and a radio. Thermal imagers can help firefighters see through smoke, thus speeding up rescue efforts.

**21.** What should a firefighter do to reduce the risk of danger while searching burning structures?
  **a.** Carry a thermal imager.
  **b.** Train, practice, and plan for searches.
  **c.** Evaluate the type of occupancy, time of day, and fire conditions.
  **d.** Ensure a charged hose line is ready to go in if needed.

**22.** A firefighter should carry all of the following equipment EXCEPT a
  **a.** flashlight.
  **b.** radio.
  **c.** forcible-entry tool.
  **d.** thermal imager.

**23.** The two-in/two-out rule
  **a.** mandates a minimum of two fully equipped firefighters be ready to assist if needed.
  **b.** reduces the risk and danger for firefighters searching burning structures.
  **c.** allows for the use of thermal imagers.
  **d.** permits firefighters to evaluate fire and smoke conditions.

Answer questions 24–28 based solely on the information in the following passage.

Firefighters know that the dangers of motor vehicle fires are too often overlooked. In the United States, one out of five fires involves motor vehicles, resulting each year in 600 deaths, 2,600 civilian injuries, and 1,200 injuries to firefighters. The reason for so many injuries and fatalities is that a vehicle can generate heat of up to 1,500° F. (The boiling point of water is 212° F, and the cooking temperature for most foods is 500° F.)

Because of the intense heat generated in a vehicle fire, parts of the car or truck may burst, causing debris to travel great distances and turning bumpers, tire rims, drive shafts, axles, and even engine parts into lethal shrapnel. Gas tanks may rupture and spray highly flammable fuel. In addition, hazardous materials such as battery acid can cause serious injury even if they do not ignite.

Vehicle fires can also produce toxic gases. Carbon monoxide, which is produced during a fire, is an odorless and colorless gas that is deadly in high concentrations. Firefighters must wear SCBA and full personal protective equipment when attempting to extinguish a vehicle fire.

**24.** One reason that firefighters wear SCBA is to protect themselves against
  **a.** flying car parts.
  **b.** intense heat.
  **c.** flammable fuels.
  **d.** carbon monoxide.

**25.** The passage suggests that most injuries in motor-vehicle fires are caused by
  **a.** battery acid.
  **b.** odorless gases.
  **c.** extremely high temperatures.
  **d.** firefighters' errors.

**26.** The main focus of this passage is
  **a.** how firefighters protect themselves against motor-vehicle fires.
  **b.** the dangers of motor-vehicle fires.
  **c.** the amount of heat generated in motor-vehicle fires.
  **d.** the dangers of odorless gases in motor-vehicle fires.

**27.** The cooking temperature for food (500° F) is most likely included in the passage to show the reader

    **a.** how hot motor-vehicle fires really are.

    **b.** at what point water boils.

    **c.** why motor-vehicle fires produce toxic gases.

    **d.** why one out of five fires involves a motor-vehicle.

**28.** One reason that firefighters must be aware of the possibility of carbon monoxide in motor-vehicle fires is because carbon monoxide

    **a.** is highly concentrated.

    **b.** cannot be seen or smelled.

    **c.** cannot be protected against.

    **d.** can shoot great distances into the air.

Answer questions 29 and 30 based on your best judgment and common sense.

**29.** When a firefighter uses a ladder to rescue a citizen, the firefighter should assist the person down the ladder. The most important reason for giving this assistance is that

    **a.** even the best fire ladders tend to be unstable.

    **b.** firefighters should do everything they can to improve public relations.

    **c.** if there is an accident, the fire department might be held liable.

    **d.** firefighters should keep individuals being rescued as safe as possible.

**30.** When firefighters remove a refrigerator from an apartment, the door, or door lock, is removed. The chief reason for this action is that

    **a.** children may play in the refrigerator and lock themselves inside.

    **b.** passersby may use the refrigerator to store their belongings.

    **c.** a disreputable company may attempt to resell the refrigerator.

    **d.** the refrigerator will develop unhealthy fumes if the door is tightly closed.

**31.** Choose the sentence that is most clearly written.

    **a.** For three weeks, the Merryville Fire Chief received taunting calls from an arsonist, who would not say where he intended to set the next fire.

    **b.** The Merryville Fire Chief received taunting calls from an arsonist, but he would not say where he intended to set the next fire, for three weeks.

    **c.** He would not say where he intended to set the next fire, but for three weeks the Merryville Fire Chief received taunting calls from an arsonist.

    **d.** The Merryville Police Chief received taunting calls from an arsonist for three weeks, not saying where he intended to set the next fire.

**32.** Choose the sentence that is most clearly written.

    **a.** Kate Meyers received a recent well-deserved promotion and several firefighters also.

    **b.** Having received a well-deserved promotion, recently Kate Meyers was included with several other firefighters.

    **c.** Kate Meyers, and including several firefighters recently, they all received a well-deserved promotion.

    **d.** Several firefighters, including Kate Meyers, have recently received well-deserved promotions.

Answer questions 33–35 based solely on the information in the following passage.

A number of specialized tools are available to firefighters to assist with or conduct forcible entry. The bam bam, or dent puller, is used to pull apart lock cylinders. The duckbill lock breaker is designed to break open heavy-duty padlocks. The K tool is used to perform through-the-lock forcible entry. The K tool is designed to pull out lock cylinders and expose their mechanisms so as to open the lock. Key tools used to open the lock include the bent, square, and screwdriver types; as well as a pick, to slide open the shutter on some rim locks. To perform the task of forcible entry, most of the tools or groups of tools discussed are used in combination with other tools.

**33.** The duckbill lock breaker forcible-entry tool is designed to break

  **a.** lock cylinders.

  **b.** rim locks.

  **c.** heavy-duty padlocks.

  **d.** lock mechanisms.

**34.** Key tools used for through-the-lock forcible entry include all of the following EXCEPT

  **a.** bent type.

  **b.** pick type.

  **c.** square type.

  **d.** round type.

**35.** Which of the following is the main subject of the passage?

  **a.** Specialized forcible-entry tool types

  **b.** Procedures used for forcible entry

  **c.** How to use a K-Tool

  **d.** How to perform through-the-lock forcible entry

Answer questions 36 and 37 based on your best judgment and common sense.

**36.** When the firehouse receives an alarm, all the firefighters should immediately put their personal protective equipment on. The most important reason for this rule is that

  **a.** it allows the firefighters to be ready to respond immediately upon arriving at the scene.

  **b.** the firefighters may not be recognized by civilians at the scene of the emergency.

  **c.** it is too difficult for firefighters to dress on the truck.

  **d.** if the firefighters on the truck cannot be identified by their attire, other vehicles may not yield.

**37.** Firefighter Jackson has been called back to work at 8:00 P.M. to replace a colleague who had to leave because of a family emergency. While driving in, she passes an abandoned warehouse that has had a number of small, unexplained fires, and notices a group of children playing inside the security fence. What is the proper action for Firefighter Jackson to take?

  **a.** Pull over, stop, identify herself as a firefighter, and wait until the children leave the area.

  **b.** Continue on her way and report the incident to her shift supervisor.

  **c.** Pull over, stop, and make a 911 call to report the situation, identifying herself and asking for police assistance.

  **d.** Ignore the situation because the children are only having fun.

**38.** Leaving work an hour after a windstorm, Firefighter Garcia is driving north on Washington Street when he comes upon a large tree limb that has fallen and is blocking his lane. About 50 yards north is the intersection of Washington and Fourth Avenue. Firefighter Garcia carefully drives around a fallen limb and stops at this intersection to phone in a report. Which of the following statements most clearly and accurately reports this situation?

   **a.** I'm at the corner of Fourth Avenue in my truck, and a tree limb fell, which is blocking my lane.

   **b.** A large tree limb has fallen across the road north of Washington Street near Fourth Avenue.

   **c.** There is a fallen tree limb blocking one lane of Washington Street, about 50 yards south of Fourth Avenue.

   **d.** In the northbound lane of Fourth Avenue and Washington Street, I had to drive around a limb that fell off a tree obstructing traffic.

**39.** Firefighter Davis is returning to the station after a call. He is driving east on First Avenue when a large dog runs in front of his truck. Firefighter Davis slams on his brakes but is unable to keep from hitting the dog. Hearing the screeching of the brakes, the dog's owner, James Ramsey, runs out of his house on the corner of First Avenue and Highland Court and discovers that his dog has a leg injury. Firefighter Davis helps put the dog into Mr. Ramsey's car so that Mr. Ramsey can take the animal to the vet. Later, Firefighter Davis files a report. Which of the following reports describes the incident most clearly and accurately?

   **a.** The dog's owner, James Ramsey, whose leg appeared to be hurt, took him to the vet after I helped him into the car on First Avenue at Highland Court.

   **b.** Near the intersection of First Avenue and Highland Court, a dog ran out in front of my truck and I could not avoid hitting it. I stopped to help the dog's owner, James Ramsey, who took the injured animal to the vet.

   **c.** I was driving along First Avenue when I hit a dog. We picked the dog up with a leg injury and put him in the car, which then drove to the vet. James Ramsey was the man's name.

   **d.** James Ramsey, who owned a dog, came running out of his house at First and Highland and saw me hit him with my truck. Though I didn't mean to do it, I helped him into a car so that Ramsey could get to the vet for medical treatment.

Answer questions 40 and 41 based on the following information.

When obtaining water from a hydrant, the firefighters should perform the following steps in this order:

1. Remove hydrant wrench and tool kit with prepacked supply hose from engine.

2. Wrap hose one turn around the hydrant and signal driver to begin laying out supply line.

3. Remove hydrant steamer cap with the hydrant wrench, then open the hydrant to flush it. Shut off hydrant.

4. Attach supply line and signal engine that the hose is connected.

5. Await pump operator's order to charge the supply line.

**40.** After the firefighter assigned to the hydrant has flushed the hydrant, he or she must
   **a.** activate the pump.
   **b.** attach the supply line.
   **c.** wrap the hydrant.
   **d.** signal the motor pump operator that the supply line is ready.

**41.** What mechanical device is used to turn on the fire hydrant valve?
   **a.** a pump
   **b.** a hose
   **c.** a hydrant wrench
   **d.** a holding tank

Answer questions 42–46 based solely on the information in the following passage.

## Standard Operational Guideline Response to High-Rise Buildings

Procedures set forth here may be varied or improved upon because of additional information obtained on specific buildings. These are basic operational procedures intended to assist the officer in charge (OIC).

### Confirmed Fire/Smoke Condition High-Rise Building

1. The first arriving engine will provide an initial size up and implement Incident Command System (ICS) procedures immediately. Standpipe supply connections will be immediately supported by the application of dual 3" lines to the standpipe supply siamese, an initial pump pressure of 150 psi will be pumped to standpipes during operations. A maintenance or building engineer should be contacted for consultation and shall remain at the command post. The initial engine should determine the location of the fire or emergency. Evac-uation will be ordered at this time if not already done so.

2. First-alarm companies shall pick up any "in-house" jack phones from the building personnel to aid in communications. Each floor will need to be checked for smoke.

3. The first arriving engine companies shall initiate actions to locate the fire and get the first line advanced into best position as well as to secure all elevators, including service elevators, obtain necessary master keys for windows, doors, and so on. The status of the HVAC (heating, ventilating, air conditioning) system should also be checked to see if it is still in operation: if so, it will need to be shut down unless it is designed to handle products of combustion. Stair towers should be pressurized using positive pressure fans prior to fire attack. Upon arrival of the second engines, the initial engine will need to be supplied using a single 5" supply line.

4. Prior to leaving the lobby for fire-suppression activities, all members will be wearing full personal protective equipment including SCBA, and will have cylinder valves opened. In addition, each person will have a personal light along with hand tools prior to entering the stair tower for suppression operations.

5. The staging floor shall be designated one floor below the fire floor and shall be used to stage equipment and manpower. There will be a sector officer at this location.

6. The first attack crew shall use the stairway to go one floor below the fire floor and connect to the standpipe outlet at this level, using department standpipe packs with a gated wye fitting. The line will then be advanced to the fire floor and one person shall be assigned to remain at the valve to adjust pressure. The next hose line placed into service will connect on the fire floor using

department standpipe packs with a gated wye fitting and will back up the original attack crew.

**42.** All of the following actions should be taken by the first arriving engine companies at the scene of a confirmed fire in a high-rise building EXCEPT
  **a.** initiate actions to locate the fire.
  **b.** establish a water supply to the initial engine with a single 5" supply line.
  **c.** pressurize stair towers with positive pressure fans prior to fire attack.
  **d.** control all building elevators.

**43.** Several firefighters are ready to leave the lobby area and enter the stair tower for fire-suppression activities. What should they do next?
  **a.** report to the staging floor
  **b.** report to the sector officer
  **c.** relieve the first attack crew
  **d.** ensure cylinder valves are open

**44.** Firefighters operating the backup line will connect to the standpipe outlet at this level using department standpipe packs with a gated wye fitting.
  **a.** one floor below the fire
  **b.** on the fire floor
  **c.** on the staging floor
  **d.** at the lobby staging area

**45.** The first attack crew shall use the stairway to go one floor below the fire floor and connect to the standpipe outlet at this level using department standpipe packs with a gated wye fitting. The line will then be advanced to the fire floor and one person shall be assigned to remain at the valve. The main reason for one firefighter to remain at that valve is that
  **a.** the backup line firefighters need assistance with their line.

  **b.** the pressure may be adjusted as needed.
  **c.** the sector officer can direct the backup line in an orderly manner.
  **d.** the backup line needs to be connected at the fire floor.

**46.** Firefighters have just arrived on the scene of a confirmed fire in a high-rise building. What should they do first?
  **a.** provide an initial size up and implement ICS procedures immediately
  **b.** connect dual 3" lines to the standpipe supply siamese
  **c.** order a building evacuation
  **d.** find a building or maintenance engineer

Answer question 47 based on your best judgment and common sense.

**47.** No level of risk is acceptable where there is no potential to save lives or property. Firefighters shall not be committed to interior offensive fire-fighting operations in abandoned or derelict buildings. The most important reason for this is that
  **a.** no building or property is worth the life of a firefighter.
  **b.** firefighting is inherently risky.
  **c.** some risk is acceptable during firefighting operations.
  **d.** measures need to be taken to control or eliminate hazards.

Answer questions 48–50 solely on the basis of this map. The arrows indicate traffic flow; one arrow indicates a one-way street going in the direction of the arrow; two arrows represent a two-way street. You are not allowed to go the wrong way on a one-way street.

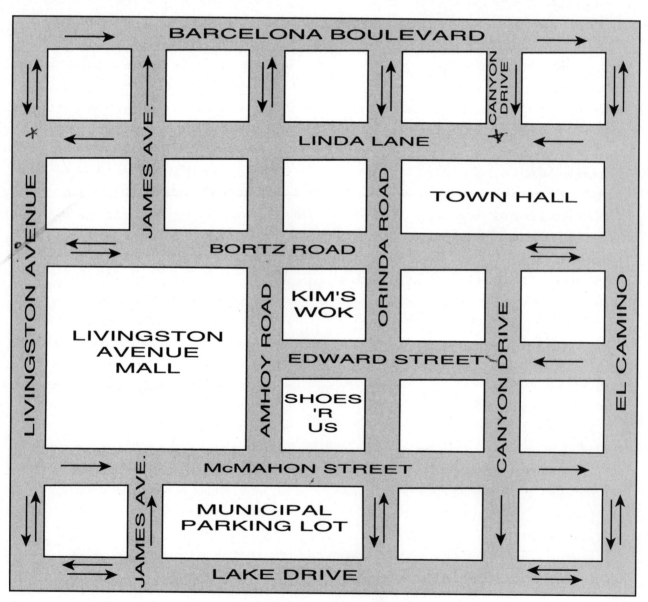

**48.** Engine 6 has been called to a trash can fire in the Livingston Avenue Mall at the southeast corner of the building. Dispatch notifies them of an alarm going off in a residence located at the northwest corner of Canyon Drive and Linda Lane. What is the quickest route for the fire engine to take from the mall to the residence?

   **a.** Turn north on Amhoy Road, then east on Linda Lane, then north on Canyon Drive.

   **b.** Turn east on McMahon Street, then north on El Camino, then west on Linda Lane, then north on Orinda Road, then east on Barcelona Boulevard to Canyon Drive, and south on Canyon Drive.

   **c.** Turn north on Amhoy Road, then east on Barcelona Boulevard, then south on Canyon Drive.

   **d.** Turn north on Amhoy Road, then east on Bortz Road, then north on Orinda Road, then east on Barcelona Boulevard, and south on Canyon Drive.

**49.** Returning from a false alarm, Engine 8 is southbound on Canyon Drive and has just crossed Edward Street, when a call comes in that someone has set fire to a bus parked at a bus stop located at Livingston Avenue and Bortz Road. What is the quickest route for the engine to take to the bus stop?

   **a.** Continue south on Canyon Drive, then turn west on McMahon Street, then north on Orinda Road, then west on Edward Street, then north on Amhoy Road, then west on Bortz Road to Livingston.

   **b.** Continue south on Canyon Drive, then turn west on Lake Drive, then north on Livingston Avenue to Bortz Road.

   **c.** Make a U-turn on Canyon Drive, then go west on Bortz Road to Livingston Avenue.

   **d.** Continue south on Canyon Drive, then turn east on Lake Drive, then north on El Camino, and then west on Bortz Road to Livingston Avenue.

**50.** Firefighter Ricardo has just come off duty and is driving west on Bortz Road. She makes a right onto James Avenue, then a left onto Linda Lane, then a right onto Livingston, and then a right onto Barcelona Boulevard. What direction is she facing?

   **a.** east

   **b.** south

   **c.** west

   **d.** north

Answer questions 51 and 52 based on your best judgment and common sense.

**51.** A woman walks into the firehouse and tells Firefighter Robinson she has locked her keys in the car. She is frantic because her three-year-old daughter is in the back seat. He should
  **a.** leave the firehouse and break the car window.
  **b.** advise the woman to call a locksmith, and then go stand by the car to reassure the child.
  **c.** ask the woman the location of her car, and inform his superior officer immediately.
  **d.** suggest that the woman call a locksmith, and advise her not to be so careless in the future.

**52.** The fire department has replaced its wooden ladders with aluminum ladders. Which of the following is NOT a sensible reason for this change?
  **a.** Wooden ladders are harder to repair and keep clean.
  **b.** Wooden ladders are less expensive than aluminum ladders.
  **c.** Wooden ladders are heavier than aluminum ladders.
  **d.** Wooden ladders catch on fire more readily than aluminum ladders.

Answer questions 53–55 based solely on the information in the following passage.

If a building is to be left in a safe condition, firefighters must search for hidden fires that may rekindle. Typically, this process, known as overhaul, begins in the area of actual fire involvement. Before searching for hidden fires, however, firefighters must first determine the condition of the building.

The fire's intensity and the amount of water used to fight the fire are both factors that affect a building. Fire can burn away floor joists and weaken roof trusses. Heat from the fire can weaken concrete and the mortar in wall joints and elongate steel roof supports. Excess water can add dangerous weight to floors and walls.

Once it has been determined that it is safe to enter a building, the process of overhauling begins. A firefighter can often detect hidden fires by looking for discoloration, peeling paint, cracked plaster, and smoke emissions; by feeling walls and floors with the back of the hand; by listening for popping, cracking, and hissing sounds; and by using electronic sensors to detect heat variances.

**53.** The main purpose of overhauling a building is to
  **a.** make sure the fire will not start up again.
  **b.** strengthen wall joints and roof supports.
  **c.** make sure excess water has not damaged floors.
  **d.** test for heat damage by using electronic sensors.

**54.** Before overhauling a building, what is the first thing a firefighter should do?
a. Look for discoloration in the paint.
b. Detect differences in heat along walls and floors.
c. Listen for sounds that may indicate a fire.
d. Determine whether the building is safe enough to carry out overhaul.

**55.** According to the passage, cracked plaster is a sign that
a. a wall may be about to fall in.
b. a fire may be smoldering inside a wall.
c. a wall is dangerously weighted with water.
d. firefighters should exit the building immediately.

Answer question 56 based on your best judgment and common sense.

**56.** While reading the latest edition of *Firefighters Magazine*, Firefighter Pitt sees an article that explains a faster, more efficient way to connect a hose to a standpipe. She thinks this is a terrific idea that will save precious time at the scene of a fire. Which of the following is the most appropriate first action for her to take?
a. At the next fire, implement the procedure she read about.
b. Write a letter to the fire commissioner reporting her findings.
c. Show the article to her superior officer and ask if her company can change its procedure.
d. Call the union and ask them if she can advise the fire department to change its procedure.

**57.** The fire department's home fire safety escape trailer will be at your station during the month of June. At that time, each family in the community will be able to purchase up to three smoke alarms at a cost of only $3 each. Each family is also entitled to one fire extinguisher at a cost of $8. Which of the following statements describes the city's new program most clearly and accurately?
a. In June, every person in the community will purchase three smoke alarms and fire extinguishers that cost $3 and $8 each.
b. During the month of June, each family may buy one fire extinguisher for $8 and up to three smoke alarms, which cost $3 each.
c. During the fire safety drive in June, families can purchase fire extinguishers and smoke alarms, up to three of these, costing $3 and $8.
d. The purchase of up to three smoke alarms at a cost of $3 each and one fire extinguisher at $8 each may be bought in June at the fire station's safety drive.

**58.** During a major snowstorm, Firefighter O'Neal is driving a fire truck along the 1200 block of Arden Drive, one of the city's main snow routes. When the snow is more than two inches deep, residents are restricted from parking on streets that are designated snow routes. The snow on this day is already four inches deep. Suddenly, Firefighter O'Neal sees a parked car on the left side of the street and barely manages to drive the truck around it. When she returns to the station, she phones in a request to have the car towed. Which of the following most clearly and accurately describes the situation?

  **a.** Because I almost did not see the car on Arden Drive during this snowstorm, it should be removed immediately.

  **b.** I am calling for a tow truck in the 1200 block of a main snow route because I almost hit a car with the snow falling, which made it impossible to see cars on my left side.

  **c.** As I was driving on the 1200 block of Arden Drive, I almost ran into an illegally parked car. Please send a tow truck and have the car removed.

  **d.** There is a car in the 1200 block of Arden Drive. The snow is four inches deep, which may cause an accident and should be towed immediately.

**59.** Firefighter Caruso is washing a fire truck in front of the station when nine-year-old Joey Tremont asks if he would help get Joey's kitten, Sugar, down from a tree across the street. After checking with his chief, Firefighter Caruso walks across the street and sees that he can easily reach the limb where the kitten is trapped. As he is pulling the kitten to safety, the kitten scratches him on the face. The next day, Firefighter Caruso's face is swollen; the scratch has become infected. He must file a medical report. Which of the following reports describes the incident most clearly and accurately?

  **a.** A kitten scratched me as I was washing the truck in front of the station when a boy named Joey asked me to retrieve Sugar. The scratch has become infected.

  **b.** Joey Tremont asked me to save his kitten, but when he did he scratched me on the face and an infection ensued.

  **c.** While I was washing the truck in front of the station, a boy named Joey asked me to rescue his kitten from a tree across the street. As I was lifting the kitten, it scratched me, and the scratch became infected.

  **d.** Having rescued a kitten named Sugar from a tree across the street after washing the truck, Joey, the boy's name, had asked me to. The kitten then scratched me on the face, which became infected the next day.

Answer questions 60–62 solely on the basis of this map. The arrows indicate traffic flow; one arrow indicates a one-way street going in the direction of the arrow; two arrows represent a two-way street. You are not allowed to go the wrong way on a one-way street.

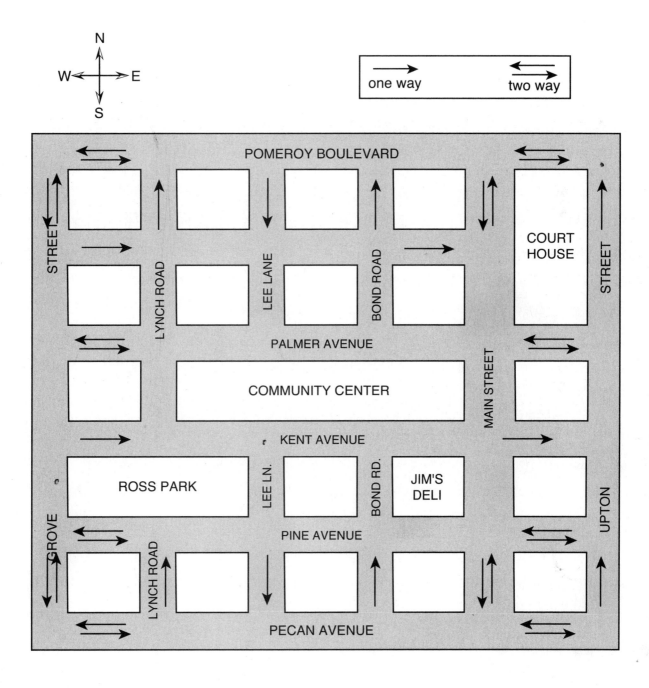

**60.** Engine 1 is eastbound on Kent Avenue at Lee Lane when a call comes in from dispatch about a gas heater explosion at a residence located at the northeast corner of Lynch Road and Mill Road. What is the quickest route for the engine to take?

**a.** Continue east on Kent Avenue, then turn north on Main Street to Mill Road, then west on Mill Road to the northeast corner of Lynch Road and Mill Road.

**b.** Continue east on Kent Avenue, then turn north on Main Street, then east on Pomeroy Boulevard, then south on Lynch Road.

**c.** Continue east on Kent Avenue, then turn south on Main Street, then west on Pine Avenue, then north on Grove Street, then east on Mill Road to Lynch Road.

**d.** Continue east on Kent Avenue, then turn north on Main Street, then west on Palmer Avenue, then north on Lynch Road to Mill Road.

**61.** Firefighter McElhaney is off duty and driving by the court house, northbound on Upton Street. He receives a call on his cell phone about a bomb having gone off at Ross Park on the Grove Street side of the park. He decides he may be able to be of some help. What is the most direct route for Firefighter McElhaney to take?

**a.** Continue north on Upton Street, turn west on Pomeroy Boulevard, then south on Main Street, then west on Kent Avenue to Grove Street.

**b.** Continue north on Upton Street, then turn west on Pomeroy Boulevard, then south on Grove Street to Ross Park.

**c.** Continue north on Upton Street, then turn west on Pomeroy Boulevard, then south on Main Street, then west on Palmer Avenue, then south on Grove Street to Ross Park.

**d.** Make a U-turn on Upton Street, then go west on Palmer Avenue, then south on Grove Street to Ross Park.

**62.** Firefighter Kearney has just had lunch at Jim's Deli and is now heading west on Pine Avenue. She turns left on Lee Lane, then left again onto Pecan Avenue. She turns left on Main Street and finally turns right on Palmer Avenue. What direction is she facing?

**a.** west

**b.** south

**c.** north

**d.** east

Answer question 63 based on your best judgment and common sense.

**63.** Firefighter Green arrives at an apartment building for a routine inspection. During the inspection, she notices several fire safety violations in the building across the street. The best course of action for her to take would be to

**a.** notify the police to arrest the owner of the building across the street.

**b.** issue violation orders for the building across the street.

**c.** disregard the building across the street, since it is not due for inspection.

**d.** call her company into the building across the street to fix the violations.

Answer questions 64–67 solely on the basis of this map. The arrows indicate traffic flow; one arrow indicates a one-way street going in the direction of the arrow; no arrows represent a two-way street. You are not allowed to go the wrong way on a one-way street.

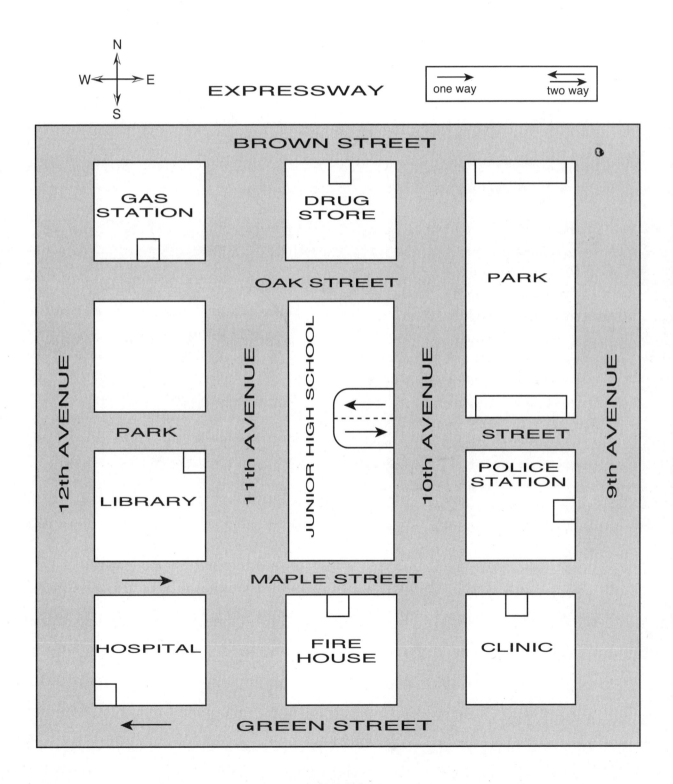

**64.** There is a vehicular accident at the corner of Brown Street and 9th Avenue, and a fire has started. What is the most direct legal way for the fire engine to travel from the fire station to the accident scene?

    **a.** Go east on Maple Street and north on 9th Avenue to the accident.

    **b.** Go west on Maple Street, north on 12th Avenue, and east on Brown Street to the accident.

    **c.** Go east on Maple Street and north on 11th Avenue to the accident.

    **d.** Go west on Maple Street, north on 11th Avenue, and east on Brown Street to the accident.

**65.** What streets run north and south of the park?

    **a.** Brown Street and Oak Street

    **b.** Maple Street and Park Street

    **c.** Brown Street and Park Street

    **d.** Green Street and Oak Street

**66.** A civilian leaving the clinic needs to drive to the drug store. What is the most direct route for her to take?

    **a.** Go east on Maple Street, north on 9th Avenue, and west on Brown Street to the store entrance.

    **b.** Go west on Maple Street, north on 10th Avenue, and west on Brown Street to the store entrance.

    **c.** Go west on Green Street, north on 12th Avenue, and east on Brown Street to the store entrance.

    **d.** Go east on Oak Street, north on 11th Avenue, and east on Brown Street to the store entrance.

**67.** Someone at the junior high school has been injured and needs to go to the hospital. What directions would you give to the ambulance driver?

    **a.** Go north on 10th Avenue, west on Brown Street, and south on 12th Avenue to the hospital entrance.

    **b.** Go south on 10th Avenue and west on Green Street to the hospital entrance.

    **c.** Go north on 10th Avenue and south on Brown Street to the hospital entrance.

    **d.** Go south on 10th Avenue, south on Maple Street, and east on Green Street to the hospital entrance.

Answer questions 68 and 69 based on your best judgment and common sense.

**68.** Firefighters operating outside buildings raising ladders, directing hose streams, or performing other external activities are not required to use respiratory protective equipment initially, but such use will be mandatory when operating on vehicle, trash, or dumpster fires; large uncontained brush fires; and while conducting roof ventilation operations. Additionally, any firefighter may use respiratory protective equipment at any incident to which such firefighter responds. Firefighter Smith is unsure if he should put on his respiratory protection during a fire incident, what should he do?

    **a.** Ask his superior officer.

    **b.** Leave his respiratory protection off.

    **c.** Use his respiratory protection, according to the directive, it is warranted.

    **d.** Follow his partner's actions.

**69.** During an EMS call, Firefighter Jones has a direct blood exposure with a patient who has a bloodborne disease. Which of the following actions should Firefighter Jones take immediately?
  **a.** Document the exposure with the proper documentation back at the station.
  **b.** Call the medical officer and report the exposure to the doctor.
  **c.** Cleanse the wound or wash off the blood.
  **d.** Ignore it until returning to the station after the EMS call.

Answer questions 70–73 based solely on the information in the following passage.

Firefighters, in the normal course of their duties, may find themselves exposed to infectious/communicable diseases including hepatitis, meningitis, HIV, and tuberculosis. Potentially infectious persons may have no specific signs, symptoms, or complaints, and they may have no awareness of their potential to transmit their disease to others. Therefore, firefighters must take preventative and protective measures with each and every person to whom they respond to prevent or reduce the risk of direct exposure to communicable diseases.

**Protective Equipment**

Nonsterile latex and nitrile gloves are provided by the department and shall be worn when firefighters are dealing with all patients, blood, or bodily fluids in the course of their duties. If the firefighter has any open cuts or lesions on his/her hands, they should be bandaged.

When applying dressings to the wounds of injured patients or removing burn victims, direct contact with blood secretions should be as minimal as possible. Avoid handling other equipment or objects with contaminated gloves. Gloves are to be changed between different patient contacts; goggles shall be worn when splattering of any fluid may occur.

When disposable gloves have been used, they are to be removed as soon as patient handling and exposure to body fluids is terminated. Firefighters shall not get back on the apparatus wearing contaminated gloves.

During extrication of trapped patients in vehicles, disposable latex or nitrile gloves shall be worn under leather rescue gloves.

All gloves, masks, shields, and TiVek gowns are disposable and should be left with the responding EMS crew in the appropriate biohazard bag obtained from such crew. In the event that no EMS crew is present, all contaminated disposable equipment shall be collected, put in a red plastic biohazard bag, and disposed of at a hospital.

**70.** According to the passage, which of the following statements is NOT accurate?
  **a.** Potentially infectious persons may have specific signs, symptoms, or complaints.
  **b.** Firefighters should not get back on the apparatus wearing contaminated gloves.
  **c.** Disposable latex or nitrile gloves shoud be worn under leather rescue gloves.
  **d.** When no EMS crew is present, contaminated equipment shoud be disposed of at a hospital.

**71.** What does the term *preventative* mean in the context of this directive?
  **a.** regulatory
  **b.** mandatory
  **c.** participatory
  **d.** anticipatory

**72.** Firefighters must wear personal protective equipment when handling patients who are ill or seem ill and when any suspected trauma is involved. What are four pieces of equipment that will be used for personal protection during EMS calls when providing care to patients?

   a. nonsterile latex gloves, red plastic biohazard bag, masks, nitrile gloves
   b. disposable latex gloves, nitrile gloves, masks, TiVek gowns
   c. sterile gloves, vinyl gloves, masks, shields
   d. level A suits, nitrile gloves, goggles, butyl gloves

**73.** If the firefighter has any open cuts or lesions on his/her hands, he/she
   a. should not engage in any EMS activities.
   b. should notify the medical officer prior to providing EMS care.
   c. should inform the patient prior to performing EMS duties.
   d. should be bandaged prior to performing EMS duties

Answer questions 74 and 75 based on the following information.

Firefighters must routinely fight structure fires that require more water than is carried on the fire truck. Water must be obtained from a fire hydrant. This water is fed through fire hoses to the truck holding tank and then pumped through additional hoses to the fire as needed. Several mechanical devices are used in this process.

1. Wrenches are used to attach the hose to the truck and the hydrant and to turn the hydrant valve.
2. Centrifugal pumps are the most common pumps used by fire engines to pump water to the fire.

3. A power take-off arrangement from the internal combustion engine is used to drive the centrifugal pumps.
4. Electric motors are frequently used to drive small piston pumps that prime the main centrifugal pumps.
5. Pressure gauges are used to ensure that the system is operating properly.
6. Valves are used to control the flow of water from the hydrant and from the fire truck.

**74.** Firefighters respond to an industrial fire. Water must be obtained from a hydrant one block away. What are four of the mechanical devices that will be used to get the water from the hydrant to the fire?
   a. electric motors, pumps, temperature gauges, and valves
   b. pumps, pulleys, internal combustion engine, and electric motors
   c. pressure gauges, centrifugal pumps, wrenches, and internal combustion engine
   d. internal combustion engine, a winch, valves, and pressure gauges

**75.** Which of the following is used to drive the centrifugal pumps?
   a. small piston pumps
   b. an internal combustion engine
   c. pressure gauges
   d. valves

Answer questions 76–81 based on your best judgment and common sense.

**76.** After a fire is extinguished, the water in the hose lines must be removed before the hose lines are reloaded on the fire truck. The best place to remove this water is
   **a.** near a large body of water if there is one close by.
   **b.** inside the building where the fire was.
   **c.** back at the fire station.
   **d.** just outside the building where the fire was.

**77.** Fires below grade, such as in a building's cellar, are difficult to attack and present a severe hazard of injury to firefighters. Access to and ventilation of this type of fire is frequently very restricted. What would be your first action to ensure safety in a cellar fire incident?
   **a.** Conduct a quick survey of the scene by walking around the entire structure.
   **b.** Commence cutting holes in the floor to gain access.
   **c.** Determine whether any lives are at stake.
   **d.** Start searches on the floors above the fire.

**78.** Lieutenant James has ordered Firefighter Kimmel to clean his breathing apparatus. While cleaning the apparatus, Firefighter Kimmel drops it and thinks he may have damaged it. The best course of action would be to
   **a.** keep quiet unless he is certain it is badly damaged.
   **b.** watch Lieutenant James when he goes to the next fire, to make sure the equipment is working properly.
   **c.** keep quiet because Lieutenant James may bring him up on charges for damaging his equipment.
   **d.** tell Lieutenant James about the suspected damage.

**79.** In responding to an automobile accident on a limited access highway, Firefighter Venezia finds that the vehicles involved stick out and partially block the left lane and shoulder of the highway. Traffic is very heavy. What should be the first thing he does upon arrival?
   **a.** Conduct a rapid triage of the injured parties.
   **b.** Position responding apparatus to shield his personnel while working.
   **c.** Wait until police shut the highway down and clear the area.
   **d.** Charge a hose line to ensure that he can fight a potential car fire.

**80.** A fire company is called to a house fire. When the engine arrives at the street supplied by the caller, there is no house at the number given, nor is there a fire elsewhere on the street. Which of the following is NOT a reasonable assumption about false alarms?

   **a.** False alarms waste the time and money of the fire department.

   **b.** The fire department cannot answer another call while out on a false alarm.

   **c.** Sometimes what seems to be a false alarm is simply a mistake made by the caller.

   **d.** False alarms, although illegal, serve a positive role in keeping firefighters alert.

**81.** Firefighter Abbas's company is doing a building inspection of your favorite restaurant. She knows the owner and all of the servers. She discovers that the restaurant's permits have all expired; therefore, she should

   **a.** take the owner aside out of courtesy and issue a verbal warning, without writing a formal summons.

   **b.** inform her superior officer, and let that officer handle the situation.

   **c.** leave the restaurant immediately because her involvement with the owner might reflect badly on the fire department.

   **d.** call the police and have the owner arrested.

Answer questions 82–84 based on the following information.

After a fire is put out, the firefighter must routinely write a report on what occurred at the scene. This is normally done back at the firehouse in the following manner:

1. Log on to the computer.
2. Go to the directory that contains the report forms.
3. If there were injuries on the scene, complete report form 103.
4. If there was a death on the scene, complete report form 111.
5. If there was loss of or damage to equipment, complete form 107.
6. If there was no injury, death, equipment loss, or equipment damage, complete form 101.
7. If form 107 and form 103 are required, complete form 122 also.
8. Complete form 106, which is a general report and must be filled out for ALL fire reports.
9. Print and file all forms that have been completed, and fax a copy to division headquarters.

**82.** A firefighter has just returned to the firehouse after a fire and is preparing the necessary report forms. One of the residents of the house that burned was injured and sent to the hospital. Also, one of the fire hoses was damaged. There were no deaths at the fire. Which forms must the firefighter complete?

   **a.** forms 101 and 106

   **b.** forms 111 and 107

   **c.** forms 106, 111, and 122

   **d.** forms 103, 106, 107, and 122

**83.** A firefighter is filling out fire reports on a fire in which there was one death, no equipment damage or loss, and one injury in addition to the death. Which forms must the firefighter complete?
 **a.** forms 103, 106, and 122
 **b.** forms 103 and 111
 **c.** forms 101, 106, and 122
 **d.** forms 103, 106, and 111

**84.** A firefighter is preparing a report on a grass fire that was put out with no injuries, no deaths, and no equipment damage or loss. Which form, in addition to form 101, must the firefighter complete?
 **a.** form 106
 **b.** form 111
 **c.** form 107
 **d.** form 103

Answer question 85 based on your best judgment and common sense.

**85.** Firefighter Li is at the scene of a fire caused by damaged wiring. The civilian who owns the building approaches her and complains about the windows broken by firefighters extinguishing the fire. She should
 **a.** deny the firefighters did it unless she is absolutely sure they did.
 **b.** chastise the civilian for being reckless and causing the fire, and then direct him to her superior officer.
 **c.** advise the civilian to write a letter to the fire commissioner.
 **d.** explain that breaking the window was necessary in order to release heat and smoke from the fire.

Answer questions 86–90 based solely on the information in the following passage.

Although preserving evidence is not the firefighter's main priority, certain steps can be taken, while fighting a fire, to maintain site integrity and maximize the efforts of investigators.

Try to determine the point of origin from wind direction or the way the fire is spread. Take note, mentally and on paper, of suspicious people or vehicles. Use ribbon or other practical material to flag potential evidence, such as tracks near the suspected point of origin and items such as matches, bottles, rags, cigarette butts, lighters, paper, or exposed wires. Keep other personnel away from these areas unless doing so would hamper firefighting efforts.

After flagging the evidence, notify the commanding officer as soon as possible. If evidence must be removed, handle it carefully to maintain fingerprint integrity.

Once the fire is declared under control, create a map of the scene, indicating the point of origin and areas where evidence is or was located. Compose an inventory of any evidence that was removed. Record any other useful information, such as conversations with witnesses, names, and descriptions. Before leaving, share your findings with the lead investigator.

Remember, safety is the main priority while you are fighting the fire. But by keeping an alert eye for clues, you can also contribute to an efficient investigation into its cause.

**86.** According to the passage, which of the following is the main responsibility of a firefighter?
 **a.** to maintain the integrity of the site
 **b.** to flag evidence and keep an inventory of it
 **c.** to operate in a safe manner
 **d.** to provide support for investigators

**87.** The passage suggests that the first step the fire-fighter should take after evidence is flagged is to
   a. bring it to the attention of the officer in command.
   b. create a map of the scene.
   c. see how it relates to the point of origin.
   d. indicate its location to investigators.

**88.** Which of the following would a firefighter NOT necessarily do after the fire is brought under control?
   a. create an inventory
   b. carefully remove the evidence from the scene
   c. log witness descriptions
   d. record flagged evidence areas

**89.** Which of the following best expresses the main idea of this passage?
   a. how to aid investigation into the cause of a fire
   b. how to maintain safety while investigating a fire
   c. the importance of flagging evidence during the fighting of a fire
   d. what to do with flagged evidence of the cause of a fire

**90.** According to the passage, fire personnel should be instructed to avoid areas where evidence is found
   a. only after the fire has been brought under control.
   b. only if the fire can also be fought effectively.
   c. only if the evidence points directly to the cause of the fire.
   d. only until the commanding officer is informed.

Answer question 91 based on your best judgment and common sense.

**91.** One of the duties of the fire department is to raise public awareness of fire prevention methods. To this end, firefighters often speak with the public at schools, churches, and other meeting places. When speaking to the public, which of the following would NOT be an appropriate subject for a firefighter to address?
   a. how to advise one's neighbors on fire prevention
   b. how to choose the most effective fire protection equipment
   c. how to purchase tickets for the firefighters' charity ball
   d. how to make an escape plan in case of a fire in one's home

Answer questions 92-94 based on the following information.

The personal safety rope is an important tool in the fire service; it serves as a last resort rescue tool for trapped firefighters and fire victims. For that reason, the rope must never be used for any other purpose than life safety. Each firefighter is issued a safety rope and storage bag that must be carried into an incident as part of his or her personal protective equipment. Each firefighter must take personal responsibility for the care of the rope and bag and is responsible for inspecting the rope prior to each shift to ensure it is in good condition and properly stored. A firefighter must remove a safety rope from service if any of the following conditions are met:
   1. The rescue rope has been used in an escape or to carry out a rescue.
   2. The strands are found to be frayed.
   3. The rope shows any sign of abrasion or fraying of strands.

4. The rope has been exposed to flame or extreme heat.
5. The rope is stained or discolored.
6. The rope has been frozen.
7. The rope has been exposed to any chemical.
8. There is any doubt or uncertainty as to the rope's suitability for service.

**92.** Which of the following situations would NOT be a reason to place your personal rescue rope out of service?
   **a.** Paint thinner was spilled on the rope.
   **b.** The rope is nine months old.
   **c.** Rope strands appear to be frayed.
   **d.** The rope was used in a rescue.

**93.** Firefighter Kwon used his rescue rope to act as a safety line for a mother and child exiting from the third floor to the aerial ladder just below. After he recovers the rope, it should be
   **a.** washed clean and dried.
   **b.** inspected and repacked for use.
   **c.** taken out of service.
   **d.** used at the next drill.

**94.** During a preshift inspection of the rescue rope, Firefighter Suarez notices a slight discoloration on some of the strands. According to the passage, she must
   **a.** have the shift captain inspect it.
   **b.** wash it and once dry, place it back in service.
   **c.** repack it and place it back in service.
   **d.** place it out of service.

**95.** While he is on his way to work at 6:40 A.M., Firefighter Marshall's car gets a flat tire. He manages to pull the car over to the shoulder of the road and decides to change the tire himself. Though his shift begins at 7:00 A.M., he now estimates that he will not arrive on the job until about 7:20 A.M. He phones his supervisor to report that he will be late. Which of the following reports most clearly and accurately describes the situation?
   **a.** I was driving to work. I won't be there until about 20 minutes later than was expected.
   **b.** On my way to work, there was a flat tire, which I am about to fix. It is now about 6:40.
   **c.** I would have been on time, but now I am unable to make it by 7:00 because the car is on the shoulder of the road.
   **d.** I am stuck on the side of the road with a flat tire. I will change it and should be able to report to work around 7:20.

**96.** Firefighters Ellis and Wong have responded to what appears to be a false alarm in the alley behind the building at 1412 Longview Avenue. They are about to return to the station when Firefighter Wong notices a suspicious-looking receptacle in one of the dumpsters. When Firefighter Ellis agrees that this receptacle may possibly contain an explosive, the two workers follow department policy by keeping people away from the area and phoning the police department. Which of the following reports describes the situation most clearly and accurately?

　**a.** There may be an explosive in a dumpster in the alley behind 1412 Longview Avenue.

　**b.** Something looks suspicious on Longview Avenue, which could possibly explode.

　**c.** There is a receptacle in a dumpster in the alley on Longview Avenue, and it is in the trash.

　**d.** At 1412 Longview, there is something suspicious-looking sitting behind it in the dumpster in the alley.

**97.** Firefighter Camillo is driving to a high school to speak to students. He stops for a red light at Lucas Drive, and when the light turns green, he drives slowly forward into the intersection of Lucas Drive and Manchester Way. There, his truck is broadsided from the left by a gray, late-model station wagon. Although he is shaken, Firefighter Camillo has not been injured. The driver of the car is also uninjured, but he accuses Firefighter Camillo of having driven through the red light. Someone in a nearby building saw the accident and phoned the police, who arrive within minutes. Which of the following reports would Firefighter Camillo give to the police to describe the accident most clearly and accurately?

　**a.** I was on Lucas, completely stopped for the red light. Then, when the light turned green, I pulled forward and was immediately broadsided by the wagon.

　**b.** He's accusing me of going through a red light, but before I drove through I stopped. I didn't see the station wagon as it hit the left side of the truck coming down Manchester Way.

　**c.** The station wagon drove into the side of my truck when I tried to drive forward on Lucas Drive. It was after the red light. Then he accused me of causing the accident.

　**d.** I was driving straight ahead on Lucas Drive, and when I was at the light at the intersection of Manchester Way, I pulled forward and he hit me. It was a gray station wagon.

Answer questions 98–100 based on the following information.

Managing the trench rescue incident is the key to maintaining control. When you manage the trench you run a very good chance of working eight hours or more. Incident complexity and risk demand strong command and control. Typically, at the start of an operation, the Incident Commander will be from a local fire/rescue service, most likely a high-risk manager with a low frequency of incident exposure. When you take charge, you need to immediately set up four teams to carry out crucial trench operations. Designate them for:

- Excavation: Your excavation team should coordinate the plans for a dewatering operation.
- Monitoring: Your monitoring team can continue to move fresh air with a confined space blower and use the air from multiple levels.
- Shoring: Establish a shoring team.
- Rescue: You also need a rescue team, which should prepare for disentanglement procedures, patient packaging, and removal. A rope rescue sector may be needed.

**Making the Trench Safe**

There are three ways to "safe" a trench: The first method is to slope to the angle of repose; the second is benching; and the third is shoring. The first two are accomplished with backhoes and live workers, the third with well-trained and organized rescuers. Here is some advice about shoring operations:

- Shores should be located 18 to 24 inches from the floor and the lip of the trench.
- Shores should be no more than 48 inches apart vertically.
- Placement of the first shore should be from outside the trench using pneumatic and/or

hydraulic-powered shores. The first shore should be placed in the middle of the upright, then the top, followed by the bottom. Never ever lean on shoring materials.

- Timber shoring is a difficult and time-consuming task. The first shore is placed on the top and requires the rescuer to enter the trench on a ladder. A retrieval line is essential. The first set of panels belongs with the patient to protect him in the event of a secondary collapse. Be prepared to place panels on either side of the initial set of panels.
- Trench ends greater than 48 inches wide need to be shored if they are located in close proximity to the trapped victim.

**98.** Firefighter Lane has successfully placed the first pneumatic shore in the middle of the upright in the trench. What should he do next?
   a. place a pneumatic shore by the bottom of the upright
   b. place a pneumatic shore at the top of the upright
   c. place a set of panels on either side of the initial set of panels
   d. place a hydraulic shore in the same area as the first pneumatic shore

**99.** All of the following statements about shoring operations are correct EXCEPT

    **a.** the first timber shore is placed on top of the
upright.

    **b.** shores should be located 18 to 24 inches
from the floor and the lip of the trench.

    **c.** shores should be no more than 60 inches
apart vertically.

    **d.** timber shoring is a difficult and time-
consuming task.

**100.** Which of the following statements regarding
making the trench safe is INCORRECT?

    **a.** Sloping and benching are performing by
backhoes and live workers.

    **b.** There are four accepted methods to safe a
trench.

    **c.** Well-trained rescuers will be needed for
shoring operations.

    **d.** Sloping the angle of repose is the first
method of making a trench safe

# ► Answers

1. **d.** In the drawing, flames are leaping from the second and third floors.
2. **c.** Two victims can be seen in the second and third floors of the fire building.
3. **d.** The business next door to the fire scene is Al's Paint Store; the address is #28.
4. **d.** The drawing shows a clothesline and a smoke stack on the roof of the fire building.
5. **c.** Three adults and two babies can be seen in the windows of the building on the left.
6. **b.** The drawing does not show that fire has spread to the paint store.
7. **a.** The window on the first floor is blocked by security bars.
8. **b.** A living room, a dining room, a kitchen, three bedrooms, and a bathroom are shown in the diagram.
9. **a.** The living room is the first room off the entryway.
10. **b.** A smoke detector is located in the master bedroom.
11. **a.** Two windows can be found in bedroom 3.
12. **d.** The fireplace is in the living room, and the dining room is closest to the living room.
13. **c.** The smoke detector in the master bedroom is the first to be activated.
14. **b.** The diagram indicates that there are eight windows in the apartment.
15. **b.** All may provide means of entry.
16. **c.** Interior stairs are the preferred method of removal.
17. **c.** The last item in the order of removal is the rescue rope.
18. **c.** The adjoining building immediately follows fire escape in the order.
19. **b.** Rescue rope is the last method on the list.

20. **a.** Maximum time in the fire area will allow a firefighter to operate more efficiently and extinguish the fire faster, a priority. Choices **b** and **d** are much less important. A full air tank will not necessarily protect against heat, flame, and toxic gases (choice **c**).
21. **b.** While searching involved structures, the best way to reduce the risk of danger is through training, practicing, and planning.
22. **d.** When conducting a search, firefighters should carry a forcible-entry tool, a flashlight, and a radio.
23. **a.** The paragraph clearly states firefighters must always work in teams of two or more and a minimum of two fully equipped firefighters and a charged hose line should be ready to go in and assist the team if needed. This is defined as the two-in/two-out rule.
24. **d.** The discussion of carbon monoxide in the last paragraph serves to demonstrate why firefighters should wear breathing apparatus.
25. **c.** The dangers outlined in the first and second paragraphs of the passage are all caused by extreme heat.
26. **b.** The other choices are mentioned in the passage but are not the main idea.
27. **a.** The cooking temperature is given to show the difference of 1,000 degrees of heat between a motor-vehicle fire and cooking.
28. **b.** The last paragraph states that carbon monoxide is odorless and colorless.
29. **d.** A priority of firefighting is always the safety of members and civilians.
30. **a.** Safety of the public is a firefighter's main concern.
31. **a.** The other choices are unclear because they are awkwardly constructed, obscuring who intends to set the fire.

**32. d.** This is the only clear statement. In choice **a**, it is not clear that several firefighters received the promotion. Choice **b** makes no logical sense. Choice **c** is grammatically unsound.

**33. c.** The duckbill lock breaker is designed to break open heavy-duty padlocks.

**34. d.** The passage does not mention a round type of key tool used for through-the-lock forcible entry.

**35. a.** See the first sentence of the passage: *A number of specialized tools are available to firefighters to assist with or conduct forcible entry.*

**36. a.** Firefighters must arrive at the scene ready to work. If they are not ready, precious minutes can be lost, and lives and property are at stake.

**37. c.** Firefighter Jackson knows that, at the very least, the building is not safe, and the children should not be inside the security fence. The small unexplained fires indicate possible juvenile fire setting. By calling the police, Firefighter Jackson is getting assistance from the agency that is able to enforce trespass laws. When she calls the situation in, she can tell the operator she is on the way to work and ask what they want her to do. They can then in turn have someone advise her supervisor.

**38. c.** This is the only clear and accurate statement. Choice **a** is incorrect because it leaves out information; choices **b** and **d** give incorrect information with regard to the location.

**39. b.** This is the only accurate statement. Choice **a** is incorrect because it implies that Mr. Ramsey broke his leg. Choice **c** leaves out information. In choice **d**, it is not clear who was helped into the car.

**40. b.** See step 4 of the procedure.

**41. c.** See step 3 of the procedure.

**42. b.** Upon the arrival of the second engine, the initial engine will need to be supplied using a single 5" supply line.

**43. d.** See procedural step 4.

**44. b.** The next hose line placed into service will connect on the fire floor using department standpipe packs with a gated wye fitting and will back up the original attack crew.

**45. b.** See procedural step 6.

**46. a.** The first arriving engine will provide an initial size up and implement ICS procedures immediately.

**47. a.** No level of risk is acceptable where there is no potential to save lives or property.

**48. c.** This is the simplest way around the one-way streets and Town Hall. Because Linda Lane is a one-way going the wrong way, some backtracking is inevitable. However, the residence is only one block off of Barcelona Boulevard, so turning eastbound on Barcelona requires the least amount of backtracking. Choice **a** directs the engine to turn the wrong way down a one-way street. Choice **b** requires too much backtracking because Barcelona Boulevard is a one-way street going east. Choice **d** requires too many turns and is the least direct route.

**49. b.** This route is most direct because it requires the fewest turns. Choice **a** requires the engine to go the wrong way on McMahon Street. Choice **c** is not correct because Canyon Drive is a one-way street south. Choice **d** is a much longer route.

**50. a.** If Firefighter Ricardo turns right onto James Avenue, she will be facing north. A left turn onto Linda Lane turns her west again, and a right turn onto Livingston Avenue turns her north. The final right turn onto Barcelona Boulevard turns her east.

**51. c.** In any emergency situation, teamwork is necessary because firefighters work as a unit. Responding on one's own (choices **a** and **b**) would be improper. Choice **d** is inappropriate because a firefighter should treat others with respect and take all requests for help seriously.

**52. b.** The lower cost is an advantage of wooden ladders over aluminum. The other statements are negative statements regarding wooden ladders.

**53. a.** The answer is found in the first sentence of the passage. The other choices give information from the passage, but they do not indicate the main purpose of an overhaul.

**54. d.** The answer is in the third sentence of the first paragraph in combination with the conditions described in the second paragraph.

**55. b.** The answer can be found in the last sentence. Choices **a**, **c**, and **d** are not in the passage.

**56. c.** A firefighter must always go to the superior officer before making any changes in standard operating procedures; therefore, this would be the first course of action.

**57. b.** This is the only clear choice. Choice **a** gives incorrect information; choice **c** is unclear; choice **d** leaves out information.

**58. c.** This is the only clear and accurate description. Choice **a** is incorrect because it leaves out important information; choices **b** and **d** are unclear.

**59. c.** This is the only clear and accurate report. Choice **a** implies that Firefighter Caruso was rescuing the kitten at the same time as he was washing the truck. Choice **b** sounds as though the boy made the scratch. Choice **d** is unclear.

**60. d.** This is the most direct route because it does not require any backtracking. Choice **a** is not correct because it would require the engine to go the wrong way on Mill Road. Choice **b** requires the engine to go the wrong way on Lynch Road. Choice **c** is not as direct because it requires the engine to move in the opposite direction from the call.

**61. b.** This is the fastest route, requiring the fewest turns. Choice **a** is not correct because Kent is a one-way street going east. Choice **c** requires too many turns and is not the most direct route. Choice **d** is not correct because Upton Street is one-way going north.

**62. d.** A left turn onto Lee Lane turns Firefighter Kearney south. Another left turn onto Pecan Avenue turns her east. Left onto Main Street turns her north and the final right turn onto Palmer turns her back east.

**63. b.** A firefighter should not ignore violations that he or she can see from across the street. They are likely to pose a threat to civilians as well as to firefighters responding to an alarm at the location.

**64. a.** The other routes are impossible or illegal.

**65. c.** Brown Street and Park Street are the two streets that run north and south of the park.

**66. a.** The other routes are impossible or illegal.

**67. b.** The other routes are impossible (choices **c** and **d**) or circuitous (choice **a**).

**68. c.** According to the directive, any firefighter may use respiratory protection for any incident.

**69. c.** Cleansing the wound or washing off the blood affords Firefighter Jones the best possibility of not getting contaminated immediately after exposure.

**70. a.** Potentially infectious persons may have no specific signs, symptoms, or complaints, and they may have no awareness of their potential to transmit their disease to others.

**71. d.** *Anticipatory* is a synonym for *preventative*.

**72. b.** Disposable latex gloves, nitrile gloves, masks, and TiVek gowns are all mentioned in the passage. No reference is made to butyl gloves or Level A suits. Red plastic biohazard bags are not personal protective equipment.

**73. d.** See directive #1.

**74. c.** The procedure does not mention the use of temperature gauges (choice **a**), pulleys (choice **b**), or a winch (choice **d**).

**75. a.** See step 3 of the procedure.

**76. d.** Hoses are drained outside the fire building. Dumping into a large body of water nearby (choice **a**) could cause pollution and would probably be illegal. Draining inside (choice **b**) would cause unnecessary damage, and transporting the hoses full of water (choice **c**) is not feasible.

**77. a.** Life and responder safety are the number one concern. Firefighters must take a look all around to know the extent of the incident and exactly what is at stake. Choice **c** is part of this, but not all, as victims in the rear might be in more danger. Choices **b** and **d** are unsafe actions if a firefighter does not have a survey of the situation.

**78. d.** Damaged equipment should never be used in an emergency situation, regardless of the circumstances.

**79. b.** Safety of victims and responders is always the number one concern. The actions in choices **a** and **d** should not be undertaken until the safety of those personnel who are working and being rescued are ensured. Choice **c** might require delay, endangering the victims.

**80. d.** Firefighters don't need false alarms to keep them alert—real alarms will do that. Choices **a** and **b** are reasonable criticisms of false alarms. Choice **c** is reasonable because people do make mistakes, especially if they are in a panic.

**81. b.** The superior officer must be made aware of any situation that is a potential hazard to firefighters or the public. Again, safety has priority.

**82. d.** There was an injury, so form 103 must be completed, as stated in step 3 of the procedure. There was equipment damage, so form 107 must be completed, as stated in step 5 of the procedure. Step 8 says that form 106 must be completed for all fire reports. Step 7 says that form 122 must be completed because forms 107 and 103 were both required.

**83. d.** There was an injury, so form 103 must be completed, as stated in step 3 of the procedure. Because there was a death on the scene, form 111 must be completed, according to step 4 of the procedure. As always, form 106 must be completed, as stated in step 8 of the procedure.

**84. a.** Because there were no injuries, deaths, or equipment loss or damage, step 8 indicates that form 106 must be completed.

**85. d.** A polite and direct explanation of the necessity of breaking windows for ventilation will help the civilian understand the company's actions. Firefighters should always be honest and courteous when dealing with the public.

**86. c.** See the next-to-last sentence.

**87. a.** See the third paragraph.

**88. b.** The fourth paragraph gives the steps to take after the fire is brought under control, and removal of evidence is not one of them.

**89. a.** The first sentence states that, while fighting a fire, firefighters can take steps to maximize efforts of investigators. Virtually all of the passage deals with those steps. Do not confuse the main idea of the passage with the

## FIREFIGHTER PRACTICE EXAM 1

| Question Type | Question Numbers | Chapter |
|---|---|---|
| Memory and Observation (15 questions) | 1–15 | 7, "Memory and Observation" |
| Reading Text (25 questions) | 24–28, 33–35, 42–46, 53–55, 70–73, 86–90 | 6, "Reading Text, Tables, Charts, and Graphs" |
| Map Reading (10 questions) | 48–50, 60–62, 64–67 | 11, "Spatial Relations" |
| Following Procedures (20 questions) | 16–19, 21–23, 40–41, 74–75, 82–84, 92–94, 98–100 | 9, "Judgment and Reasoning" |
| Judgment (20 questions) | 20, 29–30, 36–37, 47, 51–52, 56, 63, 68–69, 76–81, 85, 91 | 9, "Judgment and Reasoning" |
| Verbal Expression (10 questions) | 31–32, 38–39, 57–59, 95–97 | 12, "Verbal Expression" |

firefighter's main responsibility (choice **b**). Choices **c** and **d** are only details relating to the main idea.

**90. b.** The second paragraph states that personnel shall be kept away from flagged evidence, unless doing so would hamper firefighting efforts.

**91. c.** Soliciting the public is not a good method of encouraging fire prevention and is detrimental to the reputation of the department.

**92. b.** Age is not listed as one of the reasons for removing a rope from service.

**93. c.** The first reason listed for taking a personal rescue rope out of service is when it has been used in an escape or to carry out a rescue.

**94. d.** The information states that when a firefighter finds a discoloration on some of the strands, he or she should take the rope out of service.

**95. d.** This is the only clear and accurate report. Choice **a** doesn't report why Firefighter Marshall will be late for work. Choice **b** doesn't say when he will report to work. Choice **c** doesn't say what happened.

**96. a.** This is the only clear and accurate statement. Choice **b** implies that Longview Avenue could explode. Choices **c** and **d** do not mention that there might be an explosive in the dumpster.

**97. a.** This is the only clear and accurate statement. Choices **b**, **c**, and **d** are incorrect because they leave out information and distort what really happened.

**98. b.** The second pneumatic shore is placed at the top of the upright.

**99. c.** Shores should be no more than 48 inches apart vertically.

**100. b.** There are three accepted methods to safe a trench.

## ► Scoring

Generally, you need a score of 70–80% on the written exam to pass. But just passing isn't likely to be enough to ensure that you will be called for the next steps in the process. Often, a score of 95% or higher is necessary to go on to the physical ability test. Once you take the physical test, your score on that test may be combined with your score on the written exam to determine your rank on the eligibility list. Or your written exam score alone may determine your rank on the list. So your goal should be to achieve the highest score you possibly can.

If you want to raise your score, you should review your exam results carefully. Use the table on the preceding page to find the number of questions you answered correctly in each of the five question types. Then calculate the percentage for each type. For example, if you answered 15 judgment questions correctly, your percentage is 75%. Next, rank your performance according to question type. In which types were your results highest? Which were lowest? Once you have ranked your performance, you can set priorities in your study plan. For instance, if your lowest score was in Following Procedures, you should plan on spending the most time reviewing the appropriate section in Chapter 9. Use the following suggestions to help direct your test preparation between now and the day of the exam:

- If you had trouble with memory and observation questions, then you should plan to spend a lot of time on Chapter 7, "Memory and Observation."

- If the verbal expression questions were the most difficult, carefully review Chapter 12, "Verbal Expression."
- If you had difficulty understanding the reading passages, then you should plan to spend more time on Chapter 6, "Reading Text, Tables, Charts, and Graphs."
- If you had difficulty with the questions on reading maps, then you should spend a longer period of time on Chapter 11, "Spatial Relations and Map Reading."
- If you had trouble with the questions testing judgment and following procedures, then you should spend a lot of time on Chapter 9, "Judgment and Reasoning."

Each of these chapters includes lots of tips and hints for doing well on the given kind of question. As you probably noticed, the various kinds of questions are all mixed up together on the exam. So take out your completed answer sheet and compare it to the table on the previous page to find out which kinds of questions you did well in and which kinds gave you more trouble. Then you can plan to spend more of your preparation time on the chapters in this book that correspond to the questions you found hardest, and less time on the chapters in areas in which you did well.

Even if you got a perfect score on a particular kind of question, you will probably want to at least glance through the relevant chapter. After you work through all the chapters, take Practice Exam 3 in Chapter 13 to see how much you've improved.

# 5 ▶ Firefighter Practice Exam 2

## CHAPTER SUMMARY

This is the second of four practice exams in this book covering the areas most often tested on firefighter exams. If your exam tests the basic skills you need to be trained as a firefighter, the test that follows will give you the practice you need.

The practice exam that follows is another type of test often used to see if firefighter candidates have what it takes to do the job. A test like this mostly tries to assess whether you have what it takes to *learn* the job; it tests some of the basic skills you need to be able to do well in your firefighter training program. This practice exam includes five areas: reading comprehension, verbal expression, logical reasoning, mathematics, and mechanical aptitude.

Normally, you would have about two hours to take an exam like this, but for now, don't worry about timing; just take the test in as relaxed a manner as you can. The answer sheet you should use is on the next page. After the exam is an answer key, with an explanation for each correct answer, followed by a section on scoring your exam.

# Practice Exam 2

| 1. | ⓐ | ⓑ | ⓒ | ⓓ | | 36. | ⓐ | ⓑ | ⓒ | ⓓ | | 71. | ⓐ | ⓑ | ⓒ | ⓓ |
|---|---|---|---|---|---|---|---|---|---|---|---|---|---|---|---|---|
| 2. | ⓐ | ⓑ | ⓒ | ⓓ | | 37. | ⓐ | ⓑ | ⓒ | ⓓ | | 72. | ⓐ | ⓑ | ⓒ | ⓓ |
| 3. | ⓐ | ⓑ | ⓒ | ⓓ | | 38. | ⓐ | ⓑ | ⓒ | ⓓ | | 73. | ⓐ | ⓑ | ⓒ | ⓓ |
| 4. | ⓐ | ⓑ | ⓒ | ⓓ | | 39. | ⓐ | ⓑ | ⓒ | ⓓ | | 74. | ⓐ | ⓑ | ⓒ | ⓓ |
| 5. | ⓐ | ⓑ | ⓒ | ⓓ | | 40. | ⓐ | ⓑ | ⓒ | ⓓ | | 75. | ⓐ | ⓑ | ⓒ | ⓓ |
| 6. | ⓐ | ⓑ | ⓒ | ⓓ | | 41. | ⓐ | ⓑ | ⓒ | ⓓ | | 76. | ⓐ | ⓑ | ⓒ | ⓓ |
| 7. | ⓐ | ⓑ | ⓒ | ⓓ | | 42. | ⓐ | ⓑ | ⓒ | ⓓ | | 77. | ⓐ | ⓑ | ⓒ | ⓓ |
| 8. | ⓐ | ⓑ | ⓒ | ⓓ | | 43. | ⓐ | ⓑ | ⓒ | ⓓ | | 78. | ⓐ | ⓑ | ⓒ | ⓓ |
| 9. | ⓐ | ⓑ | ⓒ | ⓓ | | 44. | ⓐ | ⓑ | ⓒ | ⓓ | | 79. | ⓐ | ⓑ | ⓒ | ⓓ |
| 10. | ⓐ | ⓑ | ⓒ | ⓓ | | 45. | ⓐ | ⓑ | ⓒ | ⓓ | | 80. | ⓐ | ⓑ | ⓒ | ⓓ |
| 11. | ⓐ | ⓑ | ⓒ | ⓓ | | 46. | ⓐ | ⓑ | ⓒ | ⓓ | | 81. | ⓐ | ⓑ | ⓒ | ⓓ |
| 12. | ⓐ | ⓑ | ⓒ | ⓓ | | 47. | ⓐ | ⓑ | ⓒ | ⓓ | | 82. | ⓐ | ⓑ | ⓒ | ⓓ |
| 13. | ⓐ | ⓑ | ⓒ | ⓓ | | 48. | ⓐ | ⓑ | ⓒ | ⓓ | | 83. | ⓐ | ⓑ | ⓒ | ⓓ |
| 14. | ⓐ | ⓑ | ⓒ | ⓓ | | 49. | ⓐ | ⓑ | ⓒ | ⓓ | | 84. | ⓐ | ⓑ | ⓒ | ⓓ |
| 15. | ⓐ | ⓑ | ⓒ | ⓓ | | 50. | ⓐ | ⓑ | ⓒ | ⓓ | | 85. | ⓐ | ⓑ | ⓒ | ⓓ |
| 16. | ⓐ | ⓑ | ⓒ | ⓓ | | 51. | ⓐ | ⓑ | ⓒ | ⓓ | | 86. | ⓐ | ⓑ | ⓒ | ⓓ |
| 17. | ⓐ | ⓑ | ⓒ | ⓓ | | 52. | ⓐ | ⓑ | ⓒ | ⓓ | | 87. | ⓐ | ⓑ | ⓒ | ⓓ |
| 18. | ⓐ | ⓑ | ⓒ | ⓓ | | 53. | ⓐ | ⓑ | ⓒ | ⓓ | | 88. | ⓐ | ⓑ | ⓒ | ⓓ |
| 19. | ⓐ | ⓑ | ⓒ | ⓓ | | 54. | ⓐ | ⓑ | ⓒ | ⓓ | | 89. | ⓐ | ⓑ | ⓒ | ⓓ |
| 20. | ⓐ | ⓑ | ⓒ | ⓓ | | 55. | ⓐ | ⓑ | ⓒ | ⓓ | | 90. | ⓐ | ⓑ | ⓒ | ⓓ |
| 21. | ⓐ | ⓑ | ⓒ | ⓓ | | 56. | ⓐ | ⓑ | ⓒ | ⓓ | | 91. | ⓐ | ⓑ | ⓒ | ⓓ |
| 22. | ⓐ | ⓑ | ⓒ | ⓓ | | 57. | ⓐ | ⓑ | ⓒ | ⓓ | | 92. | ⓐ | ⓑ | ⓒ | ⓓ |
| 23. | ⓐ | ⓑ | ⓒ | ⓓ | | 58. | ⓐ | ⓑ | ⓒ | ⓓ | | 93. | ⓐ | ⓑ | ⓒ | ⓓ |
| 24. | ⓐ | ⓑ | ⓒ | ⓓ | | 59. | ⓐ | ⓑ | ⓒ | ⓓ | | 94. | ⓐ | ⓑ | ⓒ | ⓓ |
| 25. | ⓐ | ⓑ | ⓒ | ⓓ | | 60. | ⓐ | ⓑ | ⓒ | ⓓ | | 95. | ⓐ | ⓑ | ⓒ | ⓓ |
| 26. | ⓐ | ⓑ | ⓒ | ⓓ | | 61. | ⓐ | ⓑ | ⓒ | ⓓ | | 96. | ⓐ | ⓑ | ⓒ | ⓓ |
| 27. | ⓐ | ⓑ | ⓒ | ⓓ | | 62. | ⓐ | ⓑ | ⓒ | ⓓ | | 97. | ⓐ | ⓑ | ⓒ | ⓓ |
| 28. | ⓐ | ⓑ | ⓒ | ⓓ | | 63. | ⓐ | ⓑ | ⓒ | | | 98. | ⓐ | ⓑ | ⓒ | ⓓ |
| 29. | ⓐ | ⓑ | ⓒ | ⓓ | | 64. | ⓐ | ⓑ | ⓒ | | | 99. | ⓐ | ⓑ | ⓒ | ⓓ |
| 30. | ⓐ | ⓑ | ⓒ | ⓓ | | 65. | ⓐ | ⓑ | ⓒ | | | 100. | ⓐ | ⓑ | ⓒ | ⓓ |
| 31. | ⓐ | ⓑ | ⓒ | ⓓ | | 66. | ⓐ | ⓑ | ⓒ | ⓓ | | | | | | |
| 32. | ⓐ | ⓑ | ⓒ | ⓓ | | 67. | ⓐ | ⓑ | ⓒ | ⓓ | | | | | | |
| 33. | ⓐ | ⓑ | ⓒ | ⓓ | | 68. | ⓐ | ⓑ | ⓒ | ⓓ | | | | | | |
| 34. | ⓐ | ⓑ | ⓒ | ⓓ | | 69. | ⓐ | ⓑ | ⓒ | ⓓ | | | | | | |
| 35. | ⓐ | ⓑ | ⓒ | ⓓ | | 70. | ⓐ | ⓑ | ⓒ | ⓓ | | | | | | |

# ► Section 1: Reading Comprehension

Answer questions 1–5 based solely on the information in the following passage.

Ventilation is necessary to improve the fire environment for firefighters to approach a fire with a hose line for extinguishment. Additionally, smoke, heat, and gases should be vented above the fire to prohibit conditions necessary for a flashover. This should be completed as soon as possible. Vertical ventilation will delay heat buildup at the ceiling level of the burning room and it may also delay flashover long enough to allow a quick search for a victim. In addition, it may assist in the advancement of an attack hose line. Ventilation decisions should be part of initial size-up. If it is determined that ventilation cannot be completed because of unsafe areas or conditions (e.g., spongy roof, trusses exposed to fire, etc.), then firefighters should not be exposed or operate under the unsafe areas or conditions.

1. The main purpose of this passage is to
   a. alert firefighters to the danger posed by a flashover.
   b. emphasize the importance of ventilation.
   c. point out unsafe conditions.
   d. discuss the initial size-up conference.

2. According to the passage, how should smoke, heat, and gases be ventilated?
   a. by using only the first-floor windows
   b. by waiting for a flashover
   c. by venting above the fire
   d. by first using a hose line to reduce heat buildup

3. According to the passage, vertical ventilation
   a. will delay a possible flashover.
   b. will delay those making a fire attack.
   c. must be done even if crews are exposed to unsafe conditions.
   d. is not important.

4. You arrive on scene at a structure fire before any other apparatus. According to the passage, when should you set up a plan to ventilate the structure?
   a. after your crew stretches the first hose line
   b. as soon as the crew starts the initial search
   c. after the first floor windows are broken out
   d. at the initial size-up

5. With which of the following statements would the author most likely agree?
   a. Flashovers are a concern at today's fires.
   b. Fire attack should go ahead without a plan.
   c. If people are trapped, no effort should be made to rescue them until vertical ventilation has been accomplished.
   d. No matter what the conditions are at the fire scene, ventilation must be carried out.

Answer questions 6–9 by referring to the following table, which provides information on alarm incident response times.

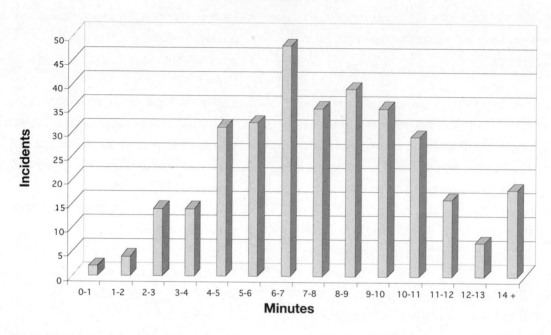

**Alarm Response Times**

**6.** According to the chart, the greatest number of incidents had a response time of
   a. 5–6 minutes.
   b. 6–7 minutes.
   c. 7–8 minutes.
   d. 8–9 minutes.

**7.** About how many incidents had a response time of over 14 minutes?
   a. 10
   b. 30
   c. 18
   d. 50

**8.** Which of the following response times had the lowest number of incidents?
   a. 0–1
   b. 1–2
   c. 2–3
   d. 3–4

**9.** On the average, which two response times had the same number of incidents?
   a. 0–1 and 1–2
   b. 2–3 and 3–4
   c. 6–7 and 7–8
   d. 12–13 and 14+

Answer questions 10–14 based solely on the information in the following passage.

The physiological effects of excessive noise exposure have been found in both animal and human studies. In one study, the exposure of guinea pigs to a siren-like noise for fairly long periods of time eventually caused the onset of endocrine and metabolic deficits that decreased the animals' ability to deal with the noise stress. These deficits will reduce the ability to respond to another startle response situation. Additional siren exposure brought about gastrointestinal ailments, cardiovascular disease, and even tissue damage in the kidneys and livers of the animals. Although the results of this study and similar animal studies have been critiqued, they do demonstrate the existence of extra-auditory effects.

Studies of firefighters' reactions to the alarm signal indicate that the onset of both physiological and psychological stress induces measurable biological effects. Although the physical activity necessary to get into a truck following an alarm signal should not increase the heart rate to more than around 100 beats per minute, studies have found that heartbeats, particularly among younger firefighters, increased to as many as 130 to 150 beats per minute. Several studies have shown increases in pulse rate after the alarm signals from between 47 to 61 beats per minute. It has been theorized that such excited responses to the alarm signal could cause an excessive discharge of catecholamines, which have been shown to disrupt the integrity of the arteries' endothelial lining in animals. A disruption in the integrity of the endothelial lining is believed to cause premature atherosclerosis, and could be a contributing factor to the higher incidence of cardiovascular disease among firefighters.

**10.** What is the most likely meaning of *physiological* as used in this passage?
   **a.** life processes
   **b.** physical restraints
   **c.** abnormal functions
   **d.** appearances

**11.** The basic idea expressed in this passage is that
   **a.** the reaction of firefighters to excessive loud noises can be directly predicted by the reaction of guinea pgs.
   **b.** there is evidence that loud noises have extra-auditory effects on firefighters.
   **c.** the alarm signal has no negative effect on firefighter health.
   **d.** excessive noise, especially among younger firefighters, assists in preparing the body for response to alarms.

**12.** According to the passage, when the alarm signal sounds,
   **a.** older firefighters exhibit serious gastrointestinal distress due to the startle response.
   **b.** younger firefighters exhibit greater signs of stress-related ailments than older firefighters.
   **c.** all firefighters experience elevated heart rates, regardless of age.
   **d.** firefighters' extra-auditory response is the sole factor that explains a higher rate of cardiovascular disease.

**13.** Which of the following is the best title for this passage?
   **a.** Animal Reactions to Sound Stress Predict Human Response
   **b.** Workplace Stress Can Harm Health of Responders
   **c.** Findings Sound Biological Stress Alarm
   **d.** Sound Stress May Contribute to Health Stress

**14.** You can infer from the article that firefighters
   **a.** are in a relaxed state as they respond to an emergency.
   **b.** should realize that they are responding in a stressed-out state.
   **c.** should realize that their heart rates are increased when they are responding.
   **d.** have no health stress due to their response to the alarm.

Answer questions 15–18 by referring to the following table, which shows forest fires in a certain region during the month of June.

| FOREST FIRES, TRI-COUNTY REGION, JUNE 2006 | | | |
|---|---|---|---|
| DATE | AREA | ACRES BURNED | PROBABLE CAUSE |
| June 2 | Burgaw Grove | 115 | Lightning |
| June 3 | Fenner Forest | 200 | Campfire |
| June 7 | Voorhees Air Base Training Site | 400 | Equipment Use |
| June 12 | Murphy County Nature Reserve | 495 | Children |
| June 13 | Knoblock Mountain | 200 | Misc. |
| June 14 | Cougar Run Ski Center | 160 | Unknown |
| June 17 | Fenner Forest | 120 | Campfire |
| June 19 | Stone River State Park | 526 | Arson |
| June 21 | Burgaw Grove | 499 | Smoking |
| June 25 | Bramley Acres Resort | 1,200 | Arson |
| June 28 | Hanesboro Crossing | 320 | Lightning |
| June 30 | Stone River State Park | 167 | Campfire |

**15.** According to the table, suspected arson fires
  **a.** occurred at Stone River State Park and Hanesboro Crossing.
  **b.** consumed over 1,700 acres.
  **c.** occurred less frequently than fires caused by smoking.
  **d.** consumed fewer acres than fires caused by lightning.

**16.** One week after the Voorhees Air Base fire, where did a fire occur?
  **a.** Knoblock Mountain
  **b.** Fenner Forest
  **c.** Cougar Run Ski Center
  **d.** Burgaw Grove

**17.** Which fire consumed the most acreage in June 2006?
  **a.** Bramley Acres Resort
  **b.** Fenner Forest
  **c.** Burgaw Grove
  **d.** Knoblock Mountain

**18.** Which of the following was the most common cause of fires?
  **a.** arson
  **b.** lightning
  **c.** smoking
  **d.** campfires

Answer questions 19–23 based solely on the information in the following passage.

Accountability on the fire ground is paramount and may be accomplished by several methods. It is the responsibility of every officer to account for every firefighter assigned to his or her company and to relay this information to the Incident Commander. Firefighters should not work beyond the sight or sound of the supervising officer unless they are equipped with portable radios. The crew leader should communicate with the supervising officer by portable radio to ensure accountability and indicate completion of assignments and duties. When the assigned duties are completed, the crew should radio this information to the supervisor, then return to the supervisor for additional duties. As a fire escalates and additional fire companies respond, a communication assistant with a command board should assist the Incident Commander with accounting for all firefighter companies at the fire, at the staging area, and at rehabilitation. One of the most important aids for accountability at an incident is the Incident Command System. The ICS is a management tool that defines the roles and responsibilities of all units responding to an incident. It enables one individual to have better control of the incident scene. This system works on an understanding among the crew that the person in charge will be standing back from the incident, focusing on the entire scene.

**19.** The main purpose of this passage is to
   **a.** demonstrate how one individual can control the fire ground.
   **b.** emphasize the importance of accountability for responders on the fire ground.
   **c.** show the paramount importance of portable radios to firefighters.
   **d.** show some methods that can accomplish the primary goal of accountability on the fire ground.

**20.** According to the passage, what should the crew leader communicate to the supervisor?
   **a.** the location and members of the crew
   **b.** that the crew is out of sight of the supervisor and is returning
   **c.** that the supervisor has to leave the command post and join the team
   **d.** that the crew is not going to be part of the Incident Command System

**21.** According to the passage, the Incident Command System is important because it
   **a.** allows a large number of incident commanders to function at a fire.
   **b.** allows crews to work on their own without having to report to a supervisor.
   **c.** is a tool that can account for personnel on the fire ground.
   **d.** allows the crews to keep a distance from the scene.

**22.** According to the passage, which of the following items is most vital for personnel accountability?
   **a.** a well-laid-out staging area
   **b.** a communications assistant
   **c.** a well-laid-out command board
   **d.** a means of communication with the supervisor

**23.** Which of the following does the passage suggest is the greatest problem for the fire ground commander?
   **a.** extinguishing the fire
   **b.** accounting for all personnel
   **c.** defining roles and responsibilities
   **d.** handling the arrival of additional companies

Answer questions 24–27 by referring to the following table, which shows arson statistics for 2005 and 2006.

| SEASON | MONTH | DAILY AVERAGE | DAILY SEASONAL AVERAGE |
|--------|-------|---------------|------------------------|
| **DAILY INCIDENCE OF FIRES IN THE UNITED STATES BY MONTH AND BY SEASON (ESTIMATED AVERAGE 2005-2006)** | | | |
| Winter | January | 4.203 | |
| | February | 4,604 | 4,548 |
| | March | 4,842 | |
| Spring | April | 5,291 | |
| | May | 4,787 | 4,986 |
| | June | 4,886 | |
| Summer | July | 5,683 | |
| | August | 4,897 | 4,932 |
| | September | 4,191 | |
| Fall | October | 4,103 | |
| | November | 4,664 | 4,285 |
| | December | 4,101 | |

**24.** On the average, what two months have the lowest number of daily fires?
a. April and July
b. January and September
c. September and December
d. October and December

**25.** Statistics show that incendiary and suspicious fires account for 22% of all fires on the average. Using the daily seasonal averages, how many fires were of incendiary and suspicious origin?
a. 4,125
b. 4,285
c. 4,548
d. 5,291

**26.** During the winter, heating fires account for 27% and cooking fires account for 17% of the structure fires. Using the Daily Seasonal Average, how many fires of these types could you expect on an average winter day in the United States?
a. 4,842
b. 4,548
c. 2,547
d. 2,001

**27.** Which of the following is the best explanation for the jump in the average daily incidence of fire during July?
a. home cooking
b. heating unit failures
c. lightning strikes and fireworks
d. barbecues

Answer questions 28–32 based solely on the information in the following passage.

Slowly, the fire service is shedding light on a situation that rarely occurs but is nevertheless serious: Some firefighters intentionally start fires. A very small percentage of otherwise trustworthy firefighters cause the very flames they are dispatched to put out. Most fire departments will never have a member indicted for arson. But for those that do, the impact is significant. Research conducted by the National Center for the Analysis of Violent Crime suggests that a telltale sign that a firefighter may be setting fires is a sudden increase in nuisance fires within a company's first due area. The research also indicates that firefighter arson offenders tend to be relatively new to the department, typically with fewer than three years as a member. An FBI study of firefighter arson showed that the top motive was excitement, especially among young firefighters who were eager to put their training to practical use, and to be seen as heroes to fellow firefighters and the communities they served.

Firefighter arsonists often escalate their fires over time. The report indicates that firefighter arsonists, as is typical of most arsonists, generally start with nuisance fires, such as dumpsters, trash piles, or vegetation. Eventually, the firefighter arsonist graduates to other targets that have more damage potential, such as abandoned vehicles or unoccupied structures. Sometimes, even occupied structures are threatened by the arsonist's actions.

Given the far-reaching effects that criminal fire setting by a firefighter can cause, awareness and action are clearly necessary. The impact of firefighter arson can be severe. People die or are seriously injured, including fellow firefighters who respond to the call. Homes are destroyed. An arsonist from within the fire department can disgrace the whole department, and his or her actions diminish public trust. Firefighter arson task forces have been organized to prevent the crime. Education, training, and appropriate criminal background and reference checks are key components of the programs.

**28.** Which of the following is not true about firefighter arsonists?
   a. Their top motive is excitement.
   b. They always set the same type of fire.
   c. A certain telltale sign is a sudden increase in nuisance fires.
   d. Fortunately, they are not a common problem.

**29.** Which of the following best expresses the main idea of the passage?
   a. Firefighter arson is a common problem in today's fire service.
   b. Young firefighters are the first people to be questioned when there is an unexplained increase in nuisance fires.
   c. Firefighter arson is a rare occurrence, but one that can have a serious impact on the department.
   d. Firefighter arsonists set fires only so that they can be seen as heroes.

**30.** Which of the following is <u>not</u> a key component of a program to prevent this crime?
   a. education and training
   b. hiring only older firefighters
   c. criminal background checks
   d. checking all references

**31.** The passage discusses education and training as part of a program to prevent firefighter arson. What do you think is the purpose of this part of the program?
   **a.** to heighten awareness of the problem
   **b.** to show that help is available for those who are fire starters
   **c.** train firefighters to properly investigate nuisance fires
   **d.** to assist those who set fires to stop their fire-setting behavior

**32.** One of the main problems with all types of arson is that
   **a.** arson fires are only a nuisance.
   **b.** the fires are always small and rarely threaten life.
   **c.** the crime is rarely investigated.
   **d.** arson fires threaten both citizens' and firefighters' lives during response and on the fire ground.

Answer questions 33–35 by referring to the following table, which lists numerical data regarding fire department call volume.

|  | Fires | Rescue/EMS | Haz-cond | Co/smoke | Service | Auto Alarm | Total |
|---|---|---|---|---|---|---|---|
| December | 1 | 7 | 4 | 3 | 1 | 6 | |
| January | 1 | 5 | 3 | 4 | 1 | 11 | |
| February | 5 | 4 | 3 | 8 | 2 | 11 | |
| March | 2 | 2 | 2 | 3 | 0 | 11 | |
| April | 3 | 11 | 2 | 7 | 0 | 6 | |
| May | 4 | 17 | 3 | 6 | 1 | 10 | |
| June | 2 | 13 | 1 | 4 | 0 | 17 | |
| July | 1 | 12 | 4 | 5 | 0 | 8 | |
| August | 0 | 7 | 1 | 5 | 0 | 21 | |
| September | 1 | 17 | 2 | 8 | 1 | 7 | |
| October | 0 | 18 | 3 | 8 | 1 | 11 | |
| November | 0 | 8 | 2 | 8 | 1 | 4 | |
| **Totals 2007** | **20** | **121** | **30** | **69** | **8** | **123** | **371** |
| | | | | | | | |
| Totals 2006 | 24 | 89 | 38 | 33 | 14 | 111 | **309** |
| Totals 2005 | 15 | 76 | 39 | 13 | 16 | 137 | **296** |
| Totals 2004 | 17 | 30 | 38 | 9 | 12 | 99 | **205** |
| Totals 2003 | 21 | 25 | 28 | 10 | 12 | 88 | **184** |
| Totals 2002 | 15 | 24 | 26 | 22 | 16 | 96 | **199** |
| Totals 2001 | 21 | 28 | 34 | 15 | 11 | 81 | **190** |
| Totals 2000 | 32 | 39 | 32 | 19 | 9 | 80 | **211** |
| Totals 1999 | 14 | 38 | 29 | 18 | 8 | 82 | **189** |

**33.** In which of the following years did the greatest number of fire incidents occur?
a. 2004
b. 2002
c. 2000
d. 1999

**34.** Which of the following years had the lowest number of total Rescue/EMS incidents?
a. 2005
b. 2004
c. 2003
d. 2002

**35.** In 2007, which month had the greatest number of Rescue/EMS incidents?
a. July
b. August
c. September
d. October

## ▶ Section 2: Verbal Expression

For numbers 36–40, choose the word that most nearly means the same as the italicized word.

**36.** Remember to always try to have an *alternative* method to what you think will probably work when conducting forcible-entry operations.
a. proven
b. single
c. resourceful
d. substitute

**37.** Firefighters must also be *proficient* in the safe use of SCBA, donning and doffing procedures, individual limitations, and limitations of the SCBA unit prior to use in suppression activities.
a. unskilled
b. competent
c. incapable
d. indifferent

**38.** New advancements in computer hardware and software have made it possible for many departments to *incorporate* the use of computers into their communication systems.
a. exclude
b. alleviate
c. integrate
d. eliminate

**39.** Collapse of burning buildings has killed and injured many firefighters engaged in *aggressive* fire ground operations.
a. hesitant
b. apprehensive
c. timid
d. uncompromising

**40.** He based his conclusion on what he *inferred* from the evidence, not on what he actually observed.

a. intuited

b. imagined

c. surmised

d. implied

For numbers 41–43, choose the word that best fills the blank.

**41.** A fire hose has two _____, the hose itself and the couplings that connect the hose sections or appliances used with them

a. uses

b. components

c. connections

d. liners

**42.** Rapid intervention teams (RIT) are being formed by many fire departments as a _____ practice to rescue lost or trapped firefighters.

a. proactive

b. reckless

c. irresponsible

d. imprudent

**43.** The spokesperson must _____ the philosophy of an entire department so that outsiders can understand it completely.

a. entrust

b. defend

c. verify

d. articulate

For numbers 44–47, replace the underlined portion with the phrase that best completes the sentence. If the sentence is correct as is, choose option **a**.

**44.** The news reporter who <u>had been covering the story suddenly became ill, and I was called</u> to take her place.

a. had been covering the story suddenly became ill, and I was called

b. was covering the story suddenly becomes ill, and they called me

c. is covering the story suddenly becomes ill, and I was called

d. would have been covering the story suddenly became ill, and I am called

**45.** The troposphere is the lowest layer of Earth's <u>atmosphere, it extends</u> from ground level to an altitude of seven to ten miles.

a. atmosphere, it extends

b. atmosphere of which it extends

c. atmosphere. Extending

d. atmosphere; it extends

**46.** <u>Along with your membership to our health club and</u> two months of free personal training.

a. Along with your membership to our health club and

b. Along with your membership to our health club comes

c. With your membership to our health club,

d. In addition to your membership to our health club being

**47.** <u>To determine the speed of automobiles, radar is often used by the state police.</u>

    **a.** To determine the speed of automobiles, radar is often used by the state police.

    **b.** In determining the speed of automobiles, the use of radar by state police is often employed.

    **c.** To determine the speed of automobiles, the state police often use radar.

    **d.** Radar by state police in determining the speed of automobiles is often used.

**48.** Which choice expresses the idea most clearly and accurately?

    **a.** Ethics and the law having no true relationship.

    **b.** There is no true relationship between ethics and the law.

    **c.** Between ethics and the law, no true relationship.

    **d.** Ethics and the law is no true relationship.

**49.** Which of these expresses the idea most clearly and accurately?

    **a.** Some people say jury duty is a nuisance that just takes up their precious time and that we don't get paid enough.

    **b.** Some people say jury duty is a nuisance that just takes up your precious time and that one doesn't get paid enough.

    **c.** Some people say jury duty is a nuisance that just takes up precious time and that doesn't pay enough.

    **d.** Some people say jury duty is a nuisance that just takes up our precious time and that they don't get paid enough.

**50.** Which of these expresses the idea most clearly and accurately?

    **a.** By the time they are in the third or fourth grade, the eyes of most children in the United States are tested.

    **b.** Most children by the time they are in the United States have their eyes tested in the third or fourth grade.

    **c.** Most children in the United States have their eyes tested by the time they are in the third or fourth grade.

    **d.** In the United States by the time of third or fourth grade, there is testing of the eyes of most children.

## ▶ Section 3: Logical Reasoning

**51.** Look at this series: 10, 34, 12, 31, __, 28, 16, . . . What number should fill the blank?

    **a.** 14

    **b.** 18

    **c.** 30

    **d.** 34

**52.** Look at this series: 17, __, 28, 28, 39, 39, . . . What number should fill the blank?

    **a.** 50

    **b.** 39

    **c.** 25

    **d.** 17

**53.** Look at this series: 0.15, 0.3, __, 1.2, 2.4, . . . What number should fill the blank?

    **a.** 4.8

    **b.** 0.006

    **c.** 0.6

    **d.** 0.9

**54.** Look at this series: J14, L16, __, P20, R22, . . .
What letter and numbers should fill the blank?
a. S24
b. N18
c. M18
d. T24

**55.** Look at this series: QPO, NML, KJI, ___,
EDC, . . . What letters should fill the blank?
a. HGF
b. CAB
c. JKL
d. GHI

For numbers 56–58, find the missing item in the pattern.

**56.**

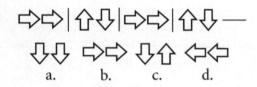

a.    b.    c.    d.

**57.**

a.    b.    c.    d.

**58.**

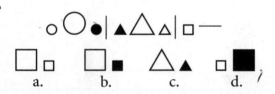

a.    b.    c.    d.

For numbers 59–62, complete the analogy.

**59.** Communication is to telephone as transportation is to
a. aviation.
b. travel.
c. information.
d. bus.

**60.** Bicycle is to pedal as canoe is to
a. water.
b. kayak.
c. oar.
d. fleet.

**61.** Tactful is to diplomatic as bashful is to
a. timid.
b. confident.
c. uncomfortable.
d. bold.

**62.** Odometer is to mileage as compass is to
a. speed.
b. hiking.
c. needle.
d. direction.

**63.** City A has a higher population than City B.
City C has a lower population than City B.
City A has a lower population than City C.
If the first two statements are true, the third statement is
a. true.
b. false.
c. uncertain.

**64.** The Shop and Save Grocery is south of Greenwood Pharmacy.

Rebecca's house is northeast of Greenwood Pharmacy.

Rebecca's house is west of the Shop and Save Grocery.

If the first two statements are true, the third statement is

a. true.

b. false.

c. uncertain.

**65.** Oat cereal has more fiber than corn cereal but less fiber than bran cereal.

Corn cereal has more fiber than rice cereal but less fiber than wheat cereal.

Of the five kinds of cereal, rice cereal has the least amount of fiber.

If the first two statements are true, the third statement is

a. true.

b. false.

c. uncertain.

## ▶ Section 4: Mathematics

**66.** Water towers are tall to provide pressure. Each foot of height provides 0.43 psi of pressure. How much pressure would be created by a 110 foot water tower?

a. 35.2 psi

b. 43 psi

c. 56.9 psi

d. 47.3 psi

**67.** The friction loss per 100 feet of $1\frac{1}{2}$ " of fire hose is 24 psi. What is the total friction loss through 250 feet of $1\frac{1}{2}$ " fire hose?

a. 48 psi

b. 36 psi

c. 60 psi

d. 72 psi

As of January 1, 2006, 81% of the nation's fire departments had responded to a national fire department census. As of that date, 24,296 departments had responded, representing 44,100 fire stations across the United States. Ninety-five percent of the responding departments were local fire departments, including career, combination, and volunteer fire departments and fire districts. The remaining 5% of responders were made up of federal and state government fire departments, contract fire departments, private or industrial fire brigades, and transportation authority or airport fire departments. The fire departments who registered with the census were staffed by approximately 1,112,000 personnel. This figure includes career, volunteer, and paid per call firefighters who represent about 88% of the registered department's personnel.

**68.** According to the information in the passage, approximately how many fire departments are in the United States?

a. 19,680

b. 29,995

c. 33,210

d. 44,100

**69.** Using the data provided, how many firefighters are employed by the registered departments?
a. 1,263,636
b. 1,112,000
c. 978,560
d. 133,440

**70.** If 13% of the responding departments listed themselves as career or mostly career, how many departments does this represent?
a. 1,869
b. 3,159
c. 21,137
d. 24,427

**71.** A firefighter checks the gauge on a cylinder that normally contains 45 cubic feet of air and finds that the cylinder has only 10 cubic feet of air. The gauge indicates that the cylinder is
a. $\frac{1}{4}$ full.
b. $\frac{2}{9}$ full.
c. $\frac{1}{3}$ full.
d. $\frac{4}{5}$ full.

**72.**

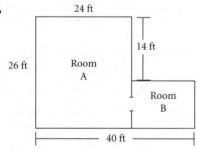

The smallest waterproof tarpaulin that will entirely cover Room B is
a. 10 feet × 14 feet.
b. 12 feet × 14 feet.
c. 10 feet × 16 feet.
d. 12 feet × 16 feet.

**73.** A fire station receives an alarm at 10:42 P.M. on August 3 and another alarm at 1:19 A.M. on August 4. How much time has elapsed between alarms?
a. 1 hour 37 minutes
b. 2 hours 23 minutes
c. 2 hours 37 minutes
d. 3 hours 23 minutes

**74.** Each sprinkler head in an office sprinkler system sprays water at an average of 16 gallons per minute. If 5 sprinkler heads are flowing at the same time, how many gallons of water will be released in 10 minutes?
a. 80
b. 160
c. 800
d. 1,650

**75.**

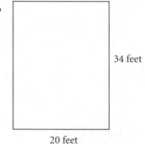

How many feet of rope will a firefighter need to tie off a protective area that is 34 feet long and 20 feet wide?
a. 54
b. 88
c. 108
d. 680

**76.** Several considerations must be weighed when raising a ladder. The heel or foot of the ladder must be a certain distance from the building for stability. To determine this distance, the ladder should be placed $\frac{1}{4}$ of its working length from the building. A 28-foot extension ladder should be placed how many feet from the building for stability?
- **a.** 5 feet
- **b.** 6 feet
- **c.** 7 feet
- **d.** 8 feet

**77.** A two-person load for rope rescue is anticipated to be 600 lbs. If firefighter standards require a safety ratio of 15:1 to use a rope for rescue, what must the minimum breaking strength of a $\frac{1}{2}$ " piece of rescue rope be before using the rope
- **a.** 9,000 lbs.
- **b.** 6,000 lbs.
- **c.** 11,000 lbs.
- **d.** 9,000 lbs.

**78.** What is the average weight of four firefighters in full personal protective gear who weigh 190 pounds, 230 pounds, 260 pounds, and 280 pounds?
- **a.** 240 pounds
- **b.** 225 pounds
- **c.** 260 pounds
- **d.** 200 pounds

**79.** Kilonewtons (kN) are stamped on rescue gear to give firefighters a measurement of what kind of forces the gear can withstand, or how strong it is. If 1 kN = 225 lbs., what is the strength rating on a 25 kN carabiner?
- **a.** 6,000 lbs.
- **b.** 5,625 lbs.
- **c.** 4,200 lbs.
- **d.** 6,325 lbs.

**80.** The 2.5 gallon pressurized water extinguisher is highly effective on Class A or ordinary combustible fires. If water weighs 8.34 lbs. per gallon, what is the weight of a Class A extinguisher?
- **a.** 16.68
- **b.** 25.02
- **c.** 20.85 lbs.
- **d.** 12.51 lbs.

## ▶ Section 5: Mechanical Aptitude

Use the information provided in the question, as well as any diagrams provided, to answer the following questions.

**81.** A fire engine has become stuck in a ditch. Which of the following tools would most likely be used to help extract the fire engine from the ditch?
- **a.** a clamp
- **b.** an electric winch
- **c.** a speedometer
- **d.** a centrifugal pump

**82.**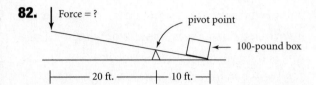

In the diagram shown above, Firefighter King must lift a 100-pound box using a lever. How many pounds of force must she apply to the left side of the lever to lift the box? (The product of the weight of the box times the distance of the box from the pivot point must be equal to the product of the required force times the distance from the force to the pivot point): ($w \times d_1 = f \times d_2$)
a. 100 pounds
b. 200 pounds
c. 50 pounds
d. 33 pounds

**83.** The purpose of a spark plug in an internal combustion engine is to provide
a. lubrication of the engine.
b. rotation of the piston.
c. cooling of the manifold.
d. ignition of the fuel.

**84.** A carpenter's square is used primarily to
a. ensure that a cut is straight.
b. measure the length of a stud.
c. saw a board to the correct length.
d. check that a building is level.

**85.**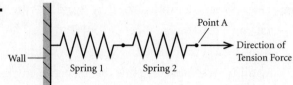

Two springs are arranged in series as shown above. Spring 1 is very stiff and will become 1 inch longer when a tension force of 10 pounds is applied to it. Spring 2 is very soft and will become 2 inches longer when a tension force of 5 pounds is applied to it. What will be the change in length of the two springs when a force of 20 pounds is applied—that is, how far will point A move to the right?
a. 10 inches
b. 6 inches
c. 8 inches
d. 3 inches

**86.** The fuel in a diesel engine is ignited by the
a. spark plug.
b. glow plug.
c. injector.
d. heat of compression.

**87.** Which of the following items is used to measure angles?
a. a lever
b. a tachometer
c. a gear
d. a protractor

**88.**

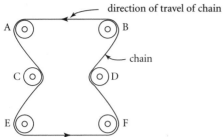

In the diagram shown above, which gears are turning clockwise?
- **a.** A, C, and E
- **b.** B, D, and F
- **c.** C and D
- **d.** E and F

**89.** Which of the following is NOT a type of wrench?
- **a.** crescent
- **b.** box end
- **c.** ratchet
- **d.** drill

**90.** What type of gauge is read in units of psi (pounds per square inch)?
- **a.** pressure gauge
- **b.** depth gauge
- **c.** speed gauge
- **d.** RPM gauge

**91.**

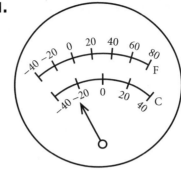

The gauge shown above is
- **a.** a pressure gauge.
- **b.** an altitude gauge.
- **c.** a temperature gauge.
- **d.** a flow meter gauge.

**92.** If a truck is traveling at constant speed of 50 miles per hour for a total time period of 1 hour and 30 minutes, how many miles does it travel? (Distance = Rate × Time)
- **a.** 75 miles
- **b.** 50 miles
- **c.** 5 miles
- **d.** 130 miles

**93.** What common mechanical device is typically used on a push button—such as that found on a push-button telephone, a computer keyboard, or an electric garage door opener—to return the button to its original position?
- **a.** a wheel
- **b.** a pulley
- **c.** a spring
- **d.** a gear

**94.**

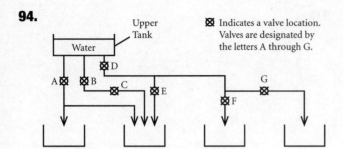 

In the diagram shown above, all valves are initially closed. Gravity will cause the water to drain down into the barrels when the valves are opened. Which barrels will be filled if valves A, B, E, F, and G are opened and valves C and D are left closed?

**a.** barrels 1 and 2

**b.** barrels 3 and 4

**c.** barrels 1, 2, 3, and 4

**d.** barrels 1, 2, and 3

**95.** Which of the mechanical devices listed below is used to control the flow of liquids and gases in a piping system?

**a.** a gear

**b.** a valve

**c.** a piston

**d.** a spring

**96.** The purpose of a radiator on a car is to

**a.** cool the engine.

**b.** maximize gas mileage.

**c.** increase the engine horsepower.

**d.** reduce engine noise.

**97.**

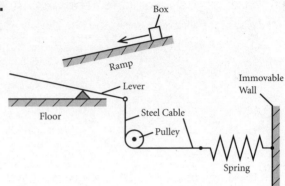

In the diagram shown above, if the box slides down the ramp and drops onto the left side of the lever, what will happen to the spring?

**a.** It will touch the box.

**b.** It will remain as it is.

**c.** It will be compressed or shortened.

**d.** It will be stretched or lengthened.

**98.** Which mechanical device is NOT typically found on an automobile?

**a.** a valve

**b.** a pump

**c.** a drill

**d.** a fan

**99.** A solar panel, a windmill, an atomic reactor, a dam on a river, and a steam turbine are all examples of methods that could be used to create
  **a.** ice.
  **b.** electricity.
  **c.** steel.
  **d.** rain.

**100.**

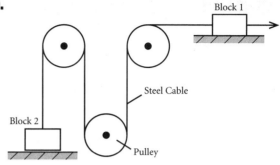

In the diagram shown above, if block 1 is moved 10 feet to the right, how far upward is block 2 lifted?
  **a.** 3 feet
  **b.** 5 feet
  **c.** 10 feet
  **d.** 20 feet

# ▶ Answers

## Section 1:
## Reading Comprehension

**1. b.** Ventilation is the best way to reduce heat buildup and reduce dangers in a structure fire.

**2. c.** Ventilation is most effective when it removes the heat trapped over the fire.

**3. a.** Vertical ventilation is an effective way to reduce heat and reduce flashover risks.

**4. d.** Ventilation must be part of the initial size-up. Proper ventilation can ease the firefighting team's work and relieve the stress on trapped victims.

**5. a.** Flashovers are a real danger today due to the amount of petrochemicals in today's furnishings and homes.

**6. b.** 6–7 minutes is the greatest total of incidents according to the chart.

**7. c.** Eighteen incidents had a response time of 14+ minutes.

**8. a.** 0–1 minutes had the smallest number of incidents.

**9. b.** 2–3 and 3–4 had the same number of incidents.

**10. a.** Physiological is defined as relating to physiology, which is the study of an organism's healthy or normal functioning. Here, it means that the alarm signal causes stress to the normal functions of body and mind.

**11. b.** The passage explains that there is evidence of extra-auditory effects on firefighters' health due to loud noises.

**12. c.** The most correct statement is that all firefighters experience elevated heart rates when the alarm sounds.

**13. b.** The best title that is broad enough and correct is "Workplace Stress Can Harm Health of Responders."

**14. c.** The passage makes it clear that the stress induced by the responder answering an alarm increases the heart rate.

**15. b.** 1,200 acres at Bramley Acres Resort and 526 acres at Stone River Park adds up to 1,726 acres.

**16. c.** The Voorhees fire occurred June 7. The Cougar Run fire occurred June 14.

**17. a.** The Bremley Acres Resort fire burned up 1,200 acres.

**18. d.** Campfires accounted for three of the fires listed, more than any other cause.

**19. d.** The passage clearly states that "accountability on the fire ground is paramount," narrowing the choices to **b** and **d**. Although **b** is correct, the majority of the passage reviews ways to accomplish the primary goal of accounting for all personnel on the fire ground.

**20. a.** The supervisor must be able to account for all the personnel undertaking operations. Only choice **a** conveys that. The other three choices would not accomplish the purpose, and they are also not found in the passage.

**21. c.** The Incident Command System provides for command, control, and communications at any size emergency incident. It provides a framework so that each person has a clear line of command and a clear chain of accountability. Although there are types of incident command that will allow for more than one commander, that is rare and it does not change the use of ICS as a tool to account for personnel on the fire ground.

**22. d.** The text of the passage tells us that a communications assistant can help with the communications to and from the staging area, operations, etc., but the most vital tool is a means of communication.

**23. b.** Roles and responsibilities are set out in the ICS, so the fire ground commander does not need to develop them. The arrival of companies and the extinguishing of the fire are part of normal operations. The passage makes it clear that the most difficult task is to account for all personnel at the emergency.

**24. d.** The average number of daily fires is 4,103 in October and 4,101 in December.

**25. a.** To find the answer, add 4,548 + 4,986 + 4,932 + 4,285 = 18,751 × 0.22 = 4,125.22.

**26. d.** 17% + 27% = 44%, so 4,548 × 0.44 = 2,001.12, which is close to 2,001.

**27. c.** Of the answers given, this is the most correct. The use of fireworks and the increase in lightning storms account for the increase. While barbeques are a possibility, and they do cause fires, for the most part these are not common. Home cooking is about the same each season, and we can assume that heating units are not a large factor in July.

**28. b.** According to the passage, firefighter arsonists progress to bigger fires over a period of time.

**29. c.** Firefighter arson is rare and an increase in nuisance fires just means that a fire setter is present, so choices **a** and **b** are false. Choice **d** states that the only reason they set fires is a need to be a hero. Although this need for excitement is the top reason cited, the passage makes it clear that there are other reasons. Choice **c** best states the main idea: Firefighter arson is both rare and a serious problem.

**30. b.** Hiring only older firefighters does not guarantee that there would be no firefighter arsonists among the new hires, so this is the false answer. The others answers are part of passage's recommendations.

**31. a.** The purpose is to heighten awareness of the problem and to train those in the fire service to recognize the problem. Fire setters are subject to dismissal, so while they might get help or might stop, they would be out of the

department. The investigation of nuisance fires is part of fire investigation training.

**32. d.** Arson is a crime that threatens life. Firefighters are in danger when they are responding to a fire. Everyone's safety is threatened by arson fires.

**33. c.** According to the chart, the year 2000 had the greatest number of fire incidents.

**34. d.** According to the chart, the year 2002 had the lowest number of Rescue/EMS incidents.

**35. d.** According to the chart, the month of October had the greatest number of Rescue/EMS incidents.

## Section 2: Verbal Expression

**36. d.** *Alternative* used in this context relates to having additional means if the primary method fails. *Substitute* has the closest meaning in this sentence.

**37. b.** *Proficient* means having or showing knowledge and skill or aptitude. *Competent* closely matches proficient.

**38. c.** *Incorporate* used in this context means to unite or merge with something already in existence. *Integrate* is the best choice.

**39. d.** Of the choices listed, *uncompromising* is the choice that is closest in meaning to *aggressive*.

**40. c.** To *infer* something is to *surmise* it or deduce it from the evidence.

**41. b.** The statement is defining the pieces that compose a fire hose section, thus, *components* would be the proper selection.

**42. a.** *Reckless, irresponsible,* and *imprudent* are all poor choices because of the context of the question. *Proactive* would be the best selection.

**43. d.** To *articulate* something is to give words to it or express it. The other choices do not fit the context of the sentence.

**44. a.** When constructing sentences, unnecessary shifts in verb tenses should be avoided. Choice **a** is best because all three verbs in the sentence indicate that the action occurred in the past (*had been covering*, *became*, and *was called*). In choice **b**, there is a shift to the present (*becomes*). Choice **c** begins in the present (*is covering*, *becomes*), then shifts to the past (*called*). Choice **d** makes two tense shifts.

**45. d.** The correct punctuation between two independent clauses is a semicolon. Choice **a** is wrong because it creates a comma splice. Choice **b** creates faulty subordination. Choice **c** creates a sentence fragment.

**46. b.** This is the correct choice because it is the only one that is a complete sentence.

**47. c.** Choice **c** is best because it is written in the active voice, and the sentence is constructed so that all modifiers are appropriately placed.

**48. b.** Choices **a** and **c** are sentence fragments. Choice **d** represents confused sentence structure as well as lack of agreement between subject and verb.

**49. c.** The other choices contain unnecessary shifts in person, from *people* to *their* and *we* in choice **a**, to *your* and *one* in choice **b**, and to *our* and *they* in choice **d**.

**50. c.** This is the only choice that is clear and logical. Choice **a** reads as though the eyes are in the third or fourth grade. Choices **b** and **d** are unclear.

### Section 3: Logical Reasoning

**51. a.** This is an alternating addition and subtraction series. The first series begins with 10 and adds 2; the second begins with 34 and subtracts 3.

**52. d.** In this addition with repetition series, each number in the series repeats itself, and then increases by 11 to arrive at the next number.

**53. c.** This is a multiplication series. Each number is 2 times greater than the previous number.

**54. b.** In this series, the letters progress by 2, and the numbers increase by 2.

**55. a.** This series consists of letters in a reverse alphabetical order.

**56. b.** Look at each segment. In the first segment, the arrows are both pointing to the right. In the second segment, the first arrow is up and the second is down. The third segment repeats the first segment. In the fourth segment, the arrows are up and then down. Because this is an alternating series, the two arrows pointing right will be repeated, so option **b** is the only possible choice.

**57. b.** Notice that in each segment, the figures are all the same shape, but the one in the middle is larger than the two on either side. Also, notice that one of the figures is shaded and that this shading alternates first right and then left. To continue this pattern in the third segment, you will look for a square. Choice **b** is correct because this choice will put the large square between the two smaller squares, with the shading on the right.

**58. d.** This is an alternating series. The first and third segments are repeated. The second segment is simply upside down.

**59. d.** The telephone is a means of communication. The bus is a means of transportation. Aviation (choice **a**) is not the answer because it is a type of transportation, not a means. The answer is not choice **b** or choice **c** because neither of these represents a means of transportation.

**60. c.** A bicycle is put in motion by means of a pedal. A canoe is put into motion by means of an oar. The answer is not choice **a** because water does not necessarily put the canoe into motion. Kayak (choice **b**) is incorrect because it is a type of boat similar to a canoe. Choice **d** is incorrect because a fleet is a group of boats.

**61. a.** *Tactful* and *diplomatic* are synonyms (they mean about the same thing). *Bashful* and *timid* are also synonyms. The answer is not choice **b** or **c** because neither of these means the same as *bashful*. Choice **d** is incorrect because *bold* means the opposite of *bashful*.

**62. d.** An odometer is an instrument used to measure mileage. A compass is an instrument used to determine direction. Choices **a**, **b**, and **c** are incorrect because none are instruments.

**63. b.** From the first two statements we know that of the three cities, City A has the highest population, so the third statement must be false.

**64. b.** Because the first two statements are true, Rebecca's house is also northeast of the Shop and Save Grocery, which means that the third statement is false.

**65. a.** From the first statement, we know that bran cereal has more fiber than both oat cereal and corn cereal. From the second statement, we know that rice cereal has less fiber than both corn and wheat cereals. Therefore, rice cereal has the least amount of fiber.

## Section 4: Mathematics

**66. d.** $110 \times .43$ psi $= 47.3$ psi

**67. c.** $24$ psi $\times 2.5 = 60$ psi

**68. b.** Careful; the question asks about departments, not stations. The passage says that 81% of the fire departments responded to the survey, and 24,296 departments responded, so $\frac{24,296}{0.81} = 29,995.1$.

**69. c.** According to the passage, the departments that responded had 1,112,200 employees, of

which 88% were firefighters. $1,112,000 \times 0.88 = 978,560$.

**70. b.** 13% of 24,296 gives the following: $24,296 \times 0.13 = 3,158.48$ or 3,159.

**71. b.** Because the answer is a fraction, the best way to solve the problem is to convert the known to a fraction: $\frac{10}{45}$ of the cylinder is full. By dividing both the numerator and the denominator by 5, you can reduce the fraction to $\frac{2}{9}$.

**72. d.** To solve the problem, the dimensions of Room B must be determined. The width of Room B is determined by subtracting 14 feet from 26 feet. The length is determined by subtracting 24 feet (the width of Room A) from 40 feet (the length of Room A and Room B together).

**73. c.** Subtraction and addition will solve this problem. From 10:42 to 12:42, two hours have elapsed. From 12:42 to 1:00, another 18 minutes have elapsed ($60 - 42 = 18$). Then from 1:00 to 1:19, there is another 19 minutes.

**74. c.** Multiply 16 times 5 to find out how many gallons all five sprinklers will release in one minute. Then multiply the result (80 gallons per minute) by the number of minutes (10) to get 800 gallons.

**75. c.** There are two sides 34 feet long and two sides 20 feet long. Using the formula $P = 2L + 2W$ will solve this problem. Therefore, you should multiply 34 times 2 and 20 times 2, and then add the results: $68 + 40 = 108$.

**76. c.** $28/4 = 7$ feet

**77. a.** $600 \times 15 = 9000$ lbs.

**78. a.** $190 + 230 + 260 + 280 = 960, 960/4 = 240$ lbs.

**79. b.** $225$ lbs. $\times 25 = 5625$ lbs.

**80. c.** $2.5 \times 8.34$ lbs. $= 20.85$ lbs.

## Section 5: Mechanical Aptitude

**81. b.** An electric winch would be used to remove a fire truck from a ditch. The other devices would not be useful in this situation.

**82. c.** The distance from the pivot point to the point of application of the force (20 feet) is twice the distance from the pivot point to the box (10 feet). Therefore, in order to lift the box, the required force will be one half of the weight of the box (100 pounds), or 50 pounds.

**83. d.** The spark plug produces a spark inside the cylinder of the engine. This spark causes the fuel to burn.

**84. a.** A carpenter's square is typically an L-shaped piece of metal used to draw a straight line on a board on which a cut is to be made.

**85. a.** Because the springs are in series, their amount of stretch is additive. Spring 1 will stretch 1 inch under 10 pounds, so its total stretch under 20 pounds will be 2 inches. Spring 2 is being subjected to a load of 20 pounds, which is four times the load that will stretch it 2 inches. Therefore, its total stretch will be 8 inches. Adding the amount of stretch for the two springs together gives you 10 inches.

**86. d.** The fuel in a diesel engine is sprayed into the cylinder by the injectors, but the actual ignition of the fuel is caused by the heat of compression of the air in the cylinder. A spark plug is used in a gasoline engine, and a glow plug is used to preheat a diesel engine for quick starting in cold weather.

**87. d.** A protractor is typically a half circle made of metal or plastic that has marks around the edge spaced at one-degree intervals—a complete circle has 360 degrees. The protractor can be used to measure angles of various geometric shapes, plots of land, and other items.

**88. c.** The other gears are turning counterclockwise. It helps to follow the direction of the chain, which is directly connected to all of the gears.

**89. d.** A drill is not a type of wrench. A drill is used to create holes in such materials as wood, plastic, metal, or concrete.

**90. a.** A pressure gauge is measured in psi. The other gauges are read in the following units: A depth gauge uses a unit of length such as feet or meters; a speed gauge uses a unit of velocity such as miles per hour (mph) or kilometers per hour (kph); the RPM gauge measures revolutions per minute.

**91. c.** That this gauge measures temperature can be determined by the units of degrees Fahrenheit and degrees Celsius shown on the gauge. These are units of temperature.

**92. a.** The truck travels for 1 hour and 30 minutes, which is 1.5 hours. According to the formula, then, the distance traveled is 1.5 hours times 50 mph, or 75 miles.

**93. c.** A compression coil spring is typically placed behind the button. When the button is pressed, the spring is compressed and then springs back to return the button to its original position.

**94. a.** Since valve D is closed, water will not flow to barrels 3 and 4. Water will flow through valve B but be stopped at valve C. Water will flow through valve A into barrels 1 and 2.

**95. b.** A valve is used to control the flow of liquids and gases in a piping system. An example is the faucet on a sink.

**96. a.** The radiator contains fluid (water and antifreeze) that is circulated around the engine block by the water pump. The fluid becomes hot as it passes around the engine and is then cooled as air passes through the radiator.

**97. d.** The box will force the left side of the lever down and the right side of the lever up, which will pull the cable up. The cable will pass across the pulley and apply a pulling force on the spring, so the spring will stretch.

**98. c.** A drill is a common carpenter's hand tool. The other items are common parts of a car.

**99. b.** The systems listed produce electric power; none generate ice, steel, or rain.

**100. c.** The two blocks are directly connected by a fixed length of steel cable. Therefore, regardless of the number of pulleys between the two blocks, the distance moved by one block will be the same as that moved by the other block.

## FIREFIGHTER PRACTICE EXAM 2

| Question Type | Question Numbers | Chapter |
|---|---|---|
| Reading Text (20 questions) | 1–5, 10–14, 19–23, 28–32 | 6, "Reading Text, Tables, Charts, and Graphs" |
| Reading Tables, Charts, and Graphs (15 questions) | 6–9, 15–18, 24–27, 33–35 | 6, "Reading Text, Tables, Charts, and Graphs" |
| Verbal Expression (5 questions) | 36–50 | 12, "Verbal Expression" |
| Logical Reasoning (10 questions) | 51–60 | 9, "Judgment and Reasoning" |
| Mathematics (15 questions) | 66–80 | 8, "Math" |
| Mechanical Aptitude (20 questions) | 81–100 | 10, "Mechanical Aptitude" |

## ► Scoring

In most cities, a score of 70 or higher places you onto the eligibility list, and anything less than a 70 usually eliminates you from the selection process. But your goal shouldn't be just to get a 70 and make it onto the list. Although in some cities the written exam is only pass/fail, other cities use the test scores to rank candidates in the beginning stages of the selection process. Whether your city ranks candidates after this exam or not, your score is usually recorded in the file that will be reviewed before final firefighter selection. Thus, the higher you score on the exam, the better.

To best help you prepare, you should review your exam results carefully. First of all, you can apply your total score to the self-evaluation section of the LearningExpress Test Preparation System in Chapter 3 of this book to help you decide on a study plan.

Next, calculate the percentage of questions you answered correctly in each section. In which section were your results highest? Lowest? Rank the sections in order of performance so you can set priorities in your study plan. For example, if your lowest score was in reading text, you should plan on paying the most attention to that chapter. The following suggestions will help direct your preparation between now and the day of the exam:

- If you had difficulty understanding the passages in the reading text section, then you should plan to spend a lot of time on Chapter 6, "Reading Text, Tables, Charts, and Graphs."
- If you had trouble with the vocabulary or grammar questions, plan to review Chapter 12, "Verbal Expression," carefully.
- If you had trouble with logical reasoning questions, spend a lot of time on Chapter 9.
- If you had trouble with the mechanical aptitude questions, carefully review Chapter 10.
- If you had difficulty with the math problems, focus on Chapter 8.

Each of these chapters includes lots of tips and hints for doing well on the given kind of question. You should decide how much time to spend on each chapter based on the results of this exam. Of course, if your exam doesn't include all of the kinds of questions included in this practice exam, you don't need to spend much time on the chapters covering those kinds of questions—though all of these skills will be useful to you when you become a firefighter.

When you have finished these chapters, take the third and fourth practice exams in Chapters 13 and 14 to see how much you have improved.

# Reading Text, Tables, Charts, and Graphs

## CHAPTER SUMMARY

Because reading is such a vital skill, most firefighter exams include a reading comprehension section that tests your ability to understand what you read. The tips and exercises in this chapter will help you improve your comprehension of written passages as well as of tables, charts, and graphs, so that you can increase your score in this area.

Memos, policies, procedures, reports—these are all things you will be expected to understand if you become a firefighter. Understanding written materials is part of almost any job. That's why most firefighter tests attempt to measure how well applicants understand what they read.

Reading comprehension tests are usually in a multiple-choice format and ask questions based on brief passages, much like the standardized tests that are offered in schools. For that matter, almost all standardized test questions test your reading skills. After all, you can't answer the question if you can't read it! Similarly, you can't study your training materials or learn new procedures once you are on the job if you can't read well. So, reading comprehension is vital not only on the test but also for the rest of your career.

## ▶ Types of Reading Comprehension Questions

You have probably encountered reading comprehension questions before. These are the kind that supply a passage to read and then ask multiple-choice questions about it. These kinds of questions give you two advantages as a test taker:

1. You don't have to know anything about the topic of the passage.
2. You are being tested only on the information the passage provides. Remember, even if you believe the information is not right, use only the information given in the passage.

The disadvantage is that you have to know where and how to find that information quickly in an unfamiliar text. This makes it easy to fall for one of the wrong answer choices, especially since they are designed to mislead you.

The best way to do well on a passage/question format like this is to be very familiar with the kinds of questions that are typically asked on the test. Questions most frequently ask you to

1. identify a specific **fact or detail** in the passage.
2. note the **main idea** of the passage.
3. make an **inference** based on the passage.
4. define a **vocabulary** word from the passage.

For you to do well on a reading comprehension test, you need to know exactly what each of these question types is asking you to do. **Facts and details** are the specific pieces of information that support the passage's main idea. The **main idea** is the thought, opinion, or attitude that governs the whole passage. Generally speaking, facts and details are indisputable—things that don't need to be proven, like statistics (18

million people) or descriptions (a green overcoat). Let's say, for example, you read a sentence that says "After the department's reorganization, workers were 50% more productive." A sentence like this, which gives you the **fact** that 50% of workers were more productive, might support a main idea that says, "Every department should be reorganized." Notice that this **main idea** is not something indisputable; it is an opinion. The writer thinks all departments should be reorganized, and because this is his or her opinion (and not everyone shares it), he or she needs to support this opinion with facts and details.

An **inference**, on the other hand, is a conclusion that can be drawn based on fact or evidence. For example, you can infer—based on the fact that workers became 50% more productive after the reorganization, which is a dramatic change—that the department had not been efficiently organized. The fact sentence, "After the department's reorganization, workers were 50% more productive," also implies that the reorganization of the department was the reason workers became more productive. There may, of course, have been other reasons, but we can infer only one from this sentence.

As you might expect, **vocabulary** questions ask you to determine the meaning of particular words. Often, if you have read carefully, you can determine the meaning of such words from their context; or how the word is used in the sentence or paragraph.

## Practice Passage 1: Recognizing the Four Question Types

The following is a sample test passage, followed by four questions. Read the passage carefully and then choose the best answers based on your reading of the text. Refer to the list on this page of types of reading comprehension questions, and note under your answer which type of question has been asked. Correct answers appear immediately after the questions.

The National Incident Management System (NIMS) is a comprehensive national approach to the way our nation prepares for and responds to domestic emergency incidents. This system will enable responders at all jurisdictional levels and across all disciplines to work together more effectively and efficiently. One of the most important components of the system is the Incident Command System, which provides a standard, on-scene, all-hazards incident management system. Long accepted for use by firefighters, hazardous materials teams, rescue organizations, and emergency medical teams, ICS is a cornerstone of NIMS.

Although compliance with the new system is voluntary, federal funding is tied to compliance with NIMS. Those agencies and jurisdictions that receive federal funds must institutionalize the use of ICS. To accomplish this, a jurisdiction must ensure that all government officials, incident managers, and emergency response organizations adopt the Incident Command System and ensure that it is used at all incident response operations. To comply, the use must be at two levels—policy and organizational/operational. At the policy level, the government officials of the jurisdiction must issue a directive that ICS is the jurisdiction's official incident response system, and direct that anyone who manages an incident and the response organization in the jurisdiction train, exercise, and apply ICS in their response operations. At the organizational/operational level, the jurisdiction must integrate ICS into functional and system-wide emergency operations policies, plans, and procedures; provide ICS training for responders, supervisors, and command level officers; and ensure that all responders are participating in and/or coordinating ICS-oriented exercises that involve responders from multiple disciplines and jurisdictions.

**1.** The cornerstone of the National Incident Management System is
   **a.** the first responders.
   **b.** the Incident Command System.
   **c.** federal funding.
   **d.** the National Response Plan.

   Question type: _____

**2.** The phrase *institutionalize the use of ICS* in this passage suggests that to be compliant
   **a.** only the fire department has to use ICS.
   **b.** all officials and organizations at all jurisdictional levels must be trained in, be exercised in, and use ICS at all responses.
   **c.** only the emergency responders of the jurisdiction must be trained in ICS.
   **d.** agencies may simply request federal funding.

   Question type: _____

**3.** What would be the best title for this passage?
   **a.** The Key to NIMS Compliance—ICS
   **b.** Is NIMS Compliance Required for Your Jurisdiction?
   **c.** Is ICS Needed at All?
   **d.** What You Need to Know for FEMA Response

   Question type: _____

**4.** The word *comprehensive* in the first sentence of the passage most nearly means
   **a.** compressed or abbreviated.
   **b.** small in content.
   **c.** large in scope.
   **d.** misdirected.

   Question type: _____

## Answers

Don't just look at the right answers and move on. The explanations are the most important part, so read them carefully. Use these explanations to help you understand how to tackle each kind of question the next time you come across it.

1. **b.** Question type: fact or detail. The passage clearly states that the Incident Command System is the cornerstone of the National Incident Management System. Some of the other answers are mentioned and are part of the requirements of NIMS, but not the most important part. Do not allow additional information to confuse you.

2. **b.** Question type: inference. The phrase *institutionalize the use of ICS* refers to what a jurisdiction has to do in order to be compliant with the requirements of the National Incident Management System. In this case, the other answers included two that are partially true (**a** and **c**).

3. **a.** Question type: main idea. The title always expresses the main idea. The third sentence states that ICS is the cornerstone of NIMS. The remainder of the passage discusses the importance of ICS to NIMS compliance and goes on to describe the process needed to be compliant. So, since ICS is the cornerstone of NIMS, choice **a** is the best title for the passage.

4. **c.** Question type: vocabulary. The word *comprehensive* is a modifier to *national*. The next sentence uses the phrase *all jurisdictional levels and across all disciplines.* Even if you did not know that *comprehensive* meant large in scope or content, extensive, you could deduce its meaning from these contextual clues.

## ▶ Main Idea and Fact or Detail Questions

Main idea questions and fact or detail questions are both asking you for information that's right there in the passage. All you have to do is find it.

### Fact or Detail Questions

In fact or detail questions, you have to identify a specific item of information from the test. This is usually the simplest kind of question. You just have to be able to separate important information from less important information. However, the choices may often be very similar, so you must be careful not to get confused.

Be sure you read the passage and questions carefully. In fact, it is usually a good idea to read the questions first, before you even read the passage, so you will know what details to look out for.

### Main Idea Questions

The main idea of a passage, like that of a paragraph or a book, is what it is *mostly* about. The main idea is like an umbrella that covers all of the ideas and details in the passage, so it is usually something general, not specific. For example, in Practice Passage 1, question 3 asked you what title would be best for the passage, and the correct answer was "The Key to NIMS Compliance—ICS." This is the best answer because it is the only one that links the importance of ICS to NIMS and the requirement for jurisdictions to be compliant.

Sometimes the main idea is stated clearly, often in the first or last sentence of the passage. For example, the main idea is expressed in the third sentence of Practice Passage 1, and then it is further emphasized by the context of the remainder of the passage. The sentence that expresses the main idea is often referred to as the **topic sentence**.

At other times, the main idea is not stated in a topic sentence but is implied in the overall passage, and you will need to determine the main idea by inference.

Because there may be a great deal of information in the passage, the trick is to understand what all that information adds up to—the gist of what the author wants you to know. Often some of the wrong answers on main idea questions are specific facts or details from the passage. A good way to test yourself is to ask, "Can this answer serve as a net to hold the whole passage together?" If not, chances are you've chosen a fact or a detail, not a main idea.

## Practice Passage 2:
## Main Idea and Fact or Detail
## Questions

Practice answering main idea and fact or detail questions by working on the questions that follow this passage. Circle the answers to the questions, and then check your answers against the key that appears immediately afterward.

There are three different kinds of burns: superficial, partial thickness, and full thickness.

It is important for firefighters to be able to recognize each type of burn so that they can be sure burn victims are given proper medical treatment. The least serious burn is the superficial burn, which causes the skin to turn red but does not cause blistering. Mild sunburn is a good example of a superficial burn, and, like mild sunburn, superficial burns generally do not require medical treatment other than a gentle cooling of the burned skin with ice or cold tap water.

Partial-thickness burns, on the other hand, do cause blistering of the skin and should be treated immediately. These burns should be immersed in warm water and then wrapped in a sterile dressing or bandage. (Do not apply butter or grease to these burns; despite the old adage, butter does not help burns heal and actually increases the chance of infection.) If partial-thickness burns cover a large part of the body, the patient should be taken to the hospital for immediate medical care.

Full-thickness burns are those that char the skin and turn it black, or burn so deeply that the skin shows white. These burns usually result from direct contact with flames and have a great chance of becoming infected. All full-thickness burns should receive immediate hospital care. They should not be immersed in water, and charred clothing should not be removed from the victim. If possible, a sterile dressing or bandage should be applied to burns before the victim is transported to the hospital.

1. Which of the following would be the best title for this passage?
   a. Dealing with Full-Thickness Burns
   b. How to Recognize and Treat Different Burns
   c. Burn Categories
   d. Preventing Infection in Burns

2. Partial-thickness burns should be treated with
   a. butter.
   b. nothing.
   c. cold water.
   d. warm water.

3. Superficial burns turn the skin
   a. red.
   b. blue.
   c. black.
   d. white.

4. Which of the following best expresses the main idea of the passage?
   a. There are three different types of burns.
   b. Firefighters should always have cold compresses on hand.
   c. Different burns require different types of treatment.
   d. Butter is not good for healing burns.

## Answers

**1. b.** A question that asks you to choose a title for a passage is a main idea question. This main idea is expressed in the second sentence, the topic sentence: "It is important for firefighters to be able to recognize each of these types of burns so that they can be sure burn victims are given proper treatment." Choice **b** expresses this idea and is the only title that encompasses all of the ideas expressed in the passage. Choice **a** is too limited; it deals only with one of the kinds of burns discussed in the passage. Likewise, choices **c** and **d** are also too limited. Choice **c** covers types of burns but not their treatment, and **d** deals only with preventing infection, which is only a secondary part of the discussion of treatment.

**2. d.** The answer to this fact question is clearly expressed in the sentence, "These burns should be immersed in warm water and then wrapped in a sterile dressing or bandage." The hard part is keeping track of whether "these burns" refers to the kind of burns in the question, which is partial-thickness burns. It's easy to choose a wrong answer here because all of the answer choices are mentioned in the passage. You need to read carefully to be sure you match the right burn to the right treatment.

**3. a.** This is another fact or detail question. The passage says that a superficial burn "causes the skin to turn red." Again, it's important to read carefully because all of the answer choices (except **b**, which can be eliminated immediately) are listed elsewhere in the passage.

**4. c.** Clearly, this is a main idea question, and **c** is the only choice that encompasses the whole passage. Choices **b** and **d** are limited to *particular*

burns or treatments, and choice **a** discusses only burns and not their treatment. In addition, the second sentence tells us that "It is important for firefighters to be able to recognize each of these types of burns so that they can be sure burn victims are given proper medical treatment."

## ▶ Inference and Vocabulary Questions

Questions that ask you about the meaning of vocabulary words in the passage and those that ask what the passage suggests or implies (inference questions) are different from detail or main idea questions. In vocabulary and inference questions, you usually have to pull ideas from the passage, sometimes from more than one place in the passage.

### Inference Questions

Inference questions can be difficult to answer because they require you to draw meaning from the text when that meaning is implied rather than directly stated. Inferences are conclusions that you draw based on the clues the writer has given you. When you draw inferences, you have to be something of a detective, looking for such clues as word choice, tone, and specific details that suggest a certain conclusion, attitude, or point of view. You have to read between the lines to make a judgment about what an author was implying in the passage.

A good way to test whether you have drawn an acceptable inference is to ask, "What evidence do I have for this inference?" If you can't find any, you probably have the wrong answer. You need to be sure that your inference is logical. It should be based on something that is suggested or implied in the passage itself—not on something you or others might think. Like a good detective, you need to base your conclusions on evidence—facts, details, and other information—not on random hunches or guesses.

## Vocabulary Questions

Questions designed to test vocabulary are really trying to measure how well you can figure out the meaning of an unfamiliar word from its context. *Context* refers to the words and ideas surrounding a vocabulary word. If the context is clear enough, you should be able to substitute a nonsense word for the one being sought, and you would still make the right choice because you could determine meaning strictly from the sense of the sentence. For example, you should be able to determine the meaning of the italicized nonsense word below based on its context:

> The speaker noted that it gave him great *terivinix* to announce the winner of the Outstanding Leadership Award.

> In this sentence, *terivinix* most likely means

**a.** pain.
**b.** sympathy.
**c.** pleasure.
**d.** anxiety.

The context of an award makes **c**, pleasure, the best choice. Awards don't usually bring pain, sympathy, or anxiety.

When confronted with an unfamiliar word, try substituting a nonsense word and see if the context gives you the clue. If you are familiar with prefixes, suffixes, and word roots, you can also use this knowledge to help you determine the meaning of an unfamiliar word.

You should be careful not to guess at the answer to a vocabulary question based on how you may have seen the word used before or what you *think* it means.

Many words have more than one possible meaning, depending on the context in which they are used, and a word you have seen used one way may mean something else in a test passage. Also, if you don't look at the context carefully, you may make the mistake of confusing the vocabulary word with a similar word. For example, the vocabulary word may be *taut* (meaning *tight*), but if you read too quickly or don't check the context, you might think the word is *tout* (meaning *publicize* or *praise*) or *taunt* (meaning *tease*). Always make sure that you read carefully and that what you think the word means fits into the context of the passage you are being tested on.

## Practice Passage 3: Inference and Vocabulary Questions

The questions that follow this passage are strictly vocabulary and inference questions. Circle the answers to the questions, and then check your answers against the key that appears immediately afterward.

When fire chiefs talk about firefighter recruitment, they usually mean the effort that is made, shortly before an application period opens, to get candidates to apply for job openings. Recruitment is the way a fire department attracts new members. Fire chiefs who wish to diversify their department's workforce or attract specific groups of people (college graduates, licensed paramedics) have learned to target those groups in the recruiting effort. A productive recruitment drive is just part of what it takes to increase the diversity of a fire department. For recruitment to be really effective, managers must establish a positive climate within the department before encouraging candidates from traditionally underrepresented groups to become firefighters. Fire departments also must begin to recognize and take advantage of the recruitment impact of most of their public activities. Expanding the concept of recruitment in these two directions will make the recruitment drive itself more productive and will increase the likelihood that those who are recruited actually will become firefighters. The skills and dedication of the people working in the recruitment unit, the creativity that goes into designing the program, and the verbal, logistical, and financial backing given to the effort by top management all play important parts in the success of a department's recruitment drive. All of this effort and investment must be supported. The recruiters' message will be that the fire department wants to diversify its membership. But if other aspects of the department give out a conflicting message, or if the department is unprepared for a workforce that includes men and women from diverse backgrounds, much of your recruitment effort will go for nothing.

**1.** The word *climate* as it is used in the passage most nearly means
   **a.** weather conditions.
   **b.** prevailing conditions.
   **c.** temperature.
   **d.** employment.

**2.** The passage suggests that a fire chief
   **a.** should leave recruitment to others.
   **b.** has to establish a welcoming atmosphere for all recruits.
   **c.** is better off not seeking to diversify.
   **d.** should ensure that each group hears the message they wish to hear.

**3.** A *concept* is most likely
   **a.** a belief.
   **b.** a development.
   **c.** work.
   **d.** an idea.

**4.** Which of the following best expresses the writer's views about recruitment?
   **a.** Recruiting campaigns must be general in nature.
   **b.** In order for a recruiting campaign to be successful, a fire department must leave the support of the program to professional recruiters.
   **c.** The chief must ensure that there is an atmosphere that is nonthreatening and positive for all recruits.
   **d.** The recruiter must not make it known that the department wants to diversify its workforce.

## Answers

**1. b.** This is a vocabulary question. *Climate* has three different definitions—*meteorological conditions*, *a region with particular meteorological conditions*, and *a prevailing condition or atmosphere*. Choice **a**, while correct, does not fit the sentence, which is about recruiting, not weather. Choice **c**, though it relates to weather, is not applicable to this sentence. Choice **d**, *employment*, does not fit the sentence's full context.

**2. b.** This is an inference question, as the phrase *the passage suggests* might have told you. The passage as a whole is advising fire chiefs on what needs to be done in order to conduct a successful recruiting program and diversify employment. The passage makes it clear that the chief sets the tone and that diversity is desirable. It also makes it clear that recruiting must be part of everything that the department does, so choice **b** represents this attitude by stating that a welcoming atmosphere is necessary.

**3. d.** This is a vocabulary question. Even if you had no clue that a *concept* was an idea, just refer back to the statement that productive recruitment programs need positive climate and a new look of the impact of public activities. These are ideas, so you have a good clue in these sentences. Although *belief* is part of an idea, it is not the idea itself. A *development* does not fit here and neither does *work*. *Idea* is the best fit.

**4. c.** This is an inference question. The writer of this passage keeps adding on to the initial premise that a good recruitment program is vital to a department's efforts to diversify. Because the chief officer is the manager most responsible for the department's direction, choice **c** is the most correct. Choice **d** infers that the recruiters are not supposed to tell anyone that they are looking for a diverse candidate pool. That goes against the statement that recruiters should make it known that the department wants to diversify. The author also states that a recurring campaign must target specific groups, not just recruit in general, and it is necessary that a recruiting campaign have departmental support or it will fail.

## ▶ Review: Putting It All Together

A good way to solidify what you've learned about reading comprehension questions is for you to write the questions. Here's a passage followed by space for you to write your own questions. Write one question of each of the four types: fact or detail, main idea, inference, and vocabulary.

The "broken window" theory was originally developed to explain how minor acts of vandalism or disrespect can quickly escalate to crimes and attitudes that break down the entire social fabric of an area. It is a theory that can easily be applied to any situation in society. The theory contends that if a broken window in an abandoned building is not replaced quickly, soon all the windows will be broken. In other words, a small violation, if condoned, leads others to commit similar or greater violations. Thus, after all the windows have been broken, the building is likely to be looted and perhaps even burned down.

According to this theory, violations increase exponentially. Thus, if disrespect to a superior is tolerated, others will be tempted to be disrespectful as well. A management crisis could erupt literally overnight. For example, if one firefighter begins to disregard proper housewatch procedure by neglecting to keep up the housewatch administrative journal, and this firefighter is not reprimanded, others will follow suit by committing similar violations of procedure, thinking, "If he can get away with it, why can't I?" So what starts out as a small thing, a violation that may not seem to warrant disciplinary action, may actually ruin the efficiency of the entire firehouse, putting the people the firehouse serves at risk.

**1.** Detail question:_____
   **a.**
   **b.**
   **c.**
   **d.**

**2.** Main idea question:_____
   **a.**
   **b.**
   **c.**
   **d.**

# If English Is Not Your First Language

When nonnative speakers of English have trouble with reading comprehension tests, it's often because they lack the cultural, linguistic, and historical frame of reference that native speakers have. People who have not lived in or been educated in the United States often don't have the background information that comes from reading American newspapers, magazines, and textbooks.

A second problem for nonnative English speakers is the difficulty in recognizing vocabulary and idioms (expressions like "chewing the fat") that assist comprehension. To read with good understanding, it is important to have an immediate grasp of as many words as possible in the text. Test takers need to be able to recognize vocabulary and idioms immediately so that the ideas those words express are clear.

## The Long View

Read newspapers, magazines, and other periodicals that deal with current events and matters of local, state, and national importance. Pay special attention to articles related to the career you want to pursue.

Be alert to new or unfamiliar vocabulary or terms that occur frequently in the popular press. Use a highlighter to mark new or unfamiliar words as you read. Keep a list of those words and their definitions. Review them for 15 minutes each day. At first, you may find yourself looking up a lot of words, but don't be frustrated—you will look up fewer and fewer as your vocabulary expands.

## During the Test

When you are taking the test, make a picture in your mind of the situation being described in the passage. Ask yourself, "What did the writer mainly want me to think about this subject?"

Locate and underline the topic sentence that contains the main idea of the passage. Remember that the topic sentence—if there is one—may not always be the first sentence. If there doesn't seem to be one, try to determine what idea summarizes the whole passage.

---

**3.** Inference question:_____
- **a.**
- **b.**
- **c.**
- **d.**

**4.** Vocabulary question:_____
- **a.**
- **b.**
- **c.**
- **d.**

### Possible Questions

Here is one sample question of each type based on the passage you just read. Your questions may be very different, but these will give you an idea of the kinds of questions that could be asked.

**1.** Detail question: According to the passage, which of the following could happen "overnight"?
- **a.** The building may be burned down.
- **b.** The firehouse may become unmanageable.
- **c.** A management crisis might erupt.
- **d.** The windows may all be broken.

**2.** Main idea question: Which of the following best expresses the main idea of the passage?

  **a.** Even minor acts of disrespect can lead to major problems.

  **b.** Broken windows must be repaired immediately.

  **c.** People shouldn't be disrespectful to their superiors.

  **d.** Housewatch procedures must be taken seriously.

**3.** Inference question: With which of the following statements would the author most likely agree?

  **a.** The broken window theory is inadequate.

  **b.** Managers need to know how to handle a crisis.

  **c.** Firefighters are lazy.

  **d.** People will get away with as much as they can.

**4.** Vocabulary question: In the first paragraph, *condoned* most nearly means

  **a.** punished.

  **b.** overlooked.

  **c.** condemned.

  **d.** applauded.

## Answers

  **1.** c.

  **2.** a.

  **3.** d.

  **4.** b.

## ▶ Reading Tables, Graphs, and Charts

Depending on what position you are testing for, your firefighter exam may also include a section testing your ability to read tables, charts, and graphs. These sections are really quite similar to regular reading comprehension exams, but instead of pulling information from a passage of text, you will need to answer questions about a graphic representation of data. The types of questions asked about tables, charts, and graphs are actually quite similar to those about reading passages, though there usually aren't any questions on vocabulary. The main difference in reading tables, charts, or graphs is that you are reading or interpreting data represented in tabular (table) or graphic (picture) form rather than textual (sentence and paragraph) form.

### Tables

Tables present data in rows and columns. Here is a simple table that shows the number of firefighter fatalities by age. Use it to answer the question that follows.

| FIREFIGHTER FATALITIES BY AGE (2007) | |
|---|---|
| **AGE** | **FATALITIES** |
| Under 21 | 5 |
| 21 to 25 | 6 |
| 26 to 30 | 7 |
| 31 to 35 | 9 |
| 36 to 40 | 14 |
| 41 to 45 | 11 |
| 46 to 50 | 12 |
| 51 to 60 | 19 |
| 61+ | 12 |

**1.** Based on the information provided in this table, what age group suffered the most fatalities in 2007?

**a.** 26 to 30

**b.** 51 to 60

**c.** 46 to 50

**d.** 41 to 45

The correct answer, of course, is **b**. The age group with the highest number of fatalities (19) in 2007 is 51–60.

## Graphs

Here is the same information presented as a line graph. This type of graph uses two axes, rather than columns and rows, to create a visual representation of the data.

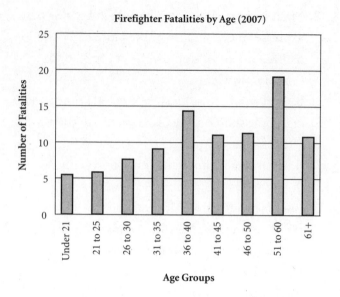

**Firefighter Fatalities by Age (2007)**

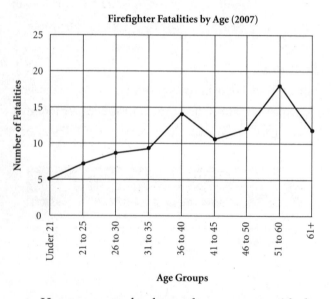

**Firefighter Fatalities by Age (2007)**

Here, you can clearly see the age group with the highest fatalities, represented by a point that corresponds to intersection of the value of the age range of the firefighters and the number of fatalities in 2007. These numbers can also be represented by a box in a bar graph, as shown in the next graph.

**2.** What is the probable cause for the higher fatality rate among firefighters in the 51 to 60 age group?

**a.** They are more likely to have serious hidden medical conditions.

**b.** They are more likely to be working in hazardous locations.

**c.** They are more likely to be in stressful leadership positions.

**d.** They are at greater risk for vehicular accidents.

The answer is **a**. A question like this tests your common sense as well as your ability to read the graph. Since all firefighters work in hazardous locations, and all firefighting is physically and emotionally stressful, these are factors that all firefighters, whether in leadership positions or not, are subject to, so choices **b** and **d** cannot account for the higher fatality figures of this age group. Choice **c** is another factor that affects all firefighters and would cause fatalities for all age groups. Choice **a** is the best answer because firefighters in this age group, as in the general population, are more likely to have a serious, undiagnosed chronic health condition.

**3.** What is the total number of firefighter fatalities?

 a. 96

 b. 104

 c. 95

 d. 93

The answer is **c.** This question tests your basic math skills. Using the information given in the bar graph, you need to determine the value of each bar and then add those members together.

## Charts

Finally, you may be presented information in the form of a chart like the following pie chart. Here, the accident figures have been converted to percentages. In this figure, you don't see the exact number of fatalities, but you see how each of the age groups relates to the others as part of the overall number of fatalities.

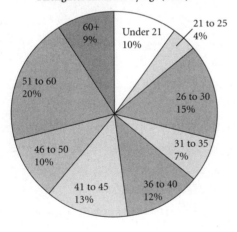

Firefighter Fatalities by Age (2005)

## Practice

Try the following questions to hone your skill at reading tables, graphs, and charts.

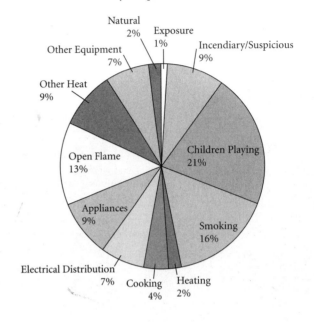

Injuries per 1,000 Fires

**1.** What is the number of injuries per 1,000 caused by smoking?

 a. 53

 b. 63

 c. 72

 d. 160

**2.** Based on the information provided in the chart, which cause of ignition is responsible for the most number of injuries in residential fires?

 a. electrical distribution

 b. other equipment

 c. open flame

 d. appliances

Answer questions 3 and 4 on the basis of the following graph.

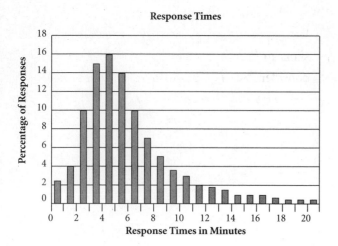

**Response Times**

3. To what percentage of fires is the response time 5 minutes?

   a. 15

   b. 14

   c. 16

   d. 10

4. What percentage of fires was responded to in less than 6 minutes?

   a. 61

   b. 71

   c. 37

   d. 47

## Answers

1. **d.** Smoking accounts for 16% of the losses, so 16% of 1,000 = 1,000 × 0.16 = 160 injuries per 1,000 fires.

2. **c.** "Electrical Distribution" and "Other Equipment" account for 7% of the injuries each. The category "Appliances" accounts for 9%. "Open Flame," the correct answer, accounts for 13% of the injuries in residential fires. This is not the largest cause overall, but it is the largest of the choices given.

3. **b.** Although it is not labeled, 5 minutes is the column between 4 and 6 minutes. Its value is 14%.

4. **a.** You have to be very careful reading this question. The question wants you to find out the total percentage of fires responded to in *less than 6 minutes*, which includes all percentages from 0 minutes to 5 minutes, but does NOT include 6 minutes. The sum of percentages is therefore 2.5% (0 minutes) + 4% (1 minute) + 10% (2 minutes) + 15% (3 minutes) + 16% (4 minutes) + 14% (5 minutes) = 61.5%. The closest answer is 61%.

## ▶ Additional Resources

Here are some other ways you can build the vocabulary and knowledge that will help you do well on reading comprehension questions.

- Practice formulating questions of these four types about passages you read for information or pleasure.

- If you have computer access, search out articles related to the career you'd like to pursue. Exchange views with others on the Internet. All of these exchanges will help expand your knowledge of job-related material that may appear in a passage on the test.

- Use your library. Many public libraries have departments, sometimes called "Lifelong Learning Centers," that contain materials for adult learners. In these sections you can find books with exercises in reading and study skills. It is also a good idea to enlarge your base of information by reading related books and articles. Library personnel will show you how to use the computers and find books and periodicals about firefighting.

- Begin building a broad knowledge of your potential profession. Get in the habit of reading articles in newspapers and magazines on job-related issues. Keep a clipping file of those articles. This will help keep you informed of trends in the profession and familiarize you with pertinent vocabulary.

■ Consider reading or subscribing to professional journals. Being an active reader makes you a better reader. This skill can only help improve your test scores. Chapter 1 lists several journals written for a general readership of people working in your desired profession. They are available for an annual subscription fee, and may also be available in your public library.

■ If you need more help building your reading skills and taking reading comprehension tests, consider *Reading Comprehension Success in 20 Minutes a Day* and *501 Reading Comprehension Questions*, both published by LearningExpress.

CHAPTER

# 7 ▶ Memory and Observation

## CHAPTER SUMMARY

This chapter contains hints and tips to help you answer questions that test your memory and observation skills. Seeing and observing are skills that make a good firefighter a better firefighter. This chapter will help you sharpen those skills.

I t's amazing what your mind will file away in that cabinet we call memory. You remember every snippet of dialogue uttered in some obscure movie you saw years ago, but you can't remember which bus route you used yesterday to get to the dentist. Some people remember names well, but can't put them with the right faces. Others forget names quickly, but know exactly when, where, and why they met the person whose name they have forgotten. There are a few lucky individuals with what is commonly referred to as total recall—and then there are those of us who wake up every morning to a radio alarm so we can find out what day of the week it is. Fortunately for most of us, a good memory is actually a skill that can be developed—with the right incentive. A high score on the firefighter exam is plenty of incentive.

Firefighter exams commonly test your short-term memory by presenting you with questions based on drawings or diagrams. Firefighters face situations daily that require split-second decisions based on a glance or a brief study of diagrams, so short-term memory is an important skill. You may be shown a sketch of a building on fire with people at the windows needing rescue, or you may be given a diagram showing the floor plan of a building. Usually you will be given a set amount of time (five minutes is common) to look at the drawing or diagram, and then you will be asked to answer test questions about what you saw without looking back at the drawing. Your goal is to memorize as much of the drawing or diagram as you can in the allotted time.

This chapter includes tips and techniques for dealing with drawings and diagrams, so you will be prepared to deal with them effectively.

## ▶ Kinds of Memory and Observation Questions

Firefighter exams include two kinds of memory and observation sections: questions based on a drawing of a fire scene, and questions based on a floor plan or similar kind of diagram.

### Questions Based on Drawings

Having you look at a sketch of a building on fire is a common way for firefighter exams to test your short-term memory. This is a simple test of your ability to recall details. You won't be asked to suggest ways to fight fires, use judgment skills, or draw conclusions about what you see.

You will be asked to look at the drawing until a specific time limit is up. Then you will turn to a set of questions in the test booklet. You have to answer the questions without looking at the drawing. Let's assume you are presented with a drawing showing a building on fire. Several people are standing in windows, including an adult figure holding an infant. You might be asked:

1. A figure in one of the windows is holding something. What is it?
   a. a suitcase
   b. a dog
   c. a book
   d. a baby

The questions and their answers are simple. If you don't remember what the adult figure was holding, or didn't notice that figure in the five minutes you had to study the drawing, then you will have to give this question your best guess.

### Questions Based on Diagrams

Similarly, you may be presented with a diagram of a floor plan of a building, perhaps filled with smoke. Again, this is a test of your ability to remember details. As mentioned in Chapter 11, "Spatial Relations," the ability of a firefighter to read a floor plan is crucial, as you may someday find yourself making your way through hallways and rooms filled with smoke. When presented with a floor plan, you will want to note the location of potential hazards and dead ends; you may be asked the placement of exits or smoke alarms or where to position a ladder for rescue.

For example, the diagram might show a center hallway with doors leading into certain rooms, and the question might be something like this:

2. You are proceeding east to west down the center hallway and have just passed the den. What is the next room you will pass?
   a. bedroom 1
   b. bathroom
   c. bedroom 2
   d. sewing room

At the end of this chapter, you will find a floor plan and several questions about it that you can use to practice.

# ▶ How to Approach Memory and Observation Questions

## What to Do

Use a methodical approach to studying what you see. When you read sentences on a page, you read from left to right. This skill is as unconscious as breathing for most English-language readers. Approach memorizing a diagram the same way you read, taking in the information from left to right. Instead of staring at the diagram with the whole picture in focus, make yourself start at the left and work your way across the page until you get to the right.

## What Not to Do

- **Do not** freeze or let yourself get overwhelmed when you first see the diagram. Take a deep breath and decide to be methodical.
- **Do not** try to start memorizing with a shotgun approach, letting your eyes roam all over the page without really taking in the details.
- **Do not** read the questions too quickly. Be sure to read them carefully, so that you answer the question that was actually asked. Haste can produce easily avoidable errors.

# ▶ Memorization Tips

Memorization is much easier if you approach the task with the expectation that you will remember what you see. Call it positive thinking, self-hypnosis, or concentration—it doesn't really matter as long as you get results. When you run through the practice questions in this book, prepare your mind before you start. Tell yourself over and over that you will remember what you see as you study the images. Your performance level will rise to meet your expectations.

Yes, it's easy for your brain to freeze up when you see a drawing or diagram filled with details, a test section full of questions, and a test proctor standing above you with a stopwatch in one hand, intoning, "You have five minutes to study this picture. You may begin." But if you have programmed yourself to stay calm and alert, and execute your plan, you will remember the details when you need them.

Plan? Yes, you need a plan. If you have a method for memorizing, say, a diagram of a second-floor hallway, then you will be more likely to relax and allow yourself to retain what you have seen long enough to answer the test questions. Keep in mind that you aren't trying to memorize the scene to learn it for life, you are doing it to retain the information long enough to answer the test questions. What will it matter if you remember the scene three months from now? Your goal is to retain the information long enough to get through this test.

# ▶ Observation Tips

It is almost impossible to talk about memorization without bringing up observation. Sherlock Holmes said, "You see but you do not observe." Some people are naturally observant. Some frequently drift off and have no awareness of the world around them. Whatever category you think you are in, it is never too late to sharpen, or acquire, strong observation skills. How? Practice, of course.

Newspaper photos make great practice tools. News photos are action-oriented and usually include more than one person. Sit down in a quiet place, clear your mind, remind yourself for several minutes that you will retain all the details you need when you study the picture, and then turn to a picture and study it for about five minutes. At the end of the time, turn the picture over, get a piece of paper and a pencil, then write down all the details you can think of in the picture. Or you might go to the library and check out a book on architecture that shows the floor plans of buildings. Go over the floor plans and memorize as many details as you can, then put away the book and write down all you remember. You may even have someone else quiz you. Make yourself do this as often as possible before the test.

You can tone up your observation skills on the way to work or school, too. Instead of sitting in your car waiting for the light to change with a blank stare on your face, look around you and say out loud what you see. "On my left is a three-story building with a bank of four windows on the first floor. There are two doorways, one on either side of the bank of windows." (If you are riding a train or subway, note details inside and recite them silently to yourself.) Not only are you practicing a basic skill to become an excellent firefighter, you are also training your mind to succeed at whatever memory questions the test maker throws your way.

Another excellent means to improve your recall is a game developed by the British Secret Service to train agents in the time of Queen Victoria. It involved a tray on which a number of small items were spread out and then covered by a paper or towel. One person then brought in the tray and uncovered it in front of the trainee, and the trainee would study the objects on the tray. At first, a trainee was given all the time he or she felt was needed; however, as the training went on, not only were the objects changed, but the time was reduced, until at the end the trainee was given only a glance at the tray. The trainee not only had to tell the trainer the objects, but each time, the number of details increased, until the trainee could not only tell what was there with a glance but could also describe each item in detail. This simple game is a great way to build your memory and observation skills: The better your skills, the bigger advantage you will have on an examination.

# ▶ Memory and Observation Practice

Below is a floor plan like those found on some firefighter exams. Following the floor plan are several questions asking about details of the floor plan. Use this diagram to practice your memory skills. Take five minutes to study the diagram, and then answer the questions that follow without looking back at the diagram.

Check your answers by looking back at the diagram. If you get all the questions right, you know you are well prepared for memory questions. If you miss a few, you know you need to spend more time practicing, using the tips outlined previously. Remember, you *can* improve your memory with practice.

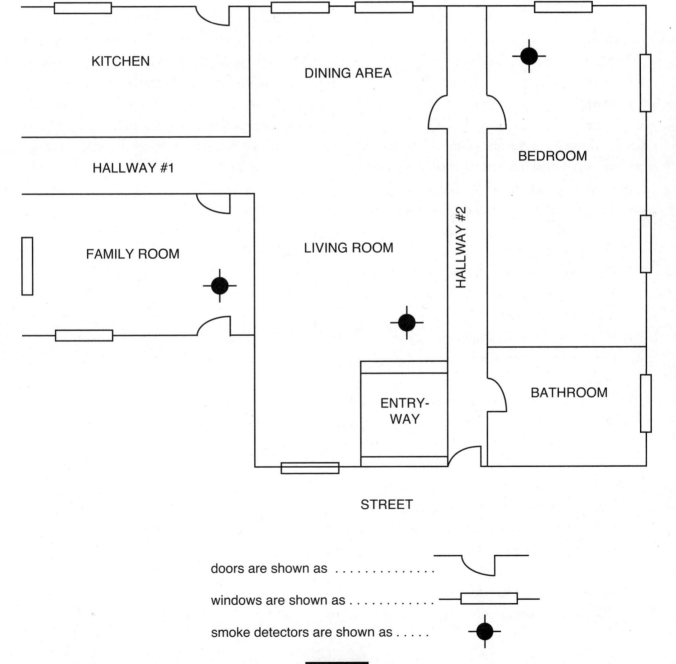

1. Which rooms or areas of the dwelling do NOT have smoke detectors?
   a. kitchen, family room, dining area, and bathroom
   b. kitchen, dining area, and bathroom
   c. family room, dining area, bedroom, and bathroom
   d. kitchen, living room, and bathroom

2. How many doorways lead off of the family room?
   a. one
   b. two
   c. three
   d. four

3. You are in the smoke-filled dining area and hear moaning coming from the kitchen. How do you proceed to get into the kitchen?
   a. Go into hallway #1, straight ahead, and through the door on your right into the kitchen.
   b. Go into the living room, through the family room, across hallway #1, and through the door into the kitchen.
   c. Go into hallway #2, straight ahead, and through the door on your left into the kitchen.
   d. Go straight through the door leading from the dining room into the kitchen.

4. You are on the street in front of the dwelling. You cannot go into the dwelling through the entryway because it is ablaze. To enter directly from the street, what other alternatives do you have?
   a. two windows and one doorway
   b. three windows
   c. two windows and two doorways
   d. one window and one doorway

5. You are in hallway #2. One of your coworkers shouts that there is a person overcome by smoke in the family room. Which of the following is your most direct route to the family room?
   a. through the doorway into the bedroom, and straight ahead through the doorway into the family room
   b. through the doorway into the entryway, then through the doorway into the living room, down hallway #1, and left through the doorway into the family room
   c. through the doorway into the bathroom, then through the doorway into hallway #1, and then left into the doorway leading into the family room
   d. through the doorway into the dining area/living room, straight ahead into hallway #1, and then left through the doorway into the family room

6. How many smoke detectors are in the dwelling?
   a. two
   b. three
   c. four
   d. five

## Tips for Memory and Observation Questions

- Use a methodical approach to memorization.
- Read the picture from left to right.
- Read the questions carefully; make sure you are answering the question that's being asked.
- Practice your memory and observation skills in your daily routine.

▶ **Answers**

**1.** b.
**2.** b.
**3.** a.
**4.** a.
**5.** d.
**6.** b.

# 8 ▶ Math

## CHAPTER SUMMARY

This chapter gives you some important tips for dealing with math questions on a firefighter exam and reviews some of the most commonly tested concepts. If you have forgotten most of your high school math or have math anxiety, this chapter is for you.

**N**ot all firefighter exams test your math knowledge, but many do. Knowledge of basic arithmetic, and the more complex kinds of reasoning necessary for algebra and geometry problems, are important qualifications for almost any profession. You have to be able to add up dollar figures, evaluate budgets, compute percentages, and perform other such tasks, both in your job and in your personal life. Even if your exam doesn't include math, you will find that the material in this chapter will be useful on the job.

The math portion of the test covers the subjects you probably studied in grade school and high school. Although every test is different, most emphasize arithmetic skills and word problems.

## ► Math Strategies

- **Don't work in your head! Use your test book or scratch paper to take notes, draw pictures, and calculate.** Although you might think that you can solve math questions more quickly in your head, that's a good way to make mistakes. Write out each step.

- **Read a math question in chunks rather than straight through from beginning to end.** As you read each chunk, stop to think about what it means and make notes or draw a picture to represent that chunk.

- **When you get to the actual question, circle it.** This will keep you more focused as you solve the problem.

- **Glance at the answer choices for clues.** If they are fractions, you probably should do your work in fractions; if they are decimals, you should probably work in decimals.

- **Make a plan of attack** to help you solve the problem.

- **If a question stumps you, try one of the backdoor approaches** explained in the next section. These are particularly useful for solving word problems.

- **When you get your answer, reread the circled question to make sure you have answered it.** This helps avoid the careless mistake of answering the wrong question.

- **Check your work after you get an answer.** Test takers get a false sense of security when they get an answer that matches one of the multiple-choice answers. Here are some good ways to check your work if you have time:
  - Ask yourself if your answer is reasonable, if it makes sense.
  - Plug your answer back into the problem to make sure the problem holds together.
  - Do the question a second time, but use a different method.

- **Carry your units.** If you are working on a problem that involves working with units, carry them through the problem. The units of the problem must work out for the answer to be correct.

- **Approximate when appropriate.** For example:
  - $5.98 + $8.97 is a little less than $15. (Add: $6 + $9)
  - .9876 × 5.0342 is close to 5. (Multiply: 1 × 5)

- **Skip hard questions and come back to them later.** Mark them in your test book so you can find them quickly.

### Backdoor Approaches for Answering Questions That Puzzle You

Remember those word problems you dreaded in high school? Many of them are actually easier to solve by backdoor approaches. The two techniques that follow are terrific ways to solve multiple-choice word problems that you don't know how to solve with a straightforward approach. The first technique, *nice numbers*, is useful when there are unknowns (like *x*) in the text of the word problem, making the problem too abstract for you. The second technique, *working backward*, presents a quick way to substitute numeric answer choices back into the problem to see which one works.

### Nice Numbers

1. When a question contains unknowns, like *x*, plug nice numbers in for the unknowns. A nice number is easy to calculate with and makes sense in the problem, such as 5, 10, 25, or even 1 or 2.
2. Read the question with the nice numbers in place. Then solve it.

3. If the answer choices are all numbers, the choice that matches your answer is the right one.

4. If the answer choices contain unknowns, substitute the same nice numbers into all the answer choices. The choice that matches your answer is the right one. If more than one answer matches, do the problem again with different nice numbers. You will only have to check the answer choices that have already matched.

**Example:** Judi went shopping with $p$ dollars in her pocket. If the price of shirts was $s$ shirts for $d$ dollars, what is the maximum number of shirts Judi could buy with the money in her pocket?

$$\textbf{a. } psd \qquad \textbf{b. } \frac{ps}{d} \qquad \textbf{c. } \frac{pd}{s} \qquad \textbf{d. } \frac{ds}{p}$$

To solve this problem, let's try these nice numbers: $p = \$100$, $s = 2$; $d = \$25$. Now reread it with the numbers in place:

Judi went shopping with **$100** in her pocket. If the price of shirts was **2** shirts for **$25**, what is the maximum number of shirts Judi could buy with the money in her pocket?

Since 2 shirts cost $25, that means that 4 shirts cost $50, and 8 shirts cost $100. So your answer is 8. Let's substitute the nice numbers into all 4 answers:

$$\textbf{a. } 100 \times 2 \times 25 = 5000 \qquad \textbf{b. } \frac{100 \times 2}{25} = 8 \qquad \textbf{c. } \frac{100 \times 25}{2} = 1250 \qquad \textbf{d. } \frac{25 \times 2}{100} = \frac{1}{2}$$

The answer is **b**, because it is the only one that matches your answer of **8**.

## Working Backward

You can frequently solve a word problem by plugging the answer choices back into the text of the problem to see which one fits all the facts stated in the problem. The process is faster than you think because you will probably only have to substitute one or two answers to find the right one.

This approach works only when:

- All of the answer choices are numbers.
- You are asked to find a simple number, not a sum, product, difference, or ratio.

Here's what to do:

1. Look at all the answer choices and begin with one in the middle of the range. For example, if the answers are 14, 8, 20, and 25, begin by plugging 14 into the problem.

2. If your choice doesn't work, eliminate it. Determine if you need a bigger or smaller answer.

3. Plug in one of the remaining choices.

4. If none of the answers work, you may have made a careless error. Begin again or look for your mistake.

Example: Juan ate $\frac{1}{3}$ of the jellybeans. Maria then ate $\frac{3}{4}$ of the remaining jellybeans, which left 10 jellybeans. How many jellybeans were there to begin with?

$$\textbf{a. } 60 \qquad \textbf{b. } 90 \qquad \textbf{c. } 120 \qquad \textbf{d. } 140$$

Starting with one of the middle answers, let's assume there were **90** jellybeans to begin with:

Since Juan ate $\frac{1}{3}$ of them, that means he ate 30 ($\frac{1}{3} \times 90 = 30$), leaving 60 of them (90 − 30 = 60). Maria then ate $\frac{3}{4}$ of the 60 jellybeans, or 45 of them ($\frac{3}{4} \times 60 = 45$). That leaves 15 jellybeans (60 − 45 = 15).

The problem states that there were **10** jellybeans left, and you wound up with **15** of them. That indicates that you started with too big a number. Thus, 90, 120, and 140 are all wrong! So, let's try **60**:

Since Juan ate $\frac{1}{3}$ of them, that means he ate 20 ($\frac{1}{3} \times 60 = 20$), leaving 40 of them (60 − 20 = 40). Maria then ate $\frac{3}{4}$ of the 40 jellybeans, or 30 of them ($\frac{3}{4} \times 40 = 30$). That leaves 10 jellybeans (40 − 30 = 10).

The right answer is **a**, because this result of **10** remaining jellybeans agrees with the problem.

## ▶ Word Problems

Many of the math problems on tests are word problems. A word problem can include any kind of math, including simple arithmetic, fractions, decimals, percentages, and even algebra and geometry.

The hardest part of any word problem is translating the text into math. When you read a problem, you can frequently translate it word for word from text statements into mathematical statements. At other times, however, a key word in the problem hints at the mathematical operation to be performed. Here are some translation rules:

**EQUALS**　key words: is, are, has

| English | Math |
|---|---|
| Bob **is** 18 years old. | $B = 18$ |
| There **are** 7 hats. | $H = 7$ |
| Judi **has** 5 books. | $J = 5$ |

**ADDITION**　key words: sum; more, greater, or older than; total; altogether

| English | Math |
|---|---|
| The **sum** of two numbers is 10. | $X + Y = 10$ |
| Karen has $5 **more than** Sam. | $K = 5 + S$ |
| The base is 3" **greater than** the height. | $B = 3 + H$ |
| Judi is 2 years **older than** Tony. | $J = 2 + T$ |
| The **total** of three numbers is 25. | $A + B + C = 25$ |
| How much do Joan and Tom have **altogether**? | $J + T = ?$ |

**SUBTRACTION**　key words: difference, less or younger than, fewer, remain, left over

| English | Math |
|---|---|
| The **difference** between two numbers is 17. | $X - Y = 17$ |
| Mike has 5 **fewer** cats **than** twice the number Jan has. | $M = 2J - 5$ |
| Jay is 2 years **younger than** Brett. | $J = B - 2$ |
| After Carol ate 3 apples, $R$ apples **remained**. | $R = A - 3$ |

**MULTIPLICATION**     key words: **of, product, times**

| English | Math |
|---|---|
| 20% **of** Matthew's baseball caps | $.20 \times M$ |
| Half **of** the boys | $\frac{1}{2} \times B$ |
| The **product** of two numbers is 12. | $A \times B = 12$ |

**DIVISION**     key word: **per**

| English | Math |
|---|---|
| 15 drops **per** teaspoon | $\frac{15 \text{ drops}}{\text{teaspoon}}$ |
| 22 miles **per** gallon | $\frac{22 \text{ miles}}{\text{gallon}}$ |

## Distance Formula: Distance = Rate × Time

The key words are movement words such as: plane, train, boat, car, walk, run, climb, swim, travel. It is also helpful to carry units on distance problems.

- How far did the **plane** travel in 4 hours if it averaged 300 miles per hour?

    $D = \dfrac{300 \text{ miles}}{\text{hour}} \times 4 \text{ hours}$

    $D = 1{,}200 \text{ miles}$

- Ben **walked** 20 miles in 4 hours. What was his average speed          $20 \text{ miles} = r \times 4 \text{ hours}$

    $\dfrac{20 \text{ miles}}{4 \text{ hours}}$

    $5 \text{ miles per hour} = r$

## Solving a Word Problem Using the Translation Table

Remember the problem at the beginning of this chapter about the jellybeans?

Juan ate $\frac{1}{3}$ of the jellybeans. Maria then ate $\frac{3}{4}$ of the remaining jellybeans, which left 10 jellybeans. How many jellybeans were there to begin with?

        **a.** 60          **b.** 90          **c.** 120          **d.** 140

We solved it by working backward. Now let's solve it using our translation rules.

Assume Juan started with $J$ jellybeans. Eating $\frac{1}{3}$ **of** them means eating $\frac{1}{3} \times J$ jellybeans. Maria ate a fraction of the **remaining** jellybeans, which means we must **subtract** to find out how many are left: $J - \frac{1}{3} \times J = \frac{2}{3} \times J$. Maria then ate $\frac{3}{4}$, leaving $\frac{1}{4}$ of the $\frac{2}{3} \times J$ jellybeans, or $\frac{1}{4} \times \frac{2}{3} \times J$ jellybeans. Multiplying out $\frac{1}{4} \times \frac{2}{3} \times J$ gives $\frac{1}{6} J$ as the number of jellybeans left. The problem states that there were 10 jellybeans left, meaning that we set $\frac{1}{6} \times J$ equal to 10: $\frac{1}{6} \times J = 10$

Solving this equation for *J* gives *J* = **60**. Thus, the right answer is **a** (the same answer we got when we worked backward). As you can see, both methods—working backwards and translating from text to math—work. You should use whichever method is more comfortable for you.

## Practice Word Problems

You will find word problems using fractions, decimals, and percentages in those sections of this chapter. For now, practice using the translation table on problems that just require you to work with basic arithmetic.

_____ **1.** Joan went shopping with $100 and returned home with only $18.42. How much money did she spend?

   **a.** $81.58       **b.** $72.68       **c.** $72.58       **d.** $71.68

_____ **2.** Mary invited 10 friends to a party. Each friend brought 3 guests. How many people came to the party, excluding Mary?

   **a.** 3           **b.** 10           **c.** 30           **d.** 40

_____ **3.** The office secretary can type 80 words per minute on his word processor. How many minutes will it take him to type a report containing 760 words?

   **a.** 8           **b.** $8\frac{1}{2}$           **c.** $9\frac{1}{2}$           **d.** 10

_____ **4.** Mr. Wallace is writing a budget request to upgrade his personal computer system. He wants to purchase 4 mb of RAM, which will cost $100, two new software programs at $350 each, a tape backup system for $249, and an additional tape for $25. What is the total amount Mr. Wallace should write on his budget request?

   **a.** $724       **b.** $974       **c.** $1,049       **d.** $1,074

## Answers

   **1.** a.
   **2.** d.
   **3.** c.
   **4.** d.

## ▶ Fraction Review

Problems involving fractions may be straightforward calculation questions, or they may be word problems. Typically, they ask you to add, subtract, multiply, divide, or compare fractions.

## Working with Fractions

A fraction is a part of something.

**Example:** Let's say that a pizza was cut into 8 equal slices and you ate 3 of them. The fraction $\frac{3}{8}$ tells you what part of the pizza you ate. The pizza below shows this: 3 of the 8 pieces (the ones you ate) are shaded.

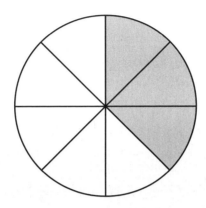

## Three Kinds of Fractions

Proper fraction: The top number is less than the bottom number:

$\frac{1}{2}$; $\frac{2}{3}$; $\frac{4}{9}$; $\frac{8}{13}$

The value of a proper fraction is less than 1.

Improper fraction: The top number is greater than or equal to the bottom number:

$\frac{3}{2}$; $\frac{5}{3}$; $\frac{14}{9}$; $\frac{12}{12}$

The value of an improper fraction is 1 or more.

Mixed number: A fraction is written to the right of a whole number:

$3\frac{1}{2}$; $4\frac{2}{3}$; $12\frac{3}{4}$; $24\frac{3}{4}$

The value of a mixed number is more than 1: It is the sum of the whole number plus the fraction.

## Changing Improper Fractions into Mixed or Whole Numbers

It's easier to add and subtract fractions that are mixed numbers rather than improper fractions. To change an improper fraction, say $\frac{13}{2}$, into a mixed number, follow these steps:

1. Divide the bottom number (2) into the top number (13) to get the whole number portion (6) of the mixed number:

$$\begin{array}{r} 6 \\ 2\overline{)13} \\ -12 \\ \hline 1 \end{array}$$

2. Write the remainder of the division (1) over the old bottom number (2): $6\frac{1}{2}$

3. Check: Change the mixed number back into an improper fraction (see the following steps).

## Changing Mixed Numbers into Improper Fractions

It's easier to multiply and divide fractions when you are working with improper fractions rather than mixed numbers. To change a mixed number, say $2\frac{3}{4}$, into an improper fraction, follow these steps:

1. Multiply the whole number (2) by the bottom number (4). $2 \times 4 = 8$

2. Add the result (8) to the top number (3). $8 + 3 = 11$

**3.** Put the total (11) over the bottom number (4).  $\frac{11}{4}$

**4.** Check: Reverse the process by changing the improper fraction into a mixed number. If you get back the number you started with, your answer is right.

## Reducing Fractions

Reducing a fraction means writing it in **lowest terms**, that is, with smaller numbers. For instance, 50¢ is $\frac{50}{100}$ of a dollar, or $\frac{1}{2}$ of a dollar. In fact, if you have a 50¢ piece in your pocket, you say that you have a half dollar. Reducing a fraction does not change its value.

Follow these steps to reduce a fraction:

1. Find a whole number that divides evenly into both numbers that make up the fraction.
2. Divide that number into the top of the fraction, and replace the top of the fraction with the quotient (the answer you got when you divided).
3. Do the same thing to the bottom number.
4. Repeat the first 3 steps until you can't find a number that divides evenly into both numbers of the fraction.

For example, let's reduce $\frac{8}{24}$. We could do it in 2 steps: $\frac{8 \div 4}{24 \div 4} = \frac{2}{6}$; then $\frac{2 \div 2}{6 \div 2} = \frac{1}{3}$. Or we could do it in a single step: $\frac{8 \div 8}{24 \div 8} = \frac{1}{3}$.

**Shortcut:** When the top and bottom numbers both end in zeros, cross out the same number of zeros in both numbers to begin the reducing process. For example, $\frac{300}{4,000}$ reduces to $\frac{3}{40}$ when you cross out 2 zeros in both numbers. Also, remember that any number that ends with an even number (0, 2, 4, 6, or 8) can be divided by 2. Any fraction in which both the top and bottom numbers end with even numbers can be reduced

Whenever you do arithmetic with fractions, reduce your answer. On a multiple-choice test, don't panic if your answer isn't listed. Try to reduce it and then compare it to the choices. Reduce the following fractions to lowest terms. The answers appear at the end of this section on page 162.

_____ **5.**  $\frac{3}{12}$

_____ **6.**  $\frac{14}{35}$

_____ **7.**  $\frac{27}{72}$

## Raising Fractions to Higher Terms

Before you can add and subtract fractions, you have to know how to raise a fraction to higher terms. This is actually the opposite of reducing a fraction.

Follow these steps to raise $\frac{2}{3}$ to 24ths:

1. Divide the old bottom number (3) into the new one (24):

$$3\overline{)24} = 8$$

2. Multiply the answer (8) by the old top number (2):

$$2 \times 8 = 16$$

3. Put the answer (16) over the new bottom number (24):

$$\frac{16}{24}$$

4. Check: Reduce the new fraction to see if you get back the original one:

$$\frac{16 \div 8}{24 \div 8}$$

Raise these fractions to higher terms:

_____ **8.** $\frac{5}{12} = \frac{}{24}$

_____ **9.** $\frac{2}{9} = \frac{}{27}$

_____ **10.** $\frac{2}{5} = \frac{}{500}$

## Adding Fractions

If the fractions have the same bottom numbers, just add the top numbers together and write the total over the bottom number.

**Examples:** $\frac{2}{9} + \frac{4}{9} = \frac{2+4}{9} = \frac{6}{9}$  Reduce the sum: $\frac{2}{3}$

$\frac{5}{8} + \frac{7}{8} = \frac{12}{8}$  Change the sum to a mixed number: $1\frac{4}{8}$; then reduce: $1\frac{1}{2}$

There are a few extra steps to add mixed numbers with the same bottom numbers, say $2\frac{3}{5} + 1\frac{4}{5}$:

1. Add the fractions:  $\frac{3}{5} + \frac{4}{5} = \frac{7}{5}$

2. Change the improper fraction into a mixed number:  $\frac{7}{5} = 1\frac{2}{5}$

3. Add the whole numbers:  $2 + 1 = 3$

4. Add the results of steps 2 and 3:  $1\frac{2}{5} + 3 = 4\frac{2}{5}$

## Finding the Least Common Denominator

If the fractions you want to add don't have the same bottom number, you will have to raise some or all of the fractions to higher terms so that they all have the same bottom number, called the **common denominator**. All of the original bottom numbers divide evenly into the common denominator. If it is the smallest number that they all divide evenly into, it is called the **least common denominator (LCD)**.

Here are a few tips for finding the LCD, the smallest number that all the bottom numbers evenly divide into:

- See if all the bottom numbers divide evenly into the biggest bottom number.
- Check out the multiplication table of the largest bottom number until you find a number that all the other bottom numbers evenly divide into.
- When all else fails, multiply all the bottom numbers together.

**Example:** $\frac{2}{3} + \frac{4}{5}$

1. Find the LCD. Multiply the bottom numbers:

$$3 \times 5 = 15$$

2. Raise each fraction to 15ths:

$$\frac{2}{3} = \frac{10}{15}$$
$$+ \frac{4}{5} = \frac{12}{15}$$
$$\overline{\phantom{xx}\frac{22}{15}}$$

3. Add as usual:

Try these addition problems:

_____**11.** $\frac{3}{4} + \frac{1}{6}$

_____**12.** $\frac{7}{8} + \frac{2}{3} + \frac{3}{4}$

_____**13.** $4\frac{1}{3} + 2\frac{3}{4} + \frac{1}{6}$

## Subtracting Fractions

If the fractions have the same bottom numbers, just subtract the top numbers and write the difference over the bottom number.

**Example:** $\frac{4}{9} - \frac{3}{9} = \frac{4-3}{9} = \frac{1}{9}$

If the fractions you want to subtract don't have the same bottom number, you will have to raise some or all of the fractions to higher terms so that they all have the same bottom number, or LCD. If you forgot how to find the LCD, just read the section on adding fractions with different bottom numbers.

**Example:** $\frac{5}{6} - \frac{3}{4}$

1. Raise each fraction to 12ths because 12 is the LCD, the smallest number

that 6 and 4 both divide into evenly:

$$\frac{5}{6} = \frac{10}{12}$$
$$- \frac{3}{4} = \frac{9}{12}$$
$$\overline{\phantom{xx}\frac{1}{12}}$$

2. Subtract as usual:

Subtracting mixed numbers with the same bottom number is similar to adding mixed numbers.

**Example:** $4\frac{3}{5} - 1\frac{2}{5}$

1. Subtract the fractions: $\quad \frac{3}{5} - \frac{2}{5} = \frac{1}{5}$
2. Subtract the whole numbers: $\quad 4 - 1 = 3$
3. Add the results of steps 1 and 2: $\quad \frac{1}{5} + 3 = 3\frac{1}{5}$

Sometimes there is an extra borrowing step when you subtract mixed numbers with the same bottom numbers, say $7\frac{3}{5} - 2\frac{4}{5}$:

1. You can't subtract the fractions the way they are because $\frac{4}{5}$ is bigger than $\frac{3}{5}$.
   So you borrow 1 from the 7, making it 6, and change that 1 to $\frac{5}{5}$ because
   5 is the bottom number:    $7\frac{3}{5} = 6\frac{5}{5} + \frac{3}{5}$

2. Add the numbers from step 1:    $6\frac{5}{5} + \frac{3}{5} = 6\frac{8}{5}$

3. Now you have a different version of the original problem:    $6\frac{8}{5} - 2\frac{4}{5}$

4. Subtract the fractional parts of the two mixed numbers:    $\frac{8}{5} - \frac{4}{5} = \frac{4}{5}$

5. Subtract the whole number parts of the two mixed numbers: $6 - 2 = 4$

6. Add the results of the last two steps together: $4 + \frac{4}{5} = 4\frac{4}{5}$

Try these subtraction problems:

_____**14.** $\frac{4}{5} - \frac{2}{3}$

_____**15.** $\frac{7}{8} - \frac{1}{4} - \frac{1}{2}$

_____**16.** $4\frac{1}{3} - 2\frac{3}{4}$

Now let's put what you've learned about adding and subtracting fractions to work in some real-life problems.

_____**17.** Officer Peterson drove $3\frac{1}{2}$ miles to the police station. Then he drove $4\frac{3}{4}$ miles to his first assignment. When he left there, he drove 2 miles to his next assignment. Then he drove $3\frac{2}{3}$ miles back to the police station for a meeting. Finally, he drove $3\frac{1}{2}$ miles home. How many miles did he travel in total?
   **a.** $17\frac{5}{12}$        **b.** $16\frac{5}{12}$        **c.** $15\frac{7}{12}$        **d.** $15\frac{5}{12}$        **e.** $13\frac{11}{12}$

_____**18.** Before leaving the fire station, Firefighter Sorensen noted that the mileage gauge on Engine 2 registered $4{,}357\frac{4}{10}$ miles. When she arrived at the scene of the fire, the mileage gauge registered $4{,}400\frac{1}{10}$ miles. How many miles did she drive from the station to the fire scene?
   **a.** $42\frac{3}{10}$        **b.** $42\frac{7}{10}$        **c.** $43\frac{7}{10}$        **d.** $47\frac{2}{10}$        **e.** $57\frac{3}{10}$

## Multiplying Fractions

Multiplying fractions is actually easier than adding them. All you do is multiply the top numbers and then multiply the bottom numbers.

**Examples:** $\frac{2}{3} \times \frac{5}{7} = \frac{2 \times 5}{3 \times 7} = \frac{10}{21}$        $\frac{1}{2} \times \frac{3}{5} \times \frac{7}{4} = \frac{1 \times 3 \times 7}{2 \times 5 \times 4} = \frac{21}{40}$

Sometimes you can cancel before multiplying. Cancelling is a shortcut that makes the multiplication go faster because you are multiplying with smaller numbers. It's very similar to reducing: If there is a number that divides evenly into a top number and bottom number, do that division before multiplying. If you forget to cancel, you will still get the right answer, but you will have to reduce it.

**Example:** $\frac{5}{6} \times \frac{9}{20}$

1. Cancel the 6 and the 9 by dividing 3 into both of them: $6 \div 3 = 2$ and $9 \div 3 = 3$. Cross out the 6 and the 9.

$$\frac{5}{\cancel{6}} \times \frac{\cancel{9}^{3}}{20}$$
$$\quad_{2}$$

2. Cancel the 5 and the 20 by dividing 5 into both of them: $5 \div 5 = 1$ and $20 \div 5 = 4$. Cross out the 5 and the 20.

$$\frac{\cancel{5}^{1}}{\cancel{6}} \times \frac{\cancel{9}^{3}}{\cancel{20}}$$
$$\quad_{2} \qquad _{4}$$

3. Multiply across the new top numbers and the new bottom numbers:

$$\frac{1 \times 3}{2 \times 4} = \frac{3}{8}$$

Try these multiplication problems:

_____**19.** $\frac{1}{5} \times \frac{2}{3}$

_____**20.** $\frac{2}{3} \times \frac{4}{7} \times \frac{3}{5}$

_____**21.** $\frac{3}{4} \times \frac{8}{9}$

To multiply a fraction by a whole number, first rewrite the whole number as a fraction with a bottom number of 1:

**Example:** $5 \times \frac{2}{3} = \frac{5}{1} \times \frac{2}{3} = \frac{10}{3}$ (Optional: Convert $\frac{10}{3}$ to a mixed number: $3\frac{1}{3}$)

To multiply with mixed numbers, it's easier to change them to improper fractions before multiplying.

**Example:** $4\frac{2}{3} \times 5\frac{1}{2}$

1. Convert $4\frac{2}{3}$ to an improper fraction: $4\frac{2}{3} = \frac{4 \times 3 + 2}{3} = \frac{14}{3}$
2. Convert $5\frac{1}{2}$ to an improper fraction: $5\frac{1}{2} = \frac{5 \times 2 + 1}{2} = \frac{11}{2}$
3. Cancel and multiply the fractions: $\frac{\cancel{14}^{7}}{3} \times \frac{11}{\cancel{2}_{1}} = \frac{77}{3}$

4. Optional: Convert the improper fraction to a mixed number: $\frac{77}{3} = 25\frac{2}{3}$

Now try these multiplication problems with mixed numbers and whole numbers:

_____**22.** $4\frac{1}{3} \times \frac{2}{5}$

_____**23.** $2\frac{1}{2} \times 6$

_____**24.** $3\frac{3}{4} \times 4\frac{2}{5}$

Here are a few more real-life problems to test your skills:

_____**25.** After driving $\frac{2}{3}$ of the 15 miles to work, Mr. Stone stopped to make a phone call. How many miles had he driven when he made his call?

    **a.** 5         **b.** $7\frac{1}{2}$         **c.** 10         **d.** 12         **e.** $15\frac{2}{3}$

_____**26.** If Henry worked $\frac{3}{4}$ of a 40-hour week, how many hours did he work?

    **a.** $7\frac{1}{2}$         **b.** 10         **c.** 20         **d.** 25         **e.** 30

_____**27.** Technician Chin makes $14.00 an hour. When she works more than 8 hours in a day, she gets overtime pay of $1\frac{1}{2}$ times her regular hourly wage for the extra hours. How much did she earn for working 11 hours in one day?

    **a.** $77         **b.** $154         **c.** $175         **d.** $210         **e.** $231

## Dividing Fractions

To divide one fraction by a second fraction, invert the second fraction (that is, flip the top and bottom numbers) and then multiply. That's all there is to it!

    **Example:** $\frac{1}{2} \div \frac{3}{5}$

**1.** Invert the second fraction ($\frac{3}{5}$):       $\frac{5}{3}$

**2.** Change the division sign ($\div$) to a multiplication sign ($\times$)

**3.** Multiply the first fraction by the new second fraction:     $\frac{1}{2} \times \frac{5}{3} = \frac{1 \times 5}{2 \times 3} = \frac{5}{6}$

    To divide a fraction by a whole number, first change the whole number to a fraction by putting it over 1. Then follow the division steps above.

    **Example:** $\frac{3}{5} \div 2 = \frac{3}{5} \div \frac{2}{1} = \frac{3}{5} \times \frac{1}{2} = \frac{3 \times 1}{5 \times 2} = \frac{3}{10}$

    When the division problem has a mixed number, convert it to an improper fraction and then divide as usual.

    **Example:** $2\frac{3}{4} \div \frac{1}{6}$

**1.** Convert $2\frac{3}{4}$ to an improper fraction: $2\frac{3}{4} = \frac{2 \times 4 + 3}{4} = \frac{11}{4}$

**2.** Divide $\frac{11}{4}$ by $\frac{1}{6}$:     $\frac{11}{4} \div \frac{1}{6} = \frac{11}{4} \times \frac{6}{1}$

**3.** Flip $\frac{1}{6}$ to $\frac{6}{1}$, change $\div$ to $\times$, cancel, and multiply:     $\frac{11}{\underset{2}{4}} \times \frac{\overset{3}{6}}{1} = \frac{11 \times 3}{2 \times 1} = \frac{33}{2}$

Here are a few division problems to try:

_____**28.**  $\frac{1}{3} \div \frac{2}{3}$

_____**29.**  $2\frac{3}{4} \div \frac{1}{2}$

_____**30.**  $\frac{3}{5} \div 3$

_____**31.** $3\frac{3}{4} \div 2\frac{1}{3}$

Let's wrap this up with some real-life problems.

_____**32.** If four friends evenly split $6\frac{1}{2}$ pounds of candy, how many pounds of candy does each friend get?

    **a.** $\frac{8}{13}$      **b.** $1\frac{5}{8}$      **c.** $1\frac{1}{2}$      **d.** $1\frac{5}{13}$      **e.** 4

_____**33.** How many $2\frac{1}{2}$-pound chunks of cheese can be cut from a single 20-pound piece of cheese?

    **a.** 2      **b.** 4      **c.** 6      **d.** 8      **e.** 10

_____**34.** Ms. Goldbaum earned \$36.75 for working $3\frac{1}{2}$ hours. What was her hourly wage?

    **a.** \$10.00      **b.** \$10.50      **c.** \$10.75      **d.** \$12.00      **e.** \$12.25

## Answers

| | | | | | | |
|---|---|---|---|---|---|---|
| **5.** | $\frac{1}{4}$ | **15.** | $\frac{1}{8}$ | **25.** | c. |
| **6.** | $\frac{2}{5}$ | **16.** | $\frac{19}{12}$ or $1\frac{7}{12}$ | **26.** | e. |
| **7.** | $\frac{3}{8}$ | **17.** | a. | **27.** | c. |
| **8.** | 10 | **18.** | b. | **28.** | $\frac{1}{2}$ |
| **9.** | 6 | **19.** | $\frac{2}{15}$ | **29.** | $5\frac{1}{2}$ |
| **10.** | 200 | **20.** | $\frac{8}{35}$ | **30.** | $\frac{1}{5}$ |
| **11.** | $\frac{11}{12}$ | **21.** | $\frac{2}{3}$ | **31.** | $\frac{45}{28}$ or $1\frac{17}{28}$ |
| **12.** | $\frac{55}{24}$ or $2\frac{7}{24}$ | **22.** | $\frac{26}{15}$ or $1\frac{11}{15}$ | **32.** | b. |
| **13.** | $7\frac{1}{4}$ | **23.** | 15 | **33.** | d. |
| **14.** | $\frac{2}{15}$ | **24.** | $\frac{33}{2}$ or $16\frac{1}{2}$ | **34.** | b. |

## ▶ Decimals

### What Is a Decimal?

A decimal is a special kind of fraction. You use decimals every day when you deal with money—\$10.35 is a decimal that represents 10 dollars and 35 cents. The decimal point separates the dollars from the cents. Because there are 100 cents in one dollar, 1¢ is $\frac{1}{100}$ of a dollar, or \$.01.

Each decimal digit to the right of the decimal point has a name:

**Example:** .1 = 1 tenth = $\frac{1}{10}$

.02 = 2 hundredths = $\frac{2}{100}$

.003 = 3 thousandths = $\frac{3}{1,000}$

.0004 = 4 ten-thousandths = $\frac{4}{10,000}$

When you add zeros after the rightmost decimal place, you don't change the value of the decimal. For example, 6.17 is the same as all of these:

6.170

6.1700

6.17000000000000000

If there are digits on both sides of the decimal point (such as 10.35), the number is called a mixed decimal. If there are digits only to the right of the decimal point (such as .53), the number is called a decimal. A whole number (such as 15) is understood to have a decimal point at its right (15.). Thus, 15 is the same as 15.0, 15.00, 15.000, and so on.

## Changing Fractions to Decimals

To change a fraction to a decimal, divide the bottom number into the top number after you put a decimal point and a few zeros on the right of the top number. When you divide, bring the decimal point up into your answer.

**Example:** Change $\frac{3}{4}$ to a decimal.

1. Add a decimal point and 2 zeros to the top number (3):

$\quad$ 3.00

2. Divide the bottom number (4) into 3.00:

$\quad$ Bring the decimal point up into the answer:

$$\begin{array}{r} .75 \\ 4\overline{)3.00} \\ \underline{2\,8} \\ 20 \\ \underline{20} \\ 0 \end{array}$$

3. The quotient (result of the division) is the answer:

$\quad$ .75

Some fractions may require you to add many decimal zeros for the division to come out evenly. In fact, when you convert a fraction like $\frac{2}{3}$ to a decimal, you can keep adding decimal zeros to the top number forever because the division will never come out evenly! As you divide 3 into 2, you will keep getting 6's:

$$2 \div 3 = .6666666666 \text{ etc.}$$

This is called a **repeating decimal** and it can be written as $.66\overline{6}$ or as $.66\frac{2}{3}$. You can approximate it as .67, .667, .6667, and so on.

## Changing Decimals to Fractions

To change a decimal to a fraction, write the digits of the decimal as the top number of a fraction and write the decimal's name as the bottom number of the fraction. Then reduce the fraction, if possible.

**Example:** .018

1. Write 18 as the top of the fraction:   $\dfrac{18}{}$

2. Three places to the right of the decimal means *thousandths,* so write 1,000 as the bottom number:   $\dfrac{18}{1,000}$

3. Reduce by dividing 2 into the top and bottom numbers:   $\dfrac{18 \div 2}{1,000 \div 2} = \dfrac{9}{500}$

Change the following decimals or mixed decimals to fractions. The answers can be found at the end of this section on page 168.

_____**35.**  .005

_____**36.**  3.48

_____**37.**  123.456

## Comparing Decimals

Because decimals are easier to compare when they have the same number of digits after the decimal point, tack zeros onto the end of the shorter decimals. Then all you have to do is compare the numbers as if the decimal points weren't there:

**Example:**  Compare .08 and .1

1. Tack one zero at the end of .1:   .10
2. To compare .10 to .08, just compare 10 to 8.
3. Since 10 is larger than 8, .1 is larger than .08.

## Adding and Subtracting Decimals

To add or subtract decimals, line them up so their decimal points are aligned. You may want to tack on zeros at the end of shorter decimals so you can keep all your digits evenly lined up. Remember, if a number doesn't have a decimal point, then put one at the end of the number.

**Example:**  1.23 + 57 + .038

1. Line up the numbers like this:

$$\begin{array}{r} 1.230 \\ 57.000 \\ + \phantom{0}.038 \\ \hline \end{array}$$

2. Add:

$$58.268$$

**Example:**  1.23 − .038

1. Line up the numbers like this:

$$1.230$$

$$\begin{array}{r} - \ .038 \\ \hline 1.192 \end{array}$$

**2.** Subtract:

Try these addition and subtraction problems:

_____**38.** .905 + .02 + 3.075

_____**39.** .005 + 8 + .3

_____**40.** 3.48 − 2.573

_____**41.** 123.456 − 122

_____**42.** Officer Watson drove 3.7 miles to the state park. She then walked 1.6 miles around the park to make sure everything was all right. She got back into the car, drove 2.75 miles to check on a broken traffic light, and then drove 2 miles back to the police station. How many miles did she drive in total?
   **a.** 8.05      **b.** 8.45      **c.** 8.8      **d.** 10      **e.** 10.05

_____**43.** The average number of emergency room visits at City Hospital fell from 486.4 per week to 402.5 per week. By how many emergency room visits per week did the average fall?
   **a.** 73.9      **b.** 83      **c.** 83.1      **d.** 83.9      **e.** 84.9

## Multiplying Decimals

To multiply decimals, ignore the decimal points and just multiply the numbers. Then count the total number of decimal digits (the digits to the right of the decimal point) in the numbers you are multiplying. Count off that number of digits in your answer beginning at the right side and put the decimal point to the left of those digits.

   **Example:** 215.7 × 2.4

**1.** Multiply 2157 times 24:

$$\begin{array}{r} 2157 \\ \times \ 24 \\ \hline 8628 \\ 4314 \ \\ \hline 51768 \end{array}$$

**2.** Because there are a total of 2 decimal digits in 215.7 and 2.4, count off 2 places from the right in 51768, placing the decimal point to the *left* of the last 2 digits:

   517.68

   If your answer doesn't have enough digits, tack zeros on to the left of the answer.

**Example:** .03 × .006

1. Multiply 3 times 6: 3 × 6 = 18
2. You need 5 decimal digits in your answer, so tack on 3 zeros: 00018
3. Put the decimal point at the front of the number (which is 5 digits in from the right): .00018

You can practice multiplying decimals with these problems.

_____**44.** .05 × .6

_____**45.** .053 × 6.4

_____**46.** 38.1 × .0184

_____**47.** Joe earns $14.50 per hour. Last week he worked 37.5 hours. How much money did he earn that week?
   **a.** $518.00      **b.** $518.50      **c.** $525.00      **d.** $536.50      **e.** $543.75

_____**48.** Nuts cost $3.50 per pound. Approximately how much will 4.25 pounds of nuts cost?
   **a.** $12.25      **b.** $12.50      **c.** $12.88      **d.** $14.50      **e.** $14.88

## Dividing Decimals

To divide a decimal by a whole number, set up the division $(8\overline{).256})$ and immediately bring the decimal point straight up into the answer $(8\overline{)\overset{.}{1}256})$. Then divide as you would normally divide whole numbers:

**Example:**
$$
\begin{array}{r}
.032 \\
8\overline{)1256} \\
-0 \phantom{56} \\
\hline
25 \phantom{6} \\
-24 \phantom{6} \\
\hline
16 \\
-16 \\
\hline
0
\end{array}
$$

To divide any number by a decimal, there is an extra step to perform before you can divide. Move the decimal point to the very right of the number you are dividing by, counting the number of places you are moving it. Then move the decimal point the same number of places to the right in the number you are dividing into. In other words, first change the problem to one in which you are dividing by a whole number.

**Example:** $.06\overline{)1.218}$

1. Because there are two decimal digits in .06, move the decimal point two places to the right in both numbers and move the decimal point straight up into the answer:

$$.06\overline{)1.21\overset{.}{1}8}$$

2. Divide using the new numbers:

$$
\begin{array}{r}
20.3 \\
6\overline{)121.8} \\
-12 \\
\hline
01 \\
-00 \\
\hline
18 \\
-18 \\
\hline
0
\end{array}
$$

Under certain conditions, you have to tack on zeros to the right of the last decimal digit in a number you are dividing into:

- if there aren't enough digits for you to move the decimal point to the right
- if the answer doesn't come out evenly when you do the division
- if you are dividing a whole number by a decimal, you will have to tack on the decimal point as well as some zeros.

Try your skills on these division problems:

_____ **49.** $7\overline{)9.8}$

_____ **50.** $.0004\overline{).0512}$

_____ **51.** $.05\overline{)28.6}$

_____ **52.** $.14\overline{)196}$

_____ **53.** If Officer Worthington drove his truck 92.4 miles in 2.1 hours, what was his average speed in miles per hour?

    **a.** 41      **b.** 44      **c.** 90.3      **d.** 94.5      **e.** 194.04

_____ **54.** Firefighter Sanders walked a total of 18.6 miles in 4 days. On average, how many miles did she walk each day?

    **a.** 4.15      **b.** 4.60      **c.** 4.65      **d.** 22.60      **e.** 74.40

## Answers

| | | | | | | |
|---|---|---|---|---|---|---|
| **35.** | $\frac{5}{1,000}$ or $\frac{1}{200}$ | **42.** | b. | **49.** | 1.4 | |
| **36.** | $3\frac{12}{25}$ | **43.** | d. | **50.** | 128 | |
| **37.** | $123\frac{456}{1,000}$ or $123\frac{57}{125}$ | **44.** | .03 | **51.** | 572 | |
| **38.** | 4 | **45.** | .3392 | **52.** | 1,400 | |
| **39.** | 8.305 | **46.** | .70104 | **53.** | b. | |
| **40.** | .907 | **47.** | e. | **54.** | c. | |
| **41.** | 1.456 | **48.** | e. | | | |

# ▶ Percents

## What Is a Percent?

A percent is a special kind of fraction or part of something. The bottom number (the denominator) in such a fraction is always 100. For example, 17% is the same as $\frac{17}{100}$. Literally, the word *percent* means *per 100 parts*. The root *cent* means 100: A century is 100 years, there are 100 cents in a dollar, etc. Thus, 17% means 17 parts out of 100. Because fractions can also be expressed as decimals, 17% is also equivalent to .17, which is 17 hundredths.

You come into contact with percents every day. Sales tax, interest, and discounts are just a few common examples.

If you are shaky on fractions, you may want to review the fraction section before reading further.

## Changing a Decimal to a Percent and Vice Versa

To change a decimal to a percent, move the decimal point two places to the **right** and tack on a percent sign (%) at the end. If the decimal point moves to the very right of the number, you don't have to write the decimal point. If there aren't enough places to move the decimal point, add zeros on the **right** before moving the decimal point.

To change a percent to a decimal, drop off the percent sign and move the decimal point two places to the left. If there aren't enough places to move the decimal point, add zeros on the **left** before moving the decimal point.

Try changing the following decimals to percent. The answers can be found at the end of this section on page 174.

_____ **55.** .45

_____ **56.** .008

_____ **57.** $.16\frac{2}{3}$

Now change these percents to decimals:

_____**58.**  12%

_____**59.**  $87\frac{1}{2}\%$

_____**60.**  250%

## Changing a Fraction to a Percent and Vice Versa

To change a fraction to a percent, there are two techniques. Each is illustrated by changing the fraction $\frac{1}{4}$ to a percent:

Technique 1:   Multiply the fraction by 100%.
Multiply $\frac{1}{4}$ by 100%:

$$\frac{1}{\underset{1}{4}} \times \frac{\overset{25}{\cancel{100}}\%}{1} = 25\%$$

Technique 2:   Divide the fraction's bottom number into the top number; then move the decimal point two places to the **right** and tack on a percent sign (%).
Divide 4 into 1 and move the decimal point 2 places to the right:

$$\overset{.25}{4\overline{)1.00}} \quad .25 = 25\%$$

To change a percent to a fraction, remove the percent sign and write the number over 100. Then reduce if possible.

**Example:**  Change 4% to a fraction.

**1.** Remove the % and write the fraction 4 over 100:       $\frac{4}{100}$
**2.** Reduce:     $\frac{4 \div 4}{100 \div 4} = \frac{1}{25}$

Here's a more complicated example: Change $16\frac{2}{3}\%$ to a fraction.

**1.** Remove the % and write the fraction $16\frac{2}{3}$ over 100:
**2.** Since a fraction means "top number divided by bottom number,"
   rewrite the fraction as a division problem:     $16\frac{2}{3} \div 100$
**3.** Change the mixed number ($16\frac{2}{3}$) to an improper fraction ($\frac{50}{3}$):       $\frac{50}{3} \div \frac{100}{1}$
**4.** Flip the second fraction ($\frac{100}{1}$) and multiply:     $\frac{\overset{1}{\cancel{50}}}{3} \times \frac{1}{\underset{2}{\cancel{100}}} = \frac{1}{6}$

Try changing these fractions to percents:

_____**61.**  $\frac{1}{8}$

_____**62.** $\frac{13}{25}$

_____**63.** $\frac{7}{12}$

Now, change these percents to fractions:

_____**64.** 95%

_____**65.** $37\frac{1}{2}$%

_____**66.** 125%

Sometimes it is more convenient to work with a percent as a fraction or a decimal. Rather than have to calculate the equivalent fraction or decimal, consider memorizing the equivalence table on page 171. Not only will this increase your efficiency on the math test, but it will also be practical for real-life situations.

## Percent Word Problems

Word problems involving percents come in three main varieties:

- Find a percent of a whole.

    **Example:** What is 30% of 40?

- Find what percent one number is of another number.

    **Example:** 12 is what percent of 40?

- Find the whole when the percent of it is given.

    **Example:** 12 is 30% of what number?

Although each variety has its own approach, there is a single shortcut formula you can use to solve each of these:

$$\frac{is}{of} = \frac{\%}{100}$$

The **is** is the number that usually follows or is just before the word **is** in the question.
The **of** is the number that usually follows the word **of** in the question.
The **%** is the number that is in front of the **%** or **percent** in the question.

Or you may think of the shortcut formula as:

$$\frac{part}{whole} = \frac{\%}{100}$$

| CONVERSION TABLE | | |
|---|---|---|
| **DECIMAL** | **%** | **FRACTION** |
| .25 | 25% | $\frac{1}{4}$ |
| .50 | 50% | $\frac{1}{2}$ |
| .75 | 75% | $\frac{3}{4}$ |
| .10 | 10% | $\frac{1}{10}$ |
| .20 | 20% | $\frac{1}{5}$ |
| .40 | 40% | $\frac{2}{5}$ |
| .60 | 60% | $\frac{3}{5}$ |
| .80 | 80% | $\frac{4}{5}$ |
| .33$\overline{3}$ | 33$\frac{1}{3}$% | $\frac{1}{3}$ |
| .66$\overline{6}$ | 66$\frac{2}{3}$% | $\frac{2}{3}$ |

To solve each of the three varieties, we are going to use the fact that the **cross-products** are equal. The cross-products are the products of the numbers diagonally across from each other. Remembering that *product* means *multiply*, here's how to create the cross-products for the percent shortcut:

$$\frac{part}{whole} = \frac{\%}{100}$$
$$part \times 100 = whole \times \%$$

Here's how to use the shortcut with cross-products:

- Find a percent of a whole.

   What is 30% of 40?

   30 is the % and 40 is the *of* number:

   Cross-multiply and solve for *is*:

   $$\frac{is}{40} = \frac{30}{100}$$
   $$is \times 100 = 40 \times 30$$
   $$is \times 100 = 1{,}200$$
   $$\mathbf{12} \times 100 = 1{,}200$$

   Thus, **12 *is*** 30% of 40.

- Find what percent one number is of another number.

   12 is what percent of 40?

   12 is the *is* number and 40 is the *of* number:

   Cross-multiply and solve for %:

   $$\frac{12}{40} = \frac{\%}{100}$$
   $$12 \times 100 = 40 \times \%$$
   $$1{,}200 = 40 \times \%$$
   $$1{,}200 = 40 \times \mathbf{30}$$

   Thus, 12 is **30%** of 40.

- Find the whole when the percent of it is given.

12 is 30% of what number?

12 is the *is* number and 30 is the %:

$\frac{12}{of} = \frac{30}{100}$

Cross-multiply and solve for the *of* number:

$12 \times 100 = of \times 30$

$1,200 = of \times 30$

$1,200 = \mathbf{40} \times 30$

Thus, 12 is 30% ***of* 40**.

You can use the same technique to find the percent increase or decrease. The *is* number is the actual increase or decrease, and the *of* number is the original amount.

**Example:** If a merchant puts his \$20 hats on sale for \$15, by what percent does he decrease the selling price?

1. Calculate the decrease, the *is* number:          $\$20 - \$15 = \$5$

2. The *of* number is the original amount, \$20

3. Set up the equation and solve for *of* by cross-multiplying:

$\frac{5}{20} = \frac{\%}{100}$

$5 \times 100 = 20 \times \%$

$500 = 20 \times \%$

$500 = 20 \times \mathbf{25}$

4. Thus, the selling price is decreased by **25%**.

If the merchant later raises the price of the hats from \$15 back to \$20, don't be fooled into thinking that the percent increase is also 25%! It's actually more, because the increase amount of \$5 is now based on a lower original price of only \$15:

$\frac{5}{15} = \frac{\%}{100}$

$5 \times 100 = 15 \times \%$

$500 = 15 \times \%$

$500 = 15 \times \mathbf{33\frac{1}{3}}$

Thus, the selling price is increased by 33%.

Find a percent of a whole:

_____**67.** 1% of 25

_____**68.** 18.2% of 50

_____**69.** $37\frac{1}{2}$% of 100

_____**70.** 125% of 60

Find what percent one number is of another number.

_____**71.** 10 is what percent of 20?

_____**72.** 4 is what percent of 12?

_____**73.** 12 is what percent of 4?

Find the whole when the percent of it is given.

_____**74.** 15% of what number is 15?

_____**75.** $37\frac{1}{2}$% of what number is 3?

_____**76.** 200% of what number is 20?

Now try your percent skills on some real-life problems.

_____**77.** The deputy chief, after reviewing the roll call, finds that 15% of the 115 members of B shift are absent due to illness and approved vacation. How many personnel have to be called in to fill in for the absent personnel?
a. 15          b. 17          c. 115          d. 132

_____**78.** Twenty percent of Engine 5's firefighters are women. If there are 30 women on the roster, how many total members are there?
a. 36          b. 70          c. 100          d. 150

_____**79.** During June, Firefighter Hanson's company responded to 150 alarms. Of these, 26 were wildland responses. What percent of the total alarms were wildland responses?
a. 12%          b. 17%          c. 22%          d. 26%

_____**80.** Chief Smith has approved a purchase of new turnout gloves at $25.50 a pair. If his company received a government discount of 15%, what was the original price per pair?
a. $25.50          b. $27.50          c. $28.45          d. $30.00

## Answers

| | | | | | | |
|---|---|---|---|---|---|---|
| **55.** | 45% | **64.** | $\frac{19}{20}$ | **73.** | 300% | |
| **56.** | .8% | **65.** | $\frac{3}{8}$ | **74.** | 100 | |
| **57.** | 16.67% or $16\frac{2}{3}$% | **66.** | $\frac{5}{4}$ or $1\frac{1}{4}$ | **75.** | 8 | |
| **58.** | .12 | **67.** | $\frac{1}{4}$ or .25 | **76.** | 10 | |
| **59.** | .875 | **68.** | 9.1 | **77.** | b. | |
| **60.** | 2.5 | **69.** | $37\frac{1}{2}$ or 37.5 | **78.** | d. | |
| **61.** | 12.5% or $12\frac{1}{2}$% | **70.** | 75 | **79.** | b. | |
| **62.** | 52% | **71.** | 50% | **80.** | d. | |
| **63.** | 58.33% or $58\frac{1}{3}$% | **72.** | $33\frac{1}{3}$% | | | |

# ► Length, Weight, and Time Units

The questions involving length, weight, and time on the math test will ask you either to convert between different measurement units or to add or subtract measurement values.

## Common Terms

You may encounter questions that expect you to understand basic geometric concepts, such as the following:

- **perimeter:** the distance around a two-dimensional figure. To determine the perimeter of a shape, add the lengths of each side.
- **square footage:** unit of measurement used to define the size of an area. To determine the square footage of a rectangular area, multiply length by width.

## Converting

You may encounter questions that ask you to convert between units of measurement in length, weight, or time. To convert from a smaller unit (such as inches) to a larger unit (such as feet), divide the smaller unit by the number of those units necessary to equal the larger unit. To convert from a larger unit to a smaller unit, multiply the larger unit by the conversion number.

 **Example:** Convert 36 inches to feet.

- Since 1 foot = 12 inches, divide 36 by 12:   36 ÷ 12 = 3 feet

 **Example:** Convert 4 feet to inches.

- Since 1 foot = 12 inches, multiply 4 by 12:   4 × 12 = 48 inches

**Example:** Convert 32 ounces to pounds.

- Since 1 pound = 16 ounces, divide 32 by 16:  $32 \div 16 = 2$ pounds

**Example:** Convert 2 pounds to ounces.

- Since 1 pound = 16 ounces, multiply 2 by 16:  $2 \times 16 = 32$ ounces

**Example:** Convert 180 minutes to hours.

- Since 1 hour = 60 minutes, divide 180 by 60:  $180 \div 60 = 3$ hours

**Example:** Convert 4 hours to minutes.

- Since 1 hour = 60 minutes, multiply 4 by 60:  $4 \times 60 = 240$ minutes

Now try some on your own. Convert as indicated. The answers are at the end of this section on page 177.

_____**81.** 2 feet = _____ inches

_____**83.** 3 pounds = _____ ounces

_____**82.** 2 hours = _____ minutes

_____**84.** 120 minutes = _____ hours.

## Calculating with Length, Weight, and Time Units

On the test, you may be asked to add or subtract length, weight, and time units. The only trick to doing this correctly is to remember to convert the smaller units to larger units and vice versa, if need be.

**Example:** Find the perimeter of the figure:

To add the lengths, add each column of length units separately:

```
      5 feet    7 inches
      2 feet    6 inches
      6 feet    9 inches
   +  3 feet    5 inches
     16 feet   27 inches
```

3 feet 5 inches

6 feet 9 inches

5 feet 7 inches

2 feet 6 inches

Since 27 inches is more than 1 foot, the total of 16 feet 27 inches must be simplified:

- Convert 27 inches to feet and inches:

  27 inches $\times \frac{1 \text{ foot}}{12 \text{ inches}} = \frac{27}{12}$ feet $= \frac{23}{12}$ feet = 2 feet 3 inches

- Add:
```
          16 feet
       +   2 feet   3 inches
          18 feet   3 inches
```

Thus, the perimeter is **18 feet 3 inches.**

Finding the length of a line segment may require subtracting lengths of different units. For example, find the length of line segment $\overline{AB}$:

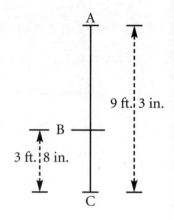

To subtract the lengths, subtract each column of length units separately, starting with the rightmost column.

```
  9 feet   3 inches
− 3 feet   8 inches
```

**Warning:** You can't subtract 8 inches from 3 inches because 8 is larger than 3! As in regular subtraction, you have to *borrow* 1 from the column on the left. However, borrowing *1 ft.* is the same as borrowing *12 inches*; adding the borrowed 12 inches to the 3 inches gives 15 inches. Thus:

```
        15
  8    12
  9 feet  3 inches
− 3 feet  8 inches
  5 feet  7 inches
```

Thus, the length of $\overline{AB}$ is **5 feet 7 inches**.

Add and simplify. Answers are at the end of this chapter.

**85.**     5 feet 3 inches
     +  2 feet 9 inches

**86.**     7 pounds 12 ounces
     +  5 pounds 14 ounces

Subtract and simplify.

**87.**     2 feet 9 inches
     −  1 feet 1 inches

**88.**     5 hours 38 minutes
     −  3 hours 45 minutes

Now, try these time word problems.

_____**89.**  At the beginning of your shift you have been assigned to run a calibration test on the company's three gas meters. Each test took you 50 minutes. Just as you are finishing, the captain brings in another meter from the chief's office. When you finish that calibration, you find that you have spent a total of $3\frac{1}{4}$ hours on this assignment. How long did it take to calibrate the fourth meter?

**a.** $\frac{1}{2}$ hour          **b.** $\frac{3}{4}$ hour          **c.** 1 hour          **d.** $1\frac{1}{4}$ hours

_____**90.** The total person-hours spent at a hazardous materials incident is 9 hours and 20 minutes, and a total of 20 firefighters are assigned. What is the average time per firefighter?

    **a.** 35 minutes    **b.** $\frac{5}{8}$ hour    **c.** 0.28 hours    **d.** 28 minutes

## Answers

| | | | | | |
|---|---|---|---|---|---|
| **81.** | 24 | **85.** | 8 feet | **89.** | b. |
| **82.** | 120 | **86.** | 13 pounds. 10 ounces | **90.** | c. |
| **83.** | 48 | **87.** | 1 foot 8 inches | | |
| **84.** | 2 | **88.** | 1 hour 53 minutes | | |

## ▶ Dimensional Analysis and Conversions

### What Is Dimensional Analysis?

Dimensional analysis is a technique for solving problems that involve units or conversions that is taught in many engineering schools. It is a very useful technique in some areas of the emergency services, especially in EMS, where drug and fluid administration rates need to be calculated.

Dimensional analysis is based on multiplication of improper fractions. The key to using it is to keep the units with the numbers. The units cancel out in much the same way as fractions do when multiplying. Writing out your work using dimensional analysis makes it much easier to keep track of what you are doing, and to double check your work. If your units do not properly cancel out to give you the unit that you want for the answer, your answer is wrong.

### How Is It Used?

Dimensional analysis is most useful in doing conversions of numbers from one unit to another, such as in converting a value in miles per hour to feet per second. Most people probably do not know that to convert miles per hour to feet per second, you multiply by 1.4666667. However, you can perform this conversion using more commonly known information.

To use dimensional analysis, you need to examine the information that you are given in a problem and convert it into an improper fraction. Say you want to convert 45 miles per hour to feet per second. You know, or need to know, the following information:

- What is the speed in mph (45 miles / hour)?
- How any minutes are in an hour (60 minutes / hour)?
- How many seconds are in a minute (60 seconds / minute)?
- How many feet are in a mile (5,280 feet / mile)?

You can write these values with either unit on top or bottom. It depends on what you are starting with and what you want to end up with. Miles per hour and feet per second both have a distance unit on top and a time unit on bottom. Therefore, you should set the start of the problem this way:

$$\frac{45 \text{ miles}}{1 \text{ hour}}$$

You then need to write the other conversions as fractions so that the units cancel out:

$$\frac{45 \text{ miles}}{1 \text{ hour}} \times \frac{5,280 \text{ feet}}{1 \text{ miles}} \times \frac{1 \text{ hour}}{60 \text{ minutes}} \times \frac{1 \text{ minute}}{60 \text{ seconds}} = \frac{66 \text{ feet}}{1 \text{ second}}$$

Remember, any whole number that you use as a conversion can be written as a fraction either over 1 or 1 over itself. You need to make sure the units cancel out. Once you cancel the units you do the math in the same way that you do multiplication of fractions. You multiply the top numbers together, in this case $45 \times 5,280 \times 1 \times 1 = 237,600$, and the bottom numbers together, $1 \times 1 \times 60 \times 60 = 3,600$, and divide the top number by the bottom number. The result can be written over 1, or can be written in a more common form as 66 feet / second (fps).

Here are a few problems to try in which dimensional analysis would be useful:

_____**91.** If your truck is pumping water at 700 gallons per minute, how many gallons of water are pumped in 2 hours?

**Answer:** 84,000 gallons

_____**92.** Convert 250 feet per minute to miles per hour.

**Answer:** 2.84 miles per hour

_____**93.** If a grass fire burns a total of 320 acres of farmland, how many square miles of farmland were burned? (Hint : 1 acre = 43,560 square feet; a square mile is the same as a square that is 5,280 feet on each side)

**Answer:** $\frac{1}{2}$ square miles

# ▶ The Metric System

## What Is the Metric System?

The metric system, or Système International d'Unités (SI system as it is commonly known), is the predominant system of measurement in the world. In fact, the United States is one of only about three countries that do not commonly use the metric system. The metric system attempts to eliminate odd and often difficult-to-remember conversions for measurements (5,280 feet in a mile, for example). It is a decimal-based system with standard terminology for measurements of length, volume, and mass (weight). It also uses standard prefixes to measure multiples of the standard units.

The standard unit of length in the SI system is the meter. One meter equals about 3.048 ft. The standard unit of volume is the liter. One liter is a little over a quart. Soda has been sold in 2-liter bottles for many years in the United States, one of the few areas that the SI system has penetrated our daily lives. The standard unit of mass is the gram. Technically, mass and weight are not the same, however, this distinction tends to be ignored often in practice. One thousand grams is about 2.2 pounds.

## Prefixes

The most common prefixes used in medicine are kilo, which is 1,000 times the base unit, centi, which is 1/100 of the base unit, and milli, which is 1/1,000 times the base unit. These prefixes are attached to the base unit to give the multiple of the base unit being measured. Therefore, a kilogram is 1,000 grams. A centimeter is 1/100 of a meter. A milliliter is 1/1,000 of a liter.

## Common Use in Emergency Services

The SI system is used extensively in the medical field, including emergency medicine, in the United States. Drug dosages are typically measured in either grams or milligrams. Weight (mass) is reported in kilograms. Length such as a patient's height is measured in centimeters. Volumes of fluids are measured in either milliliters or liters, but can also be measured in cubic centimeters (cc). One cubic centimeter is the same as 1 milliliter.

There have been periodic attempts to convert the United States to the SI system. For example, in the 1990s, the federal government mandated that federally funded projects such as road construction projects have to use the SI system. This mandate was reversed after a few years. It is unlikely that a wholesale change to the SI system will occur in the United States in the foreseeable future.

## Conversions

There are two important conversions that you should remember between English units and the SI system. They are:

      1 pound = 2.2 kilograms

      1 inch = 2.54 centimeters

Volume conversions are not commonly used or needed.

When making these conversions in the field, it is often helpful to make approximations or estimates. One pound is a little more then 2 kilograms, so divide the persons weight in pounds by 2 and subtract an appropriate approximation for the decimal amount. For example, 176 pounds is 80 kilograms: 176/2 = 88. You can approximate to deduct about 8 kilograms for the 0.2 decimal and subtract it to get the result, which is 80. Refer back to the section on dimensional analysis. This technique is very helpful in many of these problems.

Practice using the SI prefixes and units and conversions below:

_____**94.**  300 milliliters = _____ liters

_____**95.**  1,200 grams = _____ kilograms

_____**96.**  350 millimeters = _____ centimeters

_____**97.**  170 pounds is about how many kilograms? _____

_____**98.**  65 kilograms is about how many pounds? _____

_____**99.**  A child who is 40 inches tall is about how many centimeters tall? _____

_____**100.** 2 feet is about how many millimeters (hint: use dimensional analysis)? _____

## Answers:

| | | | |
|---|---|---|---|
| **94.** | 0.3 | **98.** | 143 (140 would be a good estimate) |
| **95.** | 1.2 | **99.** | 1,016 (1,000 would be a good estimate) |
| **96.** | 35 | **100.** | 609.6 |
| **97.** | 77 (80 would be a good estimate) | | |
| | 100. 610 | | |

CHAPTER

# 9 ▶ Judgment and Reasoning

## CHAPTER SUMMARY

This chapter will familiarize you with questions on the firefighter exam that test your judgment and reasoning ability. It shows you a systematic approach to answering these questions, using sample questions as examples.

**F**irefighters have to be able to make sound judgments under pressure: Lives can and do depend on it. Firefighters who react without thinking endanger themselves, their fellow firefighters, and the people they are trying to protect. Judgment and reasoning questions on a firefighter exam are designed to measure your ability to use reason in firefighting situations. Judgment and reasoning questions ask you to play the game "What if?" If you were a firefighter in a given situation, what would you do? The fire department wants to know whether, given a certain set of job-related conditions, you can think on your feet, follow directions, take orders from superiors, and interact with the public. To arrive at the correct answer to this kind of question, you have to analyze a situation and use good judgment and common sense to arrive at a course of action.

## ▶ What Judgment and Reasoning Questions Are Like

Judgment and reasoning questions may be based on any number of different situations and are presented in varying formats. The following are examples of various kinds of judgment and reasoning questions as they may appear on the test.

- **Firefighting operations.** After a fire is extinguished, the water in the hose lines must be removed before the hose lines are repacked onto the fire truck. The best place to remove this water is. . . .
- **Firehouse routines.** Each shift, on arriving at the firehouse, performs a thorough inspection of the tools and equipment. Which of the following best expresses the reason for this procedure?
- **Public relations.** A man enters the firehouse and tells you he has locked his keys in the car with the ignition running. His puppy is in the car, and it is a very hot day. Which of the following should you do?
- **Interpersonal skills.** Your superior officer has asked you to give a car a summons for parking in a fire zone at a local shopping mall. When you get to the car, you recognize that it belongs to your neighbor. The best course of action for you to take is to. . . .

There may also be questions that test your ability to follow directions. You might, for instance, be given a list of procedures to follow in ventilating the roof of a fire building. You would then be given a situation in which a roof needs to be ventilated and be asked which step is the next one you should take, according to the procedure you read.

## ▶ A Systematic Approach to Judgment Questions

To answer judgment and reasoning questions, use decision-making techniques to help you think through the best course of action. Use a systematic approach:

1. **Read the question more than once.** Be sure you understand what is being asked. Look for and underline key words such as *all*, *always*, *every*, *never*, *except*, and *not*.

2. **Read all the answer choices.** Eliminate answers intelligently. Use common sense to rule out the choices that cannot possibly be correct. Try to use the information from the question to select the correct answer. When faced with two or more answers that seem correct, try to select the one that is *always* correct rather than the one that is only *sometimes* correct. Look for answers that are opposite; there is a good chance that one of these is correct.

3. **Make a decision.** After careful consideration, select the best possible choice.

4. **Reread the question.** Make absolutely certain that the answer you have chosen satisfies all conditions of the question.

### Watch for Tricky Wording

Use caution! There is more than one way to ask the same question, and the correct answer may depend on the way the question is worded. You might be asked to choose the *best* possible answer, but, on the other hand, you might instead be asked which choice is NOT correct or what would NOT be the best course of action. Each of these questions is based on the same situation, but choosing the correct answer depends on a careful reading of the way the question is worded:

■ While you are on your way to work, you see a gasoline truck with fluid apparently leaking from the rear tank. You suspect that the leak is gasoline but are not certain. **Which of the following actions is the most appropriate for you to take?**

■ While you are on your way to work, you see a gasoline truck with fluid apparently leaking from the rear tank. You suspect that the leak is gasoline but are not certain. **You would be correct in doing all of the following EXCEPT. . . .**

■ While you are on your way to work, you see a gasoline truck with fluid apparently leaking from the rear tank. You suspect that the leak is gasoline but are not certain. **Which of the following would NOT be the best course of action for you to take?**

In the first version of this question, you are simply being asked to choose the best course of action. In the other two versions, however, you must choose the least appropriate action. In these cases, three out of four answer choices are likely to be actions that would be more or less appropriate, whereas another—the correct answer—will be an inappropriate, perhaps dangerous or careless, thing you might do.

### Example: How to Use the Systematic Approach

This first sample question is followed by a step-by-step analysis that shows you how to use common sense and a systematic problem-solving approach to select the best possible answer. You might want to try working out the answer yourself before you read the explanation that follows.

1. While on your way to work, you see flames shooting out a second-floor window of a six-story apartment building. What should you do?
   a. Immediately evacuate the building.
   b. Proceed to work and report the fire as soon as you get there.
   c. Ignore the fire because you are not yet on duty.
   d. Report the fire at the nearest phone and then try to evacuate the building.

Here's how to use the systematic approach to answer the question.

1. **Read the question carefully.** What is the question asking? Stated simply, the question is asking, "What would you do if you saw a building on fire?"
2. **Read all the answer choices.** Read and evaluate each answer choice, eliminating choices that are clearly wrong.
   a. "Immediately evacuate the building." Common sense tells you that getting the people out of a burning building is a good course of action. Your reaction may save the lives of the people inside the building. This sounds like a possible answer.
   b. "Proceed to work and report the fire as soon as you get there." It is never a good idea to delay reporting a fire. There may be people who need help. Obviously this is not a good option, so eliminate it.
   c. "Ignore the fire because you are not yet on duty." A building fire should never be ignored. The fact that you are not on duty is irrelevant: As a firefighter, on or off duty, you are sworn to protect the public. Discard this option as well.
   d. "Report the fire at the nearest phone and then try to evacuate the building." Reporting the fire would bring help from other firefighters, as well as equipment for rescuing the occupants. After that, evacuating the building will save lives, due

to your quick response and sure knowledge. This appears to be a very good choice.

3. **Make a decision.** You eliminated options **b** and **c.** Now you should review choices **a** and **d.** They are very similar to each other, but choice **d** is the better answer because you are getting the proper help and equipment to the scene of the fire as well as trying to remove the residents from the building on fire. It is therefore the most correct answer.

4. **Reread the question.** Once you have made a decision, review the question to make sure the answer you have chosen meets the conditions set out in the situation. Sure enough, choice **d** represents the best course of action for an off-duty firefighter who sees a building fire.

You will get more practice in using this kind of systematic approach as you read the sections that follow on the types of situations and questions you might encounter in a judgment and reasoning section of the firefighter exam.

## ▶ Questions on Firefighting Operations

The most frequently asked questions require candidates to place themselves in the position of a firefighter at the scene of a fire or emergency. In answering a question of this type, you must consider a firefighter's priorities: saving lives, preserving property, and extinguishing the fire. In any emergency situation, the safety of responders and civilians is the first priority. All operations are conducted under the Incident Command System, which ensures a chain of command in which response is structured and measured.

Keep these priorities in mind as you try to answer these sample questions on firefighting operations.

2. A fire company responds to a report of a multi-vehicle accident. When they arrive on the scene, they see that one car is turned upside-down with at least two civilians trapped inside. The other car seems to have less damage; however, it is leaking what appears to be gasoline. What should they do?
   a. Set up a hose line as a protection for rescue personnel and trapped civilians.
   b. Immediately remove the trapped civilians from their car.
   c. Disregard the gasoline, since nothing is currently on fire.
   d. Call for a tow truck.

Good judgment and common sense should enable you to eliminate choice **c.** You should also reject choice **d,** since it does not address the urgency of the situation. Choice **b** may be appealing at first; however, you should consider the whole situation. A gasoline leak always raises the possibility of a fire or an explosion, which could injure not only the people trapped in the car but also you and your fellow firefighters. The safety of all concerned should be your first priority. Keeping this principle in mind, you should eliminate choice **b** and pick **a** instead. Setting up a standby hose line, charged with water and ready to go, will protect the responders and the trapped civilians.

Now try another question, this one based on more routine operations. Remember, safety is still a firefighter's first concern.

3. Firefighters must do inspections of any buildings, hospitals, factories, and schools in their area. They check the premises for any violations of fire safety regulations. All of the following should be checked for violations EXCEPT the
   a. automatic sprinkler system.
   b. electrical wires and outlets.
   c. fire extinguishers.
   d. food safety measures.

The first thing you should notice when you read the question is that word *EXCEPT*. It tells you to look for something that the firefighters will *not* check for violations as the answer.

The correct answer is choice **d**. The firefighters would check all of the other choices when they do an inspection, keeping in mind that people's safety can depend on the proper functioning of sprinkler systems, electrical wires and outlets, and fire extinguishers.

## ▶ Questions on Firehouse Routine

If equipment that is used in fighting fires does not work properly, lives may be lost. Thus, firefighters have to check and maintain their equipment and apparatus, usually at the firehouse at the beginning of each shift. Some questions on the firefighter exam may ask questions about the routine of examining and maintaining equipment.

Even though the operations described in these questions are routine, the firefighter's priorities of life, property, and extinguishment, as well as safety and authority, are still paramount. For this reason, firefighters follow specific procedures in maintaining equipment and always replace damaged equipment or bring it to the attention of superior officers. Keeping that in mind, try to answer the following sample questions.

**4.** At the beginning of each shift, the power saw must be filled with gasoline and tested to make sure it works properly. The best reason for this requirement is that it
   **a.** gives the firefighters something to do every day.
   **b.** makes the firefighters' job easier than if they waited until the tank was empty.
   **c.** ensures that the power saw is ready for maximum use if needed at a fire.
   **d.** ensures that the power saw is always ready for inspection by the fire chief.

You can eliminate choices **a** and **b** because they do not give good common sense reasons for this procedure. And while it is true that the chief may order an inspection of equipment at any time, choice **d** is not the best reason, either. That leaves choice **c** as the best answer. If a tool is not ready to be used on arrival at the scene of an emergency, people's lives may be at risk.

Try your hand at another question based on routine procedures.

**5.** When a fire truck is leaving or returning to the firehouse, firefighters are required to stand on the street, one on the sidewalk and one inside the station. Which of the following is the most important reason for following this procedure?
   **a.** to let the neighbors know that the firefighters are leaving so that the neighbors will watch the station while they are gone
   **b.** to let pedestrians and automobiles know the truck is moving and to guide the truck's driver
   **c.** to test the truck's lights and sirens before leaving the station to make sure they work efficiently
   **d.** to give the firefighters time to get dressed and to show the neighborhood how their tax money is being used

You can eliminate choices **a** and **d** pretty quickly, because they do not use good judgment or common sense. Choice **c** looks a little better, but common sense should tell you that the moment the truck is leaving for a fire is not a good time to run an equipment check; anyway, the lights and siren shouldn't have to be checked every time the truck leaves or enters.

Choice **b** is the best answer. For their safety and the safety of others, firefighters stand outside in the street and on the sidewalk to warn motorists and pedestrians that the truck is in motion. The firefighter standing inside the firehouse helps to guide the truck's driver as the truck backs into the station.

## ► Public Relations Questions

Another part of exercising good judgment and common sense involves dealing with the public. Firefighters hold a position of public trust and must act in a manner consistent with such a position. People must feel they can call on firefighters for help. Children should be able to look up to firefighters as role models and protectors. Although firefighters cannot be expected to know and do everything, they can be and are expected to treat civilians with respect at all times. Keep these ideas in mind as you try some sample questions.

**6.** A neighborhood woman enters the firehouse and asks Firefighter Ross to cut down a tree in her yard because it is too close to the utility lines. She claims that this is a fire hazard and that, therefore, he should handle it. He should
   **a.** get the ax and chop down the tree.
   **b.** tell her to call her utility company so that they can handle the problem properly.
   **c.** refuse her request but tell her his brother will do it for $50.00.
   **d.** tell her to stop bothering the fire department unless there is a fire.

Good judgment and common sense, not to mention common courtesy, should lead you to eliminate choices **c** and **d** as inappropriate responses. The problem-solving approach should help you to reason that choice **a** is not appropriate. If you chop down a tree near utility lines, the tree or the lines may cause injury to yourself or others. Because this choice does not show concern for safety, it can also be eliminated.

The best possible answer is, thus, choice **b**. A firefighter must always be polite and courteous to the public. An explanation of why the utility company is best suited to help her allows the citizen to understand your actions. Though it would be unsafe for you to do as the citizen asks, you have still taken responsibility for the request and helped in the best way possible.

Using what you know about firefighters' priorities and concern for the public, try another question:

**7.** A company arrives at the scene of a house fire with a response time of approximately five minutes. The owner of the house, however, begins to yell that his house and possessions are burning and that it has been half an hour since he called the fire department. The best response for a firefighter to give would be to
   **a.** tell the man to get control of himself; he is getting hysterical.
   **b.** explain that the response time was only five minutes and assure the man that the company will do the best they can to save his house and possessions.
   **c.** ignore the man and begin working on putting out the fire.
   **d.** tell the man he should not have been so careless in the first place, so the fire company would not have to be there putting out this fire.

The best answer is choice **b**. You need to explain to the citizen the procedures for receiving and responding to a call, as well as reassuring him that you want to prevent as much damage as possible. Your explanation will help the man understand that you are really doing all you can to help him, so that he may feel better and respect the job you are doing. Choices **a**, **c**, and **d** are not acceptable answers because they do not treat the citizen with respect. A firefighter must always be courteous and polite to the public, especially in a crisis situation when people may react inappropriately because of the stress they are under.

## ▶ Questions on Interpersonal Relations

The firefighters in a station house work as a dedicated team, entrusting their lives to one another. They also operate within a hierarchical structure. In this structure, they treat their superiors with the utmost respect, valuing their experience and knowledge. Judgment and reasoning questions that deal with interpersonal relations stress respect for authority, dedication to all firefighters, and responsibility for one's actions.

8. While replacing the hose on the fire engine toward the end of her shift, Firefighter Evans drops the nozzle and thinks it may be damaged. She should
   a. do nothing because she knows the nozzle is expensive to replace.
   b. report the damage to her superior officer so he or she can get a new one.
   c. choose not to worry about it since her shift is almost over.
   d. try to blame it on someone else so she will not get in trouble.

Keeping safety and the well-being of other firefighters in mind should enable you to eliminate choices **a**, **c**, and **d** immediately. Firefighters should never allow damaged equipment to be used, because injury can result. Firefighters must also be honest, responsible, and concerned for the safety of their fellow firefighters. Choice **b** is the only choice that shows these characteristics.

9. A firefighter enters an apartment to search for victims. While she is in the apartment, the fire spreads and blocks the stairs. The apartment is on the fifth floor and has no fire escape. What should the firefighter do?
   a. She should call for other firefighters to assist her.
   b. She should jump from the window and hope she lands on something soft.
   c. She should take the stairs one flight up to the next floor.
   d. She should wait for the fire to die down, so she can use the stairs.

Choice **a** is the best answer. All firefighters work as a team. Each firefighter who goes into a fire building knows that he or she can count on the other members to come to his or her aid. Choice **b** does not use good judgment. Choice **c** is not possible because the question clearly states that the stairs are blocked by the fire. Choice **d** is not an intelligent choice and also shows lack of teamwork.

## ▶ Questions on Following Procedures

A good firefighter has the ability to follow directions. Firefighters must follow detailed written procedures or verbal orders for everything from operating at building fires to equipment maintenance. Some firefighter exams include another kind of judgment question, one that tests your ability to follow a set of written procedures or orders to the letter.

In this kind of question, the examiners provide you with a set of directions for completing a firehouse assignment or operating at a fire scene. The directions might, for instance, provide step-by-step instructions for loading hoses on the apparatus or specify the uses and location of tools.

The list of procedures is then followed by one or more questions that ask you something about the order of the steps in the list. The answers to these questions rely less on your judgment, as in the previous types, than on your ability to read and understand the procedures. So it is important to read the procedure carefully. There may be certain conditions that have to be met before you would take a particular step; if they are not met, you would have to skip that step and go to the next. Key words to look for in this type of question are:

- "What would you do *next*?" In this case, you have to find the answer that is the next step in the procedure.
- "What did you do *before* . . . ?" In this case, you have to find the last step completed immediately *before* the step you are on now in the list of procedures.

The most important thing to remember in answering this kind of question is not to make assumptions. Instead, follow the procedure and apply the information in the procedure to the question. You will see how this process works as you go through the sample questions that follow.

Questions 10–12 refer to the following procedure.

Firefighters must often move injured or unconscious victims to get them out of danger and to a location where they can receive proper medical attention. As a firefighter, you should carry out the following steps in the order listed to properly move a victim.

1. Check to make sure there is no immediate danger to you or the victim.
2. Provide support for the victim's neck and spine.
3. Avoid bending or twisting the victim's body.
4. If at all possible, and if there is no danger to the firefighter or the victim, remain in place until additional assistance can arrive.

5. Lift the victim to a sitting position, using your knees, not your back.
6. If you are alone, drag the victim to safety, keeping the victim's body straight while protecting the victim's head and back.
7. If there are two people, use a two-handed seat carry.

10. Firefighter Ali is searching an apartment that is smoky but apparently not on fire. He finds an unconscious woman on the floor in the kitchen. He has supported the woman's neck and spine. What should he do next?
    a. Drag the woman to safety, keeping her body straight.
    b. Avoid bending or twisting the woman's body.
    c. Lift the woman to a sitting position, using his knees, not his back.
    d. Use a two-handed seat carry to remove the woman from the apartment.

The key word in the question is *next*. Reviewing the procedure, you should see that the next step after supporting the woman's neck and spine is to keep the woman's body from bending or twisting, choice **b**. The other choices do not immediately follow supporting the neck and spine.

Use the same process to arrive at the answer to another question based on the same procedure.

11. A company responds to an apartment fire. Firefighter Mendoza is alone when she finds a man unconscious on the floor. Seeing that the fire is under control, she supports the man's neck and spine and then lifts him to a sitting position without twisting his body. She determines that it is unsafe to remain in the room. What should she do next?
    a. Use a two-handed seat carry.
    b. Check to make sure there is no immediate danger to her or the victim.

c. Provide support for the man's neck and spine.

d. Drag the man, keeping his body straight.

The correct choice is **d**. The procedure tells you that when you are alone, you should drag the victim to safety, keeping the body straight. The two-handed seat carry (choice **a**) is used when there are two rescuers. The other two choices are steps that she has already accomplished, according to the situation described in the question.

**12.** A fellow firefighter has injured his ankle while climbing the stairs in a house fire. As there is no immediate danger, Firefighter Moe calls another firefighter to help him. How would they remove the injured firefighter?

a. Use a two-handed seat carry to remove the firefighter from the house.

b. Avoid bending or twisting the firefighter's body.

c. Provide support for the firefighter's neck and spine.

d. Lift the firefighter to a sitting position and drag him to safety.

The correct answer is **a** because the procedure states that, when there are two people, you should use a two-handed seat carry. The other choices are steps in the procedure that are unnecessary in the given situation.

Now try your hand at another set of questions based on a different procedure.

Questions 13–15 refer to the following procedure.

Firefighters inspect buildings for any violations of the fire safety laws. There are specific steps used when conducting an inspection. They are listed below.

1. Locate the building manager and inform him or her that you are here to inspect the premises.

2. Inspect the exits. Make sure that all doors are working properly and are not locked or blocked. Make sure that exit signs are posted above each door.

3. Check the public hallway. Ensure that it is free from accumulations of rubbish.

4. Fire extinguishers should be fully charged and properly placed.

5. Test the fire escape. It should be sturdy and in good repair.

6. Check the automatic sprinkler systems.

7. Check for the storage of flammable materials.

8. Visually examine the premises for improper wiring.

**13.** On arriving at a building to inspect, Firefighter Fox informs the building manager that she is here for the annual fire safety inspection. What should she do next?

a. Make sure there is no trash blocking the public hallway.

b. Check for the storage of flammable materials.

c. Check the doors to ensure that they work properly.

d. Make sure the fire escape is sturdy and in good repair.

Read the question, and then return to the building inspection procedure. The question states that she has met with the building manager and asks what she will do next. The key word is *next*. According to the question, she has accomplished step 1. Step 2 is to inspect the exits, so choice **c** is the answer.

**14.** The inspection of a building is almost complete. What is the last thing a firefighter should do before leaving the premises?

a. Look at the wiring.

b. Check the automatic sprinkler systems.

**c.** Ensure that the fire extinguishers are fully charged.

**d.** Tell the building manager that he is here to inspect the premises.

This time you have been asked what the last step in the inspection is. The key word is *last*. The last step given in the procedure is to visually examine the premises for improper wiring. Thus, the answer is choice **a**.

**15.** In a building inspection, a firefighter has found that the doors are satisfactory and exit signs are properly posted. What should he or she check next?
  **a.** the automatic sprinkler
  **b.** the public hallway
  **c.** the roof
  **d.** the fire escape

The key word, once again, is *next*. You have accomplished step 2 and should go on to step 3, the public hallway, which is choice **b**. Notice that choice **c**, the roof, does not appear anywhere in the inspection procedure, so it should have been easy to eliminate that choice immediately.

## ▶ Logical Reasoning Questions

Firefighters have the ability to analyze and reason. A good firefighter must use analytical and logical reasoning skills when making important decisions. Therefore, firefighter exams sometimes include questions that test critical thinking.

Analytical and logical reasoning questions take many different forms: number series, sequences, analogies, and logic problems are just some of them.

## Series and Sequences

Use your reasoning abilities as you try to answer the following sample questions.

**16.** Look at this series: 1, 1, 5, __, 9, 9, 13, . . .
  What number should fill the blank?
  **a.** 3
  **b.** 5
  **c.** 9
  **d.** 17

Number series, letter series, and sequence questions measure your ability to reason without words. To answer these questions you must determine the pattern in each one. In each number series, look for the degree and direction of change between the numbers. In other words, do the numbers increase or decrease, and by how much? In question 16, the numbers repeat once and then increase by 4. Notice also that this question asks you to fill in the blank, not to add to the end of the series. Since the number 5 is repeated once, the answer is choice **b**.

## Analogies

Another type of logical reasoning question is the verbal analogy. In an analogy, two sets of words are related to each other in a specific and similar way. Verbal analogies will test your ability to see these word relationships.

**17.** Aspirin is to headache as bandage is to
  **a.** injection.
  **b.** fracture.
  **c.** accident.
  **d.** wound.

The correct answer is choice **d**, *wound*. This is a use or function analogy; in both sets of words—*aspirin* and *headache*, *bandage* and *wound*—something is used for something else. *Aspirin* is used to treat a *headache*,

Judgment and reasoning questions are used to see how you would approach situations you may face as a firefighter on a day-to-day basis. Potential firefighters are expected to be sharp, safety conscious, respectful, and professional. When answering judgment and reasoning questions:

- Read the question slowly, and more than once if needed, so that you will understand what the question is asking as well as the scenario given to you.
- Look for key words that direct you to the correct answers.
- Read each answer carefully. Use common sense to eliminate answers that are clearly wrong.
- When faced with more than one answer you haven't been able to eliminate, choose the best answer by reasoning out the situation.
- Reread the question to be sure the answer you chose uses sound judgment.

a *bandage* is used to treat a *wound*. All the other choices in this question are loosely associated with injury, but the best answer is clearly choice **d**.

A good way to figure out the relationship in a given analogy question is to make up a sentence. You must first read each question carefully, as it is easy to mistake one kind of analogy for another. Formulating a sentence that expresses the relationship is the best way to avoid this mistake. Take question 17 as an example. The following are sentences you might make when approaching this analogy:

- *Aspirin* is used to treat a *headache*. A *bandage* is used to treat an *injection*? No. As soon as you say the sentence, you know that choice **a** is wrong. So you must try again.
- A *bandage* is used to treat a *fracture*. Again, no. A fracture requires a cast; a bandage won't help.
- A *bandage* is used to treat an *accident*. No, once again. A bandage might treat a person who has been in an accident, but it will not treat the accident itself.
- A *bandage* is used to treat a *wound*. Yes, of course. Your sentence tells you this is the right choice.

## Logic

Next, try this logic problem:

**18.** During the past year, Zoe read more books than Heather.

Jane read fewer books than Heather.

Jane read more books than Zoe.

If the first two statements are true, the third statement is

**a.** true.

**b.** false.

**c.** uncertain.

Logic problems may appear daunting at first. However, solving these problems can be done in the most straightforward way. These problems can often be solved by writing out the information using math formulas. This may allow the relationships between the information in the question to be seen more easily. For question 18, there are three individuals noted: Zoe, Jane, and Heather. Write out the information in the question as math formulas. Recall the math symbols for greater than ($<$) and less than ($>$). The open part of the symbol is always in the direction of the larger value, such as $10 > 7$ or $7 < 10$. Using this technique, the information in the question can be written like this:

Zoe > Heather (or Z > H)
Jane < Heather (or J < H); this is the same as
Heather > Jane
Jane > Zoe (or J > Z)

If the first two statements are true as the question states, Zoe would be greater than Jane because Zoe is greater then Heather and Heather is greater than Jane (remember that you can write this relationship either way as long as you turn the symbol around). Using this logic, the third statement that Jane > Zoe is obviously false.

A similar technique can be used on logic questions that involve numbers. Try this problem:

**19.** Kyle has twice as many marbles as Stan. Stan has a third as many marbles as Eric. If Eric has 21 marbles, how many does Kyle have?

   a.   25
   b.   14
   c.   7

To solve this type of problem, write out the known information using math formulas:

$K = 2 \times S$ (Kyle has twice as many marbles as Stan)
$S = E / 3$ (Stan has 1/3 as many marbles as Eric)
$E = 21$ (Eric has 21 marbles)

You can now use these fairly simple formulas to solve the problem. To find out how many marbles Stan has, plug 21 into the value for E in the second formula:

$S = 21 / 3 = 7$; Stan has 7 marbles

Plug that answer into the first formula to find how many marbles Kyle has:

$K = 2 \times 7 = 14$; Kyle has 14 marbles

Choice **b** is correct. Using these simple math techniques for logic problems can make them much clearer and easier to follow.

# 10 ▶ Mechanical Aptitude

## CHAPTER SUMMARY

Mechanical aptitude is tested on many firefighter exams. This chapter will familiarize you with commonly tested concepts by presenting definitions, study tips, and sample test questions for basic mechanical devices and systems.

Firefighters use mechanical devices every day: simple hand tools such as axes and wrenches, as well as more complex systems such as pumps and internal combustion engines. The ability to understand and use mechanical concepts is critical to a firefighter's job.

If your exam includes a section on mechanical aptitude, it may cover topics with which you are very familiar, as well as some that are new. Regardless of your background, understanding the concepts in this chapter will benefit you both during the exam and in your career as a firefighter. After an introduction to mechanical aptitude questions, this chapter summarizes some of the most commonly tested mechanical devices and mechanical systems. It also suggests ways in which you can further improve your knowledge of mechanical devices and related scientific and mathematical knowledge. Finally, it gives you an opportunity to review what you have learned by presenting a sample mechanical aptitude section like those found on firefighter exams.

## ▶ What Mechanical Aptitude Questions Are Like

Mechanical aptitude questions tend to cover a wide range of topics. The questions will usually be multiple choice with four or five possible answers. Some questions may require previous knowledge of the topic—so it is a good idea to study this chapter well! Other questions will include all of the information you will need.

Some questions will require the identification of various mechanical tools or devices. Some of the types of mechanical devices that may appear on the exam—and covered in this chapter—include hand tools, gears, pulleys, levers, fasteners, springs, valves, gauges, and pumps. In addition to individual mechanical devices, the exam may test your knowledge of various systems, or combinations of mechanical devices. A common example of a mechanical system is the internal combustion engine of an automobile.

A typical mechanical aptitude question will look something like this:

Which of the following is a common component of an internal combustion engine?
**a.** a piston
**b.** a compass
**c.** a hammer
**d.** a hydraulic jack

The answer is **a**, a piston. A compass is used to determine a direction on a map. A hammer is used to drive nails. A hydraulic jack is used to lift heavy items.

## ▶ Definition: What Is a Mechanical Device?

A mechanical device is a tool designed to make a given task easier. For example, you could drive a nail into a piece of wood with a rock. However, a long time ago, someone who spent a lot of time building things with wood figured out that it would be a lot more efficient to use something that was easier to hold on to than a rock. He or she thought that a long slender handle might be nice, and that a hard piece of metal for striking the nail would provide more accuracy and not damage the wood as easily. Thus, the hammer was born.

Most mechanical devices were invented in the same manner: People looking for easier ways to perform their everyday jobs. Some mechanical devices are thousands of years old, such as the lever, the wheel, and many hand tools. Other more complex devices, such as pumps and valves, were invented more recently. Many times, the idea of a new mechanical device exists but the technology to make it does not. For example, many years before the pump was invented, people probably discussed the need for an easier way to move water from the river to the town on the hill. However, the technology for casting metal had not yet been invented, so the pump could not possibly have been invented at that time.

Mechanical devices cover a wide range of types of tools. In general, they are tools that relate to physical work and are governed by mechanical forces and movements. You can usually see what they do and how they work—as opposed to, say, a light switch or a battery, which are electrical devices. Some tools are used to directly accomplish a specific task, as when you use a hand saw to cut a piece of wood. Others, such as pulleys and gears, may be used indirectly to accomplish certain tasks that would be possible without the device but are easier with it. Still others, such as gauges, only provide feedback information on the operation of other mechanical devices. You see and use mechanical devices many times each day, so there is no reason to be intimidated by a mechanical aptitude section on the exam.

## ► Commonly Tested Mechanical Devices

The following sections review some of the mechanical devices that are most likely to appear on firefighter exams.

### Hand Tools

Hand tools are defined as tools operated not by motors but rather by human power. There are many different types of hand tools, including carpentry tools, automotive hand tools, and hand tools used specifically by firefighters. This chapter cannot cover every conceivable hand tool, so it will be limited to tools used in everyday situations and those specific to firefighting—the ones you are most likely to be tested on.

Some of the hand tools used by carpenters and other workers, including firefighters, are listed in the table on pages 196–197, along with their most common uses and some examples of each kind.

Hand tools used in the fire and rescue service are often classified by their main function or their size. In general, a large hand tool would not fit in a standard tool box, whereas a small hand tool would. Most fire apparatus carries a supply of standard, everyday small hand tools such as wrenches, screwdrivers, and hammers. These tools are used for a variety of purposes. For example, if a fire occurs in an electrical breaker box, firefighters will need wrenches or screwdrivers to disassemble the box to check if the fire is out.

Many common larger hand tools have uses in the fire service. Automotive jacks and high-lift jacks are used in vehicle rescue to stabilize cars and trucks. Sledgehammers are used in forcible entry as well as in other applications. Tools such as axes and ladders have obvious uses in the fire service, although the versions of these tools used for fire service are typically heavier or have greater capacity than domestic models. For example, fire service ladders have much greater capac-ity than a ladder you may have in your home, and are much heavier.

Specialty tools are often classified by the main function they serve. Some examples are pulling tools such as hooks or pike poles, and prying tools such as pry bars. Some tools also have secondary uses. An axe is normally used for cutting; however, a flat-head axe can also be used as a striking tool to drive another tool.

### Gears

A gear is generally a toothed wheel or cylinder that meshes with another toothed element to transmit motion or to change speed or direction. Gears are typically attached to a rotating shaft turned by an outside energy source such as an electric motor or an internal combustion engine. Gears are used in many mechanical devices, including automotive transmissions, carpenter's hand drills, elevator lifting mechanisms, bicycles, and carnival rides such as Ferris wheels and merry-go-rounds.

Gears can be used in several different configurations. Two gears may be connected by directly touching each other, as in an automotive transmission. In this arrangement, one gear spins clockwise and the other rotates counterclockwise. Another possible configuration is to have two gears connected by a loop of chain, as on a bicycle. In this arrangement, the first gear rotates in one direction, causing the chain to move. Because the chain is directly connected to the second gear, the second gear will immediately begin to rotate in the same direction as the first gear.

Many times a system will use two gears of different sizes, as on a ten-speed bicycle. This will allow changes in speed of the bicycle or machine.

Problems about gears will always involve rotation or spinning. The easiest way to approach test questions that involve gears is to draw a diagram of what the question is describing, if one is not already provided.

## HAND TOOLS

| TOOL | DESCRIPTION/FUNCTION | EXAMPLES |
|---|---|---|
| Hammer | used primarily to drive and remove nails, as well as to pound on devices such as chisels | claw hammer, rubber mallet, ball-peen hammer |
| Saw | thin metal blade with a sharp-toothed edge used to cut wood or metal | handsaw, hacksaw, jigsaw |
| Screwdriver | used to tighten and loosen screws and bolts | slotted head (single groove or slot), Phillips head (two grooves or slots crossing at 90°) |
| Level | a tool of varying length (made of wood, plastic, or a metal beam) that contains calibrated air bubble tube or tubes, used to ensure that work is vertically plumb or horizontally level (Note: Newer leveling devices make use of laser technology and electronics and may be handheld devices that do the same job.) | hand level, laser level |
| Square | used primarily to aid in drawing a cut line on a board to ensure a straight, 90° cut | L-square, T-square |
| Plane | metal tool with a handle and an adjustable blade, used to shave off thin strips of wood for the purpose of smoothing or leveling | block plane, various sizes of carpenter's planes |
| Chisel | metal tool with a sharp, beveled edge that is struck with a hammer to cut and shape stone, metal, or wood | scoop chisel, beveled chisel, masonry chisel, cold chisel |
| Protractor | half-circle with tick marks around the edge spaced at one-degree intervals, used to measure angles | only one type, made of metal or plastic |
| C-clamp | C-shaped metallic instrument with a threaded stop that can be adjusted to clamp together pieces of material of different thicknesses | furniture clamps, many types and sizes of metallic C-clamps |

| HAND TOOLS | | |
|---|---|---|
| **TOOL** | **DESCRIPTION/FUNCTION** | **EXAMPLES** |
| Compass | instruments of two general types (made of wood, plastic, or metal) used to draw circles; both types use a pin with a sharp point on one leg, which is used to mark the center point, and the other leg has a pencil, pen, or chalk attached to mark the circumference of the circle. The first type of compass is a V-shaped instrument with two legs attached at the top; the second type, sometimes called a "beam compass," has two adjustable legs with a screw or clamp to hold the two legs in place along the length of the beam. | a number of types exist |

Use arrows next to each gear to indicate which direction (clockwise or counterclockwise) it is rotating.

## Pulleys

A pulley consists of a wheel with a grooved rim in which a pulled rope or cable is run. Pulleys are commonly used with ropes or steel cable to change the direction of a pulling force or to add mechanical advantage.

Pulleys are often used to lift things. For instance, a pulley could be attached to the ceiling of a room. A rope could be run from the floor, up through the pulley, and back down to a box sitting on the floor. The pulley would allow you to pull down on the rope and cause the box to go up. That is, the pulley causes a change in direction of the pulling force.

Another common use for a pulley is to connect an electric motor to a mechanical device such as a pump. One pulley is placed on the shaft of the motor, and a second pulley is placed on the shaft of the pump. A belt is used to connect the two pulleys. When the motor is turned on, the first pulley rotates and causes the belt to rotate, which in turn causes the second pulley to rotate and turn the pump. This arrangement is very similar to the previous example of a bicycle chain and gears.

You may have seen pulleys used in a warehouse to lift heavy loads. Another use for a pulley is on a large construction crane. The cable extends from the object being lifted up to the top of the crane boom, across a pulley, and back down to the electric winch that is used to pull on the cable. In this situation, the pulley again causes a change in direction of the pulling force, from the downward force of the winch that pulls the cable to the upward movement of the object being lifted.

## Levers

A lever is a very old mechanical device. A lever typically consists of a metal or wooden bar that pivots on a fixed point. The object of using a lever is to gain a mechanical advantage. Mechanical advantage results when you use a mechanical device to make a task easier; that is, you gain an advantage by using a mechanical device. A lever allows you to complete a task, typically lifting, that would be more difficult or impossible without the lever.

The most common example of a lever is a playground seesaw. A force (a person's weight) is applied to one side of the lever, which causes the weight on the other side (the other person) to be lifted. However, since the pivot point on a seesaw is in the center, each person must weigh the same or things do not work well. A seesaw is a lever with no mechanical advantage. If you push down on one side with a weight of 10 pounds, you can only lift a maximum of 10 pounds on the other side. This is no great advantage.

This brings us to the secret of the lever: To lift an object that is heavier than the force you want to apply to the other side of the lever, you must locate the pivot point closer to the object you want to lift. If two 50-pound children sit close to the center of the seesaw, one 50-pound child close to the end of the board on the other side will be able to lift them both.

Test questions about levers will typically require a bit of math (multiplication and division) to solve the problem. There is one simple concept that you must understand to solve lever problems: The product of the weight to be lifted times the distance from the weight to the pivot point must be equal to the product of the lifting force times the distance from the force to the pivot point. Stated as an equation: $w \times d_1 = f \times d_2$.

For example, Bill has a 15-foot long lever, and he wants to lift a 100-pound box. If he locates the pivot point 5 feet from the box, leaving 10 feet between the pivot point and the other end of the lever where he will apply the lifting force, how hard must he press on the lever to lift the box?

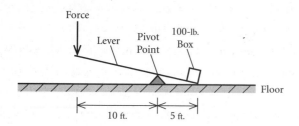

Use the lever formula, $w \times d_1 = f \times d_2$. The weight of 100 pounds times 5 feet must equal 10 feet times the force: $100 \times 5 = 10 \times force$. Using multiplication and division

to solve for the force, you get 50 pounds of force that Bill must apply to the lever to lift the box.

## Fasteners

A mechanical fastener is any mechanical device or process used to connect two or more items together. Typical examples of fastening devices are bolts, screws, nails, and rivets. Processes can be used to mechanically join items together, including gluing and welding. There are also unique mechanical fasteners such as "hook and loop," which consist of two tapes of material with many small plastic hooks and loops that stick together. Hook and eye fastening tape—Velcro©—is the most common fastener used on firefighters' turnout gear, part of the complete personal protective equipment that protects firefighters from exposure to the products of combustion.

## Springs

A spring is an elastic mechanical device, normally a coil of wire, that returns to its original shape after being compressed or extended. There are many types of springs, including the compression coil, spiral coil, flat spiral, extension coil, leaf spring, and torsional spring.

Springs are used for many applications such as car suspensions (compression coil and leaf springs), garage doors (extension coil and torsion springs), wind-up clocks (flat spiral and torsion springs), and some styles of ballpoint pens (compression coil).

In the kinds of questions you are likely to be asked on the firefighter exam, you can assume that springs behave linearly. That is, if an extension spring stretches one inch under a pull of ten pounds, then it will stretch two inches under a pull of 20 pounds. In real life, if you pull too hard on a spring, it will not return to its original shape. This is called exceeding the spring's elastic limit. Your exam is not likely to deal with this type of spring behavior.

If several springs are used for one application, they can be arranged in one of two ways—in series or in parallel. The easiest way to remember the difference is that if the springs are all hooked together, end to end, then you have a series of springs. The other option is for the springs not to be hooked together but to be lined up side by side, parallel to each other. If two springs are arranged in series, they will stretch much farther than the same two springs arranged in parallel under the same pulling force. This is because in series, the total pulling force passes through both springs. If the same springs are arranged in parallel, the pulling force is divided equally with half going through each spring.

*Springs in Series:*

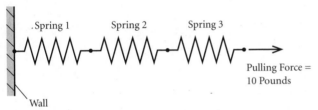

*Springs in Parallel:*

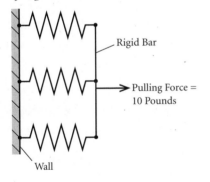

The key to solving spring problems is to draw a diagram of the arrangement, if one isn't already provided, and follow the pulling force through the system.

## Valves

A valve is a mechanical device that controls the flow of liquids, gases, or loose material through piping systems. There are many types of valves, including butterfly valves, gate valves, plug valves, ball valves, and check valves.

A valve is basically a gate that can be closed or opened to permit the fluid or gas to travel in a particular direction. The type of exam question you are likely to see that involves valves will be one in which you must follow a piping flow diagram through several sets of valves. These problems are best approached by taking your time and methodically following each branch of the piping system from start to finish.

## Gauges

Gauges are used to monitor the various conditions and performance of mechanical machines such as pumps and internal combustion engines, as well as to monitor the surrounding atmospheric conditions, which could indirectly affect a particular machine.

Gauges are usually marked with the *units* they are measuring. A few examples of different types of units are:

- degrees Celsius or Fahrenheit for temperature gauges
- pounds per square inch (psi) for pressure gauges
- meters (or sometimes feet) for elevation gauges

You must be very careful to recognize and understand the units of a gauge that appear in a test question. For instance, a temperature gauge (commonly called a thermometer) could use either degrees Fahrenheit or degrees Celsius. Mistakes on units can cause major problems, so be careful! The table on page 200 shows some common types of gauges, what they measure, and the kind of units they use.

Gauges are sometimes marked with warnings about limits of safe operation. Most gauges on fire apparatus are now color coded, and many newer pieces of apparatus are equipped with digital gauges with audible warnings. For instance, an oil pressure gauge on an internal combustion engine may show a maximum safe working pressure of 15 psi. If you are asked about the safe

| ATMOSPHERIC GAUGES | | |
|---|---|---|
| **GAUGE** | **WHAT IT MEASURES** | **UNITS** |
| Thermometer | temperature; commonly used on fire apparatus to determine engine, pump, and hydraulics temperature to ensure proper operation | degrees Fahrenheit or Celsius |
| Barometer | atmospheric pressure; in the fire service, this is used at wildland fires to detect pressure changes that could show local wind shifts and is a basic component of the pressure gauges on the pump | inches or millimeters of mercury |
| Hygrometer | relative humidity; used in wildland firefighting to determine the amount of moisture in the atmosphere and therefore in the fuel | percentage of water in air |

| MACHINE PERFORMANCE GAUGES | | |
|---|---|---|
| **GAUGE** | **WHAT IT MEASURES** | **UNITS** |
| Speedometer | velocity; used on all fire apparatus to determine speed | miles per hour (mph) or kilometers per hour (kph) |
| Tachometer | speed of rotation for equipment such as pumps, internal combustion engines, or fans; an important gauge for fire engines pumping water to prevent engine overspeed | revolutions per minute (rpm) |
| Pressure gauge | internal pressure; on an engine, one is provided for each hose line to ensure that proper pressure is maintained | pounds per square inch (psi) or inches of water |
| Flow meter | volume of flow in a piping system; used on fire apparatus to ensure the proper number of gallons are being supplied | cubic feet per minute (cfm) or gallons per minute (gpm) |

operation of a device with a gauge on it, you should pay careful attention to any markings that show such a limit.

## Pumps

A pump is a device used to transfer a liquid or a gas from one location, through a piping system, to another location. For example, a fire engine is a large, self-propelled pump capable of delivering a large volume of water at varying pressures. There are many different types of pumps, including centrifugal pumps, positive displacement pumps, metering pumps, diaphragm pumps, and progressive cavity pumps.

Generally speaking, a working pump consists of the pump itself (case, bearings, impeller, seals, shaft, base, and other components) and an outside energy source. The outside energy source could be an electric motor, internal combustion engine, or battery to provide mechanical energy to the pump. This energy causes the inner workings of the pump to propel the liquid or gas through the piping system. The flow rate at which the liquid or gas is pushed through the piping system is typically measured by a flow meter in units of gallons per minute (gpm) or cubic feet per minute (cfm).

Pumps are used for many purposes. Additional examples include gasoline pumps used to pump the gasoline from a holding tank into your car, water pumps to transfer drinking water from a reservoir to your house or business, and industrial pumps used to move industrial fluids such as chemicals or waste products from one tank to another inside a plant. A car also uses pumps to pump fuel from the gas tank to the engine and to pump coolant from the radiator to the engine block.

## ▶ Systems That Use Mechanical Devices

Many mechanical devices are actually a combination of several simple devices that work in conjunction to form a group of interacting mechanical and electrical components called a system. Some of the systems most likely to appear on the exam are discussed below.

### Internal Combustion Engines

Internal combustion engines (ICEs) are commonly used to drive many mechanical devices. However, they are very complex mechanical devices themselves. ICEs are used in cars, trucks, construction equipment, and many other devices. They can be fueled by gasoline, diesel fuel, natural gas, or other combustible fossil fuels.

An ICE is a system composed of dozens of individual mechanical (as well as electrical) systems. A few of the major systems within an ICE are discussed below.

### The Cooling System

The purpose of the cooling system is to dissipate the heat generated by the engine. The system consists of a pump that moves the coolant from the radiator through piping to the engine block, where it becomes hot, and then back out to the radiator where the liquid coolant is cooled.

### The Pistons, Tie Rods, and Crankshafts

The pistons, tie rods, and crankshafts are all parts of the inner workings of an ICE. In a gasoline-powered engine, a spark plug ignites the fuel and air mixture inside the cylinder, forcing the piston down. In a diesel engine, the ignition of the fuel is caused by the heat of compression of the air in the cylinder. At just the right time in the cycle, fuel is injected into the cylinder, causing an explosion that forces the piston down. In both types of engines, the piston is mechanically linked to a tie rod, which in turn is linked to a crankshaft. The up-and-down motion of the cylinder is changed into a rotational movement by the crankshaft. The crankshaft drives a transmission, which is a gear box. The transmission sends the power developed by the engine to the wheels of the vehicle, the workings of the pump, or whatever device the ICE is powering. Diesel power is the most common ICE installed in fire apparatus.

### The Fuel Pump

Fuel, usually gasoline or diesel fuel, is transferred to the engine from the fuel tank (or tanks) by this pump, which is either a mechanically driven device or, as is now more common, electrically driven. The fuel pump delivers fuel to a carburetor (gasoline) or fuel injection system (diesel and newer gasoline engines), which distribute the fuel under pressure in a spray to the proper cylinder. Many devices that were formerly mechanically driven are now replaced by computer-controlled devices.

### The Throttle Governor

A throttle governor is a mechanical or electronic device that is used to control the speed of an ICE. In older motor vehicles, it is a spring device that works directly on the gas pedal. In more modern motor vehicles, it is an electronic device that limits the speed of the engine. A throttle governor can be used to limit or maintain the vehicle's speed and, on fire apparatus, to maintain speed at a set rate when the vehicle is used to power pumps, hydraulics, or operate auxiliary machinery when stationary.

## Motor Vehicles

Motor vehicles are among the most complex assemblies of mechanical and electronic devices in existence. A piece of fire apparatus is among the most complex of all motor vehicles with hydraulic systems, power systems, pumps, compressed air, and lighting systems, to name a few. Today, computers have taken over more and more of the work that had previously been done by mechanical devices. All of these systems operate in addition to the normal subsystems discussed next.

## The Brakes

Motor vehicle brakes can be of several types. Originally, brakes were mechanical, using direct pressure on a brake pedal and transferring that pressure by linkages to pads that applied the pressure to a drum or rotor attached to the axle. That friction slows or stops the vehicle. To increase the pressure from the braking system on the axles to control heavier vehicles or to reduce the strain on the driver, hydraulics have replaced mechanical linkages. Now when the brake pedal is depressed, a hydraulic cylinder forces fluid through brake lines that connect the main cylinder to hydraulic cylinders at each wheel. The fluid then forces the pads onto the rotors, which slows or stops the vehicle. To further increase the pressure on the pads, pumps can be added to increase the hydraulic pressure. With large vehicles, such as fire apparatus, even this type of braking may not provide the level of safe braking that is

needed. Large vehicles use air brakes to slow or stop the vehicle. In these brakes, air is used either to keep the brake pads off the cylinder or to apply the pressure. These work in a similar way to the others described, but are designed to apply brakes any time air pressure is lost or suddenly reduced. Once again, brake systems are being computerized and now have features that prevent brakes from locking up and causing the vehicle to skid.

## The Steering Assembly

The steering wheel is attached to the tip of the steering column. In older vehicles, the bottom of the column was directly attached to the wheels by a series of gears and levers, so that if the steering wheel was turned to the right, the vehicle turned right, and vice versa. Today, the steering system of a vehicle employs hydraulics either to assist in the movement of the wheels or to actually move them. Modern steering systems allow the vehicle operator to turn the vehicle with much greater ease than older steering systems.

## The Exhaust System

As each cylinder fires, the combustion produces hot gases that expand in the confined space, forcing the piston down. For the engine to continue to function, it must exchange the burnt gases for fresh air and then, at the right moment, fuel. This exchange of combustion gases for fresh air is the job of the exhaust system. From an exhaust valve or from a series of ports, the burnt gases are drawn into a device called an exhaust manifold that gathers the gases from all the cylinders. This is connected to welded piping that passes the exhaust gases through a scrubbing device to remove harmful gases, changing them to harmless exhaust gases. This device, frequently called a *catalytic converter*, discharges the scrubbed exhaust gases through a muffler, which is an acoustical chamber that reduces the engine noise.

## Bicycles

A bicycle is not nearly as complex as an automobile. However, it too uses several mechanical devices.

- **The chain drive.** The pedals are connected to the drive gear. A chain is used to connect the drive gear to the gears on the rear wheel.
- **The frame.** Many welded joints are used to hold the frame together.
- **The suspension system.** Many newer bikes have suspension systems. The front wheel may use a hydraulic shock absorber. The rear wheel may use two springs in parallel to reduce shock to the rider.

## ▶ Brushing Up on Related Topics

Some mechanical aptitude questions may require the use of math or science to determine the correct answer. This chapter cannot cover all the possible questions you might be asked on the firefighter exam, but here are suggestions for ways to increase your knowledge of math, science, and general mechanical aptitude.

## Math

The required mathematical skills are primarily arithmetic (addition, subtraction, multiplication, and division) and geometry (angles and shapes). The arithmetic involved is almost always fairly simple. If you had trouble with arithmetic or geometry in your past schooling, you can brush up by reading the math chapter of this book. If you still want more help, pull out your old high school math book or check out a basic math book from the library.

## Science

Science subjects such as physics, materials science, thermodynamics, and chemistry are confusing for some people, but they needn't be. Science is real, seen in everyday life. You see science in action dozens of times every day. A car is stopped by brakes, which use friction (physics). A magnet adheres to the refrigerator due to the properties of the magnet and carbon steel of which the door is made (materials science). A pot of water boils when you set it on the stove and turn on the burner (thermodynamics). A tomato plant grows through the chemical reaction of sunlight, water, and food (chemistry). This chapter has reviewed many of the scientific concepts that are involved in mechanical devices. Again, as with math, you may have science books from previous schooling that you can use to help you solidify your scientific knowledge. If not, the library is full of scientific resources.

## General Mechanical Aptitude

Mechanical devices are such an integral part of everyday life that there are many real-life sources you can investigate to gain more knowledge of their design and use. A construction site is a great place to visit for a day to learn more about hand tools, cranes, pumps, and other devices. Ask the construction supervisor if you can take a tour.

Another alternative would be to visit an automotive repair shop. Internal combustion engines, lifts, levers, and hand tools are only a few of the types of mechanical devices you could see in use. Yet another possibility would be to visit a local manufacturer in your town. Examples include a foundry, a sheet metal fabricator, an automotive manufacturer, or a pump manufacturer. Look in the phone book under "manufacturing" for possibilities.

# ▶ Sample Mechanical Aptitude Questions

Now use what you have learned in this chapter by answering the following mechanical aptitude questions. Answers are found at the end of the chapter.

**1.** Which of the following tools is used to smooth or level a piece of wood?
 **a.** a wrench
 **b.** a screwdriver
 **c.** a plane
 **d.** a hammer

**2.** A compass is used for what purpose?
 **a.** to measure angles
 **b.** to tighten and loosen nuts and bolts
 **c.** to drive and remove nails
 **d.** to draw circles of various sizes

**3.** Which of the following is NOT a hand tool?
 **a.** a winch
 **b.** a level
 **c.** a compass
 **d.** a chisel

**4.** Vice grips are a type of
 **a.** ax.
 **b.** wrench.
 **c.** ladder.
 **d.** mechanical jack.

**5.** How can gears be used to change the speed of a machine?
 **a.** use more gears
 **b.** use two gears of the same size
 **c.** use two gears of different sizes
 **d.** use two large gears

**6.** What is the main function of a pulley?
 **a.** to increase the strength of a construction crane
 **b.** to override the power of an electric motor
 **c.** to add energy to a system
 **d.** to change the direction of a pulling force

**7.** Steve has a lever whose pivot point is 3 feet from the 50-pound box he wants to lift. Steve is standing at the other end of the lever, 6 feet from the pivot point. How much force must he apply to lift the box?

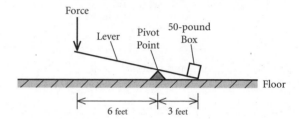

 **a.** 50 pounds
 **b.** 25 pounds
 **c.** 100 pounds
 **d.** 6 pounds

**8.** Which of the following is NOT a mechanical process for fastening?
 **a.** welding
 **b.** buttoning
 **c.** bolting
 **d.** covalent bonding

**9.** When three identical springs are arranged in series and a pulling force of 10 pounds is applied, the total stretch is 9 inches. If these same three springs were arranged in parallel and the same 10-pound force were applied to the new arrangement, what would be the total distance of stretch?

*Springs in Series:*

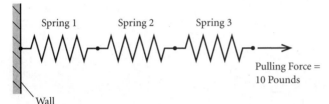

Pulling Force = 10 Pounds

Wall

*Springs in Parallel:*

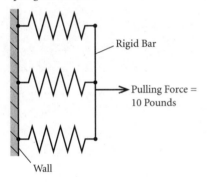

Rigid Bar

Pulling Force = 10 Pounds

Wall

**a.** 3 inches
**b.** 4.5 inches
**c.** 9 inches
**d.** 18 inches

**10.** What type of gauge uses units of rpm?
**a.** a pressure gauge
**b.** a tachometer
**c.** a speedometer
**d.** a thermometer

**11.** What type of outside energy source could be used to operate a pump?
**a.** a battery
**b.** an internal combustion engine
**c.** an electric motor
**d.** all of the above

**12.** What type of mechanical device is used to aid in cooling an internal combustion engine?
**a.** a pump
**b.** a lever
**c.** a gauge
**d.** a hammer

**13.** Of the following mechanical devices on an automobile, which one uses friction to accomplish its purpose?
**a.** the steering system
**b.** the exhaust system
**c.** the braking system
**d.** the internal combustion engine

**14.** The suspension system on a bicycle is likely to use which of the following mechanical devices?
**a.** a chain
**b.** a pulley
**c.** a gear
**d.** a spring

# How to Answer Mechanical Aptitude Questions

- **Read each problem carefully.** Questions may contain words such as *not*, *all*, or *mostly*, which can be tricky unless you pay attention.

- **Read the entire question** once or even a few times before trying to pick an answer. Decide exactly what the question is asking. Take notes and draw pictures on scratch paper. That way you won't waste time by going in the wrong direction.

- **Some questions will require the use of math** (typically addition, subtraction, multiplication, and division) and science. In these situations, think about what you have learned previously in school.

- **Use your common sense.** Some mechanical devices can seem intimidating at first but are really a combination of a few simple items. Try to break complicated questions down into smaller, manageable pieces.

- **Answer the questions that are easiest for you first.** You do not have to go in order from start to finish. Read each question and, if you are not sure what to do, move on to the next question. You can go back to harder questions if you have time at the end.

- **Many mechanical devices are commonly used in everyday life.** You do not have to be a mechanic or an engineer to use these devices. If something seems unfamiliar, try to think of items around your house that might be similar.

- **Don't be intimidated by unfamiliar terms.** In most instances, there are clues in the question that will point you toward the correct answer, and some of the answers can be ruled out by common sense.

---

**15.** The tops and caps of your department's fire hydrants have a hexagonal stud extending about an inch from the base. Which of the following basic tools could you use to open the hydrant or remove the cap?

**a.** pliers

**b.** wrench

**c.** screwdriver

**d.** lever

**16.** What gauge could be used to test the amount of water streaming from a hydrant?

**a.** tachometer

**b.** pressure gauge

**c.** speedometer

**d.** flow meter

## Answers

1. **c.** See the table under "Carpenter's Tools" earlier in this chapter for the functions of the items listed.

2. **d.** As defined under "Carpenter's Tools," a compass is used to draw circles.

3. **a.** A level, a compass, and a chisel are all carpenter's hand tools.

4. **b.** Vice grips are a kind of wrench.

5. **c.** Changing gears on a ten-speed bicycle is a good example of using different-sized gears to change speed.

6. **d.** Pulleys are used to change not the strength of a force but its direction.

7. **b.** Apply the distance formula, $w \times d_1 = f \times d_2$, to come up with the equation $50 \times 3 = f \times 6$. Solve for the unknown $f$ by multiplying 3 times 50 to get 150 and then dividing by 6 to get 25 pounds.

8. **d.** A covalent bond is a chemical bond. Welding, buttoning, and bolting are all mechanical fastening processes.

9. **a.** The total pulling force will be divided equally, with each spring experiencing one-third of the total force. Since the force is divided by 3, the amount of movement will be divided by 3 also. The original configuration stretched 9 inches, so the new arrangement will stretch only 3 inches.

10. **b.** A tachometer measures rotation in units of revolutions per minute or rpm.

11. **d.** Any of the energy sources listed could be used to operate a pump.

12. **a.** As discussed in the section "Internal Combustion Engines" earlier in this chapter, a pump is used to help cool an ICE.

13. **c.** The braking system uses friction to slow or stop the rotation of the wheels.

14. **d.** Springs are commonly used in suspension systems.

15. **b.** A wrench is used to turn a bolt-like head. Although pliers could be used, they would tend to slip. Both a lever and a screwdriver would be useless in this instance.

16. **d.** Flow meters measure the volume of flow within a piping system or flowing from a piping system. A pressure gauge would show you the pressure of the water, but you are not interested in that. You need to measure flow, the volume (amount of water), not the pressure (force of water). Tachometers and speedometers measure machinery speed, not water speed or volume.

# 11 ▶ Spatial Relations and Map Reading

## CHAPTER SUMMARY

Firefighter exams often include questions that test your ability to read maps, floor plans, and pictures. This chapter shows you how to tackle such questions on spatial relationships.

Imagine you are shopping in a local mall. You look at the store directory to find the closest restaurant. You locate the arrow that says "You Are Here." Do you know where you are? Do you know which way to go to find the restaurant?

The store directory has just presented you with a typical spatial relations question. Spatial relations is the ability to visualize in three dimensions. As the store directory example suggests, everyone needs to be able to translate a two-dimensional representation into a three-dimensional sense of where they are and where they want to go. But this ability is particularly important for firefighters, who must read maps and floor plans to get to the people who need their help.

Spatial relations questions on a firefighter exam are based on a map, a building floor plan, or a picture, usually accompanied by a short explanation of the scene. The examiners may give you a picture of a street with apartment buildings, houses, and stores, possibly including a fire scene containing apparatus and personnel. The questions require you to locate certain points or give details on objects shown in the picture. The answers to the questions can all be found in the diagram; however, you must read each question carefully and pay close attention to the details.

## ► Reading a Map

Many spatial relations questions are based on maps. Map-reading skills are essential to the work of a firefighter. Firefighters are expected to be able to figure out the quickest route to the scene of an emergency without hesitation. They are frequently stopped by lost motorists trying to find their way. Pedestrians often come into the firehouse to ask directions.

### Questions on the Most Direct Route

Map-based questions typically ask for the most direct route between two points. As you answer such questions, keep in mind that you must choose the best legal route, observing one-way streets and traffic rules. When giving directions to pedestrians, you don't have to consider the flow of traffic, so providing them with the shortest route may be easier to do. Take a systematic approach to answering this type of question, using the following procedure:

1. **Look at the map.** Take a moment to scan the buildings and streets. Locate the legend, if any; it tells you which way is north and explains any special symbols, such as those indicating one-way streets.

2. **Read the question.** Read carefully and be sure you understand what is being asked. Do not read the answer choices at this time. Read only the question so that you can plot the route yourself. That way, you are less likely to be confused by incorrect choices purposely included to distract you.

3. **Return to the map.** Locate the information asked for in the question. Look at the street names and traffic patterns.

4. **Prepare your answer by tracing your route.** Remember to observe any traffic rules that are necessary. Write down the route you have selected. Read the question again. Have you understood what was asked, and have you answered correctly?

5. **Read the answer choices.** Be very observant, as the choices may be very similar to each other. Does one of the choices match your route exactly? Some answers may almost match your route but contain one wrong direction, for example, using north when you are supposed to go south. If you do not find an answer choice that matches yours exactly, reread the question and try again. Carefully review the question to see what is being asked. Do you understand the question? Have you mapped out the correct directions in selecting this route?

A street map is on the next page. Following the map are questions that ask you to find the best route based on the map. After each question is a detailed explanation of how to use the procedure outlined above to find the correct answer.

A firefighter is often required to assist civilians who seek travel directions or referral to city agencies and facilities. The accompanying map shows a section of the city where some public buildings are located. Each of the squares represents one city block. Street names are as shown. If there is an arrow next to the street name, it means the street traffic moves one way in the direction of the arrow. If there is no arrow next to the street name, two-way traffic is allowed. Answer questions 1–4 on the basis of this map.

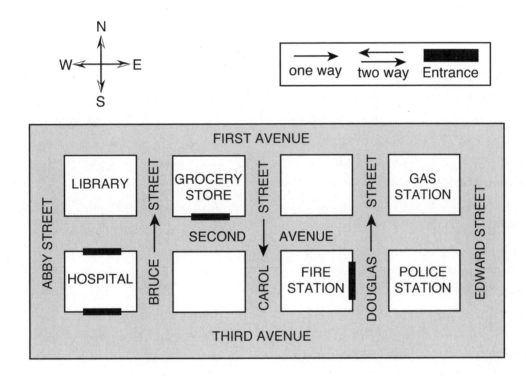

1. Your company must respond to a reported fire at the Third Avenue entrance of the hospital. What is the shortest legal route the engine can take?

   a. South on Douglas Street, west on Second Avenue, north on Carol Street, and west on Third Avenue to the hospital entrance.

   b. North on Douglas Street, west on Second Avenue, south on Bruce Street, and west on Third Avenue to the hospital entrance.

   c. North on Douglas Street, west on Second Avenue, south on Carol Street, and west on Third Avenue to the hospital entrance.

   d. North on Douglas Street, west on First Avenue, south on Abby Street, and east on Second Avenue to the hospital entrance.

Here's how you would use the map-reading procedure to answer question 1:

1. **Look at the map.** Notice that some streets are one-way only and that avenues permit two-way traffic. Locate north, south, east, and west. What are the names of the buildings shown?

2. **Read the question.** Take note of key words and directions, in this case, *shortest legal route*. You are responding to a fire alarm, so the starting point must be the fire station. The hospital has two entrances, one on Second Avenue and another on Third Avenue. You are being asked to go from the entrance of the fire station to the Third Avenue entrance of the hospital using the shortest legal route.

3. **Return to the map.** Locate the fire station entrance. It is on Douglas Street between Second Avenue and Third Avenue. Douglas Street is one way going north. The hospital entrance you are asked to report to is on Third Avenue between Abby Street and Bruce Street. Avenues allow two-way traffic, but Bruce Street is one way going north. You need to go south to get to Third Avenue. Abby Street is a two-way street, but you would have to go past the hospital to use it. Carol Street, which is one way going south, is the better option.

4. **Prepare your answer by tracing your route.** After careful consideration, you find that the shortest legal route would be to start on Douglas Street at the fire station entrance and go north to Second Avenue. Then you would proceed west on Second Avenue to Carol Street. Then you would travel south on Carol Street to Third Avenue and then west on Third Avenue to the hospital entrance. Now, reread the question. You have found the shortest legal route from the firehouse to the Third Avenue entrance of the hospital.

5. **Read the answer choices.** Choice **c** matches the route you chose, but examine the other choices to make sure. Choice **a** is incorrect because you can't legally travel south on Douglas Street, and, if you could, it wouldn't lead you to Second Avenue. Choice **b** is close to your chosen route, but it becomes incorrect when it sends you south on Bruce Street, which allows northbound traffic only. Choice **d** will get you to the hospital legally but takes you to the Second Avenue entrance of the hospital instead of the Third Avenue entrance. It also takes you out of the way by traveling on First Avenue to Abby Street.

Use the same procedure to answer the next question.

2. The deliveryperson from the grocery store calls to ask directions to the firehouse so that he can walk over with the order. You should direct him to walk
   a. west on Second Avenue to Douglas Street, make a left, and go half a block to the firehouse.
   b. east on Second Avenue to Douglas Street, make a right, and go half a block to the firehouse.
   c. west on Second Avenue to Douglas Street, make a right, and go half a block to the firehouse.
   d. east on First Avenue to Douglas Street, make a left, and go half a block to the firehouse.

The deliveryperson needs to walk from the grocery store to the firehouse. First, locate the grocery store and the firehouse. The grocery store is on Second Avenue between Bruce Street and Carol Street. The firehouse is on Douglas Street between Second and Third Avenues. Since the deliveryperson is walking, you can ignore the one-way streets. Trace a route: Beginning at the grocery store, the deliveryperson should walk east on Second Avenue to Douglas Street, turn right, and go half a block to the firehouse.

Now read the answer choices. Choice **b** is the route you would have directed the deliveryperson to use to get from the grocery store to the firehouse. Choices **a** and **c** have him walking west on Second Avenue, which is not the correct direction from the grocery store to the firehouse. Choice **d** has the deliveryperson walking on First Avenue, which is not where the entrance to the grocery store is located, and left on Douglas Street, which will not take him to the firehouse.

## Questions on Finding Your Location or Direction

Map questions may also ask you for your location after following a series of directions. These questions, although worded differently, should be answered using the same procedure:

1. Look at the map.
2. Read the question.
3. Return to the map and follow the directions given.
4. Go back to the question and examine the answer choices to see which one matches the direction or location you found in step 3.

Try this procedure on the questions that follow, using the same map given previously.

3. You are on the corner of First Avenue and Abby Street. Drive east two blocks, south one block, and west half a block. You are in front of the
   a. hospital.
   b. library.
   c. fire station.
   d. grocery store.

Trace the steps given in the question on the map, paying careful attention to the specific directions, north, south, east, and west. Turn the map as you go to help you keep track of where you are. You have arrived in front of the grocery store, choice **d**.

4. You are walking north on Bruce Street. You turn right on Second Avenue, walk two blocks to Douglas Street, and turn right. What direction are you now facing?
   a. north
   b. south
   c. east
   d. west

The answer to this question is also found by tracing the steps given in the question. Again, turn the map as you are reading the directions indicated. If you are facing north on Bruce Street, a right turn will leave you walking east. Turning right onto Douglas Street leaves you facing south, choice **b**.

## ▶ Reading a Floor Plan

A floor plan is a map of the interior of a building, apartment, or house. The ability to read floor plans and visualize your position is critical if you want to be a firefighter. Firefighters sometimes find themselves crawling down dark and smoky hallways. Knowing the location of doors, windows, and rooms in an apartment on fire may mean the difference between life and death. If fire conditions in the apartment worsen, you do not want to crawl into a closet while trying to find the exit. Firefighters also need to know the location of fire apparatus and personnel, the fire itself, and victims; furthermore, they have to be aware of the risk of the fire spreading to adjoining buildings or apartments.

Preplans are similar to floor plans except they will often show features on the outside of the building in addition to the floor plan, although they may have somewhat less detail on the interior of the building. Preplans are frequently made for businesses, churches, and similar types of commercial buildings. These plans are often carried on the trucks for reference by the crews at an incident. A preplan may include information on access roads around the building, connections to sprinkler systems, location of gas or bulk material storage, locations of fire hydrants, information on alarm systems in the building, and other critical information for the crews.

In questions based on floor plans, your ability to observe and judge location and potential hazards is being challenged to see if you have what it takes to become a firefighter. The floor plan or fire scene may be accompanied by a brief explanation of what the picture shows. The questions may ask the number of exits, windows, bedrooms, or smoke detectors. You may be asked where you would position a ladder to attempt a rescue or which room you are in based on a set of directions.

Fire departments often assign letter or number designations to buildings during an incident. This helps to avoid confusion on what is the front, back, left, or right side of the building. Usually, the "front" of the building is considered the side that fronts the main road that the trucks will use to approach the building. This side will be designated as either Side A or Side 1. The other sides of the building are then numbered sequentially clockwise around the building. For example, if you are standing in front of Side A and are looking at the building, the side on your left would be Side B or 2, the back would be Side C or 3, and the side on your right would be Side D or 4. Letter designations are probably a little more common. Corners of the building are designated using the two adjacent walls, Corner A-B, and so on. If letter designations are used, the floors of the building are numbered as divisions, starting with the ground floor as Division 1. The second floor would be Division 2, and so on. You may see exam problems that use this type of information for a spatial relations question.

Handle floor-plan questions in the same manner as those on maps. Before attempting to answer any questions, look at the diagram. Familiarize yourself with such features as doors, windows, doorways, patio doors, fire extinguishers, and smoke detectors. Read each question carefully; then return to the diagram to find the answer. After you have determined your answer, try to match it to the choices. The correct answer should be apparent, but read each choice carefully to avoid making unnecessary errors. Never jump at one option without carefully reading all the others.

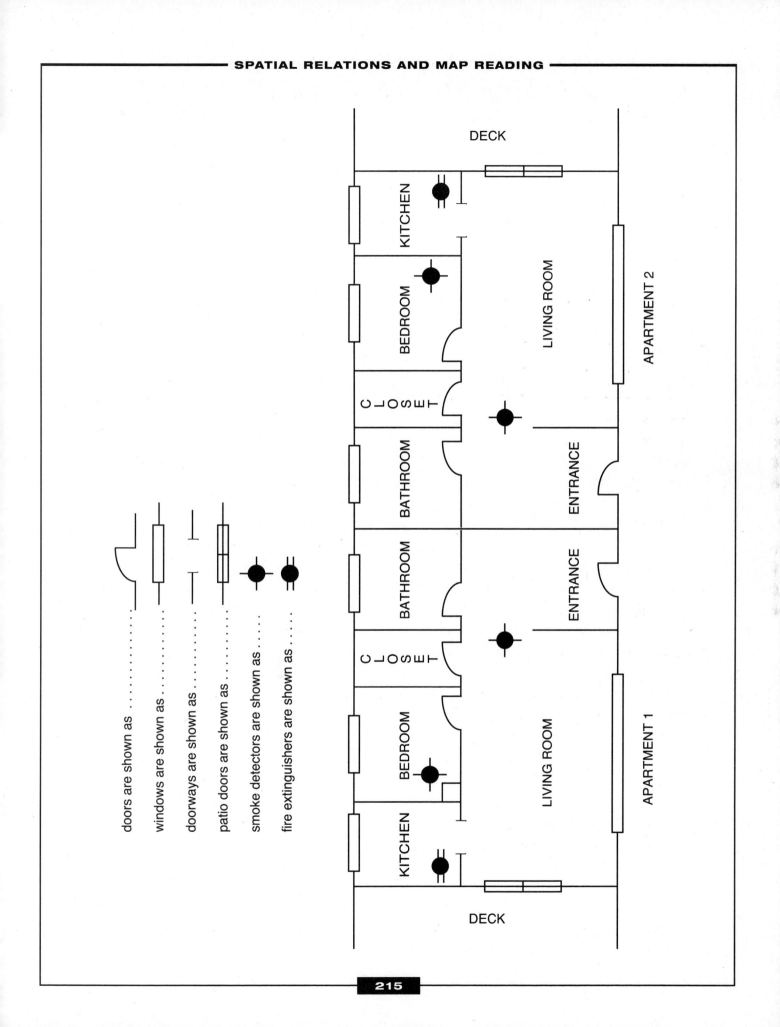

- First, familiarize yourself with the map or diagram.
- Next, read the question carefully to determine what you are being asked to do.
- Return to the diagram and find your own answer before reading the choices given.
- Reread the question and the answer choices. Don't rush; read all the possible choices. Misleading answers are placed on the test to see if you can be caught not paying attention.
- If the answer you found does not match the choices, look at the question carefully, return to the diagram, and go over your options to see what you missed.
- Remember, the answers to the questions are right there in the map or diagram. Take your time, read to understand, and think through your answers.

Examine the floor plan on page 215. Apply the procedure outlined above to answer the following questions.

Office buildings and apartment buildings may post floor plans at the front entrance or by the elevators to assist visitors. Firefighters arriving at the scene of a fire must be able to read a floor plan quickly and develop a mental picture of the interior. When there is a fire, the smoke can be very thick, so firefighters need to know their way in and out without seeing where they are. The diagram on page 215 shows two apartments on the first floor of a building. Answer questions 5–8 based on this diagram.

5. Firefighters arrive at the scene to find that there is a woman trapped in the bedroom of apartment 2. There is a fire in the living room, and the entrance to the apartment is blocked by fire. What would be the most direct way to rescue the trapped woman?
   a. Go into the apartment through the patio doors.
   b. Climb through the kitchen window.
   c. Climb through the bedroom window.
   d. Climb through the bathroom window.

The question asks for an alternate way to reach the bedroom of apartment 2, since the entrance is blocked. A look at the floor plan shows that choices **a**, **b**, and **d** would bring the firefighters through the living room, where the fire is located. Choice **c**, which brings you directly into the bedroom, is the fastest and safest means of entering the apartment and rescuing the woman with the least risk of injuring either her or the rescuers.

6. A fire in the kitchen has filled apartment 1 with smoke. You must reach the bedroom to search for sleeping occupants. Visibility is near zero as you are crawling down the entry hall. How many doors will you encounter before you reach the bedroom?
   a. none
   b. six
   c. four
   d. two

To answer this question, locate the entrance to apartment 1 and trace a route down the hall and to the bedroom. You would pass the bathroom door and a closet door before the bedroom: two doors, choice **d**.

**7.** How many bathrooms are there in apartment 1?

  **a.** one

  **b.** two

  **c.** three

  **d.** four

Review the diagram. Two apartments are shown, labeled 1 and 2. The question asks for the number of bathrooms in apartment 1. Apartment 1 contains one bathroom, choice **a**. If you counted all the bathrooms shown on the diagram, you would incorrectly choose **b**.

**8.** How many smoke detectors and fire extinguishers are there in apartments 1 and 2?

  **a.** six

  **b.** ten

  **c.** four

  **d.** three

The answer is **a**. You must read the question carefully to see that it asks you to look at both apartments and to find two items, the smoke detectors and the fire extinguishers. There are two smoke detectors and one fire extinguisher in each apartment. If you counted the smoke detectors (but not the fire extinguishers) in both apartments, you would have chosen choice **c**. On the other hand, if you counted both smoke detectors and fire extinguishers, but only in one apartment, you would have thought choice **d** was correct.

The ability to understand spatial relations is an important firefighting tool. Can you apply what you see and mentally navigate yourself through the city or a building, while paying close attention to detail? That's what these questions try to assess.

# 12 ▶ Verbal Expression

## CHAPTER SUMMARY

This chapter will help you brush up your vocabulary and grammar skills so that you will be able to do well on exam questions that test your ability to express yourself in writing.

Some questions on the firefighter exam test how well you can use words to express yourself. Basically, there are two different kinds of questions: Vocabulary questions ask you to identify the meanings of words, whereas clarity questions ask you which is the best way to express the information given in the question.

Here is an example of a **vocabulary** question:

Choose the word that most nearly means the same as the italicized word.

   **1.** The mechanic inspected the faulty hydraulic system and discovered that it was *defective*.
      **a.** efficient
      **b.** offensive
      **c.** flawed
      **d.** powerful

The answer is **c**. Something that is *defective* contains a *flaw* that keeps it from working or looking as it should.

The context clue in this sentence is the word *faulty*. Hydraulic systems may be *efficient* (choice **a**) or *powerful* (choice **d**), but these choices don't fit the context of the sentence. Choice **b** can be ruled out because *flawed* is clearly a better choice than *offensive*.

**Clarity** questions ask you to choose the sentence that states an idea most clearly and accurately.

Here is one type of clarity question:

2. A firefighter notices a leaking fire hydrant near 612 36th Street. This is between Woodland Avenue and Grand Avenue. Which of the following states the problem most clearly and accurately?
   a. The hydrant was leaking between Woodland and Grand Avenue. It's all wet and needs to be fixed.
   b. There's a leaking hydrant near 612 36th Street. That's between Grand and Woodland.
   c. At 612 between Grand and Woodland is a leaking hydrant.
   d. There's a leaking hydrant at Grand and Woodland at 36th Street. It's near 612.

The best answer is **b**. This answer choice states the problem and gives the exact location in the first sentence. It further identifies the location by mentioning the nearest cross streets.

This chapter explains in detail how to handle both vocabulary and clarity questions.

## ▶ Vocabulary

Many firefighter exams test vocabulary. There are two basic kinds of questions.

- **Synonyms:** Identifying words that mean the same as the given words
- **Context:** Determining the meaning of a word or phrase by noting how it is used in a sentence or paragraph

## Synonym Questions

A word is a *synonym* of another word if it has the same or nearly the same meaning as the other word. Test questions often ask you to find the synonym or antonym of a word. If you are lucky, the word will be included in a sentence that helps you guess what the word means. If you are less lucky, you will just get the word, and then you have to figure out what the word means without any help.

Questions that ask for synonyms can be tricky because they require you to recognize the meaning of several words that may be unfamiliar—not only the words in the questions but also the answer choices. Usually the best strategy is to *look* at the structure of the word and to *listen* for its sound. See if a part of a word looks familiar. Think of other words you know that have similar key elements. How could those words be related?

## Synonym Practice

Try your hand at identifying the word parts and related words in these sample synonym questions. Circle the word that means the same or about the same as the italicized word. Answers and explanations appear right after the questions.

3. *incoherent* answer
   a. not understandable
   b. not likely
   c. undeniable
   d. challenging

**4.** *ambiguous* questions
   **a.** meaningless
   **b.** difficult
   **c.** simple
   **d.** vague

**5.** covered with *debris*
   **a.** good excuses
   **b.** transparent material
   **c.** scattered rubble
   **d.** protective material

**6.** *inadvertently* left
   **a.** mistakenly
   **b.** purposely
   **c.** cautiously
   **d.** carefully

**7.** *exorbitant* prices
   **a.** bargain
   **b.** unexpected
   **c.** reasonable
   **d.** outrageous

**8.** *compatible* workers
   **a.** gifted
   **b.** competitive
   **c.** harmonious
   **d.** experienced

**9.** *belligerent* attitude
   **a.** hostile
   **b.** reasonable
   **c.** instinctive
   **d.** friendly

## Answers

The explanations are just as important as the answers because they show you how to go about choosing a synonym if you don't know the word.

**3. a.** *Incoherent* means *not understandable.* To *cohere* means to *connect.* A coherent answer connects or makes sense. The prefix *in-* means *not.*

**4. d.** *Ambiguous* questions are *vague* or uncertain. The key part of this word is *ambi-*, which means *two* or *both*. An ambiguous question can be interpreted two or more ways.

**5. c.** *Debris* is scattered fragments and trash.

**6. a.** *Inadvertently* means *by mistake.* The key element in this word is the prefix *in-*, which usually means *not*, the *opposite of.*

**7. d.** The key element here is *ex-*, which means *out of* or *away from.* Exorbitant literally means "out of orbit." An *exorbitant* price would be an *outrageous* one.

**8. c.** *Compatible* means *harmonious.*

**9. a.** The key element in this word is the root *belli-*, which means *warlike.* The synonym choice, then, is *hostile.*

## Context Questions

*Context* is the surrounding text in which a word is used. Most people use context to help them determine the meaning of an unknown word. A vocabulary question that gives you a sentence around the vocabulary word is usually easier to answer than one with little or no context. The surrounding text can help you as you look for synonyms for the specified words in the sentences.

The best way to take meaning from context is to look for key words in sentences or paragraphs that convey the meaning of the text. If nothing else, the context will give you a means to eliminate wrong answer choices that clearly don't fit. The process of elimination will often leave you with the correct answer.

## Context Practice

Try these sample questions. Choose the word that most nearly means the same as the italicized word in the sentence.

**10.** The fire inspector was *appalled* by the attitude of the building's owners when she pointed out the locked fire doors.
   **a.** horrified
   **b.** amused
   **c.** surprised
   **d.** dismayed

**11.** Even though he seemed rich, the defendent claimed to be *destitute*.
   **a.** wealthy
   **b.** ambitious
   **c.** solvent
   **d.** poor

**12.** The woman was *distraught* because she could not reach her child due to the amount of smoke and fire in the hallway.
   **a.** punished
   **b.** distracted
   **c.** composed
   **d.** anguished

**13.** To protect the hearing of the firefighters, the new Rescue 5 truck had features to *attenuate* the sound of the engine, horn, and sirens.
   **a.** direct
   **b.** increase
   **c.** silence
   **d.** reduce

Some tests may ask you to fill in the blank by choosing a word that fits the context. In the following questions, choose the word that best completes the sentence.

**14.** Professor Washington was a very_____ woman known for her reputation as a scholar.
   **a.** stubborn
   **b.** knowledgeable
   **c.** illiterate
   **d.** disciplined

**15.** His_____was demonstrated by his willingness to donate large amounts of money to worthy causes.
   **a.** honesty
   **b.** loyalty
   **c.** selfishness
   **d.** altruism

## Answers

Check to see whether you were able to pick out the key words that help you define the target word, as well as whether you got the right answer.

**10. a.** The key words in the question are *attitude* and *locked*. These show that the inspector was pointing out a violation and the building's owners did not seem to be concerned. *Appalled* is the proper answer, as the other words are too mild for the reaction of the inspector.

**11. d.** The key word here is *rich*, but this is a clue by contrast. The introductory *Even though* signals that you should look for the opposite of the idea of having financial resources.

**12. d.** The key phrases are *could not reach her child* and *amount of smoke and fire*, showing that she tried and failed to reach her child. She would be naturally upset and worried; therefore, she is *distraught* or *anguished* about the fate of her child.

**13. d.** *Attenuate* means to *reduce in amount*. The key is that the sentence starts with *To protect the hearing of the firefighters*. Although directing the sound might help a little, the noise would be the same. Silencing the sounds would also help, but then no one could hear the siren or horn outside. Increasing the sound would not help at all.

**14. b.** The key words here are *professor* and *scholar*.

**15. d.** The key words here are *large amounts of money to worthy causes*. They give you a definition of the word you are looking for. Even if you don't know the word *altruism*, the other choices seem inappropriate to describe someone so generous.

## For Nonnative Speakers of English

Be very careful not to be confused by the sound of words, which may mislead you. Be sure to look at the word carefully, and pay attention to the structure and appearance of the word as well as its sound. You may be used to hearing English words spoken with an accent. The sounds of those words may be misleading in choosing a correct answer.

## Word Parts

The best way to improve your vocabulary is to learn word parts: roots, which are the main part of the word; prefixes, which come before the root word; and suffixes, which come after. Any of these elements can carry meaning or change the use of a word in a sentence. For instance, the suffix *-s* or *-es* can change the meaning of a noun from singular to plural: *boy, boys*. The prefix *un-* can change the meaning of a root word to its opposite: *necessary, unnecessary*.

On the next page are some of the word elements seen most often in vocabulary tests. Simply reading them and their examples for five to ten minutes a day will give you the quick recognition you need to make a good association with the meaning of an unfamiliar word.

## Common Word Elements

Below are some common elements of English words, including root words and prefixes. Take the time to look up any unfamiliar example words in a dictionary. Expanding your vocabulary will help you recognize more words on the test.

| WORD ELEMENT | MEANING | EXAMPLE |
|---|---|---|
| ama | love | amateur |
| ambi | both | ambivalent, ambidextrous |
| aud | hear | audition |
| bell | war | belligerent, bellicose |
| bene | good | benefactor |
| cid/cis | cut | homicide, scissor |
| cogn/gno | know | agnostic, recognize |
| curr | run | current |
| flu/flux | flow | fluid, fluctuate |
| gress | to go | congress, progress |
| in/im | not, in | inconceivable, impregnate |
| ject | throw | inject, reject |
| luc/lux | light | lucid, translucent |
| neo | new | neophyte |
| omni | all | omnivorous |
| pel/puls | push | impulse, propeller |
| pro | forward | project |
| pseudo | false | pseudonym |
| rog | ask | interrogate |
| sub | under | subjugate |
| spec/spic | look, see | spectator, conspicuous |
| super | over | superfluous |
| temp | time | contemporary, temporal |
| un | not, opposite | uncoordinated |
| viv | live | vivid |

## More Vocabulary Practice

Here is another set of practice exercises with samples of each kind of question covered in this chapter. Answers are found at the end of the exercise.

Choose the word that means the same or nearly the same as the italicized word.

**16.** *congenial* company
   **a.** friendly
   **b.** dull
   **c.** tiresome
   **d.** angry

**17.** *conspicuous* mess
   **a.** secret
   **b.** notable
   **c.** visible
   **d.** boorish

**18.** *meticulous* record-keeping
   **a.** dishonest
   **b.** casual
   **c.** painstaking
   **d.** careless

**19.** *superficial* wounds
   **a.** life-threatening
   **b.** bloody
   **c.** severe
   **d.** surface

**20.** *impulsive* actions
   **a.** cautious
   **b.** sudden
   **c.** courageous
   **d.** cowardly

**21.** *tactful* comments
   **a.** polite
   **b.** rude
   **c.** angry
   **d.** confused

Using the context, choose the word that means the same or nearly the same as the italicized word.

**22.** Though flexible about homework, the teacher was *adamant* that papers be in on time.
   **a.** liberal
   **b.** casual
   **c.** strict
   **d.** pliable

**23.** The condition of the room after the party was *deplorable*.
   **a.** regrettable
   **b.** pristine
   **c.** festive
   **d.** tidy

Choose the word that best completes the following sentences.

**24.** Her position as a(n) _____ teacher took her all over the city.
   **a.** primary
   **b.** secondary
   **c.** itinerant
   **d.** permanent

**25.** Despite her promise to stay in touch, she remained _____ and difficult to locate.
   **a.** steadfast
   **b.** stubborn
   **c.** dishonest
   **d.** elusive

### How to Answer Vocabulary Questions

- The key to answering vocabulary questions is to notice and connect what you do know to what you may not recognize.
- **Know your word parts.** You can recognize or make a good guess at the meanings of words when you see some suggested meaning in a root word, prefix, or suffix.
- **Use the process of elimination.** Think of how the word makes sense in the sentence.
- **Don't be confused by words that sound like other words,** but may have no relation to the word you need.

## Answers

16. a.
17. c.
18. c.
19. d.
20. b.
21. a.
22. c.
23. a.
24. c.
25. d.

## ▶ Clarity

Your communication skills may be tested in another way, by seeing how well you can express a given idea orally or in writing. You may be asked to read two or more versions of the same information and then choose the one that most clearly and accurately presents the given information, the **best** option. The **best** option should be:

- accurate
- clear
- logical
- grammatically correct

Imagine this situation:

> It is 2:30 on Tuesday, August 22. You are driving Vehicle #25, heading west on NW 91st Street. Your coworker Alex Thorp is riding on the platform at the back of the truck. Just as you round the corner to head north on Park Place, he loses his grip and falls from the truck. You stop immediately to see if he is hurt. He says he's fine, but about an hour later his wrist hurts badly enough that he asks you to take him to the hospital. You go to the Mercy Medical Center. The doctor who examines him says the wrist is mildly fractured.

The information above can be expressed accurately or inaccurately, clearly or unclearly, logically or illogically, grammatically or ungrammatically. The following examples will show you how this works.

### Accurate

Check the facts for accuracy first. If the facts are wrong or confused in a particular answer choice, that choice is wrong, no matter how well written it is.

## Inaccurate

Alex Thorp was in #25 on NE 91st when he fell off onto Park Place because he broke his wrist. I stopped, but he wasn't hurt. Later the doctor said he had a fractured wrist. It was 3:30 on Tuesday, August 22.

## Accurate

Around 2:30 on Tuesday, August 22, Alex Thorp fell from the back platform of #25 while I was turning the corner from the west lane of NW 91st to go north on Park Place. About an hour later he asked to go to the hospital. The doctor said his wrist was fractured.

## Clear

The best answer is written in plain English in such a way that most readers can understand it the first time through. If you read through an answer choice and then need to reread it to know what it means, look for a better option.

## Unclear

On or about 2:30 on Tuesday, August 22, my coworker Alex Thorp and I were headed westbound on NW 91st Street. As I proceeded around the corner to head northbound on Park Place, he lost his grip and suffered an unknown injury. Later we went to Mercy Medical Center to seek a doctor's attention, who said it was fractured wrist, only mildly.

## Clear

Around 2:30 on Tuesday, August 22, I was driving Vehicle #25, and Alex Thorp was riding on the back platform. He lost his grip and fell as I rounded a corner from NW 91st west onto Park Place north. He thought he was all right at first, but about an hour later he asked to go to the hospital. The doctor who saw him at Mercy Medical Center said he had a mildly fractured wrist.

## Logical

The best answer will present information in logical order, usually time order. If the information seems disorganized, look for a better option.

## Illogical Order

The doctor said Alex's wrist was mildly fractured. It happened when he fell off the back of Vehicle #25. He went to the doctor later at Mercy Medical Center. It didn't hurt at first. He lost his grip. I turned from NW 91st west onto Park Place north. This was Tuesday, August 22, at around 2:30.

## Logical Order

Around 2:30 on Tuesday, August 22, Alex Thorp lost his grip while riding on the back platform of Vehicle #25 as I was driving around the corner from NW 91st west onto Park Place north. He didn't realize he was hurt until about an hour later. I took him to Mercy Medical Center where a doctor examined him and said he had a mildly fractured wrist.

In addition to accuracy, clarity, and logic, there are other characteristics of well-written, grammatically correct sentences. The next section points out some common grammar mistakes and tells you how to make the right choices on your exam.

## Pronoun Agreement

The best answer contains clearly identified pronouns (*he, she, him, her, them,* etc.) that match the number of nouns they represent. First, the pronouns should be clearly identified.

## Unclear

Ann Dorr and the supervisor went to the central office, where she made **her** report.

## Clear

Ann Dorr and the supervisor went to the central office, where **the supervisor** made her report.

An answer choice with clearly identified pronouns is a better choice than one with uncertain pronoun references. Sometimes the noun must be repeated to make the meaning clear.

In addition, the pronoun must match the noun it represents. If the noun is singular, the pronoun must be singular. Similarly, if the noun is plural, the pronoun must match.

## Mismatch

I stopped the driver to tell **them** a headlight was burned out.

## Match

I stopped the driver to tell **him** a headlight was burned out.

In the first example, *driver* is singular but the pronoun *them* is plural. In the second, the singular pronoun *him* matches the word it refers to.

## Verb Tenses

The best option is one in which the verb tense is consistent. Look for answer choices that describe the action as though it has already happened, using past tense verbs (mostly -*ed* forms). The verb tense must remain consistent throughout the passage.

## Inconsistent

I searched the room and find nothing unusual.

## Consistent

I searched the room and found nothing unusual.

The verbs *searched* and *found* are both in the past tense in the second version. In the first version, *find*, in the present tense, is inconsistent with *searched*.

It's easy to distinguish present tense from past tense by simply fitting the verb into a sentence.

| VERB TENSE | |
|---|---|
| **PRESENT TENSE** (Today, I __ . . . ) | **PAST TENSE** (Yesterday, I __ . . . ) |
| drive | drove |
| think | thought |
| rise | rose |
| catch | caught |

The important thing to remember about verb tense is to keep it consistent. If a passage begins in the present tense, keep it in the present tense unless there is a specific reason to change—to indicate that some action occurred in the past, for instance. If a passage begins in the past tense, it should remain in the past tense.

Check yourself with these sample questions. Choose the option that uses verb tense correctly. The answers follow after the questions.

**26. a.** When I cry, I always get what I want.
    **b.** When I cry, I always got what I want.
    **c.** When I cried, I always got what I want.
    **d.** When I cried, I always get what I wanted.

**27. a.** It all started after I came home and am in my room studying for a big test.

**b.** It all started after I came home and was in my room studying for a big test.

**c.** It all starts after I come home and was in my room studying for a big test.

**d.** It all starts after I came home and am in my room studying for a big test.

**28. a.** The child became excited, dashes into the house, and slams the door.

**b.** The child becomes excited, dashed into the house, and slammed the door.

**c.** The child becomes excited, dashes into the house, and slammed the door.

**d.** The child became excited, dashed into the house, and slammed the door.

## Answers
**26. a.**
**27. b.**
**28. d.**

## Clear Modifiers

The best option will use words clearly. Watch for unclear modifying words or phrases such as the ones in the next group of sentences. Misplaced and dangling modifiers can be hard to spot because your brain tries to make sense of things as it reads. In the case of misplaced or dangling modifiers, you may make a logical connection that is not present in the words.

## Dangling Modifiers

Nailed to the tree, Cedric saw a "No Hunting" sign.
Waddling down the road, we saw a skunk.

## Clear Modifiers

Cedric saw a "No Hunting" sign nailed to a tree.
We saw a skunk waddling down the road.

In the first version of the sentences, it sounds like *Cedric* was nailed to a tree and *we* were waddling down the road. The second version probably represents the writer's intentions: The *sign* was nailed to a tree and the *skunk* was waddling.

## Misplaced Modifier

A dog followed the boy that was growling and barking.

## Clear Modifiers

A dog that was growling and barking followed the boy.

Did you think the boy was growling and barking? The second version of the sentence represents the real situation.

## Efficient Language

The best option will use words efficiently. Avoid answer choices that are redundant (repeat unnecessarily) or are wordy. Extra words take up valuable time and increase the chances that facts will be misunderstood. In the following examples, the italicized words are redundant or unnecessary. Try reading the sentences without the italicized words.

## Redundant

They refunded our money *back to us*.
We can proceed *ahead* with the plan we made ahead of time.
The car was red *in color*.

## Wordy

*The reason* we left was because the job was done.
We didn't know what *it was* we were doing.
*There are* many citizens who obey the law.

In each case, the sentence is simpler and easier to read without the italicized words. When you find an answer choice that uses unnecessary words, look for a better option.

## Complete Sentences

The best option will be written in complete sentences. Sentences are the basic unit of written language. Most writing is done using complete sentences, so it's important to distinguish sentences from fragments. A sentence expresses a complete thought, whereas a fragment is only part of a complete thought.

Look at the following examples of complete and incomplete sentences.

## Fragment

The dog walking down the street.
Exploding from the bat for a home run.

## Complete Sentence

The dog was walking down the street.
The ball exploded from the bat for a home run.

These examples show that a sentence must have a subject (usually a noun) and a verb to complete its meaning. A **verb** is a word that describes an action, such as *run* or *go*. A **noun** is a person, place, or thing, such as *boy* or *kitchen* or *car*.

The first fragment has a subject and a verb, but the verb in this fragment—*walking*—needs a helping verb to make it a complete sentence. The second fragment has neither a subject nor a verb. *Exploding* looks like a verb, but it actually describes something not identified in the word group.

Now look at the next set of word groups. Mark those that are complete sentences.

**29. a.** We saw the tornado approaching.
    **b.** When we saw the tornado approaching.

**30. a.** Before the house was built in 1972.
    **b.** The house was built in 1972.

**31. a.** Since we are leaving in the morning.
    **b.** We are leaving in the morning.

If you chose **29a, 30b,** and **31b,** you were correct. You may have noticed that the groups of words are the same, but the fragments have an extra word at the beginning. These words are called subordinating conjunctions. Subordinating conjunctions make a phrase dependent upon another phrase. In other words, a group of words that would normally be a complete sentence will become dependent—it will need more information—when a subordinating conjunction is added. Subordinating conjunctions include words such as *when, since,* and *because*. Note the subordinating conjunctions in the following sentences:

- **When we saw the tornado approaching,** we headed for cover.
- **Before the house was built in 1972,** the old house was demolished.
- **Since we were leaving in the morning,** we went to bed early.

Here is a list of words that can be used as subordinating conjunctions.

| | |
|---|---|
| after | that |
| although | though |
| as | unless |
| because | until |
| before | when |
| if | whenever |
| once | where |
| since | wherever |
| than | while |

## Specific Language

Language that is specific and detailed says more than language that is general and vague.

## General

My sister and I enjoyed each other's company as we were growing up. We had a lot of fun, and I will always remember her. We did interesting things and played fun games.

## Specific

As children, my sister and I built rafts out of old barrels and tires, then tried to float them on the pond behind our house. I'll never forget playing war or hide-and-seek in the grove beside the pond.

The ideas behind both of these versions are similar, but the specific example is more interesting and memorable. Choose the option that uses specific language.

## Commonly Confused Words

The best answer uses words correctly. The following word pairs are often misused in written language. By reading the explanations and looking at the examples, you can learn to spot the correct way of using these easily confused word pairs.

### Its/it's

*Its* is a possessive pronoun that means "belonging to it." *It's* is a contraction for *it is* or *it has*. The only time you will ever use *it's* is when you can also substitute the words *it is* or *it has*.

### Who/that

*Who* refers to people. *That* refers to things.

- There is the man *who* helped me find a new pet.
- The woman *who* invented the copper-bottomed kettle died in 1995.
- This is the house *that* Harold bought.
- The magazine *that* I needed was no longer in print.

### There/their/they're

*Their* is a possessive pronoun that shows ownership. *There* is an adverb that tells where an action or item is located. *They're* is a contraction for the words *they are*. Here is an easy way to remember these words.

- *Their* means "belonging to them." With some creativity, *their* can be transformed into the word *them*. (Extend the *r* on the right side and connect the *i* and the *r* to turn *their* into *them*.) This clue will help you remember that *their* means "belonging to them."
- If you examine the word *there*, you can see from the way it's written that it contains the word *here*. Whenever you use *there*, you should be able to substitute *here*. The sentence should still make sense.
- Imagine that the apostrophe in *they're* is actually a very small letter *a*. Use *they're* in a sentence only when you can substitute *they are*.

### Your/you're

*Your* is a possessive pronoun that means "belonging to you." *You're* is a contraction for the words *you are*. The only time you will ever use *you're* is when you can also substitute the words *you are*.

### To/too/two

*To* is used as a preposition or an infinitive. As a preposition, it will suggest direction of movement; as an infinitive, it will suggest "to do."

- As a preposition: to the mall, to the bottom, to my church, to our garage, to his school, to his hideout, to our disadvantage, to an open room, to the gymnasium
- As an infinitive, *to* is followed by a verb: to walk, to leap, to see badly, to find, to advance, to read, to build, to want, to misinterpret, to peruse

*Too* means "also." Whenever you use the word *too*, substitute the word *also*. The sentence should still make sense.

*Two* is a number, as in *one, two*. This is a spelling you have to memorize.

The key is to think consciously about these words when you see them in written language. Circle the correct form of these easily confused words in the following sentences. Answers are at the end of the exercise.

**32.** (Its, It's) (to, too, two) late (to, too, two) remedy the problem now.

**33.** This is the man (who, that) helped me find the book I needed.

**34.** (There, Their, They're) going (to, too, two) begin construction as soon as the plans are finished.

**35.** We left (there, their, they're) house after the storm subsided.

**36.** I think (your, you're) going (to, too, two) win at least (to, too, two) more times.

**37.** The corporation moved (its, it's) home office.

### Answers
**32.** It's, too, to
**33.** who
**34.** They're, to
**35.** their
**36.** you're, to, two
**37.** its

The following are four sample multiple-choice questions. By applying the principles explained in this section, choose the best version of each of the four sets of sentences. The answers and a short explanation for each question follow the exercise.

**38. a.** Vanover caught the ball. This was after it had been thrown by the shortstop. Vanover was the first baseman who caught the double-play ball. The shortstop was Hennings. He caught a line drive.
  **b.** After the shortstop, Hennings, caught the line drive, he threw it to the first baseman, Vanover, for the double play.
  **c.** After the line drive was caught by Hennings, the shortstop, it was thrown to Vanover at first base for a double play.
  **d.** Vanover the first baseman caught the ball from shortstop Hennings.

**39. a.** This writer attended the movie *Casino*, starring Robert DeNiro.
  **b.** The movie *Casino*, starring Robert DeNiro, was attended by me.
  **c.** The movie *Casino*, starring Robert DeNiro, was attended by this writer.
  **d.** I attended the movie *Casino*, starring Robert DeNiro.

**40. a.** They gave cereal boxes with prizes inside to the children.
  **b.** They gave cereal boxes to children with prizes inside.
  **c.** Children were given boxes of cereal by them with prizes inside.
  **d.** Inside the boxes of cereal were prizes. The children got them.

**41. a.** After playing an exciting drum solo, the crowd rose to its feet and then claps and yells until the band plays another cut from their new album.

   **b.** After playing an exciting drum solo, the crowd rose to its feet and then clapped and yelled until the band played another cut from their new album.

   **c.** After the drummer's exciting solo, the crowd rose to its feet and then claps and yells until the band plays another cut from their new album.

   **d.** After the drummer's exciting solo, the crowd rose to its feet and then clapped and yelled until the band played another cut from their new album.

---

**The best option**

- is accurate
- is written in plain English
- presents information in a logical order
- has clearly identified pronouns that match the number of the nouns they represent
- has a consistent verb tense
- uses modifiers clearly
- uses words efficiently
- is written using complete sentences
- is specific
- uses words correctly

---

## Answers

**38. b.** Choice **a** is unnecessarily wordy and the order is not logical. Choice **c** is also wordy and unclear. Choice **d** omits a piece of important information.

**39. d.** Both choice **a** and **c** use the stuffy-sounding *this writer*. Choice **d** is best because it avoids the wordy phrase "was attended by."

**40. a.** In both choices **b** and **c**, the modifying phrase *with prizes inside* is misplaced.

**41. d.** Both choices **a** and **b** contain a dangling modifier, stating that the crowd played an exciting drum solo. Choice **c** mixes past and present verb tense. Only choice **d** has clearly written modifiers and a consistent verb tense.

## ▶ Additional Resources

One of the best resources for any adult student is the public library. Many libraries have resources for adult learners or for those preparing to enter or change careers. Those sections contain skill books and review books on a number of subjects, including vocabulary. Here are some books you might consult:

### Vocabulary

- *1001 Vocabulary & Spelling Questions* (LearningExpress)
- *601 Words You Need to Know to Pass Your Exam* by Murray Bromberg et al. (Barron's)
- *How to Build a Better Vocabulary* by Morris Rosenblum et al. (Warner Books)
- *Merriam-Webster's Vocabulary Builder* by Mary Wood Cornog (Merriam-Webster)
- *Vocabulary and Spelling Success in 20 Minutes a Day* (LearningExpress)
- *501 Synonym and Antonym Questions* (LearningExpress)
- *501 Word Analogies* (LearningExpress)

### Grammar and Writing

For more help with verbal expression, here are some books you can consult.

### For Nonnative Speakers of English

- *English Made Simple* by Arthur Waldhorn and Arthur Ziegler (Made Simple Books)

- *Basic English Grammar* by Betty Schrampfer Azar (Pearson)
- *English Grammar in Use with Answers* by Raymond Murphy (Cambridge University Press)

## For Everyone

- *501 Grammar and Writing Questions* (LearningExpress)
- *The American Heritage Book of English Usage* (Houghton Mifflin)

- *Cliffs Quick Review Writing: Grammar, Usage & Style* by Jean Eggenschwiler (Cliffs Notes)
- *The Handbook of Good English* by Edward D. Johnson (Washington Square Press)
- *Writing Skills Success in 20 Minutes a Day* (LearningExpress)
- *Writing Smart* by Marcia Lerner (Princeton Review)

# 13 ▶ Firefighter Practice Exam 3

## CHAPTER SUMMARY

This is the third practice exam in this book, based on the firefighter written exam. After working through the instructional material in the previous chapters, use this test to see how much your score has improved since you took the first exam.

**N**ow that you have been introduced to the skills tested on the firefighter exam, you should be more confident taking this third practice exam. Like Firefighter Practice Exam 1, this practice exam tests job-related skills.

The exam will test you in six areas: memory and observation, reading text, verbal expression, spatial relations, judgment, and following procedures. Though your actual exam is likely to use different categories for some of these questions, the skills tested here are similar to those tested on many firefighter exams.

For this third exam, simulate the actual test-taking experience as closely as possible. Find a quiet place to work where you won't be interrupted. Tear out the answer sheet on the next page and find some number 2 pencils. Set a timer or stopwatch, and give yourself three hours for the entire exam. When that time is up, stop, even if you haven't finished the entire test.

After the exam, use the answer key that follows to see how you did and to find out why the correct answers are correct. The answer key is followed by a section on how to score your exam.

## Practice Exam 3

| | | | | |
|---|---|---|---|---|
| 1. | ⓐ | ⓑ | ⓒ | ⓓ |
| 2. | ⓐ | ⓑ | ⓒ | ⓓ |
| 3. | ⓐ | ⓑ | ⓒ | ⓓ |
| 4. | ⓐ | ⓑ | ⓒ | ⓓ |
| 5. | ⓐ | ⓑ | ⓒ | ⓓ |
| 6. | ⓐ | ⓑ | ⓒ | ⓓ |
| 7. | ⓐ | ⓑ | ⓒ | ⓓ |
| 8. | ⓐ | ⓑ | ⓒ | ⓓ |
| 9. | ⓐ | ⓑ | ⓒ | ⓓ |
| 10. | ⓐ | ⓑ | ⓒ | ⓓ |
| 11. | ⓐ | ⓑ | ⓒ | ⓓ |
| 12. | ⓐ | ⓑ | ⓒ | ⓓ |
| 13. | ⓐ | ⓑ | ⓒ | ⓓ |
| 14. | ⓐ | ⓑ | ⓒ | ⓓ |
| 15. | ⓐ | ⓑ | ⓒ | ⓓ |
| 16. | ⓐ | ⓑ | ⓒ | ⓓ |
| 17. | ⓐ | ⓑ | ⓒ | ⓓ |
| 18. | ⓐ | ⓑ | ⓒ | ⓓ |
| 19. | ⓐ | ⓑ | ⓒ | ⓓ |
| 20. | ⓐ | ⓑ | ⓒ | ⓓ |
| 21. | ⓐ | ⓑ | ⓒ | ⓓ |
| 22. | ⓐ | ⓑ | ⓒ | ⓓ |
| 23. | ⓐ | ⓑ | ⓒ | ⓓ |
| 24. | ⓐ | ⓑ | ⓒ | ⓓ |
| 25. | ⓐ | ⓑ | ⓒ | ⓓ |
| 26. | ⓐ | ⓑ | ⓒ | ⓓ |
| 27. | ⓐ | ⓑ | ⓒ | ⓓ |
| 28. | ⓐ | ⓑ | ⓒ | ⓓ |
| 29. | ⓐ | ⓑ | ⓒ | ⓓ |
| 30. | ⓐ | ⓑ | ⓒ | ⓓ |
| 31. | ⓐ | ⓑ | ⓒ | ⓓ |
| 32. | ⓐ | ⓑ | ⓒ | ⓓ |
| 33. | ⓐ | ⓑ | ⓒ | ⓓ |
| 34. | ⓐ | ⓑ | ⓒ | ⓓ |
| 35. | ⓐ | ⓑ | ⓒ | ⓓ |

| | | | | |
|---|---|---|---|---|
| 36. | ⓐ | ⓑ | ⓒ | ⓓ |
| 37. | ⓐ | ⓑ | ⓒ | ⓓ |
| 38. | ⓐ | ⓑ | ⓒ | ⓓ |
| 39. | ⓐ | ⓑ | ⓒ | ⓓ |
| 40. | ⓐ | ⓑ | ⓒ | ⓓ |
| 41. | ⓐ | ⓑ | ⓒ | ⓓ |
| 42. | ⓐ | ⓑ | ⓒ | ⓓ |
| 43. | ⓐ | ⓑ | ⓒ | ⓓ |
| 44. | ⓐ | ⓑ | ⓒ | ⓓ |
| 45. | ⓐ | ⓑ | ⓒ | ⓓ |
| 46. | ⓐ | ⓑ | ⓒ | ⓓ |
| 47. | ⓐ | ⓑ | ⓒ | ⓓ |
| 48. | ⓐ | ⓑ | ⓒ | ⓓ |
| 49. | ⓐ | ⓑ | ⓒ | ⓓ |
| 50. | ⓐ | ⓑ | ⓒ | ⓓ |
| 51. | ⓐ | ⓑ | ⓒ | ⓓ |
| 52. | ⓐ | ⓑ | ⓒ | ⓓ |
| 53. | ⓐ | ⓑ | ⓒ | ⓓ |
| 54. | ⓐ | ⓑ | ⓒ | ⓓ |
| 55. | ⓐ | ⓑ | ⓒ | ⓓ |
| 56. | ⓐ | ⓑ | ⓒ | ⓓ |
| 57. | ⓐ | ⓑ | ⓒ | ⓓ |
| 58. | ⓐ | ⓑ | ⓒ | ⓓ |
| 59. | ⓐ | ⓑ | ⓒ | ⓓ |
| 60. | ⓐ | ⓑ | ⓒ | ⓓ |
| 61. | ⓐ | ⓑ | ⓒ | ⓓ |
| 62. | ⓐ | ⓑ | ⓒ | ⓓ |
| 63. | ⓐ | ⓑ | ⓒ | ⓓ |
| 64. | ⓐ | ⓑ | ⓒ | ⓓ |
| 65. | ⓐ | ⓑ | ⓒ | ⓓ |
| 66. | ⓐ | ⓑ | ⓒ | ⓓ |
| 67. | ⓐ | ⓑ | ⓒ | ⓓ |
| 68. | ⓐ | ⓑ | ⓒ | ⓓ |
| 69. | ⓐ | ⓑ | ⓒ | ⓓ |
| 70. | ⓐ | ⓑ | ⓒ | ⓓ |

| | | | | |
|---|---|---|---|---|
| 71. | ⓐ | ⓑ | ⓒ | ⓓ |
| 72. | ⓐ | ⓑ | ⓒ | ⓓ |
| 73. | ⓐ | ⓑ | ⓒ | ⓓ |
| 74. | ⓐ | ⓑ | ⓒ | ⓓ |
| 75. | ⓐ | ⓑ | ⓒ | ⓓ |
| 76. | ⓐ | ⓑ | ⓒ | ⓓ |
| 77. | ⓐ | ⓑ | ⓒ | ⓓ |
| 78. | ⓐ | ⓑ | ⓒ | ⓓ |
| 79. | ⓐ | ⓑ | ⓒ | ⓓ |
| 80. | ⓐ | ⓑ | ⓒ | ⓓ |
| 81. | ⓐ | ⓑ | ⓒ | ⓓ |
| 82. | ⓐ | ⓑ | ⓒ | ⓓ |
| 83. | ⓐ | ⓑ | ⓒ | ⓓ |
| 84. | ⓐ | ⓑ | ⓒ | ⓓ |
| 85. | ⓐ | ⓑ | ⓒ | ⓓ |
| 86. | ⓐ | ⓑ | ⓒ | ⓓ |
| 87. | ⓐ | ⓑ | ⓒ | ⓓ |
| 88. | ⓐ | ⓑ | ⓒ | ⓓ |
| 89. | ⓐ | ⓑ | ⓒ | ⓓ |
| 90. | ⓐ | ⓑ | ⓒ | ⓓ |
| 91. | ⓐ | ⓑ | ⓒ | ⓓ |
| 92. | ⓐ | ⓑ | ⓒ | ⓓ |
| 93. | ⓐ | ⓑ | ⓒ | ⓓ |
| 94. | ⓐ | ⓑ | ⓒ | ⓓ |
| 95. | ⓐ | ⓑ | ⓒ | ⓓ |
| 96. | ⓐ | ⓑ | ⓒ | ⓓ |
| 97. | ⓐ | ⓑ | ⓒ | ⓓ |
| 98. | ⓐ | ⓑ | ⓒ | ⓓ |
| 99. | ⓐ | ⓑ | ⓒ | ⓓ |
| 100. | ⓐ | ⓑ | ⓒ | ⓓ |

You will have five minutes to study the diagram on the following page, after which you must turn the page and answer questions 1–7 from memory. You will NOT be permitted to look back at the diagram to answer the questions.

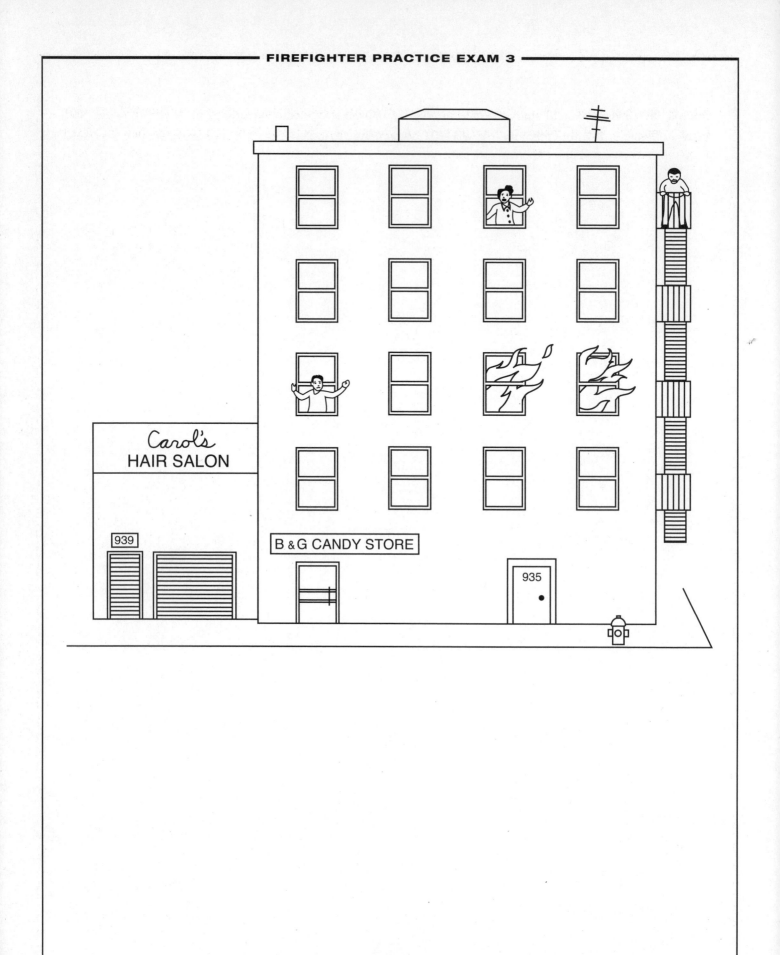

Carol's
HAIR SALON

939

B & G CANDY STORE

935

After you have spent five minutes studying the diagram on the previous page, answer questions 1–7 based on the diagram. DO NOT turn back to the diagram to answer these questions. When you have finished questions 1–7, you may go on to the next memory diagram.

1. The fire building has
   a. no fire escape or stairs on the sides of the building.
   b. one set of stairs on the outside of the building.
   c. a fire escape on the outside of the building.
   d. a fire escape and a set of stairs on the outside of the building.

2. Fire is showing at
   a. two windows in 935.
   b. one window in 939.
   c. two windows in 939.
   d. one window in 935.

3. There are three civilians in the drawing. They are located on
   a. the second, third, and fourth floors.
   b. the fourth and fifth floors and the fire escape.
   c. the third, fourth, and fifth floors.
   d. the third and fifth floors and the fire escape.

4. The closest fire hydrant can be found
   a. in front of the store.
   b. in front of the apartment building.
   c. on the side of the apartment building.
   d. on the side of the store.

5. The sign on the first floor of the apartment building reads
   a. 939.
   b. Carol's Hair Salon.
   c. Apartment 935.
   d. B & G Candy Store.

6. The firefighters need to do a roof rescue. What obstacles may be in their way?
   a. a TV antenna, a clothesline, and a smoke stack
   b. a TV antenna, a smoke stack, and two civilians
   c. a TV antenna, a smoke stack, and an air shaft
   d. a TV antenna, a clothesline, and an air shaft

7. How many people most likely need to be evacuated from the hair salon?
   a. none
   b. one
   c. two
   d. three

You will have five minutes to study the diagram on the following page, after which you must turn the page and answer questions 8–12 from memory. You will NOT be permitted to look back at the diagram to answer the questions.

BEDROOM A

LIVING
ROOM

BEDROOM B

UTILITY

KITCHEN

BATH
ROOM

PANTRY

HALLWAY

Doors are shown as...............................

Windows are shown as.........................

Smoke detectors are shown as.............

Fire extinguishers are shown as...........

After you have spent five minutes studying the diagram on the previous page, turn the page and answer questions 8–12 based on the diagram. DO NOT turn back to the diagram to answer these questions. When you have finished questions 8–12, you may go on to the next diagram and set of questions.

**8.** Which of the following rooms is NOT found in this apartment?
   **a.** Utility room
   **b.** Dining room
   **c.** Pantry
   **d.** Bedroom B

**9.** If a fire were to start in the cushions of the couch in the living room, which room in the apartment would be most affected by the spread of the fire?
   **a.** Kitchen
   **b.** Bedroom A
   **c.** Bedroom B
   **d.** Bathroom

**10.** Which room in the apartment contains a fire extinguisher?
   **a.** There is no fire extinguisher in the apartment.
   **b.** Kitchen
   **c.** Bedroom A
   **d.** Utility room

**11.** You see smoke and fire issuing from a double window in the apartment as you approach the building. In which room is the fire located?
   **a.** Living Room
   **b.** Bedroom A
   **c.** Kitchen
   **d.** Bedroom B

**12.** You are searching the apartment by entering the door into the kitchen and following the wall on your left as you enter the door. As you follow this wall, you count the number of doors you locate along the wall. Which number door, not counting the one from the hall into the kitchen, opens into Bedroom B?
   **a.** third
   **b.** second
   **c.** fifth
   **d.** fourth

N

D

LOADING DOCK 2

GAS STORAGE

SHIPPING AND RECEIVING

QUALITY CONTROL

MATERIAL PREPARATION

C

MATERIAL STORAGE

OFFICES AND LOBBY

PARKING LOT

A

SCRAP AND WASTE STORAGE

FABRICATION

COATING AND FINISHING

LOADING DOCK 1

B

Doors are shown as..............
Garage doors shown as..............
Standpipe shown as..............
Skylights shown as..............
Roof vents shown as..............

BUILDING SIDES ARE DESIGNATED A, B, C, D

You will have five minutes to study the diagram on the previous page, after which you must turn the page and answer questions 13–15 from memory. You will NOT be permitted to look back at the diagram to answer the questions.

**13.** You are responding to a fire at this facility and your engine receives an order to pump the standpipe connection for the building. Which side of the building is the standpipe connection located?

a. Side A

b. Side B

c. Side C

d. Side D

**14.** In which corner of the building is the gas storage area located?

a. Corner A-B

b. Corner B-C

c. Corner C-D

d. Corner A-D

**15.** How many skylights are there in the building?

a. 11

b. 10

c. 8

d. 4

Answer questions 16–19 based on the following information.

Our department has always been a leader in community initiatives, providing new services to the community as they are needed. Our newest service is the Fire Assistance and Support Team (FAST). In the past, we would arrive on the scene of a residential fire, put out the fire as quickly as possible, and then leave. The homeowners would be left on their own to deal with the aftermath. With our new program, the families affected are not left alone to deal with everything that needs to be done. The FAST will stay with the victims and assist them in a variety of ways. The services provided by FAST personnel include:

- explaining what is going on at the fire scene
- keeping the family informed as to when they will be able to re-enter their home
- making phone calls on the family's behalf (insurance company, family members, schools, etc.)
- assisting the family with finding a place to stay for the night
- accompanying the family as the investigator goes through their home
- assisting with the removal of any items the family may wish to retrieve
- providing the family with transportation

The team works with the Red Cross, Salvation Army, and other service organizations. The team will remain in contact with the victims until their assistance is no longer required.

**16.** What is this passage about?
   **a.** cooperation with the Red Cross and similar private agencies
   **b.** getting insurance companies to deliver on their contracts
   **c.** explaining fire department operations to the general public
   **d.** assisting victims in dealing with the aftermath of a fire

**17.** The description of the FAST in this passage has all of the following duties listed EXCEPT
   **a.** explaining fire department actions at the fire scene.
   **b.** boarding up the home after the fire.
   **c.** finding the family a place to stay for the night.
   **d.** transporting the victims to a shelter.

**18.** A synonym for *exhaustive* is
   **a.** conclusive.
   **b.** consistent.
   **c.** comprehensive.
   **d.** extortive.

**19.** What would be a possible title for this passage?
   **a.** A FAST Way to Serve Our Community
   **b.** A New Way to Assist and Support Fire Victims
   **c.** Standing Up for Victims
   **d.** Providing Help for Those in Distress

Answer questions 20–22 based on your best judgment and common sense.

**20.** You respond to a call for a chemical leaking from barrels in a warehouse. When you arrive on scene you find about a dozen barrels that are marked with this label:

Based on this marking, what would you expect to be the most critical danger associated with the chemicals in these barrels?
   **a.** They could catch fire.
   **b.** They are poisonous.
   **c.** They could explode.
   **d.** They are corrosive.

**21.** Fires in vacant buildings can cause many problems for firefighters. Which of the following factors is least likely to pose difficulty?
   **a.** The building is likely to be boarded up.
   **b.** The building's structure may be weak and unstable.
   **c.** There could be unknown combustible materials in the building.
   **d.** Probably no one lives in the building.

**22.** There has been a small fire in a first-floor apartment. The fire is now extinguished and Firefighter Neal has been assigned to the overhaul team. As he begins to work, he notices that there are discolored places on the wall marking where pictures once hung, where there are now smaller pictures or no pictures. He also notices that there are no personal possessions around and that the bookshelves are empty. In this situation, he should
   **a.** just ignore it and get the overhaul done so he can return to the station.
   **b.** look around and wait until the work is finished to tell his officer.
   **c.** leave the apartment and let a police officer know what he observed.
   **d.** immediately advise his supervisor of his observations and ask her to alert the arson squad.

Answer questions 23–26 solely on the basis of the information in the following passage.

Operating a fire department pump requires an understanding of friction loss and other factors that will reduce the amount of water pressure in a fire hose. Operating the pump at the correct pressure will ensure that the nozzle functions properly and the water stream is the most effective in extinguishing the fire. Operating pumps at excessive pressure places additional stress on equipment and on firefighters using the lines. Excessive pressure also increases nozzle reaction forces that are acting on the firefighters using the hose line making the line more difficult to control. Operating pumps at too low a pressure is also hazardous to the firefighters on the line. Inadequate pressure can also make streams ineffective and may not supply enough water volume to extinguish the fire. The fire hose will also kink more easily at lower pressures.

The basic equation for calculating pressure at the nozzle in a hose line is:

Nozzle Pressure = Pump Pressure – Friction Loss – Appliance Loss + Elevation Loss or Gain.

To find the pressure needed at the pump, the equation becomes:

Pump Pressure = Nozzle Pressure + Friction Loss + Appliance Loss + Elevation Loss or Gain.

Nozzle pressure is the optimum pressure needed to form an effective stream. Fog type nozzles typically operate at 100 psi, although some models are designed to operate at lower pressures. Hand-held solid bore nozzles typically operate at 50 psi. Solid bore master streams can operate at pressures as high as 80 psi. Pressures that exceed these values will make hose streams less effective in putting out the fire.

Pump pressure is the pressure at which the pump on the truck is operating. This is the pressure that the pump needs to be operated at to overcome the losses and provide the required nozzle pressure.

Friction loss is a reduction in pressure as water flows through a hose. It is caused by the water rubbing against the inside surface of the hose and being slowed down. Friction loss is affected by several factors, but the two most important factors are: the diameter of the hose and the amount of water flowing through the hose. Larger hose lines have lower friction loss than smaller ones flowing the same volume of water. Friction loss will increase in a given-size hose as the volume of water flowing through it increases. In general, if the flow in a given-size hose is doubled, the friction loss is also doubled.

Appliance loss is a loss in pressure caused by a hose appliance being placed in a hose line. An appliance can be a device used to split one line into two smaller lines such as a gated wye, a section of pipe in an aerial ladder truck, or a large-size nozzle such as a deluge gun that is designed to flow very large amounts of water.

Elevation loss or gain is caused by a change in elevation between the pump and the nozzle. If the nozzle is above the pump, additional pressure is required to pump the water up to overcome gravity. If the nozzle is below the pump, gravity will reduce the amount of pressure needed to pump the water.

**23.** Which of the following conditions is NOT a concern caused by using excessive pump pressures on hose lines?
   **a.** Firefighters could lose control of the hose line.
   **b.** A hose line could burst.
   **c.** The motor on the pumper could become overheated.
   **d.** The hose line could kink and cut off some of the water flow to the nozzle.

**24.** To properly operate a pump, a firefighter would need to know all of the following information EXCEPT:
   **a.** the types of nozzles being used on hose lines.
   **b.** what type of material is is on fire.
   **c.** the lengths of the hose lines.
   **d.** the floor in a multistory building in which the hose line is being used.

**25.** Two hose lines are being operated from the same pumper at a fire. One line has a fog nozzle, is 200 ft. long, and has 25 psi of friction loss per 100 ft. of hose. The second line has a hand-held solid bore nozzle, is 400 ft. long, and has 10 psi of friction loss per 100 ft. of hose. Which of the following statements is correct?
   **a.** The two lines need to be pumped at the same pressure.
   **b.** The line with the fog nozzle needs to be pumped at a higher pressure.
   **c.** The line with the hand-held solid bore nozzle needs to be pumped at a higher pressure.
   **d.** There is not enough information to determine which line needs more pressure

**26.** You are operating a pump that is supplying a hose line attached to an aerial truck. The aerial truck has raised its ladder and is flowing water from the ladder through its installed ladder pipe. The aerial truck does not have a pump; it is relying on your pump only. Which of the following factors would need to be accounted for in finding the pump pressure required?
   **a.** The height of the building that is on fire
   **b.** If there are any firefighters on the ladder while water is flowing.
   **c.** How far the aerial ladder is extended (in other words, how long it is)?
   **d.** How far away from the fire building the aerial ladder is parked?

Answer questions 27–31 solely on the basis of the map on the following page. The arrows indicate traffic flow: One arrow indicates a one-way street going in the direction of the arrow, and no arrows represent a two-way street. You are not allowed to go the wrong way on a one-way street.

**27.** While Firefighter Flores is on duty in the fire station, an elderly man asks her to help him find the Senior Citizens' Center. She should tell him to
  **a.** walk across the street to the Senior Citizens' Center.
  **b.** ask a police officer how to get to the Senior Citizens' Center.
  **c.** walk north to Avenue B, west on Avenue B to the end of the park, make a right, and go one block.
  **d.** walk north to Avenue B, west on Avenue B to Lafayette Street, make a right, and go one block.

**28.** The head librarian needs gasoline for his automobile. He is leaving the Avenue D garage exit from the library. His quickest legal route to the gas station is to go
  **a.** north on Central Street to Avenue C and west on Avenue C to the gas station.
  **b.** west on Brooklyn Street to Avenue B and north on Avenue B to the gas station.
  **c.** west on Avenue D to Grand Street and north on Grand Street to the gas station.
  **d.** west on Avenue D to Lafayette Street and north on Lafayette Street to the gas station.

**29.** Firefighter Puckett is leaving the firehouse and is on his way to the high school to pick up his son. Which is the most direct, legal way to go?
  **a.** north to Avenue B, west to Grand Street, south to Avenue D, east to Greene Street, and then north to the entrance to the high school
  **b.** south on Brooklyn Street, west on Avenue D, and north on Greene Street to the entrance of the high school
  **c.** north to Avenue A, west to Lafayette Street, south on Lafayette Street, east on Avenue C, and south on Greene Street to the entrance of the high school
  **d.** south on Brooklyn Street, west on 1st Avenue, and north on Greene Street to the entrance of the high school

**30.** Firefighter Healy's spouse is a nurse at the city hospital and goes to the public library every Monday as a volunteer. What would be the shortest legal route from the hospital to the library?
  **a.** west on Avenue A, south on Lafayette Street, east on Avenue C, and south on Central Street to the library entrance
  **b.** east on Avenue B and south on Central Street to the library entrance
  **c.** west on Avenue A, south on Lafayette Street, and east on Avenue D to the library entrance
  **d.** east on Avenue A and south on Central Street to the library entrance

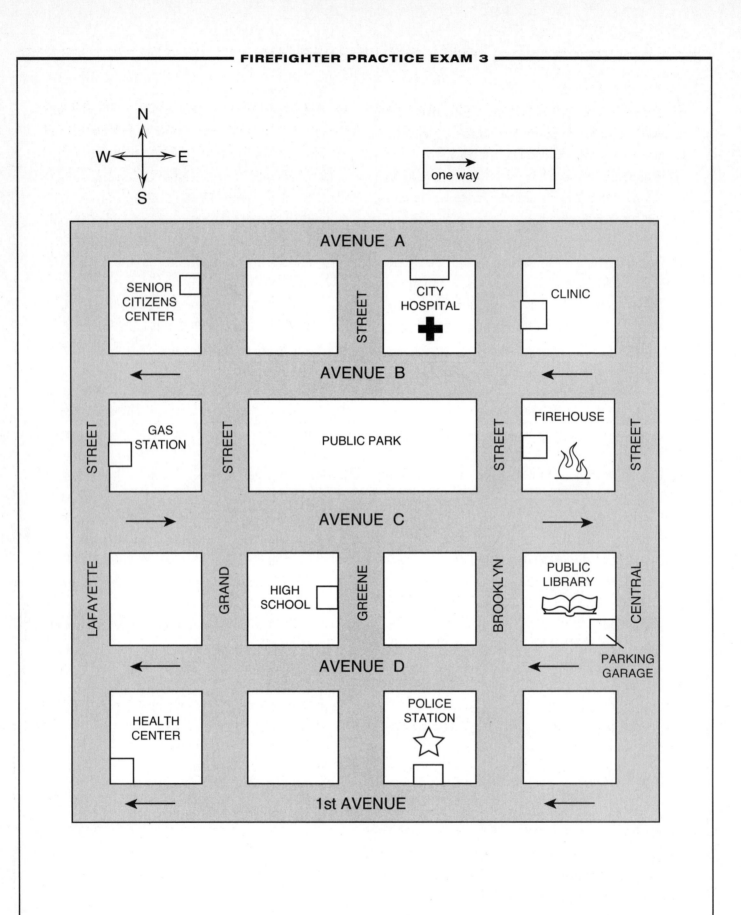

**31.** Firefighter Jones is driving an ambulance with a patient from an accident at the intersection of Avenue C and Grand Street. What is the shortest legal route to the emergency department entrance on Avenue A?

    **a.** east on Avenue C, north on Brooklyn Street and west on Avenue A

    **b.** north on Grand Street, east on Avenue B, north on Greene Street, east on Avenue A

    **c.** north on Grand Street, east on Avenue A

    **d.** east on Avenue C, north on Central Street, west on Avenue A

Answer questions 32–35 solely on the basis of the information in the following passage.

Firefighters work in an environment in which high heat and humidity put stress on their bodies. They wear gear that protects them against fire and the gases of combustion, but this leads to even further potential heat stress. A physical reaction to heat-induced stress occurs when the body loses large amounts of salt and water through the process of sweating. During fire operations, firefighters become overheated, and due to the heavy loss of fluids, their bodies cannot eliminate the heat. If not properly monitored, firefighters may be prone to conditions such as heat exhaustion and heat stress. For that reason, it is vital that all fire personnel take the time to learn the signs of heat stress.

Heat exhaustion is generally characterized by clammy skin, fatigue, nausea, dizziness, profuse perspiration, and sometimes fainting, resulting from an inadequate intake of water and the loss of fluids. First aid treatment for this condition includes having the victim lie down, raising the feet 8–12 inches, applying cool, wet cloths to the skin, and giving the victim sips of salt water (1 teaspoon per glass, half a glass every 15 minutes), over the period of an hour.

Heat stroke is much more serious; it is an immediate life-threatening situation. The characteristics of heat stroke are a high body temperature (which may reach 106° F or more); a rapid pulse; hot, dry skin; and a blocked sweating mechanism. Victims of this condition may be unconscious, and first aid measures should be directed at cooling the body quickly. The victim should be placed in a tub of cold water or repeatedly sponged with cool water until his or her temperature is lowered sufficiently. Fans or air conditioners will also help with the cooling process. Care should be taken, however, not to overly chill the victim once the temperature is below 102° F.

**32.** The most immediate goal of a person tending a victim of heat stroke should be to

    **a.** get salt into the victim's body.

    **b.** raise the victim's feet.

    **c.** lower the victim's pulse.

    **d.** lower the victim's temperature.

**33.** Which of the following is a symptom of heat exhaustion?

    **a.** a rapid pulse

    **b.** profuse sweating

    **c.** hot, dry skin

    **d.** a weak pulse

**34.** Heat stroke is more serious than heat exhaustion because heat stroke victims

    **a.** have no salt in their bodies.

    **b.** cannot take in water.

    **c.** do not sweat.

    **d.** have frequent fainting spells.

**35.** Symptoms such as nausea and dizziness in a heat exhaustion victim indicate that the person most likely needs to
   **a.** be immediately taken to a hospital.
   **b.** be given salt water.
   **c.** be immersed in a tub of water.
   **d.** sweat more.

**36.** Choose the sentence that is most clearly written.
   **a.** Less money for new fire trucks and other equipment mean the occurrence of budget cuts as well as the recession.
   **b.** Budget cuts, as well as the recession, have meant less money for new fire trucks and other equipment.
   **c.** Budget cuts, the recession as well, and there is less money for fire trucks and other equipment.
   **d.** With less money, recessive budget cuts means fewer fire trucks and other equipment.

**37.** Choose the sentence that is most clearly written.
   **a.** All day, the exhausted volunteers struggled through snake-ridden underbrush, but they still have not been found during this search.
   **b.** The exhausted volunteers struggled all day as they searched for the teenagers through snake-ridden underbrush who still had not been found.
   **c.** All day, the exhausted volunteers had struggled through snake-ridden underbrush in search of the missing teenagers, who still have not been found.
   **d.** During their search, the teenagers still have not been found all day while the exhausted volunteers struggled through the snake-ridden underbrush.

Answer questions 38–41 solely on the basis of the information in the following passage.

A recent wildland fire response led to an incident in which some firefighters were trapped, and quick action was needed to save them. The chief of the department had the incident reviewed, and the following recommendations were made:

   **Recommendation 1:** Provide firefighters with wildland personal protective equipment (e.g., fire-resistant pants or coveralls and fire shelters) and ensure its use.

   **Recommendation 2:** Firefighters who fight wildland fires should be equipped with an approved fire shelter and provided training on the proper deployment of that fire shelter at least annually with periodic refresher training.

   **Recommendation 3:** Utilize National Weather Service Fire Weather Forecasters for all fire weather predictions and immediately share with all personnel all information about significant fire weather and fire behavior events.

   **Recommendation 4:** Firefighters engaged in wildland firefighting should learn, communicate, and follow the ten standard fire orders as developed by the Forest Service.

- Fight fire aggressively but provide for safety first.
- Initiate all action based on current and expected fire behavior.
- Recognize current weather conditions and obtain forecasts.
- Ensure instructions are given and understood.
- Obtain current information on fire status.
- Remain in communication with crew members, your supervisor, and adjoining forces.
- Determine safety zones and escape routes.
- Establish lookouts in potentially hazardous situations.

- Retain control at all times.
- Stay alert, keep calm, think clearly, and act decisively.

**38.** After several older members of the company read the recommendations, they stated that all this has been tried before, but the advice was eventually ignored because any protective equipment, no matter how light, is excessive weight. In wildland firefighting, they believe that mobility is far more important than additional protective equipment. What should a firefighter do?

  **a.** Join with the older members because they have experience, and complain about the recommendations.

  **b.** Ignore the recommendations as just one more directive.

  **c.** Get a copy of the full report and look at the basis of the recommendations before he or she says anything.

  **d.** The new protocol is a direct order, so he or she should do as instructed.

**39.** Why is it important to recognize and forecast weather conditions at a wildland fire?

  **a.** Weather affects the behavior of wildland fires.

  **b.** Firefighters can predict when rain will come.

  **c.** If the weather turns cold, the department will need to get warm clothes up to the firefighters.

  **d.** Weather has an effect on radio communications.

**40.** Because Firefighter Boyle showed so much interest in the equipment and gear used in wildland firefighting, the captain has assigned her the task of showing how to deploy the shelters. While she has the instructions, she wants more information. What should she do?

  **a.** Tell the captain that she is not really interested in giving a presentation.

  **b.** Call the department training officer and get her to do the work.

  **c.** Get on the Internet and see what the forestry service has available for training in this area.

  **d.** Just use what she has and get the job over with.

**41.** All of the following are part of the ten standard fire orders EXCEPT

  **a.** aggressively fight a fire at all times.

  **b.** initiate any action based on current and expected fire behavior.

  **c.** always have an escape route.

  **d.** ensure all orders are given and understood.

Answer questions 42 and 43 solely on the basis of the following map. The arrows indicate traffic flow; one arrow indicates a one-way street going in the direction of the arrow; two arrows represent a two-way street. You are not allowed to go the wrong way on a one-way street.

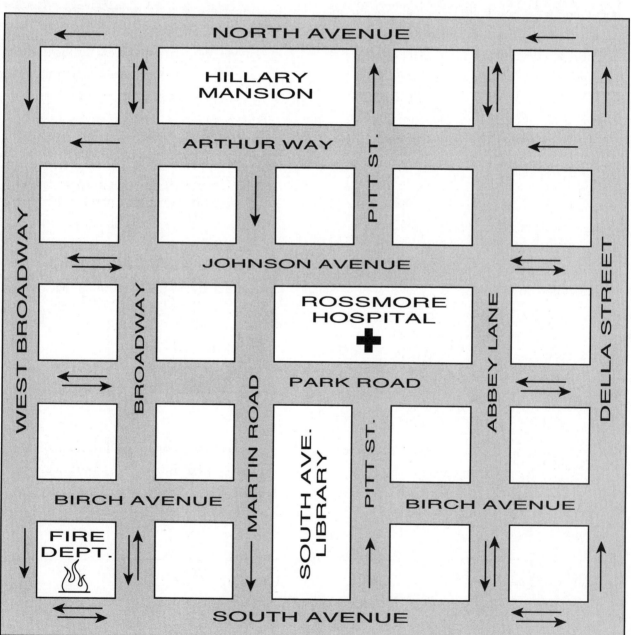

**42.** Firefighter Lazere has just had his lunch break at the South Avenue Library, which faces South Avenue. He must now go to a meeting at the North Avenue entrance to the Hillary Mansion. What is Firefighter Lazere's most direct route to the Hillary Mansion?

   **a.** Go east on South Avenue, then turn north on Abbey Lane to North Avenue, then west on North Avenue to the Hillary Mansion.

   **b.** Go east on South Avenue, then turn north on Pitt Street, then west on North Avenue to the Hillary Mansion.

   **c.** Go west on South Avenue, then turn north on West Broadway, then east on North Avenue to the Hillary Mansion.

   **d.** Go west on South Avenue, then turn north on Broadway to North Avenue, then east on North Avenue to the Hillary Mansion.

**43.** Firefighter Lew is just returning from lunch and is southbound on Martin Road. She has just crossed Park Road when she receives a call for help at a fire in a residence at the corner of Arthur Way and Della Street. What is Officer Lew's most direct route to the residence?

   **a.** Make a U-turn on Martin Road, then go north on Martin Road to Arthur Way, then east on Johnson Avenue to Della Street, then north on Della Street to the residence.

   **b.** Continue south on Martin Road, then go east on South Avenue, then north on Pitt Street, then east on Park Road, then north on Abbey Lane, and then east on Arthur Way.

   **c.** Continue south on Martin Road, then go east on South Avenue, then north on Della Street to the residence.

   **d.** Continue south on Martin Road, then go north on Abbey Lane, then east on Arthur Way to the residence.

Answer questions 44–48 based on the information in the following table. This table gives data on friction loss in 100-ft. lengths of fire hose, based on the amount of water flowing and the size of the hose.

| | Hose Line Size | | | |
|---|---|---|---|---|
| | $1\frac{3}{4}''$ | $2\frac{1}{2}''$ | 3" | 4" |
| 100 GPM | 12 psi | 3 psi | | |
| 200 GPM | 53 psi | 10 psi | | |
| 300 GPM | | 21 psi | 8 psi | |
| 400 GPM | | 36 psi | 14 psi | |
| 500 GPM | | 55 psi | 20 psi | 5 psi |

(Flow — left axis label)

**Friction Loss in 100–ft. Hose**

**44.** What is the approximate percentage difference of friction loss between a $\frac{1}{2}''$ hose and a $1\frac{3}{4}''$ hose flowing 200 GPM?

   **a.** 38%

   **b.** 19%

   **c.** 9%

   **d.** 500%

**45.** If the values in the table are based on 100 ft. of hose, how much friction loss would occur in a 3" hose flowing 400 GPM that is 600 ft. long?

   **a.** 68 psi

   **b.** 48 psi

   **c.** 80 psi

   **d.** 120 psi

**46.** A $2\frac{3}{4}$" hose line that is 300 ft. long is being pumped at a pressure of 110 psi. The hose is flowing 200 GPM. What will the approximate nozzle pressure be with this arrangement?

For this problem, Nozzle Pressure = Pump Pressure – Friction Loss

  **a.** 50 psi

  **b.** 60 psi

  **c.** 80 psi

  **d.** 120 psi

**47.** Your department is considering changing from 3" hose to 4" hose for its pumpers. For a 500 GPM flow, what is the approximate fraction of the friction loss in the 4" hose per the friction loss in the 3" hose?

  **a.** $\frac{1}{2}$

  **b.** $\frac{1}{4}$

  **c.** $\frac{1}{8}$

  **d.** 4

**48.** During a routine inspection, Firefighter Franklin discovers that an air cylinder contains about 2,500 psi of air. Fire department policy is that all air cylinders must contain between 4,000 psi and 4,500 psi of air. What is the approximate percentage of air in the cylinder compared to the minimum amount required by the policy?

  **a.** 56%

  **b.** 63%

  **c.** 45%

  **d.** 72%

Answer questions 49–51 based on your best judgment and common sense.

**49.** Firefighter Lawrence is on the fire department's softball team, and her team has advanced to the play-offs. In the bottom of the ninth inning with the bases loaded, she is up next. If she scores for her team, the game will be tied and go into extra innings. She looks at her watch and realizes she has to be at work in 20 minutes. If the game does go into extra innings, she will be late. She should

  **a.** lose the game on purpose because getting to work on time is more important.

  **b.** call her superior officer and tell him she will be late because of the game.

  **c.** keep playing and explain the circumstances to her superior officer when she gets to the firehouse.

  **d.** ask someone to take her place so she can report for duty on time.

**50.** Firefighter Ott is driving his spouse home and is planning to go straight to work from there. Unfortunately, he is in an accident. The other driver insists that they should exchange insurance information, which will make Firefighter Ott late for work. He should

  **a.** leave without delay since the public and other firefighters depend on him, and he must not be late.

  **b.** call his superior officer, explain what happened, and then proceed with exchanging information.

  **c.** tell the driver of the other car that he will be in touch later, explaining how important it is for him to be on time.

  **d.** leave the scene, but have his spouse stay and exchange the information.

**51.** Firefighter Nixey has just gotten off duty and arrived back home. When she gets out of her car, she hears her neighbors across the street yelling and sees that the husband is on a ladder near an open window. Firefighter Nixey goes over to find out if she can help. The wife explains that their two-year-old has locked herself in the bathroom. Firefighter Nixey can see that the ladder is not tall enough for the man to reach the child from the open window. Her best course of action would be to
   **a.** tell them to call the fire department, whose taller ladders will enable firefighters to rescue the child quickly and safely.
   **b.** leave them to deal with the situation on their own, so they will learn to be more responsible in the future about their child's safety.
   **c.** call the police and report them for child endangerment.
   **d.** advise them that breaking down the bathroom door would be easier than climbing the ladder.

Answer questions 52–55 solely on the basis of the information in the following passage.

Understanding the basics of fire extinguishers is a requirement for firefighters who teach fire safety to the public. Different types of fires require different types of extinguishers. Being able to clearly explain the differences can save lives and property.

Class A fires involve combustible materials such as paper, wood, and cloth. A water-filled extinguisher is the most effective in putting out these fires. Residents should direct the nozzle toward the base of the fire and spray until all involved material is wet. A dry chemical extinguisher can also be used on some Class A fires.

Fires that involve flammable liquids, such as gasoline and paint, are Class B fires. Dry chemical extinguishers are most effective on these types of fires. Residents should stand about ten feet from the fire and spray the chemical substance at the base of the fire. As the fire diminishes, they can slowly move closer. If there is no wind, carbon dioxide extinguishers, which decrease the amount of oxygen, can be used.

Energized electrical fires are in the Class C category. If it can be done quickly and safely, residents should attempt to shut off power before confronting this type of fire. Dry chemical extinguishers work well on these types of fires. Carbon dioxide extinguishers should be used for delicate electronic equipment such as computers as they will not damage the circuits. Water-filled extinguishers should only be used once the power has been turned off.

Fires involving combustible metals such as magnesium are Class D fires. Special foam compounds are needed to extinguish these fires.

Extinguishers should be kept in areas where they are easily accessible but safe from damage and out of the reach of children.

**52.** On which of the following types of fires can water-filled extinguishers be used?
   **a.** Class A and Class C
   **b.** Class B and Class D
   **c.** Class A and Class B
   **d.** Class B and Class C

**53.** If a pan of grease caught fire on top of a stove, which of the following would be the ideal extinguisher to employ?
   a. carbon dioxide unit
   b. foam unit
   c. water-filled unit
   d. dry chemical unit

**54.** If the motor in a clothes dryer caught fire in the laundry room of an apartment building, which type of extinguisher would be the best to use?
   a. water-filled unit
   b. carbon dioxide unit
   c. dry chemical unit
   d. foam unit

**55.** Which of the following is the main idea of the passage?
   a. Residents should learn how to operate extinguishers.
   b. Firefighters should understand that extinguishers can save lives.
   c. Different types of extinguishers are effective on various kinds of fires.
   d. Electrical fires require a special type of extinguisher.

**56.** Off-duty Firefighter Roth is walking her dog behind the apartment building at 4498 Cahill Avenue when she hears someone calling for help. She looks up and sees an older man at the window on the third floor. The man shouts that his wife may have had a heart attack and his phone is out of order. Roth goes into the building and calls 911 from the superintendent's phone. Which of the following statements reports the emergency most clearly and accurately?
   a. Send an ambulance to the apartment building at 4498 Cahill Avenue. A woman on the third floor may have had a heart attack.
   b. A woman may have suffered a heart attack behind 4498 Cahill Avenue and needs an ambulance.
   c. The woman's husband on the third floor of the apartment building said she had a heart attack, but his phone is out of order.
   d. An ambulance is immediately needed at 4498 Cahill Avenue. I spoke to the victim's husband in the alley behind the building where she had a heart attack.

**57.** Firefighter Delgado is returning to the station during a torrential rainstorm. As he is making a left turn onto Bartola Street from Unity Road, he slides on the slick pavement. He loses control of the truck, and it bounces up over the curb and hits a bus shelter. Fortunately, no one is waiting for the bus. The truck, however, is disabled. Which of the following statements reports this information most clearly and accurately?

**a.** At the bus shelter near Unity Road in the rain, I lost control of the truck that became disabled after hitting the curb. The bus shelter was empty.

**b.** During the rainstorm, my disabled truck attempted a left turn onto Bartola Street. When I got to the bus shelter, no one was waiting for the bus, which was fortunate when I lost control and ran up over the curb.

**c.** From Unity Road, I missed the turn onto Bartola Street after I lost control of the truck. It bounced over the curb, which hit the bus shelter. Although the truck is disabled, the shelter did not sustain injuries.

**d.** As I was turning left onto Bartola Street from Unity Road, the truck slid on the wet pavement. I lost control and hit the bus shelter. The shelter was empty, but my truck is disabled.

**58.** While taking out the trash at his home at 804 Olive Street, Firefighter Johnston slips on the icy sidewalk and twists her right ankle. Johnston is in pain and soon realizes that she cannot put weight on her ankle. Her neighbor takes her to the hospital, where a doctor tells her she has a severe sprain and should not go back to work for at least a week. The next day, Johnston calls her chief to tell her why she will not be reporting for work. Which of the following statements describes the situation most clearly and accurately?

**a.** I fell on the ice outside my home and suffered a severe ankle sprain. The doctor has advised me not to return to work for at least a week.

**b.** After falling on the ice, my neighbor took me to the hospital last night, so I will not be reporting for work all week.

**c.** I cannot put weight on my right ankle where I fell on the sidewalk at 804 Olive Street and am not coming into work as the doctor prescribed.

**d.** The right ankle is sprained. This occurred when the trash was taken out on the sidewalk, and a doctor at the hospital has warned me not to come to work for a week.

Answer questions 59–63 based solely on the information in the following passage.

Firefighters are often called upon to speak to school and community groups about the importance of fire safety, particularly fire prevention and detection. Because smoke detectors cut a person's risk of dying in a fire in half, firefighters often provide audiences with information on how to install these protective devices in their homes.

A smoke detector should be placed on each floor level of a home and outside each sleeping area. A good site for a detector would be a hallway that runs between living spaces and bedrooms.

Because of the dead air space that might be missed by turbulent hot air above a fire, smoke detectors should be installed either on the ceiling at least four inches from the nearest wall, or high on a wall at least four, but no further than 12 inches from the ceiling. Detectors should not be mounted near windows, exterior doors, or other places where drafts might direct the smoke away from the unit. Nor should they be placed in kitchens and garages, where cooking and gas fumes are likely to set off false alarms.

**59.** What is the main focus of this passage?
   a. how fire fighters carry out their responsibilities
   b. the detection of dead air space on walls and ceilings
   c. the proper installation of home smoke detectors
   d. how smoke detectors prevent fires in homes

**60.** The passage implies that dead air space is most likely to be found
   a. on a ceiling, between four and 12 inches from a wall.
   b. close to where a wall meets a ceiling.
   c. near an open window.
   d. in kitchens and garages.

**61.** The passage states that, when compared with people who do not have smoke detectors, persons who live in homes with smoke detectors are
   a. 50% more likely to survive a fire.
   b. 50% more likely to prevent a fire.
   c. 100% more likely to detect a hidden fire.
   d. 200% more likely not to be injured in a fire.

**62.** A smoke detector should not be installed near a window because
   a. outside fumes may trigger a false alarm.
   b. a wind draft may create a dead air space.
   c. a wind draft may pull smoke away from the detector.
   d. outside noises may muffle the sound of the detector.

**63.** The passage indicates that one responsibility of a firefighter is to
   a. install smoke detectors in the homes of residents in the community.
   b. check homes to see if smoke detectors have been properly installed.
   c. develop fire safety programs for community leaders and school teachers to use.
   d. speak to school children about the importance of preventing fires.

**64.** Firefighter Lopez was getting into his truck after responding to a small garage fire in the middle of the 2200 block of Howard Street when a woman suddenly ran up to the vehicle. The woman, Ina Barry, explained that her gold watch had fallen into the street the previous evening and that a street sweeper had swept it up. She wanted Firefighter Lopez to tell her where the city's street sweepers deposited what they picked up. Firefighter Lopez carefully explained that this problem was not under his jurisdiction and told her to file a report with the Sanitation Department. When he returned to the station, Firefighter Lopez reported the incident to his chief. Which of the following describes the incident most clearly and accurately?

**a.** Ina Barry is the name of the woman who said that her gold watch was confiscated by a street sweeper in the 2000 block of Howard Street. I told her to call the Sanitation Department because she was talking to the wrong department.

**b.** While I was putting out a garage fire on Howard Street, I told a woman named Ina Barry to file a report with the Sanitation Department about her gold watch.

**c.** A woman named Ina ran up to my truck as I was getting into it and said that the street sweeper was responsible for the loss of her gold watch and that this should be reported to the Sanitation Department.

**d.** As I was getting into my truck in the 2200 block of Howard Street, a woman named Ina Barry ran up and told me that her watch had been swept up by the street sweeper. I advised her to contact the Sanitation Department.

**65.** A job announcement states, "The application period for this position is from January 15 through March 1. Applications are available at the Fire Department at 600 Main Street. Application forms must be received at the department by 5:00 P.M. on the closing date of the application period." Which of the following statements describes this announcement most clearly and accurately?

**a.** Application forms for this position must be received at the Fire Department at 600 Main Street between January 15 and 5:00 P.M. on March 1.

**b.** Application forms should be picked up at 500 Main Street and returned to the same location by 6:00 P.M. on March 1 to be considered for the position.

**c.** According to the job announcement, the closing of the application is between January 15 and March 1 at the Fire Department on Main Street.

**d.** Pick up applications at the Fire Department at 600 Main Street. Return application forms on January 15 or March 1 at the same location.

Answer questions 66–68 based on your best judgment and common sense.

**66.** While on duty, Firefighter Wilson sees a fellow firefighter behaving in what seems to her a suspicious manner. She suspects that he is sabotaging another firefighter's equipment. She should

**a.** tell the firefighter to stop, and threaten to report him if she sees him doing it again.

**b.** do nothing because she is not absolutely sure of the true nature of the incident.

**c.** tell the firefighter whose equipment may have been tampered with that he should be careful.

**d.** report the incident and her impressions to her superior officer.

**67.** While searching a fire scene for hidden pockets of fire, Firefighter Morse finds a book of matches with a cigarette inside rolled up in newspaper. He shows it to the investigating officer because he is convinced that that was how the fire was started. The investigator is able to determine who the arsonist was from that evidence. Later, a reporter comes into the firehouse to ask him about the arson suspect who was just arrested. The reporter was told that evidence found at the fire scene led to the arsonist being caught and wants to give Firefighter Morse credit for helping in the case. How should he answer the reporter's questions?

**a.** Don't answer any of the questions because the arsonist may come after him.

**b.** Tell the reporter he has no comment, and call his superior officer over.

**c.** Don't answer any of the questions because this is strictly a police matter.

**d.** Tell the reporter everything he knows because his actions were truly heroic.

**68.** A company responds to a call of a car fire on the main highway. The first order the superior officer gives is to put flares on the road. The flares serve to

**a.** warn motorists that they need to use extreme caution.

**b.** give citizens confidence that their tax money is being put to good use.

**c.** educate passing motorists on just how dangerous car fires can be.

**d.** let the police know where the firefighters are working.

**69.** Firefighter Yamata is responding to a report of a smoking dumpster at an apartment building in the 700 block of Norcross Road. While he is checking the dumpster, two boys run up to his truck and spray graffiti on the driver's door. Mrs. Stanley, who is walking her dog, is the only witness to the crime. She stops Firefighter Yamata and tells him that one of the boys, Randy McGill, age 13, lives in the 800 block of Norcross. When Firefighter Yamata returns to the garage, he files a report. Which of the following statements most clearly and accurately describes what occurred?

**a.** On the 700 block of Norcross Road, which I was responding to, Mrs. Stanley told me about the graffiti on the truck. It appeared there after teenagers living on the next block ran down Norcross with a spray can. It was on the driver's side.

**b.** Mrs. Stanley was walking her dog and said that Randy McGill lived in the next block of Norcross from the one I was doing the pickup. He was 13 and spray painted the truck, but I did not get an eyewitness myself because I was busy with the dumpster.

**c.** Mrs. Stanley and her dog told me that Randy McGill lived in the 800 block of Norcross while I was responding to a call in the 700 block. He was 13 with another boy, and I was told that they were the ones to spray the graffiti. However, I did not witness this myself.

**d.** As I was responding to a call in the 700 block of Norcross Road, Mrs. Stanley witnessed two boys spraying graffiti on the driver's side of my truck. She identified one of the boys as 13-year-old Randy McGill, who lives in the 800 block of Norcross.

**70.** New county regulations for fire prevention state that all property owners must clear away dry undergrowth on or before May 15 of each year. By the same date, property owners must also trim back any tree limbs that overhang or are touching the roof of the house or any other buildings on the property. After May 15, firefighters who are making inspections may cite owners for failing to comply with the regulations. On May 1, Mr. Jacobs phones the fire station and asks Firefighter Jones to explain the new regulations. Which of the following statements is the most clear and accurate explanation?

**a.** During the next week, you should clear away the dry undergrowth and tree limbs that are touching the roof of your house and which overhang them.

**b.** By May 15, you must remove all dry undergrowth and trim back any tree limbs that overhang or are touching the roof of any building on your property.

**c.** Trim back all tree limbs and remove all dry undergrowth that overhangs or touches your house or any other building on your property by May 15 of each year.

**d.** You will be fined for any and all tree limbs that overhang your roof or for the dry undergrowth that you should have removed before May, which is the deadline.

**71.** Firefighter Jarvis is returning to the station after having spoken to students at an elementary school. There had been rain earlier in the day, but now the temperature has dropped below freezing. Firefighter Jarvis is heading east across the Livingston Bridge when his truck hits a patch of ice and slides into a guardrail. Fortunately, he is not hurt. There is slight damage, however, to the right side of the truck. Later, Firefighter Jarvis files a report on the accident. Which of the following reports describes the incident most clearly and accurately?

**a.** As I was driving on the Livingston Bridge, I hit some ice and slid into a guardrail, damaging the right side of the truck.

**b.** The guardrail damaged the right side of the truck, which was sitting on the Livingston Bridge on a patch of ice.

**c.** When I hit an icy patch along the Livingston Bridge, the guard rail hit the right side of the truck, causing me to slide into it.

**d.** Though I was not hurt, the truck was on its right side after it hit the guard rail on the bridge.

Answer questions 72–74 solely on the basis of the following map. The arrows indicate traffic flow: One arrow indicates a one-way street going in the direction of the arrow, and two arrows represent a two-way street. You are not allowed to go the wrong way on a one-way street.

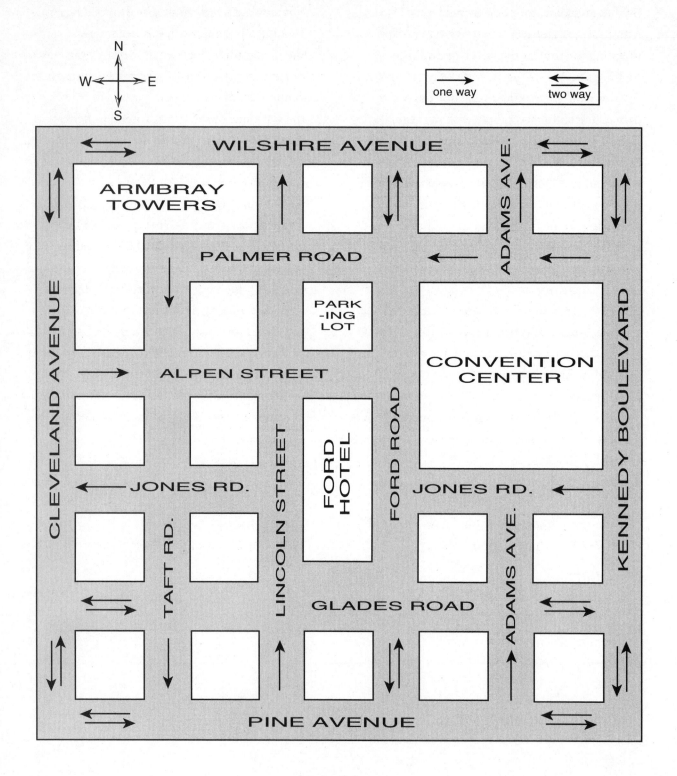

**72.** Firefighters Muldoon and Chavez have just gotten off work and are eating breakfast at Al's Cafe, which faces Jones Road. They get a call of a serious fire at the Cleveland Avenue entrance to the Armbray Towers and are asked to come and help. What is their most direct route to the Armbray Towers?

    **a.** Go east on Jones Road, then south on Kennedy Boulevard, then west on Glade Road, then north on Cleveland Avenue to the Armbray Towers.

    **b.** Go west on Jones Road to Cleveland Avenue, then north on Cleveland to the Armbray Towers.

    **c.** Go west on Jones Road, then south on Ford Road, then west on Glade Road, then north on Cleveland Avenue to the Armbray Towers.

    **d.** Go west on Jones Road, then north on Glade Road, then west on Palmer Road, then south on Taft Road, then west on Jones Road, then north on Cleveland Avenue to the Armbray Towers.

**73.** Firefighters Chang and Parker are returning from a meeting and are northbound on Lincoln Street and have just crossed Alpen Street. They hear on the radio that a pickup truck has caught fire on Adams Avenue at Pine Avenue and is blocking traffic. They decide to go see if they can be of assistance. What is their most direct route to the truck fire scene?

    **a.** Continue north on Lincoln Street, then east on Wilshire Boulevard, then south on Ford Road, then east on Glade Road, then south on Adams Avenue to the accident scene.

    **b.** Continue north on Lincoln Street, then west on Palmer Road, then south on Taft Road, then east on Pine Avenue to the accident scene.

    **c.** Make a U-turn on Lincoln Street, south on Lincoln Street, east on Pine Avenue to the accident scene.

    **d.** Continue north on Lincoln Street, then east on Wilshire Avenue, then south on Kennedy Boulevard, then west on Pine Avenue to the accident scene.

**74.** Firefighter Tananga is southbound on Kennedy Boulevard. He makes a right turn onto Glade Road, then a left onto Taft Road, a right onto Pine Avenue and another right onto Cleveland Avenue, and then a right onto Wilshire Avenue. Which direction is he facing?

    **a.** west

    **b.** south

    **c.** east

    **d.** north

Answer questions 75–78 based on your best judgment and common sense.

**75.** Firefighter Schultz is a dinner guest in a friend's home. The friend yells for help from the kitchen, and Firefighter Schultz rushes in to find that grease in a frying pan has caught fire. The first thing she should do is
- a. remind everyone she is a firefighter to avoid the danger of panic.
- b. turn off the stove and cover the pan with a metal object.
- c. pour water on the pan.
- d. throw the pan out the window.

**76.** Firefighter Rupert receive a call at the firehouse in which a citizen reports smelling gas in her home. The first thing he should advise the citizen to do is to
- a. avoid doing anything that might cause a spark, including making any more calls.
- b. turn off all gas appliances and leave the house immediately.
- c. open all the doors and windows to ventilate the house.
- d. call the gas company from the house next door.

**77.** Which of the following would be the best way for the driver of a fire truck that is responding to an alarm to approach a red light at an intersection?
- a. Stop and wait for a green light.
- b. Have firefighters riding on the truck motion other vehicles away.
- c. Drive straight through because a fire truck always has the right of way.
- d. Stop and proceed as soon as the traffic is clear.

**78.** Firefighter Muhammed is at an elementary school with his lieutenant, doing an inspection of the school. While walking through the halls, he is approached by a six-year-old boy who asks why he should bother to learn fire safety rules. Firefighter Muhammed should tell him that
- a. learning fire safety rules will help him and his family know what to do in case of emergency.
- b. he needn't memorize the rules as he might get them wrong; he should let his parents or school officials advise him what to do in case of an emergency.
- c. knowing fire safety rules can show who is the smartest student in the class.
- d. he should write a letter to the fire commissioner for a complete answer.

Answer questions 79–82 based solely on the following passage.

**Department Order 301**
**Daily Station Inspection of Fire Apparatus**

**Purpose:** All apparatus or vehicles assigned to companies must be inspected on a daily basis and the results of that inspection recorded and reported to vehicle maintenance.

**Discussion:** It is important that the apparatus assigned to the companies and personnel of this department be available to answer any and all alarms to ensure the safety of this community. Over the past few months, there have been reports that minor problems with apparatus have not been addressed in a timely manner. This is a concern due to the high number of reports of accidents and incidents involving fire service vehicles in the United States. This order will establish a method to ensure that there is a program to inspect and report the findings to the Mechanic's Office before a minor problem becomes the cause of a failure. The Mechanic's Office has an ongoing program for weekly and periodic maintenance reports and service checks, but the daily inspection of the apparatus has varied from station to station as well as shift to shift. It is the purpose of this order to ensure that all daily inspections are carried out and reported the same way, and that this report is forwarded to the Mechanic's Office for action. Maintenance schedules are the foundation of a well-planned maintenance program, but do not catch minor problems that occur on a daily basis.

**Action:** Each shift must conduct a daily inspection of the apparatus or vehicle assigned. The Mechanic's Office will forward to each company officer the manufacturer's recommendation for proper fluid levels and maintenance checks to be done on a daily basis. Weekly inspections will be done by the Mechanic's Office while the vehicle is in quarters. The officer assigned to the apparatus is responsible for ensuring that the inspection is made as soon as the shift has been relieved, or, if relieving when an alarm is in progress or being immediately dispatched, as soon as practicable after the shift begins. The officer is also responsible for ensuring that the report is forwarded promptly to the Mechanic's Office.

- The **Assigned Vehicle Operator** is responsible for the mechanical readiness of the apparatus or vehicle assigned. That inspection will include, but not be limited to, checking the oil level, coolant level, batteries, visible and audible warning signals, fuel levels, and tires for any damage. The operator is also responsible for carrying out an inspection of the any installed air system, including a test of the air brakes in accordance with the directions set forth by the Mechanic's Office, noting any failure, decrease, or fluctuation in air pressure. All of this information will be noted on the forms provided and forwarded to the officer assigned to the apparatus. Any discrepancies considered to be safety-related may require that the apparatus be taken out of service and replaced by a spare. That decision is the responsibility of the

assigned officer, guided by the recommendation of the Mechanic's Office, with the approval of the shift supervisor.

- Each **Company Member**: Each member of the company should check his or her assigned riding position to ensure that all safety equipment, such as the seat belt, is in place and operating properly. Any discrepancies will be reported to the assigned officer.

**Action:** Safety is of the first importance in the performance of duties. Safe apparatus means safe responses. It is the responsibility of all assigned personnel to work together to ensure that the apparatus is ready to respond. A safety-related deficiency may be grounds for removing the apparatus from service until the deficiency is corrected. The final determination of the suitability of any apparatus for response remains the prerogative of the chief of department, who can overrule any decision.

79. According to the passage, who is the person charged with the duty to make the final determination on whether an apparatus should be suitable for response?
    a. vehicle operator
    b. mechanic
    c. assigned officer
    d. chief of department

80. The assigned vehicle operator is responsible for the following checks EXCEPT
    a. tire damage.
    b. all riding position seat belts.
    c. oil levels.
    d. leaks.

**81.** After reading the passage, what seems to be the reason for this order?

    **a.** The chief is worried that the mechanic is not doing the job assigned.

    **b.** The department vehicles are responding with a number of unreported safety violations.

    **c.** A number of apparatus accidents around the nation made the chief want to tighten procedures to prevent similar incidents.

    **d.** The mechanic needs additional reports to the office to justify clerical help.

**82.** Engine Two has just relieved. As soon as the assigned personnel start their safety inspection, an alarm comes in for a structure fire in their first due area. What should the lieutenant on duty do?

    **a.** Continue the inspection and respond when it is complete.

    **b.** Report that Engine Two is out of service for inspection and request that the backup company respond.

    **c.** Respond, but at a reduced speed, as the truck has not been inspected.

    **d.** Respond as normal and do the inspection when the company returns to quarters.

Answer questions 83–84 based on your best judgment and common sense.

**83.** While fighting a fire at a building, Firefighter Bennett notices that cracks are developing in the walls and the ceiling starting to sag. Her best first course of action is to

    **a.** do nothing, since these are usual conditions at a fire and are to be expected.

    **b.** immediately communicate her observation to her superior officer and other firefighters.

    **c.** run out of the building immediately.

    **d.** go to the floor above to find the cause of the damage.

**84.** Firefighters should take great care when handling flammable liquids because the vapors from these liquids can travel to sources that can ignite them easily. Which of the following would NOT be advisable when refueling firefighting equipment?

    **a.** keeping as many other firefighters from entering the area as possible

    **b.** taking pains not to overfill the equipment

    **c.** allowing smoking in the area as long as it is done some distance away

    **d.** opening windows and doors in the immediate area

**85.** Firefighter Simpson's company is responding to a multi-vehicle accident at which injured citizens are trapped. He is driving an engine and has two more blocks to go when he sees a detour sign, and the road ahead is blocked off. He was just down this same block this morning, and no construction was going on. Following the detour sign will take him four blocks out of his way. He should

   **a.** proceed directly through the traffic barrier, knocking it out of the way.

   **b.** move the traffic barrier and call the fire commissioner when he returns to the firehouse to report a detour that should not exist.

   **c.** follow the detour sign because he can't be sure that construction was not begun since he last drove by this spot.

   **d.** call his superior officer and ask that officer what he should do.

Answer questions 86–88 based on the Dwelling Inspection Form on the next page. Each item on the form is numbered. The questions refer to those numbers.

**86.** The presence of a handicapped person should be marked under which number?

   **a.** 12

   **b.** 15

   **c.** 16

   **d.** 11

**87.** While inspecting a residence, a firefighter finds several electrical devices plugged into a single outlet. The resident has not used a power strip with a circuit breaker, but rather used several old plug splitters that allow more then one plug to be placed in a single socket. Which number should the firefighter mark to show this?

   **a.** 8

   **b.** 9

   **c.** 12

   **d.** 18

**88.** Which number shows the inspecting firefighter's station?

   **a.** 5

   **b.** 7

   **c.** 10

   **d.** 4

Answer questions 89–90 based on your best judgment and common sense.

**89.** An elementary school is visiting the firehouse. Some of the students begin climbing on the truck, others ask to hear the siren and see the lights, and still others want to slide down the pole. The best way to handle this is to

   **a.** ask the teacher to gather the class into a group for an organized tour of the firehouse.

   **b.** advise the teacher on how to give the tour so that the firefighters can return to more important duties directly related to firefighting.

   **c.** tell the teacher the class will have to leave but may come back when the children have learned proper behavior in a firehouse.

   **d.** scold the children for not behaving in the firehouse and advise the teacher to either bring them under control or leave.

## DWELLING INSPECTION FORM

Address: _____1_____ Date:_____2_____

The firefighter doing the inspection was: _____3_____

of Station No. _____4_____ Telephone:_____5_____

If homeowner is not in, check here:__6___

If homeowner refuses entry, check here:__7___

With your consent, a member of the fire department has just completed an inspection of your home. By eliminating any of the conditions or hazards checked below, you will make your home a safer place in which to live.

Improper use of extension cords, check here:__8___

Overfusing, check here:__9___

Improper storage of flammable or combustible liquids, check here:__10___

Defective smoke pipe vent or chimney, check here:__11___

Housekeeping, check here:__12___

Illegal burning. Burning in barrels, portable incinerators, or on the open ground is prohibited. Check here:__13___

Other conditions, check here:__14___

Remarks:_____15_____

_____

**16.** Are there invalids? Yes_____ No_____ Posted? Yes_____ No_____

**17.** Are there any smoke detectors in the home? Yes_____ No_____

**18.** Are there any fire extinguishers in the home? Yes_____ No_____

**19.** Are there any children under age 18 in the home? Yes_____ No_____ Posted? Yes_____ No_____

**20.** Are there any animals in the home? Yes_____ No_____

**90.** While Firefighter McKiernan is walking to work, dressed in her uniform, she witnesses an automobile accident. Which of the following actions is the most appropriate?

   **a.** She leaves because if she stays she will be late for work.

   **b.** She stays to offer any information about what she saw, since she is a witness.

   **c.** She leaves after giving her name to the persons involved in the accident, so she can be contacted later about what she saw.

   **d.** She leaves so that she will not involve the fire department in what may become a court case.

Answer questions 91–94 based on the following information.

Firefighters must sometimes use the aerial ladder on the fire truck to reach the upper levels of a building during a fire. This is the large ladder that is attached to the fire truck, and many can pivot and extend in excess of 100 feet. To operate the aerial ladder, firefighters must take the following steps in the order shown.

   **1.** Activate the outriggers to stabilize the truck.

   **2.** Increase the idle speed of the truck's internal combustion engine to 2,500 RPM because the engine is used to drive the motors that operate the ladder.

   **3.** To prevent electrocution, check the locations of overhead wires prior to activating the ladder.

   **4.** Observe the following with regard to the three control levers that operate the ladder: Lever 1 controls the angle of the ladder, which must not exceed 60 degrees. Lever 2 controls the extension of the ladder, which must not exceed 50 feet. Lever 3 controls the rotation of the ladder.

   **5.** In the case of strong winds, the extension limit is a matter of department policy—usually half the full extension.

**91.** Firefighters have determined that they require the use of the aerial ladder to investigate the third floor of a high-rise building that is on fire. What should they do next?

   **a.** Raise the ladder to 60 degrees.

   **b.** Turn on the pumps.

   **c.** Activate the outriggers.

   **d.** Check the wind speed.

**92.** What is the maximum allowable angle to which the aerial ladder can be raised when the wind speed is less than 30 miles per hour?

   **a.** 60 degrees

   **b.** 50 degrees

   **c.** 3 degrees

   **d.** 30 degrees

**93.** What is the recommended maximum distance the ladder may be extended when the wind speed is strong?

   **a.** 100 feet

   **b.** 25 feet

   **c.** 75 feet

   **d.** 50 feet

**94.** Firefighters who are using the aerial ladder want to extend it from 40 to 45 feet. They should use

   **a.** Lever 1.

   **b.** Lever 2.

   **c.** Lever 3.

   **d.** Lever 4.

Answer questions 95 and 96 based on your best judgment and common sense.

**95.** While on duty, Firefighter Dumaine is ordered by her superior officer to issue a summons to a car parked directly in front of a fire hydrant. A citizen is upset because the firefighter gave his neighbor a summons. What should she do?

　**a.** Put the incorrect license number on the summons and tell the citizen his neighbor will not receive a summons, but that the neighbor should not do it again.

　**b.** Tell her superior officer she does not feel it is her place to write a summons.

　**c.** Tell the citizen he must leave the scene or she will give him a summons as well.

　**d.** Explain to the citizen what a serious problem blocked fire hydrants are at fires.

**96.** A writer from *Firefighters Weekly* walks into the firehouse. She is doing a story about alcoholism in the workplace and wants Firefighter Kim to give a statement. A source has told her that a firefighter in the firehouse has had a problem with alcohol. What should he tell her?

　**a.** that he knows the firefighter she is referring to and will find out if that firefighter is willing to talk with her

　**b.** that he personally knows of no one in this firehouse who has an alcohol problem but that he will report the rumor to his superior officer

　**c.** that he does not wish to comment but will get his superior officer for her

　**d.** that as a good citizen he will tell her what she wants to know as long as his name does not appear in the article

Answer questions 97–100 based on the following information.

Moving toward a workplace in which cultural diversity is valued means challenging the comfort zones of people entrenched in the status quo. Those who promote change within an institution thus face strong reactions. The personnel who represent change often become the convenient targets of that reaction. Fire service leaders must ensure that firefighters of color, women firefighters, and others do not shoulder the entire burden of the fire service's cultural transition. Deliberate change in an organization happens from the top down. If a fire department is to move from the melting pot to the mosaic, the chief and top management must take the initiative to change their own attitudes and behavior first to redesign policy and provide the education that will implement change throughout the department.

For top management to be able to support diversity effectively, its members must understand and be able to identify the cultural differences that exist within the workforce. Managers should be aware of their own stereotypes and assumptions, and learn to listen to people positively, being careful not to discount ideas that they don't agree with or that come from someone with a different background. Managers should promote diversity education actively and see that all employees have access to the information, people, and other resources they need to do their jobs. A good manager of a diverse workforce will encourage constructive communication about differences instead of pretending everyone is alike, and will treat people in the workforce with fairness instead of with cookie-cutter uniformity.

What is the future for a fire service leader who chooses not to implement these changes? The chief of a diverse workforce who does not deal positively with diversity will find his or her leadership weakened. A chief who talks the talk about valuing diversity but fails to support its implementation loses credibility and sets the program up for failure.

**97.** What would be a good title for this passage?
  **a.** Valuing Diversity
  **b.** Making Change Deliberately
  **c.** Managing a Diverse Workforce
  **d.** Diversity Leadership: Walking the Walk

**98.** *Implement* can be replaced with
  **a.** use a tool.
  **b.** listen to.
  **c.** apply.
  **d.** act on.

**99.** If top management is to be able to support diversity, they must
  **a.** pretend that everyone is alike.
  **b.** ensure others are aware of their stereotypes.
  **c.** disregard ideas they do not agree with.
  **d.** encourage constructive communication about differences.

**100.** What does the phrase *from the melting pot to the mosaic* mean?
  **a.** For the fire department to function, every person in the department must think and act alike.
  **b.** Diversity is a problem to any fire department trying to function as a unit.
  **c.** Everyone does not have to think and act alike to work together for a common purpose.
  **d.** The sole purpose of diversity is to engage with the local community.

# ▶ Answers

**1. c.** A fire escape is visible on the right side of the diagram; there are no stairs shown in the diagram.

**2. a.** Fire can be seen in two windows of building #935.

**3. d.** The people can be seen on the third and fifth floors and on the fire escape.

**4. b.** The fire hydrant is located in the front of the apartment building.

**5. d.** The sign *B & G Candy Store* can be seen on the first floor of the apartment building.

**6. c.** A TV antenna, a smoke stack, and an air shaft can be seen on the roof.

**7. a.** No people can be seen in the hair salon.

**8. b.** There is no dining room shown on the plan, only an eat-in kitchen with a counter.

**9. a.** The kitchen is more likely to be affected first by fire spread because there is not a full wall between it and the living room.

**10. d.** The extinguisher is located in the utility room.

**11. a.** The living room is the only room with a double window.

**12. d.** Once you enter the apartment and follow the wall on your left, you would find doors to the following rooms in this order: Pantry—Utility—Bathroom—Bedroom B.

**13. b.** The standpipe connection is located on Side B near the loading dock.

**14. e.** The gas storage area is located in the upper right hand corner of the building, making it Corner C-D in this example.

**15. a.** There are a total of 11 skylights in the shop area of the building. Skylight locations are important to note on preplans since they can be used to ventilate buildings if a fire occurs.

**16. d.** The paragraph does mention the Red Cross and other agencies, and aiding the victims to call the insurance company, but the main thrust is assisting the victims of a fire to recover from a fire. Explaining fire department operations to the general public is the job of the public relations officer.

**17. b.** The team may help a victim to arrange for boarding up the fire-damaged home, but they do not do it.

**18. c.** Not *exhaustive* as used here means that it is not a *comprehensive* list of duties.

**19. b.** Although all the titles could be used here, choice **b** is the one that best fits the passage's main point.

**20. d.** The marking on the barrel, also known as a placard, indicates that the chemical will corrode skin and other objects.

**21. d.** The possibility that there is no one to rescue is not a problem for the firefighters; it is simply one less thing to worry about. The other choices are all hazards when fighting a fire in a vacant building.

**22. d.** What Firefighter Neal observed in the apartment does not make sense. Although it could be the home of a family who just moved in or has very little in the way of possessions, it could also be a sign of arson for profit. Firefighters should never ignore signs of criminal activity, and should stop overhaul until the investigators look at what was found and give permission to continue.

**23. d.** The last sentence of the first paragraph states that fire hose is more likely to kink when inadequate pressure is used. Higher pressures actually help to prevent kinking of the hose, however, excessive pressure can cause any of the other three conditions.

**24. b.** The type of material that is on fire is not needed to properly operate the pump. The other answers are all factors in determining the proper pump pressure.

**25. b.** From the third paragraph, the required nozzle pressure for a fog nozzle is 100 psi, whereas the required nozzle pressure for the solid bore nozzle is 50 psi. The first line is shorter, but has more friction loss; loss in the first line is 2 × 25 psi = 50 psi, whereas the loss in the second line is 4 × 10 psi = 40 psi. The first line requires more pressure.

**26. c.** Knowing how far the aerial ladder is extended would allow you to estimate the elevation difference and loss between the pump and the nozzle. In practice you should also consider the angle of the ladder in making this estimate. Note that some aerial trucks have nozzles that can be set at different locations along the length of the ladder. This means that the nozzle may not be at the end of the ladder but may be at some other point.

**27. c.** Choice **a** will take the man to the park, not to the Senior Citizens' Center. Telling the man to ask a police officer (choice **b**) would be unnecessary and discourteous. Choice **d** will take him to the Senior Citizens Center, but not to the entrance.

**28. d.** Choice **a** will take the librarian the wrong way on Avenue C. Choice **b** shows the wrong directions for the streets—Brooklyn Street runs north–south and Avenue B runs east–west. Choice **c** will leave the librarian one block east of the gas station.

**29. b.** The other choices will bring you to the high school legally but are not as direct.

**30. d.** Route **a** is less direct. Route **b** does not start from the hospital and, at any rate, will involve going the wrong way on Avenue B. Route **c** will be less direct and will involve going the wrong way on Avenue D.

**31. c.** Choice a is less direct and requires an additional turn. Choice b will go the wrong way on Avenue B. Choice d is the longest route.

**32. d.** This is clearly stated in the last paragraph (*first aid measures should be directed at cooling the body quickly*). The other responses are first aid for heat exhaustion victims.

**33. b.** This is clearly stated in the first sentence of the second paragraph. Choices **a** and **c** are symptoms of heat stroke. Choice **d** is not mentioned.

**34. c.** Heat stroke victims have a *blocked sweating mechanism*, as stated in the third paragraph.

**35. b.** This is an inference from the information given in the second paragraph: If the victim still suffers from the symptoms listed in the first sentence of the paragraph, the victim needs more water and salt to help with the *inadequate intake of water and the loss of fluids* that caused those symptoms.

**36. b.** This is the only clearly written sentence. Choice **a** makes no sense. Choices **c** and **d** are unclear because they are poorly worded and have misplaced modifiers.

**37. c.** This is the only clear statement. In choice **a**, it is not clear who has not been found. Choice **b** sounds like the underbrush has not been found. Choice **d** sounds like the teenagers are both lost and searching.

**38. c.** Although choices **a** and **b** are tempting because they are easy, these actions do nothing to improve safety in the department. Choice **d** is also tempting, after all, you are only a small part of a large organization, but knowledge is power, which is why **c** is the correct answer. Even if you obey the recommendations, you should be aware of why they were made and then use this knowledge to improve safety.

**39. a.** Weather is one of the major factors that determine the progress of a wildland fire. Humidity and temperature effect how fast a fire will move. Wind can drive a fire to sweep through areas and a change in wind direction can drive flames down on top of firefighters.

**40. c.** The captain asked Firefighter Boyle because he believes she has shown interest. If she tells him she is not interested, she may wind up not getting asked again. The training officer may very well be getting something prepared, but Firefighter Boyle might be able to help her out. Using just the instructions may work, but it is a better move to find what is out there and incorporate real experience from those who work with these devices all the time.

**41. a.** Although the ten standard orders contain the admonition to fight fires aggressively, that phrase ends with *but provide for safety first.*

**42. a.** This is the most direct route to the Hillary Mansion, requiring the fewest changes in direction. Choice **b** requires the firefighter to drive through the Rossmore Hospital. Route **c** takes the firefighter the wrong way up West Broadway. Choice **d** takes the firefighter the wrong way on North Avenue.

**43. c.** This route requires the fewest number of turns. Choice **a** is wrong because Martin Road is a one-way street. Choice **b** requires a number of turns and goes the wrong way on Arthur Way. Choice **d** would mean traveling the wrong way on a one-way street.

**44. b.** To find this percentage, first calculate the decimal difference between the two values. Because the problem asks for the $2\frac{1}{2}$" hose value first, that value becomes the top number, and the value for the $1\frac{1}{2}$" hose becomes the bottom number. Dividing 10 by 53 gives about 0.19. Shifting the decimal point to the right two places and tacking on the percent sign gives the correct answer of 19%. This problem can also be solved using approximations. Dividing 10 by 50 gives 0.20, which is very close to the correct answer. This tech-

nique can be very useful in questions like this.

**45. d.** To find this value, first find the value in the table. Read across the top of the table to the 3" hose, then down to the 400 GPM row to find the value of 14 psi. Recall that the table is based on 100 ft. of hose. As 600 ft. of hose is 6 times longer then 100 ft., one need multiply 14 psi × 6 = 84 psi.

**46. c.** First, assign the value of 110 psi to the Pump Pressure in the equation. Next, find the amount of friction loss in the hose. From the table, a $2\frac{1}{2}$" hose flowing 200 GPM will have 10 psi of friction loss in 100 ft. of hose. The hose in the question is 300 ft. long. The equation becomes: Nozzle Pressure = 110 psi − (3 × 10 psi) = 80 psi.

**47. b.** Find the values from the table for both the 3" and 4" hose for 500 GPM. The values are 20 psi and 5 psi, respectively. The question asks for the loss of 4" hose per the 3", therefore it is asking to divide the value for the 4" by the value for the 3"; 5 divided by 20 reduces to $\frac{1}{4}$.

**48. b.** The minimum amount of air pressure that is to be in the cylinder is 4,000 psi. The question asks for the percentage of air compared to the minimum, therefore divide the actual amount by the minimum amount and convert to a percentage. 2,500 / 4,000 = 0.625. Shifting the decimal point two places to the right and rounding gives 63%.

**49. d.** Firefighters must not neglect their responsibilities. People's lives depend on firefighters reporting for duty as scheduled. A baseball game has much lower priority.

**50. b.** If an unforeseen occurrence will hinder a firefighter's arrival at the fire station, he or she must inform the superior officer. The other choices involve leaving the scene, which would be illegal.

**51. a.** The fire department is in the best position to assist the family in this type of emergency. Choice **b** might put the child in further danger. Choice **c** is an overreaction to a somewhat common occurrence. The child's safety is more important than choosing the easiest solution (choice **d**).

**52. a.** See the second and fourth paragraphs.

**53. d.** See the third paragraph. A grease fire is considered a flammable liquid fire, therefore, a dry chemical extinguisher would be the most appropriate type to use.

**54. c.** See the fourth paragraph. Dry chemical extinguishers are the most effective type for this situation. A clothes dryer motor probably does not contain delicate electronic equipment; therefore it would not be necessary to use a carbon dioxide unit. The water unit could only be used if you were certain that the electrical power was off.

**55. c.** See the first paragraph. The other choices are too narrow.

**56. a.** Choice **b** is incorrect because it implies that the woman is in the alley. Choice **c** leaves out important information. Choice **d** is inaccurate.

**57. d.** This is the only clear and accurate statement. Choice **a** implies that Firefighter Delgado has been disabled. Choice **b** leaves out important information. Choice **c** is both inaccurate and unclear.

**58. a.** This is the only clear and accurate statement of the event. Choice **b** sounds as though the neighbor may have fallen on the ice. Choice **c** is unclear. Choice **d** doesn't say whose ankle was sprained.

**59. c.** Although the passage mentions firefighters' responsibilities (choice **a**), the main focus of the passage is the installation of smoke detec-

tors. Choice **b** is only a detail. Choice **d** is not mentioned.

**60. b.** The answer can be inferred from the first sentence of the third paragraph.

**61. a.** The answer is found in the first paragraph (*smoke detectors cut a person's risk of dying in a fire in half*).

**62. c.** The answer can be found in the next to last sentence of the passage.

**63. d.** The answer is implied by the first sentence of the passage. There is no information in the passage to indicate that the other choices are a firefighter's responsibility.

**64. d.** This is the only clear and accurate account of what happened. Choice **a** implies that the watch was stolen. Choice **b** implies that the event occurred while Firefighter Lopez was putting out a fire. Choice **c** is inaccurate and unclear.

**65. a.** This is the only clear and accurate statement. Choice **b** gives the wrong address and time. In choice **c**, the phrase "the closing of the application" is unclear. Choice **d** gives incorrect information.

**66. d.** Sabotaging another firefighter's equipment is a serious matter. If Firefighter Wilson's impression is correct, both the firefighter whose equipment has been sabotaged and the civilians who are counting on him or her would be in great danger. She must, therefore, report the incident.

**67. b.** In matters dealing with the public or press, the best course of action is to refer them to your superior officer.

**68. a.** Working on a main highway is hazardous, and for this reason, flares are standard emergency equipment. They will alert motorists to firefighters' presence.

**69. d.** This is the only clear report. Choice **a** is unclear and distorts the facts; choices **b** and **c** provide most of the information but are unclear.

**70. b.** This is the only clear and accurate explanation. Choice **a** gives a wrong deadline date; choices **c** and **d** are poorly worded and unclear.

**71. a.** This is the only clear and accurate statement. None of the other choices even indicate that Firefighter Jarvis was driving the truck. Choice **d** is inaccurate and does not say where the accident took place.

**72. c.** This is the quickest way around the Ford Hotel and then to Cleveland Avenue. Choice **a** is not correct because it requires the officers to go the wrong way on Jones, a one-way street. Choice **b** would require the firefighters to drive through the Ford Hotel and then to Cleveland Avenue. Choice **d** has too many turns to be the most direct.

**73. b.** This is correct because it is the quickest and most direct route. Choice **a** has too many turns to be the most direct. Choice **c** is a one-way street going north and wouldn't be the right choice. Choice **d** takes the firefighters several blocks out of their way and is not the most direct.

**74. c.** A right turn onto Glade Road turns Firefighter Tananga west. The left onto Taft Road turns him south. The right onto Pine Avenue turns him west, and the right onto Cleveland Avenue turns him back north. The right onto Wilshire Avenue turns him east.

**75. b.** Covering the pan is the quickest way to extinguish the flame, which is the most important thing. Grease that is very hot will explode if water is poured on it (choice **c**). Choice **a** does not solve the problem. Choice **d** would be irresponsible.

**76. a.** The most dangerous thing in this situation would be an explosion, which could be set off by a spark.

**77. d.** Caution must always be used while driving through the streets. While the fire engine does have the right of way and need not wait for a green light (choices **a** and **c**), getting into an accident en route to the fire scene would delay firefighters at best and cause damage and injury at worst. There is no way the firefighters on the truck can control traffic; their gestures might not even be noticed by other drivers (choice **b**).

**78. a.** Fire prevention and safety is something every child should know.

**79. d.** Although the order says that the assigned officer can make that decision, the final paragraph states the chief of department is the final authority.

**80. b.** Riding position seat belts are the responsibility of the member assigned to that position. The operator is responsible for his or her seat belt, but not the others.

**81. c.** In the paragraph titled *Discussion*, the concern is that there have been a number of accidents nationwide and the chief is concerned that complaints about minor problems are not being acted on in a prompt manner. There is an additional problem in that there is no standard inspection and report procedure.

**82. d.** The order provides that in the event that an alarm is in progress or the company is immediately dispatched the inspection is done *as soon as practicable.*

**83. b.** The first priority is safety, not only one's own but that of other firefighters. A natural reaction may be to run out, but firefighters must work as a team.

**84. c.** When firefighters refuel their equipment they should make sure the room is well ventilated from the fumes and should be careful not to spill the highly flammable liquid, so choices **b** and **d** are incorrect. The unnecessary presence of anyone else would be a needless hazard, so choice **a** is incorrect. On the other hand, smoking, even some distance from the refueling operation, could ignite the vapors from the liquid.

**85. c.** Driving through a closed-off area (choices **a** and **b**) could delay the truck longer than if it just went around because conditions might have changed since Firefighter Simpson passed this way in the morning. Calling the superior officer (choice **d**) would likely cause more delay than taking the detour.

**86. c.** Refer to Dwelling Inspection Form, item number 16.

**87. b.** This would be an example of overfusing, or placing an excessive number of plugs into a single outlet. This could overload the outlet's circuit.

**88. d.** Refer to Dwelling Inspection Form, item number 4.

**89. a.** A firefighter is always expected to behave in a courteous manner when dealing with civilians, especially children. Children should be taught to respect firefighters so they will turn to firefighters for help if they need it. All the other choices would be discourteous.

**90. b.** It is a firefighter's duty to be honest and upstanding on or off duty. Leaving for any of the reasons given would mean neglecting an important civic responsibility.

**91. c.** This is the first step in the procedure.

**92. a.** Though step 5 of the procedure states that the maximum angle is 35 degrees when the wind speed is more than 30 mph, step 4 is the one that covers limitations (60 degree maximum angle and 50 feet maximum extension) for situations when the wind speed is less than 30 mph.

**93. d.** See step 5 of the procedure.

**94. b.** See step 4.

**95. d.** A direct explanation is the best response to civilian complaints. Blocking a hydrant can have serious consequences, so choice **a** is not an option. Firefighters should not disobey their superior officers (choice **b**) or threaten civilians (choice **c**).

**96. c.** In matters dealing with the public or press, the best course of action is to refer them to the superior officer.

**97. d.** The paragraph talks about various issues dealing with diversity, but the greatest emphasis is on leadership that not only *talks the talk* but also *walks the walk*.

**98. c.** As used here, *implement* means to apply the changes. *Act on* comes close, but the leaders are not changing the changes needed, but rather the culture that rebels against diversity in the workplace.

**99. d.** For the department to accept a diverse workforce, the leaders have to learn to listen and encourage constructive communication about differences.

**100. c.** A melting pot means that cultural differences are mingled, and after coming together, everyone comes out with the same culture, attitudes, and way of viewing events. The phrase contrasts a melting pot with a mosaic, in which many different-colored pieces create a single picture. As used here, the phrase says that we need to build a fire department that welcomes people of diverse backgrounds, allows them to hold their beliefs and differences in culture, and works together toward a common goal.

| FIREFIGHTER PRACTICE EXAM 3 | | |
| --- | --- | --- |
| **Question Type** | **Question Numbers** | **Chapter** |
| Memory and Observation (15 questions) | 1–15 | 7, "Memory and Observation" |
| Reading Text (25 questions) | 16–19, 23–26, 32–35, 52–55, 59–63, 97–100 | 6, "Reading Text, Tables, Charts, and Graphs" |
| Map Reading (10 questions) | 27–31, 42–43, 72–74 | 11, "Spatial Relations" |
| Following Procedures (15 questions) | 38–41, 79–82, 86–88, 91–94 | 9, "Judgment and Reasoning" |
| Judgment (20 questions) | 20–22, 49–51, 66–68, 75–78, 83–85, 89–90, 95–96 | 9, "Judgment and Reasoning" |
| Verbal Expression (10 questions) | 36–37, 56–58, 64–65, 69–71 | 12, "Verbal Expression" |
| Mathematics (5 questions) | 44–48 | 8, "Math" |

## ► Scoring

In most cities, you need a score of at least 70–80% (that is, 70–80 questions answered correctly) to pass the exam. However, since you may need a much higher score than that to be called for the next step in the process, and since your rank on the eligibility list may be partly based on your score on the written exam, you should try for the highest score you can possibly reach. You have probably seen improvement between your first practice exam score and this one. If you didn't improve as much as you would like, here are some options:

- **If you scored below 60%,** you should do some serious thinking about whether you are really ready to take a firefighter exam. An adult education course in reading comprehension at a high school or community college would be a very good strategy. If you don't have time for a course,

you should at least try to get some private tutoring.

- **If your score is in the 60 to 70% range,** you need to work as hard as you can in the time you have left to boost your skills. Consider the LearningExpress book *Reading Comprehension in 20 Minutes a Day* or other books from your public library. Also, reread Chapters 6, 7, 9, 11, and 12 of this book, and make sure you take all of the advice there for improving your score. Enlist friends and family to help you by making up mock test questions and quizzing you on them.

- **If your score is between 70 and 95%,** you could still benefit from additional work to help improve your score. Go back to Chapters 6, 7, 9, 11, and 12 and study them diligently between now and test day.

- **If you scored above 95%,** congratulations! Your score should be high enough to make you an attractive candidate to the any fire department.

Be sure you don't lose your edge; keep studying this book up to the day before the exam.

If you didn't score as well as you would like, try to analyze the reasons why. Did you run out of time before you could answer all the questions? Did you go back and change your answer from the right one to a wrong one? Did you get flustered and sit staring at a hard question for what seemed like hours? If you had any of these problems, go back and review the test-taking strategies in Chapter 3 to learn how to avoid them.

You should also look at how you did on each kind of question on the test. You may have done very well on reading comprehension questions and poorly on map-reading questions, or vice versa. If you can figure out where your strengths and weaknesses lie, you will know where to concentrate your efforts in the time you have left before the exam. Take out your completed answer sheet and compare it to the table on page 284 to find out which kinds of questions you did well on and which kinds you had difficulty with. Then go back and spend extra time studying the chapters that cover the questions that gave you the most trouble.

Finally, one of the biggest factors in your success on the exam is your self-confidence. Remember, because you are using this book, you are better prepared than most of the other people who are taking the exam with you.

# 14▶ Firefighter Practice Exam 4

## CHAPTER SUMMARY

This is the last of the four practice exams in this book covering the areas most often tested on firefighter exams. Compare your score on this test with your scores on the previous practice exams to see how much you have improved after working through the instructional chapters.

Like Firefighter Practice Exam 2 in Chapter 5, the practice exam that follows tests some of the basic skills that you need to do well as a firefighter: reading comprehension, verbal expression, logical reasoning, mathematics, and mechanical aptitude. For this final exam, simulate the actual test-taking experience as much as possible. Find a quiet place to work where you won't be interrupted. Tear out the answer sheet on the next page and find some number 2 pencils to fill in the circles. Set a timer or stopwatch, and give yourself two and a half hours for the entire exam. When that time is up, stop, even if you haven't finished the entire test.

After the exam, use the answer key that follows it to see how you did and to find out why the correct answers are correct. The answer key is followed by a section on how to score your exam and suggestions for continued study.

## Practice Exam 4

| | | | | | | | | | | | | | |
|---|---|---|---|---|---|---|---|---|---|---|---|---|---|
| 1. | ⓐ | ⓑ | ⓒ | ⓓ | 36. | ⓐ | ⓑ | ⓒ | ⓓ | 71. | ⓐ | ⓑ | ⓒ | ⓓ |
| 2. | ⓐ | ⓑ | ⓒ | ⓓ | 37. | ⓐ | ⓑ | ⓒ | ⓓ | 72. | ⓐ | ⓑ | ⓒ | ⓓ |
| 3. | ⓐ | ⓑ | ⓒ | ⓓ | 38. | ⓐ | ⓑ | ⓒ | ⓓ | 73. | ⓐ | ⓑ | ⓒ | ⓓ |
| 4. | ⓐ | ⓑ | ⓒ | ⓓ | 39. | ⓐ | ⓑ | ⓒ | ⓓ | 74. | ⓐ | ⓑ | ⓒ | ⓓ |
| 5. | ⓐ | ⓑ | ⓒ | ⓓ | 40. | ⓐ | ⓑ | ⓒ | ⓓ | 75. | ⓐ | ⓑ | ⓒ | ⓓ |
| 6. | ⓐ | ⓑ | ⓒ | ⓓ | 41. | ⓐ | ⓑ | ⓒ | ⓓ | 76. | ⓐ | ⓑ | ⓒ | ⓓ |
| 7. | ⓐ | ⓑ | ⓒ | ⓓ | 42. | ⓐ | ⓑ | ⓒ | ⓓ | 77. | ⓐ | ⓑ | ⓒ | ⓓ |
| 8. | ⓐ | ⓑ | ⓒ | ⓓ | 43. | ⓐ | ⓑ | ⓒ | ⓓ | 78. | ⓐ | ⓑ | ⓒ | ⓓ |
| 9. | ⓐ | ⓑ | ⓒ | ⓓ | 44. | ⓐ | ⓑ | ⓒ | ⓓ | 79. | ⓐ | ⓑ | ⓒ | ⓓ |
| 10. | ⓐ | ⓑ | ⓒ | ⓓ | 45. | ⓐ | ⓑ | ⓒ | ⓓ | 80. | ⓐ | ⓑ | ⓒ | ⓓ |
| 11. | ⓐ | ⓑ | ⓒ | ⓓ | 46. | ⓐ | ⓑ | ⓒ | ⓓ | 81. | ⓐ | ⓑ | ⓒ | ⓓ |
| 12. | ⓐ | ⓑ | ⓒ | ⓓ | 47. | ⓐ | ⓑ | ⓒ | ⓓ | 82. | ⓐ | ⓑ | ⓒ | ⓓ |
| 13. | ⓐ | ⓑ | ⓒ | ⓓ | 48. | ⓐ | ⓑ | ⓒ | ⓓ | 83. | ⓐ | ⓑ | ⓒ | ⓓ |
| 14. | ⓐ | ⓑ | ⓒ | ⓓ | 49. | ⓐ | ⓑ | ⓒ | ⓓ | 84. | ⓐ | ⓑ | ⓒ | ⓓ |
| 15. | ⓐ | ⓑ | ⓒ | ⓓ | 50. | ⓐ | ⓑ | ⓒ | ⓓ | 85. | ⓐ | ⓑ | ⓒ | ⓓ |
| 16. | ⓐ | ⓑ | ⓒ | ⓓ | 51. | ⓐ | ⓑ | ⓒ | ⓓ | 86. | ⓐ | ⓑ | ⓒ | ⓓ |
| 17. | ⓐ | ⓑ | ⓒ | ⓓ | 52. | ⓐ | ⓑ | ⓒ | ⓓ | 87. | ⓐ | ⓑ | ⓒ | ⓓ |
| 18. | ⓐ | ⓑ | ⓒ | ⓓ | 53. | ⓐ | ⓑ | ⓒ | ⓓ | 88. | ⓐ | ⓑ | ⓒ | ⓓ |
| 19. | ⓐ | ⓑ | ⓒ | ⓓ | 54. | ⓐ | ⓑ | ⓒ | ⓓ | 89. | ⓐ | ⓑ | ⓒ | ⓓ |
| 20. | ⓐ | ⓑ | ⓒ | ⓓ | 55. | ⓐ | ⓑ | ⓒ | ⓓ | 90. | ⓐ | ⓑ | ⓒ | ⓓ |
| 21. | ⓐ | ⓑ | ⓒ | ⓓ | 56. | ⓐ | ⓑ | ⓒ | ⓓ | 91. | ⓐ | ⓑ | ⓒ | ⓓ |
| 22. | ⓐ | ⓑ | ⓒ | ⓓ | 57. | ⓐ | ⓑ | ⓒ | ⓓ | 92. | ⓐ | ⓑ | ⓒ | ⓓ |
| 23. | ⓐ | ⓑ | ⓒ | ⓓ | 58. | ⓐ | ⓑ | ⓒ | ⓓ | 93. | ⓐ | ⓑ | ⓒ | ⓓ |
| 24. | ⓐ | ⓑ | ⓒ | ⓓ | 59. | ⓐ | ⓑ | ⓒ | ⓓ | 94. | ⓐ | ⓑ | ⓒ | ⓓ |
| 25. | ⓐ | ⓑ | ⓒ | ⓓ | 60. | ⓐ | ⓑ | ⓒ | ⓓ | 95. | ⓐ | ⓑ | ⓒ | ⓓ |
| 26. | ⓐ | ⓑ | ⓒ | ⓓ | 61. | ⓐ | ⓑ | ⓒ | ⓓ | 96. | ⓐ | ⓑ | ⓒ | ⓓ |
| 27. | ⓐ | ⓑ | ⓒ | ⓓ | 62. | ⓐ | ⓑ | ⓒ | ⓓ | 97. | ⓐ | ⓑ | ⓒ | ⓓ |
| 28. | ⓐ | ⓑ | ⓒ | ⓓ | 63. | ⓐ | ⓑ | ⓒ | | 98. | ⓐ | ⓑ | ⓒ | ⓓ |
| 29. | ⓐ | ⓑ | ⓒ | ⓓ | 64. | ⓐ | ⓑ | ⓒ | | 99. | ⓐ | ⓑ | ⓒ | ⓓ |
| 30. | ⓐ | ⓑ | ⓒ | ⓓ | 65. | ⓐ | ⓑ | ⓒ | | 100. | ⓐ | ⓑ | ⓒ | ⓓ |
| 31. | ⓐ | ⓑ | ⓒ | ⓓ | 66. | ⓐ | ⓑ | ⓒ | ⓓ | | | | | |
| 32. | ⓐ | ⓑ | ⓒ | ⓓ | 67. | ⓐ | ⓑ | ⓒ | ⓓ | | | | | |
| 33. | ⓐ | ⓑ | ⓒ | ⓓ | 68. | ⓐ | ⓑ | ⓒ | ⓓ | | | | | |
| 34. | ⓐ | ⓑ | ⓒ | ⓓ | 69. | ⓐ | ⓑ | ⓒ | ⓓ | | | | | |
| 35. | ⓐ | ⓑ | ⓒ | ⓓ | 70. | ⓐ | ⓑ | ⓒ | ⓓ | | | | | |

## ► Section 1: Reading Comprehension

Answer questions 1–3 based solely on the information in the following passage.

Although hand washing remains the most fundamental measure for controlling infection, it is still not taken as seriously as it should be. Infection rates in patients, hospital personnel, and emergency responders continue to be a national problem, despite continuing improvements in medical technology. It was in the mid-1800s in Vienna, Austria, that a physician named Ignaz Semmelweis demonstrated the importance of hand washing in decreasing the incidence of infection in women following childbirth. He observed that medical students were conducting cadaver dissections in the morning and then delivering babies in the afternoon without wearing gloves or washing their hands. When the medical students were on vacation, the incidence of infection was reduced. Semmelweis traveled to other European cities to demonstrate that hand washing could reduce deaths related to infection. Even though he had reduced infection from 18% to 1% in the Vienna hospital, at the time the medical community did not take him seriously. Since then, infection control procedures have been developed and refined continuously. Unfortunately, research on the incidence of infection, the spread of infection from patient to care provider, and the incidence of infection related to contaminated medical equipment continues to be limited almost exclusively to hospital-based studies. To date, there are few studies related to the incidence of disease in the emergency response environment. As a result, recommended practice and/or procedures for emergency responders are generally modifications of those established for in-hospital personnel.

**1.** According to the passage, the basis of infection control is
   **a.** disposable sharps.
   **b.** hand washing.
   **c.** using clean instruments.
   **d.** sterilizing the ambulance.

**2.** What is the meaning of the word *incidence* as used in this passage?
   **a.** frequency
   **b.** extent
   **c.** affecting
   **d.** occurrence

**3.** What problem does the passage mention about infection control in the emergency response environment?
   **a.** Emergency responders do not take hand washing seriously.
   **b.** No new infection and control procedures have been developed since the mid-nineteenth century.
   **c.** There are few studies outside of hospital-based ones.
   **d.** It is almost impossible to reduce infections in the field.

Answer questions 4–6 by referring to the following table, which shows the results of a review of losses in confined structure fires.

| CONTENT LOSS DISTRIBUTION, CONFINED STRUCTURE FIRES (2006) | | | | | |
|---|---|---|---|---|---|
| CONTENT LOSS RANGE | FIRES WITH CONTENT LOSS ONLY | AVERAGE CONTENT LOSS (TOTAL LOSS) | ALL FIRES WITH CONTENT LOSS | AVERAGE CONTENT LOSS | AVERAGE TOTAL LOSS |
| $1–$250 | 1,306 | $84 | 2,520 | $65 | $954 |
| $251–$500 | 501 | $432 | 793 | $437 | $1,167 |
| $501–$1,000 | 285 | $923 | 613 | $949 | $2,431 |
| > $1,000 | 276 | $7,810 | 594 | $17,214 | $27,097 |
| Incidents | 2,368 | | 4,520 | | |

**4.** In fires with a content loss of $1 to $250, what percentage of those fires is categorized as "content loss only" compared to the category "all fires with content loss"?
   **a.** 9%
   **b.** 51%
   **c.** 77%
   **d.** 192%

**5.** What is the average content loss for the range of $501 to $1,000?
   **a.** $923
   **b.** $949
   **c.** $954
   **d.** $1,167

**6.** How many fires with content loss only were reported to have losses greater than $1,000?
   **a.** 594
   **b.** 501
   **c.** 285
   **d.** 276

Answer questions 7–8 based solely on the information in the following passage.

In crisis situations, concerned agencies respond differently, stemming from variations in tasks, jurisdictions, education, geographical environment, level of preparedness, and other administrative and political considerations. Consequently, they are drawn into a crisis at different moments, with varying viewpoints and purposes. Considering these divergent responsibilities, it is essential to coordinate efforts to mitigate and control civil disorders.

One means of addressing civil unrest is to develop a "menu" approach for joint action between law enforcement and fire/emergency medical service (EMS) agencies. A list of strategies that a community may adopt as is, or interchange as needed, is compiled. Even with this approach, joint action between police and fire personnel may not be the best strategy to control a particular situation. (In some circumstances, allowing the crisis to run its course may be the best policy.)

**7.** According to the passage, in a crisis situation,
- **a.** the differing responses of emergency agencies is helpful.
- **b.** allowing the crisis to run its course is always the best approach.
- **c.** joint action may not be the best strategy in all situations.
- **d.** it is not necessary to coordinate mitigation efforts.

**8.** *Mitigate*, as it is used in this passage, indicates that
- **a.** the responders should work to make the situation less intense.
- **b.** the police must end the situation by any means necessary.
- **c.** an effort to change the situation should be left up to the civil authority in charge.
- **d.** no change should be made in the situation.

Answer questions 9–12 based solely on the information in the following passage.

The physical and mental demands associated with firefighting and other emergency operations, coupled with the environmental dangers of extreme heat and humidity or extreme cold, create conditions that can have an adverse impact upon the safety and health of the individual emergency responder. Members who are not provided adequate rest and rehydration during emergency operations or training exercises are at increased risk for illness or injury, and may jeopardize the safety of others on the incident scene. When emergency responders become fatigued, their ability to operate safely is impaired. As a result, their reaction time is reduced and their ability to make critical decisions diminishes. Rehabilitation is an essential element on the incident scene to prevent more serious conditions, such as heat exhaustion or heat stroke, from occurring. The need for emergency incident rehabili-

tation is cited in several national standards. Recent studies have concluded that a properly implemented fireground rehabilitation program will result in fewer accidents and injuries to firefighters. Moreover, responders who are given prompt and adequate time to rest and rehydrate may safely re-enter the operational scene, which may reduce the requirement for additional staffing at an incident. An emergency incident rehabilitation program can be established in any department with a minimal impact on human, fiscal, and equipment-related resources. A successful rehabilitation program will improve the morale of the department and increase the level of productivity. It fits into the framework of the ICS used by fire departments, emergency medical services, hazardous materials response teams, and special rescue teams across the country.

**9.** Which of the following pieces of information is included in the passage?
- **a.** the physical and emotional demands made upon firefighters
- **b.** the procedures needed for proper rehydration
- **c.** a rehabilitation program fits into the framework of ICS
- **d.** the details of what studies have shown about injuries due to fatigue

**10.** A serious problem facing firefighters during a response is
- **a.** heat stress and physical fatigue reduces reaction time.
- **b.** due to adrenaline, firefighters are more alert after fighting a fire.
- **c.** rehabilitation takes personnel off the line, thus increasing work for others.
- **d.** the expense of starting a rehabilitation program makes it prohibitive.

**11.** Personnel who become fatigued during operations
  **a.** must get used to it, as it is part of the job.
  **b.** are at increased risk for injury or illness.
  **c.** need to take a moment to catch a breath.
  **d.** increase the staff needed at an incident.

**12.** *Rehydration* as used here means
  **a.** to rest personnel to lower their heart rate.
  **b.** to rotate tasks so personnel stay alert.
  **c.** a process to replace lost water and salts in proper proportions.
  **d.** to supply personnel with fresh air to clear their lungs.

Answer questions 13–14 based on the following pie chart, which shows the distribution of fires in schools by type.

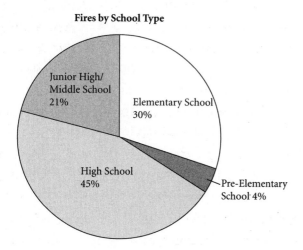

**Fires by School Type**

**13.** After reviewing the pie chart, which school type needs the most the most inspection, enforcement, and fire safety education efforts?
  **a.** pre-elementary school
  **b.** elementary school
  **c.** junior high/middle school
  **d.** high school

**14.** If there were a total of 325 fires in schools during this period, how many of these fires occurred in elementary schools?
  **a.** 68
  **b.** 98
  **c.** 146
  **d.** 228

Answer questions 15–18 based solely on the information in the following passage.

Due to recent national events, the Yardley City Government has introduced new bomb threat procedures for government buildings. This information is for department use only.

From this point on, all personnel must be on the highest alert. You must pay close attention to your surroundings. If a vehicle you do not recognize enters the parking lot, observe driver and passenger behavior. If an employee has been terminated recently, examine his or her performance evaluations and exit interview reports. If there are incidents involving visitors, notify your supervisor. Keep in mind, however, that we must not overreact. Part of being alert is exercising proper judgment.

If there is an actual bomb threat, carry out the following procedures: First, evacuate the premises. Do not fall into fire drill routines; remember, you are vacating to avoid injury stemming from premeditated violence. Leave the building immediately. Take nothing with you. Do not shut down electrical equipment. Keep movement to a minimum. If there are visitors or persons with special needs in the building, make certain they are evacuated.

Proceed to the area away from the building designated in the fire drill policy. Do not enter vehicles parked nearby. Take attendance. Make mental notes about any missing personnel or any questionable activity in or near the building. If you received the actual threat, record as much information as possible: gender, specific language, insider information, type of violence threatened. Once you reach your designated safe area, identify emergency personnel and share the information with them.

**15.** Which of the following organizational schemes does the passage mainly follow?
   **a.** hierarchical order
   **b.** chronological order
   **c.** order by topic
   **d.** cause and effect

**16.** The passage as a whole suggests that during an actual bomb threat incident, the most important priority is to
   **a.** avoid overreacting.
   **b.** follow proper procedures.
   **c.** notify the supervisor of suspicious activities.
   **d.** keep the bomb threat information inside the department.

**17.** Which of the following is NOT included in this passage?
   **a.** where to go in the event of a bomb threat
   **b.** what to do if an unknown vehicle parks near the station
   **c.** what to do with specific bomb threat information
   **d.** how to identify a potentially dangerous fired employee

**18.** If there is a bomb threat incident, and you have previously seen a visitor enter the building in a wheelchair, you should
   **a.** direct the visitor to the designated evacuation area.
   **b.** notify your supervisor.
   **c.** notify emergency personnel.
   **d.** carefully observe the visitor's behavior.

Answer questions 19–23 solely on the basis of the information in the following list of procedures.

Firefighters must learn the proper procedures for responding to residential carbon monoxide (CO) emergencies.

Upon arriving at the scene of the alarm, personnel shall put on personal protective equipment, then bring an operational, calibrated CO meter onto the premises.

Occupants of the premises shall then be examined. If they are experiencing CO poisoning symptoms—that is, headaches, nausea, confusion, dizziness, and other flu-like symptoms—an EMS crew shall be notified immediately and the occupants evacuated and administered oxygen.

To test for CO contamination, meters must be held head-high. Appliances should be operating for five to ten minutes before testing, and a check must be made near all gas appliances and vents. If vents are working properly, no CO emissions will enter the structure.

If the meters register unsafe levels—above ten parts per million (ppm)—all occupants shall be evacuated and the source of the contamination investigated. Occupants shall be interviewed to ascertain the location of the CO detector (if any), the length of time the alarm has sounded, what the occupants were doing at the time of the alarm, for example, cooking, and what electrical appliances were functioning. Occupants shall not re-enter the premises until the environment is deemed safe.

If the meter register levels lower than nine ppm, occupants shall be allowed to re-enter the building. They shall be notified of the recorded level and given a CO informational packet.

**19.** When arriving at a CO emergency, what is the first thing a firefighter should do?
  **a.** Take a CO meter reading.
  **b.** Put on protective clothing.
  **c.** Administer oxygen to the occupants of the premises.
  **d.** Interview the occupants of the premises.

**20.** If residents are experiencing carbon monoxide poisoning symptoms, which of the following steps should firefighters take immediately?
  **a.** Allow the residents to lie down.
  **b.** Determine CO levels in the household.
  **c.** Summon an EMS team.
  **d.** Investigate the source of contamination.

**21.** Carbon monoxide levels under nine ppm are considered
  **a.** relatively safe.
  **b.** very dangerous.
  **c.** capable of causing illness.
  **d.** cause for evacuation.

**22.** According to the passage, all occupants of a residence should be evacuated when
  **a.** the investigators arrive.
  **b.** an EMS crew arrives.
  **c.** the source of contamination is discovered.
  **d.** any occupant exhibits symptoms of CO poisoning.

**23.** Which of the following information is NOT included in this passage?
  **a.** potential sources of contamination
  **b.** indications of CO toxicity
  **c.** proper levels of oxygen for ailing occupants
  **d.** which pieces of equipment should be taken into homes

Answer questions 24–26 by referring to the following graph, which compares the total average percentage of fires at a given time of the day with the average percentage of those fires that cause injury.

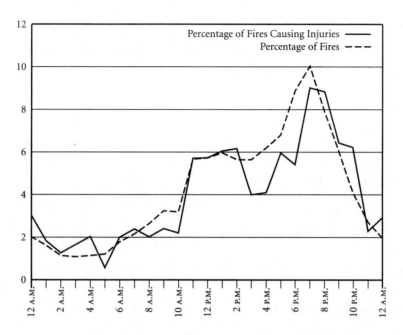

**24.** The graph shows the line for the percentage of fires causing injuries below the line for the percentage of fires for the time period from 2:00 P.M. to 7:00 P.M. What is a possible reason for this trend?

   **a.** There are fewer fires during this period of time.

   **b.** The fires during this period of time tend to be smaller.

   **c.** People are typically awake and active in the house during this time, and more aware of their surroundings.

   **d.** There is no apparent reason.

**25.** At what time is the percentage of fires the lowest?

   **a.** 4:30 A.M.

   **b.** 2:30 A.M.

   **c.** 6:00 P.M.

   **d.** 9:00 A.M.

**26.** At what time would you expect to need the most fire personnel, based on this graph?

   **a.** 12:00 A.M. to 6:00 A.M.

   **b.** 6:00 A.M. to 12:00 P.M.

   **c.** 12:00 P.M. to 6:00 P.M.

   **d.** 6:00 A.M. to 12:00 A.M.

Answer questions 27–29 by referring to the following pie chart, which shows data for automatic fire alarm responses for a year.

**Automatic Fire Alarm Responses For a Year**

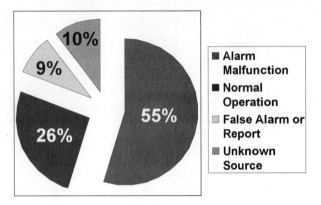

Legend:
- Alarm Malfunction
- Normal Operation
- False Alarm or Report
- Unknown Source

**27.** If there were a total of 874 automatic fire alarms reported in this year, how many of them were the result of an alarm malfunction?
   a. 522
   b. 481
   c. 275
   d. 339

**28.** Based on the information in the chart, what would be the most effective area for the fire department to concentrate its efforts to educate the public to reduce the total number of automatic fire alarms?
   a. the importance of maintaining alarm systems to prevent malfunctions
   b. to disconnect the alarm systems to eliminate these types of calls
   c. safe cooking methods to prevent burning food and setting off alarms
   d. to prevent malicious false alarms such as children pulling fire alarms.

**29.** If there were 53 automatic alarms for which the cause of the alarm could not be determined, what is the approximate total number of automatic alarms in the year?
   a. 470
   b. 530
   c. 720
   d. Cannot be determined based on this information.

Answer questions 30–33 based solely on the information in the following procedural memo.

An additional truck company shall be assigned to all working structure fires and other major incidents at the discretion of the officer in charge (OIC) to provide a rapid intervention team (RIT) for the protection of the firefighters operating at the incident. Personnel assigned to the RIT truck shall not engage in any firefighting operations not directly associated with the operation of the RIT, as this may prevent the timely response of the team to a firefighter emergency. Officers in charge of incidents should consider this before requesting additional resources for fireground operations.

The captain of the company assigned to RIT shall function as RIT Sector Operations. He or she will coordinate directly with the OIC and Safety Officer on all RIT operations. The captain will direct all operations related to a rapid intervention response, including deployment of teams, allocation of resources for RIT, monitoring of incident times, requests for additional RIT resources or companies, and coordination with firefighting operations.

The remaining four members of the truck company shall be assigned into two teams of two firefighters each and will be designated as RIT Team 1 and RIT Team 2. Full personal protective equipment, including SCBA shall be used. Additional RIT teams will be assigned identification by the RIT Sector Operations as needed.

Team 1 will function as the initial entry team should a deployment be required. On arrival at the scene of an incident, Team 1 will perform a complete walkaround of the incident scene to observe firefighting operations and safety measures already in place. On completion of the walkaround, Team 1 will report to the RIT staging area and report findings to the RIT Sector captain and Team 2. The walkaround should be repeated as often as needed to maintain an awareness of ongoing operations.

Team 2 will set up staging during the initial walkaround. Staging shall be set up in an area that is as accessible to the incident scene as possible without interfering with firefighting operations. The following types of tools should be staged:

- forcible-entry tools
- search ropes
- emergency air supplies, including spare SCBA cylinders
- emergency medical equipment
- power tools, including ventilation saws
- hand lights and portable lighting
- other equipment as deemed necessary according to the size of the incident, number of personnel operating, building construction and condition, and other factors.

Once staging and the walkaround are complete, all RIT personnel should monitor all fireground operations. Unsafe or deteriorating conditions should be immediately reported to the RIT Sector captain for relay to the Safety Officer or OIC. RIT personnel should deploy ground ladders to the greatest extent possible on all sides of any multistory building.

The RIT Sector captain shall direct the deployment of teams should an incident occur or a mayday is called. In the event of a firefighter emergency, the RIT Sector captain should obtain as much information as possible regarding the incident. This assessment should include determining the number of firefighters involved in the emergency, their location in the structure, the type of emergency (collapse, flashover, medical, etc.), and the amount of remaining air the firefighters have in their SCBA.

Team 1 will enter the structure carrying forcible-entry tools, hand lights, radios, emergency air supply, and a search line. The entry team will immediately deploy to the location of the incident. Depending on the nature of the incident, both teams may deploy simultaneously. All personnel entering the structure shall carry portable lighting and a forcible-entry tool.

Once the entry team has located the firefighter(s) involved in the incident, an assessment of the situation will be performed and a size-up given to the RIT Sector captain. Additional resources needed shall be part of the size-up. Additional resources may include additional manpower, rescue equipment, or extrication assistance. The RIT Sector captain will coordinate the deployment of additional resources with the OIC. In addition, upon any RIT deployment, a full additional alarm and an additional RIT truck company will be automatically dispatched.

Communication between the RIT teams and the RIT Sector captain are critical during the extrication of injured or ill firefighters, as fire conditions often affect escape paths or operations. All RIT personnel should be assigned portable radios if possible.

On completion of an RIT assignment, all personnel shall report to the rehab sector for medical clearance prior to returning to RIT staging.

**30.** Based on the information in the procedure, which of the following tools would not normally be found in the RIT staging area?
   **a.** axe
   **b.** medical first aid kit
   **c.** fire hose
   **d.** chain saw

**31.** Given the information in the procedure, which of the following statements is true?
   **a.** The RIT Sector captain will personally lead Team 1.
   **b.** It is not necessary to repeat the full structure walkaround.
   **c.** The RIT Team should be deployed for a firefighter who suddenly develops severe chest pain while fighting the fire.
   **d.** The RIT Team should never set up ground ladders at a building because this would technically be a fireground operation related to putting out the fire.

**32.** Which of the following details is not included in the procedure?
   **a.** procedures on how to remove an injured firefighter from a building
   **b.** what additional resources are automatically dispatched when a firefighter emergency is declared
   **c.** who the RIT Sector captain coordinates with on the scene of an incident
   **d.** who has the authority to actually deploy an RIT team

**33.** Which of the following would be important for an RIT team to observe, either during the initial walkaround or while staging and monitoring of the incident?
   **a.** Where are any injured or displaced civilians being treated?
   **b.** Which fire hydrants are being used to supply water?
   **c.** In which areas or floors of the building are firefighters working?
   **d.** All of the above would be important observations.

Answer questions 34 and 35 by referring to the following table, which shows fire fatalities statewide for certain ages.

| | **FIRE FATALITIES STATEWIDE BY AGE, RACE, AND GENDER** | | | | | | | | | |
|---|---|---|---|---|---|---|---|---|---|---|
| **Ages** | **1–4** | **5–9** | **10–14** | **15–19** | **20–24** | **25–34** | **35–44** | **45–54** | **55–64** | **Totals** |
| White Male | 7 | 1 | 0 | 2 | 2 | 9 | 8 | 7 | 4 | 40 |
| White Female | 7 | 1 | 0 | 1 | 0 | 2 | 3 | 1 | 6 | 21 |
| Non-White Male | 5 | 3 | 2 | 0 | 0 | 5 | 8 | 3 | 7 | 33 |
| Non-White Female | 3 | 3 | 0 | 0 | 2 | 3 | 3 | 2 | 1 | 17 |
| **Totals** | **22** | **8** | **2** | **3** | **4** | **19** | **22** | **13** | **18** | **111** |

*Note: For the purposes of this study, persons under 20 years of age are classified as children. Persons 20 years of age and older are classified as adults.*

**34.** According to the table, the greatest number of fatalities among children aged 1–14 occurred in which group?
  a. white males
  b. non-white males
  c. white females
  d. non-white females

**35.** If the trend shown on the table continues in future years, which of the following statements is accurate?
  a. Fewer white males than white females will die.
  b. Fewer white females over age 20 than white females under 20 will die.
  c. More adults than children will die.
  d. More non-white persons than white persons will die.

## ▶ Section 2: Verbal Expression

For questions 36–40, choose the word that most nearly means the same as the italicized word.

**36.** On the witness stand, the suspected arsonist, usually a flashy dresser, appeared uncharacteristically *nondescript*.
  **a.** lethargic
  **b.** undistinguished
  **c.** indisposed
  **d.** impeccable

**37.** According to the code of conduct, "Every firefighter will be held *accountable* for his or her decisions."
  **a.** applauded
  **b.** compensated
  **c.** responsible
  **d.** approachable

**38.** Since the townspeople were so dissatisfied, various methods to *alleviate* the situation were debated.
  **a.** ease
  **b.** tolerate
  **c.** clarify
  **d.** intensify

**39.** The fire education officer was an *indispensable* member of the department, so they had no choice but to offer him a higher salary to stay on.
  **a.** indulgent
  **b.** experienced
  **c.** essential
  **d.** apologetic

**40.** After the storm caused raw sewage to seep into the ground water, the Water Department had to take measures to *decontaminate* the city's water supply.
  **a.** refine
  **b.** revive
  **c.** freshen
  **d.** purify

For questions 41–43, choose the word that best fills the blank.

**41.** You cannot join the fire safety team without the _____ three-week training course.
  **a.** prerequisite
  **b.** optional
  **c.** preferred
  **d.** advisable

**42.** The suspect gave a(n) _____ explanation for his presence at the scene of the fire, so the police decided to look elsewhere for the arsonist.
  **a.** plausible
  **b.** incredible
  **c.** insufficient
  **d.** apologetic

**43.** The general public didn't care about the new building code and so was _____ about the outcome.
  **a.** enraged
  **b.** apathetic
  **c.** suspicious
  **d.** saddened

For questions 44–47, replace the underlined portion with the phrase that best completes the sentence. If the sentence is correct as is, select choice **a**.

**44.** An American poet of the nineteenth century, <u>Walt Whitman's collection of poems, *Leaves of Grass,*</u> celebrates nature and individualism.
   **a.** Walt Whitman's collection of poems, *Leaves of Grass,*
   **b.** *Leaves of Grass,* a collection of poems by Walt Whitman,
   **c.** Walt Whitman published a collection of poems, *Leaves of Grass,* that
   **d.** Walt Whitman published poems, collected as *Leaves of Grass,* that

**45.** <u>When two angles have the same degree measure, it is said to be congruent.</u>
   **a.** When two angles have the same degree measure, it is said to be congruent.
   **b.** When two angles has the same degree measure, it is said to be congruent.
   **c.** Two angles with the same degree measure is said to be congruent.
   **d.** When two angles have the same degree measure, they are said to be congruent.

**46.** <u>The likelihood</u> of a region's experiencing an earthquake can be estimated, earthquakes cannot be accurately predicted.
   **a.** The likelihood
   **b.** Although the likelihood
   **c.** Since the likelihood
   **d.** In fact, the likelihood

**47.** Everyone signed the petition before <u>submitting it</u> to the city counsel.
   **a.** submitting it
   **b.** you submit it
   **c.** we will submit it
   **d.** we submitted it

**48.** Which of these expresses the idea most clearly?
   **a.** As soon as she realized that the hurricane was going to strike, the mayor told the residents to evacuate the city.
   **b.** As soon as she realized that the hurricane was going to strike, the city residents were told to evacuate by the mayor.
   **c.** As soon as she realized that the hurricane was going to strike, the mayor tells the city residents of her decision to evacuate.
   **d.** As soon as she realized that the hurricane was going to strike, the residents of the city were told to evacuate by the mayor.

**49.** Which of these expresses the idea most clearly?
   **a.** A sharpshooter for many years, a pea could be shot off a person's shoulder from 70 yards away by Miles Johnson.
   **b.** A sharpshooter for many years, Miles Johnson could shoot a pea off a person's shoulder from 70 yards away.
   **c.** A sharpshooter for many years, from 70 yards away off a person's shoulder Miles Johnson could have shot a pea.
   **d.** A sharpshooter for many years, Miles Johnson could shoot from 70 yards away off a person's shoulder a pea.

**50.** Which of these expresses the idea most clearly?
   **a.** Ultraviolet radiation levels are 60% higher at 8,500 feet from the sun than they are at sea level, according to researchers.
   **b.** Researchers have found from the sun ultraviolet radiation levels 60% higher, they say, at 8,500 feet than at sea level.
   **c.** Researchers have found that ultraviolet radiation levels from the sun are 60% higher at 8,500 feet than they are at sea level.
   **d.** At 8,500 feet researchers have found that ultraviolet radiation levels are 60% higher from sea level with the sun's rays.

## ▶ Section 3: Logical Reasoning

**51.** Look at this series: 3, 9, 6, 27, 9, ___, 12, 243, …..
   What number should fill the blank?
   **a.** 54
   **b.** 81
   **c.** 30
   **d.** 84

**52.** Look at this series: 84, 89, 86, 91, 88, __, 90, . . .
   What number should fill the blank?
   **a.** 83
   **b.** 85
   **c.** 92
   **d.** 93

**53.** Look at this series: $\frac{1}{9}, \frac{1}{3}, 1, $ __$, 9, . . .$
   What number should fill the blank?
   **a.** $\frac{2}{3}$
   **b.** 3
   **c.** 6
   **d.** 27

**54.** Look at this series: F2, __, D8, C16, B32, . . .
   What letter and numbers should fill the blank?
   **a.** A16
   **b.** G4
   **c.** E4
   **d.** E3

**55.** Look at this series: RDJ, QFK, PHL, ___, NLN, ….. What letters should fill the blank?
   **a.** MIL
   **b.** QGK
   **c.** SJD
   **d.** OJM

For questions 56–58, find the pattern in the sequence.

**56.**

   a.   b.   c.   d.

**57.**

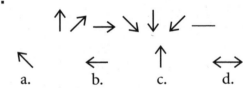

   a.   b.   c.   d.

**58.**

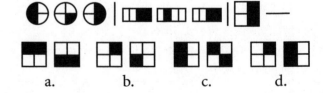

   a.   b.   c.   d.

For questions 59–62, complete the analogy.

**59.** Baker is to bread as congressperson is to
   a. senator.
   b. law.
   c. state.
   d. politician.

**60.** Approach is to retreat as provide is to
   a. present.
   b. withhold.
   c. supply.
   d. afford.

**61.** Yard is to inch as quart is to
   a. gallon.
   b. ounce.
   c. milk.
   d. liquid.

**62.** Sponge is to porous as lead is to
   a. dense.
   b. massive.
   c. hard.
   d. solid.

**63.** The temperature on Monday was lower than on Tuesday.
   The temperature on Wednesday was lower than on Tuesday.
   The temperature on Monday was higher than on Wednesday.
   If the first two statements are true, the third statement is
   a. true.
   b. false.
   c. uncertain.

**64.** Hose A flows more water than Hose B. Hose B flows less water than Hose C. Hose C flows more water than Hose A. If the first two statements are true, the third statement is
   a. false.
   b. true.
   c. uncertain.

**65.** Middletown is north of Centerville.
   Centerville is east of Penfield.
   Penfield is northwest of Middletown.
   If the first two statements are true, the third statement is
   a. true.
   b. false.
   c. uncertain.

## ▶ Section 4: Mathematics

**66.** Firefighter Green earns $26,000 a year. If she receives a 4.5% salary increase, how much will she earn?
   a. $26,450
   b. $27,170
   c. $27,260
   d. $29,200

**67.** Which of the following rooms has the greatest perimeter?
   a. a square room 10 feet × 10 feet
   b. a square room 11 feet × 11 feet
   c. a rectangular room 12 feet × 8 feet
   d. a rectangular room 14 feet × 7 feet

**68.** If it takes four firefighters 1 hour and 45 minutes to perform a particular job, how long would it take one firefighter working at the same rate to perform the same task alone?

   **a.** 4.5 hours

   **b.** 5 hours

   **c.** 7 hours

   **d.** 7.5 hours

**69.** Which of the following hose diameters is the smallest?

   **a.** $\frac{17}{20}$ inches

   **b.** $\frac{3}{4}$ inches

   **c.** $\frac{5}{6}$ inches

   **d.** $\frac{7}{10}$ inches

**70.** When a sprinkler system is installed in a home that is under construction, the system costs about 1.5% of the total building cost. The cost of the same system installed after the home is built is about 4% of the total building cost. How much would a homeowner save by installing a sprinkler system in a $150,000 home while the home is still under construction?

   **a.** $600

   **b.** $2,250

   **c.** $3,750

   **d.** $6,000

**71.** If one gallon of fluid weighs 7.3 pounds, and a steel drum weighs 22 pounds, a filled 55-gallon drum of the fluid would weigh most nearly

   **a.** 402 pounds.

   **b.** 440 pounds.

   **c.** 424 pounds.

   **d.** 395 pounds.

**72.** In doing a size-up of a building on fire, the firefighter estimates the building is 250 feet long and 60 feet wide. The building has three floors. What is the total floor area of the building?

   **a.** 15,000 square feet

   **b.** 45,000 square feet

   **c.** 18,000 square feet

   **d.** 42,000 square feet

**73.** Which of the following rope lengths is the longest? (1 inch = 25.4 millimeters)

   **a.** 1 meter

   **b.** 1 yard

   **c.** 32 inches

   **d.** 850 millimeters

**74.** A safety box has three layers of metal, each with a different width. If one layer is $\frac{1}{8}$ inch thick, a second layer is $\frac{1}{6}$ inch thick, and the total thickness is $\frac{3}{4}$ inch thick, what is the width of the third layer?

   **a.** $\frac{5}{12}$

   **b.** $\frac{11}{24}$

   **c.** $\frac{7}{18}$

   **d.** $\frac{1}{2}$

**75.** A person can be scalded by hot water at a temperature of about 122° F. At about what temperature Centigrade could a person be scalded?

   $C = \frac{5}{9}(F - 32)$

   **a.** 35.5° C

   **b.** 55° C

   **c.** 50° C

   **d.** 216° C

**76.** At 1:05 A.M., at the scene of a fire, the gauge on a fire engine's pump control panel indicated a pressure of 260 pounds per square inch (psi). By 1:20 A.M., the same gauge indicated a pressure of 110 psi. The pressure decreased, on average, about how many psi per minute?
a. 10
b. 11
c. 12
d. 20

**77.** Studies have shown that automatic sprinkler systems save about $5,700 in damages per fire in stores and offices. If a particular community has on average 14 store and office fires every year, about how much money is saved each year if these buildings have sprinkler systems?
a. $28,500
b. $77,800
c. $79,800
d. $87,800

**78.** If a firefighter weighs 168 pounds, what is the approximate weight of that firefighter in kilograms? (1 kilogram = about 2.2 pounds)
a. 76
b. 77
c. 149
d. 150

**79.** Tank A, when full, holds 555 gallons of water. Tank B, when full, holds 680 gallons of water. If Tank A is only $\frac{2}{3}$ full and Tank B is only $\frac{2}{5}$ full, how many more gallons of water are needed to fill both tanks to capacity?
a. 319
b. 593
c. 642
d. 658

**80.** Fire departments commonly use the following formula to find out how far from a wall to place the base of a ladder: (Length of ladder ÷ 5) + 2 = distance from the wall. Using this formula, if the base of a ladder is placed 10 feet from a wall, how tall is the ladder?
a. 48 feet
b. 72 feet
c. 40 feet
d. 100 feet

## ▶ Section 5: Mechanical Aptitude

Use the information provided in the question, as well as any diagrams provided, to answer the following questions.

**81.** Of the actions described below, which one best illustrates the principle of preventative maintenance?
a. fixing a device after it fails
b. making periodic adjustments on a device to keep it working smoothly
c. purchasing a new device just before an old one wears out
d. purchasing a new device after an old one wears out

**82.** A hinge is most likely to be used on which of the following?
a. a hand rail
b. a digital clock
c. an electric fan
d. a cabinet door

**83.** What would be the primary function of the tool shown below?

    **a.** striking
    **b.** disassembly
    **c.** pulling
    **d.** prying

**84.** The primary use of a fire department axe is for cutting. Which of the following could be another common use for a fire department axe?
    **a.** striking
    **b.** disassembly
    **c.** pulling
    **d.** joining

**85.** Which of the following best describes the purpose of welding?
    **a.** joining
    **b.** cleaning
    **c.** lifting
    **d.** moving

**86.**

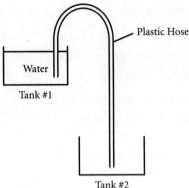

What mechanical device could be used to transfer water from tank 1 to tank 2?
    **a.** a pulley
    **b.** a siphon
    **c.** a gauge
    **d.** a spring

**87.** Which of the following mechanical devices is used to open a common soft drink can?
    **a.** a winch
    **b.** a lever
    **c.** a wrench
    **d.** a piston

**88.** Which hand tool listed below is used to tighten a nut and bolt?
    **a.** a crescent wrench
    **b.** a screwdriver
    **c.** an awl
    **d.** a hammer

**89.**

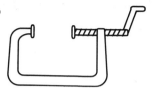

The C-clamp shown above would most likely be used to

**a.** temporarily hold two boards together.

**b.** hold up a car to repair a flat tire.

**c.** secure a nut as the bolt is tightened.

**d.** make a straight cut on a board.

**90.** The primary function of a wire mesh screen is to

**a.** transport water on a construction project.

**b.** aid in reading a directional compass.

**c.** separate large particles from smaller ones.

**d.** lift heavy loads in a warehouse.

**91.** A crane is primarily used to perform which of the following functions?

**a.** pushing

**b.** drilling

**c.** welding

**d.** lifting

**92.** Which of the following statements is true concerning the differences between an electric motor and a gas-powered engine?

**a.** There are no differences, the devices are essentially the same.

**b.** An electric motor requires an external power source other than itself to operate.

**c.** Gas-powered engines are safer to use in a confined space or area.

**d.** Electric motors tend to produce more noise then gas-powered engines.

**93.**

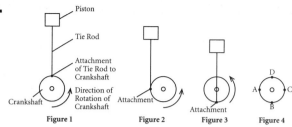

Figure 1 above shows the initial position of a piston that is connected to a crankshaft by a tie rod. Figure 2 shows the relative positions after the crankshaft is rotated 90 degrees (one quarter of a revolution) in the direction shown. Figure 3 shows the relative positions after another 90 degrees of rotation. In Figure 4, what will be the position of the tie rod attachment to the crankshaft after yet another 90 degree rotation?

**a.** position A

**b.** position B

**c.** position C

**d.** position D

**94.** A bicycle wheel has a diameter of 1.9 feet and a circumference of 6 feet. A girl rides this bicycle for two revolutions of this wheel. How far down the driveway does she travel?

**a.** 20 feet

**b.** 12 feet

**c.** 4 feet

**d.** 2 feet

**95.** The primary purpose of a pump is to

**a.** lift heavy equipment.

**b.** move fluids from one point to another.

**c.** reduce vibration of internal combustion engines.

**d.** regulate the speed of an electric motor.

**96.**

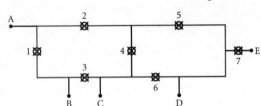

⊠  Indicates a valve
location. The valves
are numbered
1 through 7.

In the diagram shown above, all valves are initially closed. Which valves must be opened to allow water to flow from point A to points B and D but NOT to points C and E?

a. valves 2, 4, and 6
b. valves 1, 2, and 3
c. valves 1, 2, and 4
d. valves 1, 2, and 5

**97.** Which of the following is an electrical, as opposed to a mechanical, device?

a. a wrench
b. a clamp
c. a hydraulic jack
d. a battery

**98.** Newton's First Law of physics says, "A body (such as a car) that is in motion along a straight line will remain in motion, at the same speed, along the same straight line, unless acted upon by an outside force." A car is traveling down a straight, flat road at 30 miles per hour. The operation of all but one of the items listed below can help demonstrate Newton's First Law. Which item cannot be used to demonstrate this law?

a. the brakes
b. the gas pedal
c. the steering wheel
d. the radiator

**99.**

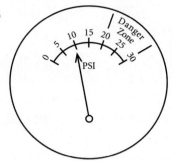

On the gauge in the diagram above, what is the maximum recommended operating pressure in psi (pounds per square inch) for the needle to remain in a safe zone?

a. 10 psi
b. 20 psi
c. 25 psi
d. 30 psi

**100.** You are cutting 18" square pieces from a four-foot by eight-foot sheet of plywood. How many pieces can be cut from a single sheet of plywood?

a. 15
b. 18
c. 10
d. 20

# ► Answers

## Section 1:
## Reading Comprehension

**1. b.** According to the passage, hand washing is still the fundamental precaution for controlling infection. The other answers will also decrease infection, but are not mentioned in the passage.

**2. d.** As used here, *incidence* is the extent or frequency of occurrence for some event, in this passage, infection. So, *occurrence* is the best answer.

**3. c.** In the last paragraph, the passage mentions that the problem about infection control in the emergency response environment is that there are few studies outside of hospital-based ones.

**4. b.** Divide 1,306 by 2,502 to get the correct answer.

**5. b.** Look under the third column at the third row of data.

**6. d.** Look under the second column at the fourth row of data.

**7. c.** The passage states that a menu approach or a joint response is not always the best strategy for every situation. Choice **c** is the best fit.

**8. a.** The purpose of emergency response is the mitigation of the incident that is lessening the impact on the community.

**9. c.** Although all four of the answers are mentioned, no details are given to support choice **a**, **b**, or **d**. Choice **c** is directly stated at the end of the passage.

**10. a.** The purpose of the paragraph is to demonstrate the advantage of rehabilitation of firefighters.

**11. b.** Fatigue, dehydration, and stress not only reduce reaction time but also lead to an increased risk for injury or illness. No one should have to get used to unsafe conditions or poor personnel management practices.

**12. c.** To hydrate means to combine with water, so the process of *rehydration* is the replacement of fluids and salts the firefighters have lost through sweat.

**13. d.** The High School category is at 45%, which is 15% above the next category, Elementary School.

**14. b.** $325 \times 0.30 = 98$.

**15. a.** Although cause-and-effect is involved in the second paragraph, the passage mainly follows a hierarchical order, beginning with evacuating the premises and ending with sharing information with the emergency personnel.

**16. b.** This choice gets broadest coverage in the passage. All other choices are mentioned, but are too narrow to be called the most important priority.

**17. d.** Choice **a** can be found in the last paragraph. Choice **b** can be found in the second paragraph. Choice **c** is mentioned in the last sentence.

**18. a.** See the last sentence of the third paragraph.

**19. b.** The answer is clearly stated in paragraph 2.

**20. c.** See the third paragraph.

**21. a.** This can be surmised based on the next-to-last sentence of the passage.

**22. d.** See the third paragraph.

**23. c.** Choice **a** is mentioned in the fourth paragraph (*a check must be made near all gas appliances* implies that they are potential sources of contamination). Choice **b** is mentioned in the third paragraph (CO *poisoning symptoms* are listed). Choice **d** is mentioned in the second paragraph (*calibrated meters should be taken onto the premises*).

**24. c.** Choice **a** is incorrect because the trend is for an increasing number of fires at this time. Choice **b** is incorrect because the graph does not provide any information regarding the size of fires. Choice **c** is a logical selection.

**25. b.** The percentage of fires is indicated by the dashed line. The line is slightly lower at 2:30 A.M. than at 4:30 A.M.

**26. c.** During the period 6:00 P.M. to midnight, the percentage of fires stays above 5% until 10:30 P.M., so this is the busiest period for the fire department.

**27. b.** To find the correct value, multiply the total number of alarms by the percentage caused by alarm malfunctions, $874 \times 0.47 = 411$.

**28. a.** Answers **a, c,** and **d** are all valid concerns that should be addressed as part of a fire prevention program. The key to this question is the term "most effective." The percentage of alarms caused by alarm malfunctions is far greater than the percentages for the other options, therefore, reducing the number of alarms caused by alarm malfunctions would have the most effect on reducing the total call volume.

**29. b.** From the chart, 10% of the alarms were the result of an unknown problem or source. To find the approximate number of total alarms, divide the number of unknown alarms by the percentage; $53 / 0.10 = 530$. This is the inverse (opposite) operation of knowing the total number of incidents and multiplying by the percentage.

**30. c.** The procedure notes that the RIT personnel should not engage in firefighting operations, therefore, a fire hose would not normally be staged.

**31. c.** The procedure notes a medical emergency as one of the types of emergencies that the team should be monitoring for; therefore, a firefighter having severe chest pain would be a valid cause for deploying the team.

**32. a.** The procedure does not contain specific details on how to remove an injured firefighter. This type of procedure would typically be discussed during hands-on training.

**33. c.** The procedure states that the RIT team will not engage in any fireground activities not directly associated with the RIT. Choices **a** and **b** would not necessarily be associated with the operation of an RIT team as defined by the procedure. Recall that the RIT team is responsible for firefighter safety, and water supply would not fall within the responsibility of the RIT team. However, where the firefighters are operating in the building is an important operational observation that may give clues to where an injured or ill firefighter will be found if an emergency occurs.

**34. b.** Ten non-white males died. The next highest number is 8.

**35. c.** Seventy-six adults died, compared with 35 children.

## Section 2: Verbal Expression

**36. b.** Something that is *nondescript* is without distinction or *undistinguished*. The keys here are the words *usually a flashy dresser* and *uncharacteristically*.

**37. c.** To be held *accountable* is to be held answerable or *responsible*.

**38. a.** To *alleviate* something is to make it more bearable or to *ease* it.

**39. c.** To be *indispensable* is to be necessary or *essential*.

**40. d.** To *decontaminate* and to *purify* both mean to remove impurities.

**41. a.** A *prerequisite* is something that is necessary or required. The fact that you can't join the team without the training course means that it is required. The other choices do not imply a hard and fast rule.

**42. a.** If something is *plausible,* it is believable or credible. This is the only logical choice.

**43. b.** To be *apathetic* is to show little or no interest or to be indifferent.

**44. c.** The opening phrase, *An American poet of the nineteenth century,* should modify a noun that identifies the poet. Only choice **c** does this. In choices **a** and **b**, either *collection* or *Leaves of Grass* is illogically credited with being the poet. Choice **d** is incorrect because the subject of the resulting dependent clause, *poems,* would not agree with its verb, *celebrates.*

**45. d.** This is the only choice in which there is agreement between the subject and verb and between the pronoun and its antecedent.

**46. b.** This is a correct choice because it makes a complete sentence that is clear and logical.

**47. d.** This is the correct choice. Choice **a** is unclear. Choices **b** and **c** make an illogical shift in verb tense.

**48. a.** This choice is clear, has no misplaced modifiers, and has no shifts in verb tense. Choices **b** and **d** have misplaced modifiers and result in unclear sentences; choice **c** has an unnecessary shift from past to present tense.

**49. b.** This is the only choice that does not have a misplaced modifier. Because Miles Johnson is the sharpshooter, his name should be placed immediately after the introductory phrase, which rules out choices **a** and **c**. Choice **d** is awkwardly constructed and unclear.

**50. c.** This is the only choice that makes logical sense.

## Section 3: Logical Reasoning

**51. b.** This series alternates in pairs of numbers. The first number has 3 added to it, and the second number is multiplied by 3, to get the next pair in the series: $3 + 3 = 6$; $9 \times 3 = 27$, and so forth.

**52. d.** This series alternates the addition of 5 with the subtraction of 3.

**53. b.** This is a multiplication series; each number is 3 times the previous number.

**54. c.** The letters decrease by 1; the numbers are multiplied by 2.

**55. d.** In this series, each letter alternates in a different order. The first letter starts at R and goes backward in the alphabet in single steps, R, Q, P, O, N. The second letter goes forward in the alphabet starting at D and skipping every other letter. The third letter starts at J and goes forward in the alphabet. Hint: For these types of problems write down the complete alphabet A through Z and look for patterns. It makes it easier to identify the patterns when you look at them written out.

**56. c.** All four segments use the same figures: two squares, one circle, and one triangle. In the first segment, the squares are on the outside of the circle and triangle. In the second segment, the squares are below the other two. In the third segment, the squares are on the inside. In the fourth segment, the squares are above the triangle and circle.

**57. b.** Each arrow in this continuing series moves a few degrees in a clockwise direction. Think of these arrows as the big hand on a clock. The first arrow is at noon. The last arrow before the blank would be 12:40. Choice **b**, the correct answer, is at 12:45.

**58. d.** In each of the segments, the figures alternate between one-half and one-fourth shaded.

**59. b.** A baker makes bread; a congressperson makes law. The answer is not choice **a** because a senator and a congressperson both make laws. Choice **c** is incorrect because a congressperson does not make a state. Politician (choice **d**) is also incorrect because a congressperson is a politician.

**60. b.** *Approach* and *retreat* are antonyms, meaning the opposite of each other. *Withhold* is an antonym of *provide*. The other choices are all synonyms.

**61. b.** A yard is a larger measure than an inch (a yard contains 36 inches). A quart is a larger measure than an ounce (a quart contains 32 ounces). Gallon (choice **a**) is incorrect because it is larger than a quart. Choices **c** and **d** are incorrect because they are not units of measurement.

**62. a.** *Sponge* is a *porous* material; *porous* would be a property of the sponge. *Lead* is commonly known as a dense material, which is why it is used for radiation shielding. Choices **b, c,** and **d** are incorrect because lead would not be commonly referred to as having any of these properties. In fact, lead is considered to be a relatively soft metal.

**63. c.** We know from the first two statements that Tuesday had the highest temperature, but we cannot know whether Monday's temperature was higher than Wednesday's.

**64. c.** The first two statements indicate that Hose B flows the least amount of water. However, it cannot be determined if Hose C flows more water than Hose A.

**65. b.** Because the first two statements are true, Penfield is west of Centerville and southwest of Middletown. Therefore, the third statement is false.

## Section 4: Mathematics

**66. b.** There are three steps involved in solving this problem. First, convert 4.5% to a decimal: 0.045. Multiply that by $26,000 to find out how much the salary increases. Finally, add

the result ($1,170) to the original salary of $26,000 to find out the new salary, $27,170.

**67. b.** First, you have to determine the perimeters of all four rooms. This is done by using the formula for a square ($P = 4S$), or for a rectangle ($P = 2L + 2W$), as follows: $4 \times 10 = 40$ for choice **a**; $4 \times 11 = 44$ for the correct choice, **b**; $(2 \times 12) + (2 \times 8) = 40$ for choice **c**; and $(2 \times 14) + (2 \times 7) = 42$ for choice **d**.

**68. c.** To solve the problem you have to first convert the total time to minutes (105 minutes), then multiply by 4 (420 minutes), then convert the answer back to hours by dividing by 60 minutes to arrive at the final answer (7 hours). Or you can multiply $1\frac{3}{4}$ hours by 4 to arrive at the same answer.

**69. d.** To solve the problem, you must first find the common denominator, in this instance 60. Then the fractions must be converted: $\frac{17}{20} = \frac{51}{60}$ (for choice **a**); $\frac{3}{4} = \frac{45}{60}$ (for choice **b**); $\frac{5}{6} = \frac{50}{60}$ (for choice **c**); and $\frac{7}{10} = \frac{42}{60}$ (for the correct choice, **d**).

**70. c.** First, you must subtract the percentage of the installation cost during construction (1.5%) from the percentage of the installation cost after construction (4%). To do this, begin by converting the percentages into decimals: 4% = 0.04; 1.5% = 0.015. Now, subtract: 0.04 − 0.015 = 0.025. This is the percentage of the total cost that the homeowner will save. Multiply this by the total cost of the home to find the dollar amount: 0.025 × $150,000 = $3,750.

**71. c.** First, find the weight of the fluid in the drum and round it off. The fluid in the drum would weigh 7.3 pounds / gallon × 55 gallons = 402 pounds. The gallon term is cancelled out by dimensional analysis. Then, add the weight of the fluid to the weight of the drum, 402 pounds + 22 pounds = 424 pounds.

**72. b.** The area of each floor is length times width, 250 feet × 60 feet = 15,000 square feet each floor. There are 3 floors in the building, therefore the total floor area is 3 × 15,000 square feet = 45,000 square feet.

**73. a.** Answers c and d can be easily disregarded. A yard is 36 inches, and a meter is 1,000 millimeters, therefore, it is obvious that neither c nor d is correct. To compare 1 yard to 1 meter, use the conversion given and dimensional analysis to convert one value into the other. For example, 1 yard = 36 inches × 25.4 millimeters / inch = 915 millimeters (the inches cancel each other out). As 915 millimeters is less than 1 meter, a meter is the longest.

**74. b.** To solve the problem, you must first find the common denominator, in this instance, 24. Then the fractions must be converted: $\frac{1}{8} = \frac{3}{24}$; $\frac{1}{6} = \frac{4}{24}$; $\frac{3}{4} = \frac{18}{24}$. Add the values for first and second layers together: $\frac{3}{24} + \frac{4}{24} = \frac{7}{24}$, then subtract the sum from the total thickness ($\frac{18}{24}$): $\frac{18}{24} - \frac{7}{24} = \frac{11}{24}$.

**75. c.** First, convert Fahrenheit to Centigrade using the formula given: $C = \frac{5}{9}(122 - 32)$; that is, $C = \frac{5}{9} \times 90$. So C = 50.

**76. a.** First, find the length of time covered by subtracting the later time from the earlier: 1:20 – 1:05 = 15 minutes. Next, find the number of psi the pressure dropped in that time: 260 – 110 = 150 psi. Now, divide the number of psi the pressure dropped (150) by the length of time covered (15 minutes): 150 ÷ 15 = 10.

**77. c.** To solve this problem, multiply the amount saved per fire, $5,700, by the average number of fires: 5,700 × 14 = 79,800.

**78. a.** To solve this problem, divide the number of pounds (168) by the number of kilograms in a pound (2.2): 168 ÷ 2.2 = 76.36. Now, round to the nearest unit, which is 76.

**79. b.** To solve this problem, find the number of gallons of water missing from each tank ($\frac{1}{3}$ of Tank A, $\frac{3}{5}$ of Tank B), and then multiply by the number of gallons each tank holds when full (555 for Tank A; 680 for Tank B): $\frac{1}{3} \times 555$ = 185 gal for Tank A; $\frac{3}{5} \times 680$ = 408 gal for Tank B. Now, add the number of gallons missing from both tanks to get the number of gallons needed to fill them: 185 + 408 = 593.

**80. c.** Since the distance from the wall is known, the formula would be: $(x \div 5) + 2 = 10$. To find $x$, start by subtracting 2 from both sides, so you have $x \div 5 = 8$. Then multiply both sides by 5, and you end up with $x = 40$.

## Section 5: Mechanical Aptitude

**81. b.** Preventive maintenance is done on a device while it is still working, to prevent its breaking down or failing. Examples of preventative maintenance include changing the oil in a car engine, adjusting the brakes on a car, lubricating the moving parts on a pump, and changing the fan belts and hoses on a truck.

**82. d.** The function of a hinge is to connect two items together and to allow rotation of one of the items relative to the other. Of the choices, a cabinet door is the most likely to use a hinge.

**83. d.** The tool shown is commonly referred to as a halligan bar or tool. It is used primarily for prying. The curved and tapered tips at each end indicate that it is a prying tool. This tool also has a blunt end, which can be used for striking, but that is not its primary purpose.

**84. a.** Fire department axes are often used as striking tools. They are frequently used in conjunction with prying tools, including the tool shown in question 83, to drive a prying tool into an opening.

**85. a.** Welding is the process of connecting two pieces of material such as metal or plastic. The two pieces to be joined are positioned next to each other, and heat is used to melt a small amount of each piece along the intersection. The melted material mixes together and then cools to form a bond that holds the pieces together.

**86. b.** To use a siphon, you would first submerge the entire length of hose in tank 1 in order to completely fill it with water. You would then place one end of the hose in tank 1 and the other end in tank 2, as shown in the diagram. Since the end of the hose in tank 2 is lower than the end in tank 1, the extra weight of the water in the right side of the hose will cause the water to flow into tank 2.

**87. b.** The little tab you use to pry open the can is a lever. You lift up one end of the lever, which rotates around a pivot point and forces the other end of the lever downward, so that the can pops open.

**88. a.** A crescent wrench is used to tighten bolts. A screwdriver is used to tighten screws, an awl to start holes in wood to accommodate nails or screws, and a hammer to drive nails.

**89. a.** The C-clamp would be placed around the two boards and tightened by turning the screw with the handle.

**90. c.** Besides being used on windows and doors—where they keep large particles such as flies out of your living room—screens are typically used in industrial applications to sift granular materials such as rock, sand, and dirt in order to separate large pieces from small pieces.

**91. d.** A crane is used to raise and lower large items that are too heavy or awkward to lift by hand.

**92. b.** An electric motor requires an external power source to operate, whereas an engine consumes fuel and powers itself, usually with an internal combustion engine. Gas-powered engines should be used with caution in confined spaces because they will produce harmful emissions, whereas electric motors typically do not. Electric motors and electrically powered tools tend to be quieter than similar gas-powered tools.

**93. c.** Figure 3 shows the attachment of the tie rod to the crankshaft at the bottom of the crankshaft. Another 90-degree counterclockwise rotation would place the attachment point on the right side of the crankshaft at position C.

**94. b.** The circumference is the distance around the outer edge of the wheel. Two revolutions of a wheel 6 feet in circumference would result in a distance traveled of 12 feet.

**95. b.** A pump is a rotating piece of machinery normally driven by an electric motor. Fluid is pulled into the front of the pump, accelerated through the pump, and discharged through the back of the pump. Pumps are used to move fluids such as water, gasoline, and waste water, as well as thick industrial slurries such as fertilizer and mine tailings.

**96. d.** Carefully follow the flow diagram to verify that you must open valves 1, 2, and 5. If you opened valves 4 and 6, water would flow to point C as well as to point D.

**97. d.** A battery is an electrical device. The other items listed are common mechanical devices.

**98. d.** Newton's First Law says that a vehicle will move at the same speed unless an outside force is applied. Both the brakes and the gas pedal could be used to apply such a force. Newton's First Law also says that the vehicle will travel along the same straight line unless an outside force—the action of the steering wheel, for instance—is applied. The radiator does not affect the speed or direction of the car's motion.

**99. b.** The gauge indicates that any pressure greater than 20 psi is in the danger zone.

**100. c.** Ten full pieces can be cut from a single sheet of plywood. The full sheet is 4' × 8'; 48" × 96". You can cut two full pieces across the width; 2 pieces × 18" wide = 36", leaving 12" remaining. You can cut five full pieces along the 8' length of the plywood; 5 pieces × 18" long = 90", leaving 6" remaining.

| FIREFIGHTER EXAM 4 | | |
| --- | --- | --- |
| **Question Type** | **Question Numbers** | **Chapter** |
| Reading Text (25 questions) | 1–3, 7–12, 15–23, 28–33 | 6, "Reading Text, Tables, Charts, and Graphs" |
| Reading Tables, Charts, and Graphs (10 questions) | 4–6, 13, 14, 24–27, 34, 35 | 6, "Reading Text, Tables, Charts, and Graphs" |
| Verbal Expression (15 questions) | 36–50 | 12, "Verbal Expression" |
| Logical Reasoning (15 questions) | 51–65 | 9, "Judgment and Reasoning" |
| Mathematics (15 questions) | 66–80 | 8, "Math" |
| Mechanical Aptitude (20 questions) | 81–100 | 10, "Mechanical Aptitude" |

## ▶ Scoring

A score of 70 is usually enough to put you on the firefighter eligibility list. But you should aim to score significantly higher, particularly if you are applying to a city that uses the written exam score to help determine your rank on the eligibility list. Check your score carefully and calculate the percentage of questions you answered correctly in each portion of the exam. Be sure to carefully review the chapters that pertain to the sections on which you received the lowest scores and try to understand why you made the mistakes you did.

In fact, unless your score was nearly perfect, you should plan to spend as much time as you can studying and practicing so your actual test results are as close to 100% as possible. Remember, not all cities test all of the skills covered in this exam. So, if your exam does not include one of the following areas, you don't have to spend much time on that section.

- If your **reading text** scores could use some improvement, review Chapter 6. You should also try to fit in as much reading as possible between now and exam day. If your city offers a study guide, review it thoroughly.
- If your scores in the **verbal expression** section could be higher, review Chapter 12. You may also want to build these skills by working with a vocabulary builder and a grammar handbook.

- If your **logical reasoning** scores need improvement, review Chapter 9. You may also want to practice working analogies and logic puzzles on your own.
- If your **math** scores were low, review Chapter 8. You may also want to seek out situations in your daily life in which you can practice your math skills. If you normally rely on a calculator to balance your checkbook, for example, do all of your calculations by hand.
- If you had difficulty with the **mechanical aptitude** section, review Chapter 10. You may also want to practice on your own by taking things apart and putting them back together or working on 3-D puzzles.

The more you can find everyday situations in which you can practice these skills and imagine the types of questions that may be asked, the higher you are likely to score on the exam.

Another key element to your success is self-confidence. The more comfortable you are with your ability to perform, the more likely you are to do well on the exam. You know what to expect, you know your strengths and weaknesses, and you can work to turn those weaknesses into strengths before the actual exam. Your preparation should give you the confidence you will need to do well on exam day.

# 15▶ The Candidate Physical Ability Test

## CHAPTER SUMMARY

This chapter describes the physical test that is required in the firefighter selection process. It focuses on the specific tasks involved, including tips from the experts about how to ace these tasks and how you can practice ahead of time.

**H**ave you ever crossed a bridge and noticed someone at the side pulling up a rope with a bookbag full of rocks attached to the end? There is a good chance that person wants to be a firefighter.

Ever walked to your car in a parking garage and noticed a person with a loaded-down backpack running up and down six flights of stairs? Probably a firefighter candidate.

Ever see someone in a harness pulling a car? Yep, another potential firefighter.

As odd as these activities may seem, these are examples of how firefighting candidates can prepare for the Candidate Physical Ability Test (CPAT). Fire departments around the country use the CPAT to determine whether candidates have the physical ability to be considered for the fire academy, which is where they learn firefighting tasks. Academy directors emphasize that all candidates must have high levels of strength and aerobic energy, or stamina.

"Fitness is a real high indicator of the ability to cope with the stress in the academy," says Al Baeta, a physical education instructor at American River College in Sacramento, California. Baeta devised a program for the Sacramento Fire Department that not only prepares academy candidates for the CPAT, but also keeps firefighters fit throughout their careers. "Academy recruits have come back and told me how surprised they were at the physical activities in the fire academy. Fire departments work them hard. It's strenuous physical work, from dawn to dusk, and it's difficult emotionally—often done in a paramilitary-type environment. The base every candidate needs is an aerobic capacity and overall body strength."

Fire academies are demanding because fires are demanding. Firefighters must work quickly, efficiently, and safely. Their job requires them to run, jump, bend, and climb while lifting, pulling, or carrying heavy weight and while wearing heavy protective gear. They carry out these tasks in a chaotic, life-threatening environment, often in extreme heat. The ability to perform and think under these conditions requires preparation, and overall physical fitness is the foundation.

## Strength + Stamina = Safety

There is no doubt, the Candidate Physical Ability Test (also called Physical Agilities Test or Physical Performance Test) is a crucial step toward becoming a firefighter. Though the type of tests may vary somewhat from state to state and city to city, academy directors agree that the CPAT requires training, particularly for upper-body strength and stamina.

"The [C]PAT tests your potential to complete a recruit academy," says Bill Wittmer, academy director of the Oakland (California) Fire Department. "If you have problems in the [C]PAT, then you are going to have a problem in the recruit academy, which is harder and runs 10 to 16 weeks. That's where you are throwing ladders, pulling hose, doing physical work all day long. They're tough."

Fire departments have answered the request of the courts in recent years to make their CPATs reflect the duties found in fighting fires. As such, more departments have moved away from CPATs that included mile-and-a-half runs and pushups. More and more CPATs around the country now include tasks that sim-

ulate the work of firefighting, such as raising ladders, hoisting bundles of hose, and dragging heavy dummies.

Departments are also quite sensitive to charges that their tests favor men. Academy directors stress that women can and do pass these tests—the Dallas (Texas) Fire Department, for example, has 60 female firefighters in its ranks. However, women may have to work more on developing strength in certain areas, particularly their arms and shoulders, to pass the physical tests. Rancho Santiago Community College in Santa Ana, California has the largest firefighting program in the state, and instructor Terri Wann notes that women who pass this program are a definite minority, "mainly due to lack of upper-body strength." However, many women do pass the tests simply by practicing technique, learning how to accomplish tasks in ways that compensate for their physical build.

## Know the Procedures

Because CPATs aren't the same at every department, it's important to find out in advance what is involved in the test you will be taking. One thing you should know is whether you will have to perform the test in heavy gear, such as boots, gloves, helmet, turnout coat, and SCBA. Not all fire departments require the gear, but if they do, it's best to practice for the test wearing clothing that is similarly heavy and restrictive.

Another variation in CPATs is that some tend to focus on upper-body strength, others on overall fitness. Some fire departments include climbing ladders to see if you are afraid of heights. Others want to know if you become claustrophobic in your breathing gear. Every department, however, wants to see if you have the physical abilities to perform safely and efficiently on the fire grounds. You can count on being tested for agility, balance, strength, and stamina.

For details about the CPAT in your municipal department, call the department office or the human resources department to find out how the test is conducted and under what conditions.

## Timing Is Everything

The current trend among fire departments is the sustained activity testing procedure. This means performing anywhere from five to ten firefighting tasks and completing all of them successfully within a prescribed time. These tests are built around a combination of strength and aerobic activity. They may include lifting ladders, running bundles of hose up several flights of stairs, and hoisting other bundles by rope up four floors of a building—one after another, with relatively little rest between.

Some departments time each event, with a pass/fail grade for each task riding on a candidate's ability to accomplish the task within the deadline. Other departments are more flexible, timing each event but compiling an overall total. This allows someone who might be slow in the hose lift to make up time with a fast stair climb.

You have to be clear about the requirements and what is meant by "successfully completing the task." Academy instructors do not want to see someone race through the exercises without being able to demonstrate control. For example, being able to raise an extension ladder to the prescribed length, but then letting it crash down to beat the deadline, won't meet the requirements of the test.

Failing to complete any part of the test generally means that the entire test has to be retaken. You may have to wait anywhere from 30 days to as long as a year to retake the test. Some departments give you two chances to complete tasks but, again, failure in any event typically means you are out.

The grading of these tests varies as well. Many departments rank candidates based on their scores in several areas, including the CPAT and the written exam. Others rank you primarily for proficiency on the CPAT, which means you can be ranked in order of how fast you completed the tasks.

The White Plains (New York) Fire Department gives candidates two shots at completing each task on its CPAT, then uses the best time in each to rank candidates. "You want to be careful on the first run and make sure you get through it," advises Deputy Chief Robert Keil. "On the next run, go for time. Then you are familiar with how it feels. The first run, you tend to be nervous."

## The Tasks

Each individual task within a CPAT may not seem that taxing. But when they are performed in succession and with heavy gear on, they can take a great toll on the body. To add to the challenge, fire departments often require you to complete tasks by walking to a finish line, or pushing a bell. This isn't designed to frustrate you, but rather to determine whether you have the composure to think clearly when you are fatigued and under stress. It can be quite disappointing to meet the required deadline for a task, only to find out you failed because you didn't walk to the finish line.

The key is knowing exactly what is required and then preparing for it. Some departments allow candidates to practice the test on the testing grounds in advance. This is a great opportunity to understand your weaknesses and improve on them for the CPAT.

The following are descriptions of various CPAT tasks, including what they test for, helpful tips, and some ways to prepare yourself. These examples may not reflect the exact CPAT you will face, but some combination of the tasks that follow will be found in most fire departments around the country. Also, it should be noted that fire departments re-evaluate their testing procedures periodically, so the test that's used now in your area could change in the near future. Photographs illustrating some of these tasks appear on pages 326 and 327.

**Ladder carry/raise:** Remove an extension ladder from a holder and carry it either around cones or through an obstacle course to a designated spot (possibly back where you began, to replace the ladder on the holder). Some tests require you to set the ladder up properly and then raise and lower the extension by pulling a rope hand over hand.

**Tests for:** Upper body strength (arms, shoulders, wrists) and agility.

**Tips:** Ladders, which can weigh from 40 to 80 pounds, may be 20 feet long, but when extended, they may stretch as high as 35 or 40 feet. Because they are difficult to maneuver, when you are carrying them, it is best to get a wide grip on the ladder and keep your balance by flexing your legs and widening your stance. Height is an advantage here because taller people tend to have a longer reach, which helps keep the ladder stable.

Raising the extension requires pulling on a rope. The higher the ladder goes, the more weight you must control. This puts great stress on the arms. Shorter candidates can lose control because they often stretch by raising up on toes, which reduces their balance and can lead to loss of control. When you are being timed, this exercise can be tough.

**Practice:** Find an extension ladder, load it up with weights and carry it around. A barbell loaded with weights is another good practice item.

For the extension pull, attach a 75-pound sack of sand to a rope (or start with a lighter weight if necessary). Throw the light end of a rope over a bar, or perhaps a high tree branch. Pull the sack up with your arms. It is best to use a rope that is a half-inch wide and to wear fire gloves as well.

**Hose drag/pull:** Grab one end of hose—usually the thick, heavy 2.5-inch-wide variety—and drag it a prescribed distance, such as 100 to 200 feet. Some departments require you to drag a "charged" line, which means it is full of water. Most prefer a dry line. After crossing the finish line, you might be required to pull the rest of the hose, hand over hand, past the line.

**Tests for:** Overall body strength, particularly legs, and endurance.

**Tips:** Get a good grasp on the end of the hose and run with a good forward lean. Building momentum early is the key because as the hose stretches out, the heavier it becomes and the more difficult it is to control. This task is often performed in firefighting gear (coat and SCBA), which can add 50 pounds to your body weight. The extra weight and the hose can take a big toll on your legs.

In pulling the hose, get a solid stance (feet just wider than the shoulders) with your knees bent. Pull from the center of your body, rotating hips back and forth to help the arms pull the weight. Use your legs more than your upper body.

**Practice:** Run uphill sprints of 30 to 50 yards. Or attach a tire filled with sand or bricks to a rope and drag it across 200 feet of asphalt. One woman who was in training attached a harness with straps to the front axle of a car, which she then pulled in 100-foot intervals.

**Hose carry/hose hoist:** Carry a bundled or rolled-up length of hose (it can weigh 55 pounds) up three to four flights of stairs. Then walk over to a ledge and use a rope to pull another bundled hose, hand over hand, to your floor. Then carry another bundled hose back down the stairs.

**Tests for:** Overall body strength and endurance.

**Tips:** Academy directors who use this task in their CPAT say it is the most draining event. It is difficult to prepare for this test since it is often done in turnout coat and SCBA, which, along with the bundled hose, make walking up and down stairs an excruciating chore. Pulling up the hose is an additional strain, particularly on the arms and shoulders. Because of the upper body strength this takes, many training directors note that women will often benefit from extra practice on the hose lifting.

Like the hose pull, it is best to work from a stable base: feet just wider than the shoulders, with the knees bent. Rotate your hips to help your arms pull up the dead weight. A steady rhythm works best.

When climbing and descending stairs, make sure you understand the requirements. Some departments demand that you take each step one by one. Others allow you to bound up (if you can!) three or four at a time.

**Practice:** For the stair climb, run stair steps with a large weight on your shoulders, such as a bag of sand or feed. Parking structures are good because they require you to turn up each flight in the stairwell. Again, if the test requires turnout coat and SCBA, you may want to practice it in restrictive clothing and with a loaded backpack on your back.

For the hose hoist, suspend weights from a railing or bridge and pull up. Here, too, it is best to wear a heavy coat and a backpack to simulate the turnout gear and SCBA.

**Attic crawl:** Crawl, with gear on, down a chute that is 5 feet wide and 3 feet high for a distance of 12 feet. You will be required to put your weight on only the rafters of the chute. If you miss, you fall through and must start over. (This task simulates crawling above a weakened ceiling.) Some departments require you to start on the floor, climb a ladder, crawl through a window into a 30-foot chute, then maneuver out and down another ladder.

**Tests:** Balance and hand and leg strength.

**Tips:** Stay low and on your hands, elbows, and knees. Keep your head up and looking forward. Speed is not as crucial as not falling through the gaps.

**Practice:** Set a ladder up on saw horses and practice crawling on it. Also, stretch string above the ladder to force you to stay low.

**Dummy drag:** Grab a life-size dummy (weighing anywhere from 150 to 180 pounds) and drag it a prescribed distance, often 100 feet. Some departments require you

to drag the dummy through a tunnel or chute with a height of four or five feet, but in this case you would generally go a shorter distance, such as 20 feet.

**Tests:** Agility, leg strength, and balance.

**Tips:** A good grip, usually behind the shoulders with your arms wrapped around the chest, is needed. Lean backward and then use your body and legs to propel yourself backward. In a tunnel or chute, you may have to lean to keep your head under the ceiling, which puts more stress on your back and legs and requires more of a backward crawl. Use your legs more than your upper body.

**Practice:** Find a friend who is willing to act as the dummy and be dragged over grass. Or you can load up a sheet with bulky, heavy objects (tires, bags of sand) to simulate the awkwardness of the human body. You can drag this around as much as you want without worrying about scrapes, nicks, and finding new friends.

**Sledge carry/roof walk:** Pick up a sledgehammer (8 to 10 pounds) and walk with it on a ladder that is suspended above the ground on sawhorses. (This simulates walking along a roof line.)

**Tests:** Overall balance.

**Tips:** Good footing can be achieved by walking on the rails of the ladder, not the rungs. Put most of your weight on the balls of your feet, with your weight spread evenly over this wide stance.

**Practice:** Put a ladder on the ground and practice walking, with sledgehammer in hand, on the rails without falling off.

**Tool use:** Some departments require you to pound a roof 20 times with a sledgehammer. Others want you to hit a weighted tire to move it 20 feet. (This tests for strength to break down doors and through walls.) Others still will require you to use a pick pole, which is thrust through ceilings to bring them down during a fire. The test will have you use this or a similar tool to latch onto a spring-loaded box and pull it down. (This takes considerable force and simulates tearing down a ceiling to get to an attic.)

**Tests:** Coordination and strength.

**Tips:** Good footing creates good balance. Take a wide stance, feet just wider than the shoulders, knees slightly flexed. Grab the handle near the bottom, with your hands slightly separated. Swing the tool with a wide arc to create momentum for the heavier head. For more control, separate your hands further.

**Practice:** Practice pounding with a sledgehammer. A softball bat, weighted down at one end, also can be used to help practice.

**Wall vault:** Vault yourself over a wall of four or six feet.

**Tests:** Balance and coordination.

**Tips:** Whether from a running or standing start, it is best to get both hands atop the wall. This will enable you to pull your lower body up and then swing over the wall. After other CPAT tasks and with heavy gear on, this can be difficult to do.

**Practice:** Again, running sprints up hills will help develop the leg strength needed to get a good initial boost over the wall. It takes explosive power to get over the higher walls. After building up your leg strength, you can experiment by vaulting over fences of various heights.

**Hang smoke ejector:** Pick up a smoke ejector (about 40 pounds), walk a prescribed distance (50 to 200 feet), and hang it on a door jamb six feet above the ground. (Note: A smoke ejector is a power-driven fan that is used to eliminate smoke.)

**Tests:** Strength and reach.

**Tips:** For shorter candidates, the smoke ejector can be difficult to manage as they raise it over their heads to hang it properly, especially when they are wearing a turnout coat and helmet. Overall upper body strength, particularly in the biceps and shoulders, is needed.

**Practice:** This is one exercise that might be best prepared for with weightlifting. Lat pulldowns will help develop the specific muscles needed.

## ▶ Further Preparation

Many departments are now electing to duplicate the standard Combat Challenge test, a timed test of four events: hose carry and hoist; using a sledge hammer to drive a weight laterally; hose drag; and dummy drag.

Additionally, some departments require candidates to climb a ladder, lift a pneumatic spreader to several different positions, and even to swim a certain distance or tread water for a certain time (this is most often found in areas with access to open waterways or where swimming pools are common).

### Fit for Fire

Just about every fire department in the country will use some form of these tasks in its CPAT. Academy instructors stress that preparation is the key. Some people may be able to come in off the street and pass one or two of the tests; it is a very rare person who can pass an entire CPAT without any advance training. It often takes months of dedicated training for most candidates to accomplish these tasks in the prescribed times.

"If you don't live the lifestyle, you will not pass the test," instructor Terri Wann says about the Rancho Santiago firefighting program, which has students who come from around the world to participate.

Like Rancho Santiago, many community colleges offer a course geared toward passing the CPAT. Students are able to assess their weaknesses and develop their skills with the tasks while improving their overall physical fitness. The final exam is passing the CPAT.

The Center for Disease Control (CDC) publishes regular NIOSH reports on the deaths and serious injuries to firefighters, and numerous monthly reports deal with death due to cardiac arrest. In the majority of these cases, the conclusions and recommendations focus on the need for a complete wellness program and the elimination of smoking.

Experienced firefighters have realized the necessity of staying in top physical shape, and for years many firehouses have had weight training or other athletic equipment as part of their inventory. However, in response to the CDC reports, a new trend is developing in fire departments throughout the United States: the trend toward a proactive approach to wellness. This plan encompasses more than simply working out each shift. In fact, these programs sometimes require a lifestyle change. For example, experts are brought in to develop healthy eating plans and teach stress reduction techniques; annual physical examinations are offered; and ergonomics are studied and changes to facilities or equipment are made.

For example, an article in one Florida city's union contract requires at least a 45-minute workout per shift (15 minutes of strength training, 15 minutes of agility training, and 15 minutes of aerobic training). Firefighters must attend an annual physical examination, including a 12-lead EKG and blood tests. Those showing any signs of cardiac abnormality are sent for further tests, which may include chest X-rays and stress tests.

It has long been understood that smoking is a major contributor of heart and lung diseases. Many fire departments prohibit smoking or the use of tobacco products. For example, Florida's "Heart and Lung" bill has been adapted in many fire departments in Florida to ban firefighters from smoking. The goal is to reduce the number of compensation cases as a result of sudden death due to heart attack.

Instructor Al Baeta, who was a track and cross-country coach for over two decades, points out that the physical demands of the job never stop. Achieving a high level of fitness at the onset of your career as a firefighter is just the start. Many departments around the country are instigating or already have programs for their personnel to stay fit. It is becoming more and more common to find weightlifting and aerobic equipment in firehouses.

"Firefighters are tremendously professional and they will rise to the occasion to meet the demands of the job," Baeta says. "However, those who are not in the condition they ought to be pay for it with accumulated stress over their lifetime. We say, Fit for Fire. Fit for Retire."

Physical fitness is a crucial part in becoming a firefighter. But staying fit plays a crucial role throughout this career.

Hose Drag/Pull

Hose Hoist

Sledge Carry/Roof Walk

Tool Use—Sledgehammer to Roof

# 16▶ The Oral Interview

## CHAPTER SUMMARY

This chapter gives you a number of guidelines, tips, and scenarios to help you imagine and prepare for your oral interview. What do you say? How do you say it? You can't know ahead of time what questions you will be asked, but there is a lot you can do to get yourself ready and boost your odds of success.

Like many candidates, you may think that the oral interview is just like any other job interview, that it's not a major part of the hiring process for firefighters, or that compared to the CPAT or the written exam, it isn't all that critical.

But did you know that many departments use the oral interview to eliminate the largest percentage of applicants? Did you know that in some places, the interview is used to choose those who will be allowed to take the CPAT? The point here is: Don't take any chances. It is not worth risking your future as a firefighter by not taking the interview seriously.

In most municipal or county departments, the oral interview is a very important part of the application process, so important that there may be two of them—a qualifying interview and a selection interview. Each jurisdiction will have different priorities, and each interviewing panel will ask different kinds of questions and have different standards in judging the answers, especially in a first interview. But all of the questions will focus on essentially the same factor: the character of the applicant—who you are as evidenced by what you have to say for yourself.

## The Qualifying Interview

The qualifying interview—also known as the screening interview—is the first, and sometimes the only, oral interview that fire departments use in their hiring process. By the time you are contacted to go through this interview, you will have completed your application form, you probably will have taken the written examination, and it is possible that you may have taken the Candidate Physical Ability Test.

In any case, just being asked to interview usually means you have been chosen from the pool of applicants to go on to the next step, that you have climbed a crucial rung up the ladder toward your career goal. You should feel encouraged and confident. Remember that feeling. Courage and confidence are two traits you will need as a firefighter—traits the interview panel will be looking for in the way you present yourself to them and the way you answer their questions.

The panel that interviews you will be made up of professionals—not just professional firefighters, but department personnel officers and interview specialists as well. They may hold any rank; a deputy chief, chief, or even a commissioner may serve on a panel. In some communities, the panel might include a civilian or two. Be aware that most community representatives are prominent citizens with some managerial experience, and they do not take this civic responsibility lightly. It is a good idea to find out in advance the makeup of the panel in your area. And always keep in mind that their experience and their position command your respect.

Remember, you are being interviewed by professionals for a professional position. Ensure that you are neatly dressed and well groomed. Be sure to wear a suit or other business attire without a lot of jewelry or other distractions. Another thing to keep in mind is the requirement for all firefighters to get a face seal when wearing self-contained breathing apparatus. That means male applicants should be clean shaven for all interviews.

## The Selection Interview

Many departments will ask you back for a second round of interviewing. This is usually called the selection interview or, in some places, the chief's interview. It can be much like the qualifying interview, only conducted by higher-level personnel. Or it can be more of a formality, in which the applicant is allowed to ask questions of the panel before officially being accepted for the job. Either way, it is important to take this interview every bit as seriously as the first.

If you are meeting the chief, treat it as an executive-level interview and be sure to dress accordingly. You will have been through the qualifying interview already, so you will have the chance to review your performance. What can you learn from it? What went well? Where could you improve? Your qualifying interview will have been evaluated by the department, and that evaluation will be among the background material the second panel refers to. For instance, there could be follow-up questions or requests for clarification of previous answers.

The selection interview is their last chance to find out about you before hiring—or disqualifying—you. But don't be intimidated. The more interviews you have, the more confidence it should give you that you have the skills and abilities they require.

## Getting Ready

It is most likely impossible, and a waste of time, to anticipate the exact questions you will be asked during the oral interview. But it is still possible, and important, to prepare yourself for it. You know the panel has the information you gave them on your application form. Think about that for a minute. What did you tell them about your background, your skills and abilities, and your character?

For example, your history of employment—what skills did you learn in the jobs you held that could help you become part of an efficient, effective team of firefighters? Do any assignments or projects you were

Standard English is the standard language of departmental command—and of the interview. So, if your English needs improvement, start studying now. College English and communications departments offer courses that can help you, as do community centers (like YMCAs) and local learning programs. Also, some fire departments that serve jurisdictions with large non-English-speaking populations give preference to applicants who, besides English, speak the languages of those populations. Check out the needs in your area.

involved in stand out as particularly challenging or representative of your capabilities? Are there gaps in your work history that need to be explained? If you were ever fired from a job, a background check will uncover that fact, and possibly the reason for it. What is your side of the story, and what is the best way to present it?

You might not know what the panel will ask you specifically, but you can get a general idea of the areas and issues that concern them from the application and exam. Did they ask about your traffic record? Drug use? Academic background? Then you had better ask yourself—was there a problem in any of these areas? What did you do about it? Know your strengths, too. Facing and solving problems can build character; sometimes you learn the most from the experiences you had the most trouble with.

This does not mean coming up with excuses and rationalizations, plotting ways to steer the conversation around to your obvious strong points, or memorizing the best possible answer to a particular type of question. These approaches are likely to make you sound insincere, and trying to remember them will just make you anxious. The idea is to think the issue through so that you understand what the experience means to you now as a potential firefighter. It is a way for you to identify and appreciate the preparation you received—on the job, on the street, in the classroom—for the demanding profession you are about to enter.

But don't stop there. In most areas, there are college degree programs in fire technology or fire protec-

tion. Many colleges offer Internet-based courses in fire and life safety. In other areas, they offer the entry training that leads to national certification accepted by many fire departments across the nation. You should take every opportunity to gain skills and certifications that will aid in your career and make you a more qualified applicant. Many persons who seek to enter the career fire service also have served in the volunteer fire service, where they have access to training and education at both the basic and advanced levels. It is also important that you look into EMT certification, as many departments respond to far more rescue and medical calls than fire calls. Many departments now require this as a prerequisite to appointment. If you know some members of the department you are interested in joining, or firefighters in other departments nearby, ask them about their interviews and the preparation that they went through before being hired. They know firsthand what it takes to prepare for a career in the fire service. Remember, it is better to be well prepared than to not prepare and be surprised.

### Presenting Yourself

Give this your serious attention. How you present yourself at the interview—your first face-to-face meeting with your prospective coworkers and bosses—is a sign of how important the job is to you and of your respect for the panel. Fire departments have a paramilitary command structure: Orders go down the ranks to mobilize a trained, disciplined fighting force, organized in companies and battalions, whose duty it is to fight fires. Respect for authority is fundamental to the occupation, and it should show in your dress and manner at the interview.

This does not necessarily mean you must wear a business suit, get a severe haircut, or sit up straight with your hands in your lap—though none of these would hurt, as long as they don't make you uncomfortable. Your appearance should be appropriate, but it should also express your personality. It does mean that male candidates should be clean shaven at this interview. Today's firefighters have to comply with strict grooming standards to meet air mask rules of the Occupational Safety and Health Administration (OSHA). You will make a good impression on those you meet and show that you are willing to comply with department orders. The panel's job is to get to know you, so dressing up like somebody you are not—just to impress them—only makes their work harder to do. They asked you to the interview because they already considered you to be a serious candidate. You should be confident that you can be yourself and succeed.

Your bearing—how you stand, sit, and carry yourself—should not be phony or self-conscious, either. Be polite, attentive, and interested. If you listen carefully, make eye contact with your questioners, and answer them directly and with respect, you should be fine. It is a job interview; attend to business.

And don't be late. It is advisable to arrive 15 to 20 minutes beforehand so you can compose yourself, relax, and get the feel of the place where the interview is being held. Arriving too early gives you too much time to wait, think, fidget, lose focus, and make yourself nervous. And showing up late—well, what would you think if you were on the panel, looking at the applicant's empty chair, then at your watch, then at the door, ready to do your part in the important task at hand, but forced to wait for someone who appar-

ently didn't think it is so important? If for some reason you are unavoidably detained, be honest, straightforward, and ready to go when you get there. This is your chance to show them who you are, and how prepared you are to take advantage of the opportunity they have presented you with. Just relax and give it your best shot.

## Answering Questions: What Works and What Doesn't

Most panels will ask most applicants a standard set of questions, which will, of course, vary from department to department. Your panel may or may not ask one of the most common questions: "Why do you want to be a firefighter?" But you should ask yourself the question. The answer covers everything from your motivation to enter the profession to the goals you ultimately hope to achieve. By thinking this through ahead of time, you will have a better idea of how to answer this and many related questions you are likely to be asked.

"I want to help people," is a good answer, but too generic. Teachers and social workers help people, too. What's different about the help firefighters provide? Well, they save property, even lives, from danger and imminent destruction. And that makes the job more exciting, and perhaps more satisfying, since you get to see the results of your labor—the saved lives, the rescued pets, the spared homes and material goods—in a more immediate and dramatic manner than most other public service workers. But then what about the work of fire prevention, public education, and equipment maintenance, which take up much more of a firefighter's time than answering fire calls? Maybe it is the varied nature of the duties and the irregular hours that appeal to you.

You may have other reasons, of course, but the answering process is the key here. At the interview, or while preparing for it, make sure to listen carefully to the question, all the way through. This will help you to present yourself as attentive and respectful, and to understand exactly what you are being asked. Don't just answer off the top of your head—think first. Does the question relate to any preparation you have done? Is it a complicated, two-or-more-part question? Is there a specific example that comes to mind?

You always want to give a thoughtful response. Once you get a job in a fire department, your advancement through the ranks is determined to a great extent by examinations, in everything from hydraulics to public administration, so your answers need to show the panel that you are a thinking person. Speak clearly and directly to the panel, so they can hear and understand your answer and get to know you. And stay focused on giving the information that answers the question. This will demonstrate to the panel your intelligence, your ability to follow orders, and your efficiency at performing the task at hand.

## Think It Through

Consider the following example: One of the panel members, while looking over a copy of your application, says to you, "You have only two years of college experience." This is a sensitive area in your life, and you are defensive about it. You have good reasons for having left school before getting your degree—family responsibilities; financial hardship; an awareness that until you really understood why you were in school, the education was not going to be meaningful to you. But these reasons are difficult for you to articulate because when somebody brings up your lack of a college degree, you always feel you are being judged negatively. So because you are quick to defend yourself, your answer comes across as a hodgepodge of emotional responses that sound like excuses.

The panel member stops you. "I was going to ask," he continues, "if, despite your limited college experience, you feel you are prepared for a career in firefighting?" This is a different question entirely from the one you thought you were being asked. And if you had not been so quick to answer, if you had taken a breath after the panel member's first statement and let him finish, if you had listened carefully, you could have given him the information he wanted and not revealed a vulnerable, defensive side to your character. And if you had considered this part of your application beforehand, and thought through this issue about your educational background, you could have prepared yourself, presented your reasons in a stronger manner, and overcome your vulnerability.

At least you have now been given a better question to answer, one that isn't negative and isn't asking about something you didn't do. Now you can be positive, telling them what you are doing to make yourself a qualified firefighter. Immediately you get an idea. You have just that morning gone through a strenuous physical workout, one designed to help you build up the strength and stamina necessary to excel at the CPAT. So, you tell them about your workout regimen, how you have set up a program of weight training for muscle development, especially in the upper body, and rotations on the stationary bike and stairmaster, along with a five-mile weekend jog, to increase your endurance. You enjoy working out; it makes you feel good and clears your mind. And you are proud of the progress you have made in lifting free weights, both in the amount of weight and the number of repetitions, and you fill the panel in, tracing the rise in pounds and reps over the last couple of months.

OK, fine—your physical condition is an essential qualification for the job. Your answer does show enthusiasm, thought, and commitment. And it is specific, which is good. However, it is enthusiastic, thoughtful, committed, and specific about working out, not about preparing for a career in a fire department. So, before you ever get to the interview, ask yourself a few thought-provoking questions. For example, how did you decide what exercises to include in your workout?

If you learned from talking to active-duty firefighters in the area that the CPAT consists of a timed hose drag, ladder lift, stair climb and tunnel crawl, all while you are wearing a turnout coat, helmet, gloves, and air bottle, and that firefighters need strong arms, shoulders, backs, and legs, should you tell the panel? After all, they already know this stuff. What they don't know, however, and what is key for them to understand, is your reasoning, your thinking process. Plus, it is evidence of your enthusiasm and your commitment to the profession that you did this research, that you went out and talked to working firefighters. The difference between a good answer and the best one you can think of is the thought you put into it.

## Show Your Stuff

If you have a clear idea of what you want to say, you are more likely to speak clearly. If you are not comfortable with public speaking, you may be self-conscious about talking to the panel. But the basics are simple. Make sure they can hear you: If they have to listen hard to follow what you are saying, you are making them work harder than they should have to and you are more of a problem than other interviewees. Make sure they understand you: Try to speak in full sentences, and don't use slang if you can help it. Also make sure they can see you: Your facial expressions can help the panel understand what you are saying, and making eye contact will help them get to know you. Don't mumble or look away if you get a little lost or confused. Keep your head up and eyes front. This is the panel's chance to meet you face-to-face—don't disappoint them.

Your answers should let the questioners know not only what you think, but how you think. If you feel as if you are getting off the subject of the question you were asked, you probably are. Recall the question—which is easier if you listened carefully in the first place—and rethink your answer. Sometimes staying focused is a matter of getting back on track, and sometimes it is a matter of considering the question again and finding a better way to answer it. In the case of the earlier question, perhaps you also tried to prepare by enrolling in a training program for firefighters at a local college, but were unable to afford the time or expense at this point in your life. You are not sure you should tell the panel about this attempt because it didn't work out, like your other try at college. But upon a moment's reflection you may decide that they should know that you investigated the possibility and hope to take advantage of it in the future. This shows that you have a plan, a goal you are working toward. It is a positive response and speaks to your qualities of patience and perseverance, which are good traits for a firefighter to have.

If you are looking into college programs to prepare for your career, you might consider a course in public speaking (see "Public Speaking 101" on the next page). Part of a firefighter's job is community outreach, educating the public on fire prevention, public safety issues, and the role of a firefighter. You may be asked to speak to workers and management in local businesses, citizen groups and neighborhood meetings, and schoolchildren at various levels. Becoming an effective speaker will help you be an effective firefighter. The lessons you learn in a public-speaking course won't hurt your interview skills, either. Let professionals help you develop better listening habits and speaking techniques, and give you a forum where you can get much-needed practice. To become a more comfortable, confident public speaker, there is no substitute for experience.

The answering process is something you can practice as part of your preparation for the interview. Remember to:

- listen carefully
- think first
- speak clearly
- stay focused

## Public Speaking 101

If speaking in public makes you nervous, or if you just need to practice and get some useful feedback, take a public-speaking course. This can be a great means to learn, study, and polish the skills necessary to ace the interview.

As an example of what is involved in a public-speaking course, the following excerpts are from the syllabus for a course on Effective Speech-Making given at the City University of New York.

**Course Objectives:**
- To develop a basic understanding of interpersonal communication
- To develop an understanding of standard American speech
- To develop an understanding of oral interpretation
- To develop knowledge of interview techniques

**Class Activities and Areas of Focus:**
- Interpersonal exercises and small-group discussions
- Verbal and nonverbal exercises
- Self-concept and perception
- Defense mechanisms and fallacies
- Breathing, posture, articulation
- Listening
- Controlling nervousness
- Informing, persuading, entertaining

**Course Rationale and Reminders:** Lessons from this class should help you interact in the public and professional worlds outside of class. Feedback is of prime concern, so ask questions. Evaluation is based on individual improvement in voice production and speech delivery. Clearly enunciate and articulate—and relax!

---

Each step of the process, in and of itself, will communicate your seriousness and self-control to the panel. You will be showing your respect for them and gaining their respect at the same time.

### Stick to the Facts

If you are scheduled for an interview, you have already been identified as someone the department thinks they want. Chances are, then, that they have done a background check on you, based on the information in your application. They may have talked to your former bosses about your employment record. Did you leave a certain job under questionable circumstances? Then they are likely to ask questions about it. Did you quit? Were you fired? In either case, why?

When a panel asks such questions, they probably have your boss's response in front of them. But even if they specifically ask you to respond to one of your employer's comments, complaints and excuses aren't the way to go. Instead, give them an answer that shows you have looked at the situation honestly, examined your actions, and learned from the experience.

If you prepared yourself to face this type of inquiry, as was suggested earlier, you will be ready for it and it will be less likely to throw you off balance. In general, what did your prior work experience—good, bad, or otherwise—mean to you at the time? And what does it mean to you now that you are on the threshold of a new career?

With questions like these, as with all the questions you are asked on application forms or in interviews, it is critical that you answer truthfully. This certainly means don't lie. But it also means don't try to scope out the panel and tell them what you think they want to hear. To begin with, it is impossible to know what even one person wants to hear you say, much less a panel of three or more people. They may not know themselves. If they ask standard questions, they may be satisfied with standard answers, but a personal response that is out of the ordinary may capture their attention and make you stand out from the other applicants.

So, should you strive for the uncommon answer that makes you different from the rest? But how would you know what "different" was without knowing how everyone else answered? As you can see, this approach can't possibly work. It's a dead end. Besides, experienced interviewers can usually recognize a false sentiment or phony tone, even if your answer isn't technically a lie. And the more sincere you act, the more your lack of sincerity will show through. In the end it is safest, and smartest, to give a personal response, to tell the panel the truth—as you see it.

## Character Counts

"It appears that your driving record over the last several years has been less than perfect." The panel member is looking down at your application, and you can tell from her tone of voice that the last phrase—"less

than perfect"—was meant to be a sarcastic understatement. You start to think through the violations you have received in the recent past, but you wait to respond until she asks a question. "Do you," she asks, "have a problem when you get behind the wheel?"

This is a question about your character, not about any specific traffic violation you committed. Your impulse may be to rise to your own defense: "No, I don't have any problems driving, none at all." But that's not the way to go—after all, the background check the department has done will provide the panel with the officers' reports and a record of the citations you have received. Again, making excuses for particular instances is not as important as the qualities of character you present to the panel.

So you are better off confronting the issue: "I like to drive and I'm confident at the wheel. But I have had a problem in the past when it comes to speed. And now I'm dealing with that. If I'm going to call myself a good driver—which in general, I believe I am—then I can't be getting speeding tickets. I don't want to endanger anybody's life, including my own, and that means obeying the speed limit." What does this answer tell the panel? That you recognized the problem and are making an effort to correct it, that you learned from the past and don't want to repeat it. If you really mean what you say, that shows character.

## Getting Personal

As much as possible, fire departments want to know the real you. They want to know something about your opinions, your habits, and your personality—as it relates to the job, of course, not because they're snoops.

For example, there might be questions about how you will cope with the lifestyle and working conditions of a firefighter: "How well do you function without sleep for a full day? Or on an irregular schedule, with four days on, 24 hours a day, then four days off?" They might ask you how you handle diversity—meaning, working and living with people from various ethnic and cultural backgrounds, both females and males. This is an important issue in many fire departments. A curt "no problem" type of answer will not be as convincing as one that refers to specific recent instances, in the workplace or the community, where you cooperated and interacted successfully with a diverse population. Some answers call for specific examples, especially if this information is not stated in your application.

In some jurisdictions, you may have taken a psychological test and an interviewer may ask questions based on that. These questions could focus, for example, on your personal beliefs, attitudes, or behavior. They may seem obscure—"How do you feel about the opposite sex?" Or probing—"How do you feel about your family?" The answers to these sorts of questions may only be significant in relation to the answers you gave during the psychological test. So, there is no way to judge what a "correct" or even an "appropriate" answer might be. Therefore, as always, it is best to be honest. You have more to lose by trying to trick or please the panel than by answering frankly and directly.

## Situational Questions

Interview panels often ask questions in which they describe a firefighting situation that raises certain ethical or professional dilemmas. They want to get a sense of how you may respond in such a situation. Some departments ask these kinds of questions almost exclusively. Some don't ask them at all, feeling that it is hard to imagine a firefighting situation until you have been in one.

Situational questions might be more difficult to anticipate and to answer than general or personal questions, but the answering process and the principles of presentation and honesty still apply. It is a good idea to prepare for this type of question in case you are asked one like the following: "You are alone in a private house with another firefighter. You see him take a wristwatch from the top of a dresser and put it in his pocket. What do you do?" Good question. Like most ethical problems, it can be answered simply or lead to difficult choices among complicated options. In the end, you have to trust yourself and your common sense.

Another kind of scenario will place you in a firehouse situation: "You are playing handball against the firehouse wall with three members of your company. A member of the local block association walks by, and stops to criticize you, loudly, for playing a game while you are on the job. What do you do?" Let's look at several potential answers.

- Answer 1: "I'd tell the person that I am doing my job."
- Answer 2: "I'd tell the person that I am doing my job, that I live at the firehouse 24 hours a day, 4 days in a row. Just because I'm taking a little time out to play a game with members of my crew doesn't mean I'm not on the job. I mean, if I hear the bell, I'm ready to go. We all are. And we'll get the job done—don't worry about it. Of course, how I say this will depend on if I know the person or not. If they're on the block association, I've probably seen them around. I might even end up inviting them to play."
- Answer 3: "I'd explain to the person, in a calm and friendly manner, that firefighting is stressful work. An occasional game of handball lets off some of the pressure, and it helps keep us in shape. The exercise is good for us, but we're ready to go as soon as that alarm bell rings."

Answer 1, while based on truth, is rather abrupt. Answer 2 shows more thought, and some cleverness, but has a somewhat confrontational tone. The speaker tries to make up for that toward the end of the answer, but trying to change the tone leads the speaker to ramble a bit. Answer 3 gets to the point, shows thought and stays focused. It is the best of the three options in terms of answering the question. (Keep in mind, however, that this is only a model—your answers need to sound like you.)

Scenarios are also used to hypothesize emergency conditions: "You arrive at the site of a fire call and find a woman in hysterics, screaming and gesticulating out of control, in the street. What do you do?" If you are unfamiliar with such situations, being confronted with one, even in an interview, can be stressful. And that's the point. Stress is an occupational hazard in firefighting. Questions that produce stress let the panel see firsthand how you handle it. This is one reason why many jurisdictions give preference to candidates with EMT or military experience. The ability to perform under conditions of stress is one of the key worker traits in the firefighting profession, and it is important that you develop and be prepared to demonstrate this ability.

## Video-Based Interviews

In addition to oral interviews, there is a new trend that is becoming more prevalent throughout the country: the use of video-based tests for observing and assessing interpersonal skills and judgment under standardized testing conditions. These sessions may be used subsequent to the oral interview, or in lieu of it, depending on the department's individual require-ments, and can be tailored toward both trained and entry-level candidates.

Candidates undergoing such sessions may be left alone in a room while a video plays, requiring them to respond to scenarios presented. The responses are recorded on videotape and are reviewed by a panel trained to measure the candidates' competency in dealing with different types of personnel-related situations.

Video-based testing may or may not be announced beforehand; many agencies post a list of specific requirements for candidate selection, such as a written examination, an oral panel interview, and video testing, and some substitute the video-based test for the preliminary interview.

## Do What It Takes

The oral interview is a crucial step on your way to becoming a firefighter. You can and should prepare for it. So, do some research both on the life and work of a firefighter. And do some research on yourself—your background, opinions, strengths and weaknesses. Self-awareness leads to self-confidence, especially in an interview situation. Seek experience in areas where you think you need it. Practice interviewing skills. Demand the best from yourself. The panel and the profession certainly will.

# NOTES

**NOTES**

## Special FREE Offer from LearningExpress!

**LearningExpress will help you be better prepared for,
and get higher scores on, the firefighter exam.**

Go to the LearningExpress Practice Center at www.LearningExpressFreeOffer.com,
an interactive online resource exclusively for LearningExpress customers.

Now that you've purchased LearningExpress's *Firefighter Exam, 4th Edition*, you
have **FREE** access to:

- **A full-length firefighter practice test** that mirrors the official firefighter exam
- **Immediate scoring** and **detailed answer explanations**
- Benchmark your skills and focus your study with our **customized diagnostic report**

Follow the simple instructions on the scratch card in your copy of *Firefighter Exam, 4th Edition*. Use your
individualized access code found on the scratch card and go to www.LearningExpressFreeOffer.com
to sign in. Start practicing online for the firefighter exam right away!

Once you've logged on, use the spaces below to write in your access code and newly created
password for easy reference:

Access Code: _____     Password: _____